RICHARD & MARIA

COSWAY

REGENCY ARTISTS OF TASTE
AND FASHION

SPONSORED BY

Mobil

and supported by
Dunard Fund

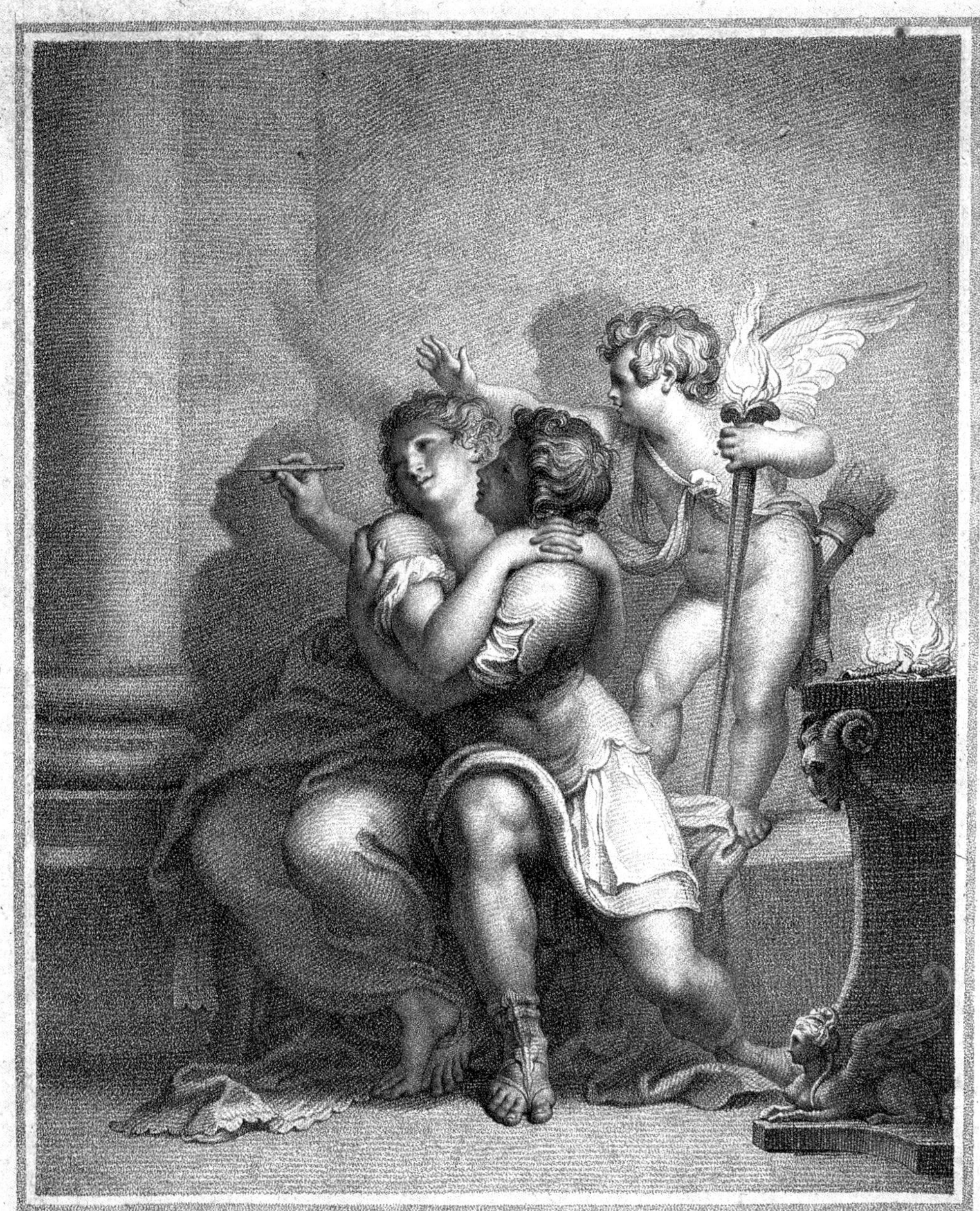

DOCET AMOR

Published as the Act directs, Ap.l 26.th 1791. by R. Cosway.

STEPHEN LLOYD

RICHARD & MARIA

COSWAY

REGENCY ARTISTS OF TASTE

AND FASHION

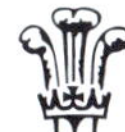

WITH ESSAYS BY

[R]ORTER & AILEEN RIBEIRO

[E]DINBURGH

[NATI]ONAL PORTRAIT GALLERY

CMXCV

Published 1995 by The Trustees of the
National Galleries of Scotland for the exhibition
held at the Scottish National Portrait Gallery, Edinburgh
from 11 August to 22 October 1995
and at the National Portrait Gallery, London
from 17 November 1995 to 18 February 1996

Designed & typeset in ITC Bodoni and FF Bodoni English Initials by Dalrymple
Printed and bound in Italy by Grafiche Milani

Cover: R. Thew after Richard Cosway
Portraits of Mr & Mrs Cosway, 1789, stipple engraving
Private Collection [**92**]
Frontispiece: J. Condé after Richard Cosway
Docet amor, 1791, stipple engraving
Private Collection [**145**]

FOREWORD

$\mathcal{R}$ICHARD and Maria Cosway were one of the most fascinating and glamorous artistic couples in Europe during the late eighteenth and early nineteenth century. Their art and lives shed considerable light on an important period of British and European cultural history and, in particular, on its concern with taste and fashion.

This is the first exhibition on the Cosways since their achievements were reassessed in an exhibition held at Moncorvo House, London, exactly a hundred years ago. In the late nineteenth and early twentieth century Richard Cosway was one of the best-known British artists, as the statue by Ernest Gillick, prominently placed on the façade of Aston Webb's Victoria and Albert Museum, testifies. Since then Richard Cosway's name has fallen from the pantheon of artists, although his miniatures have always been highly regarded. Until now Maria Cosway's art has never been properly exhibited, always remaining in the shadow of her husband's fashionable small-scale portraiture.

This current reassessment of the Cosways has been made by Stephen Lloyd, Assistant Keeper at the Scottish National Portrait Gallery, who has recently completed major research on the Cosways. The exhibition has been selected and curated by him, and he has also written the major part of this publication. We are also very grateful to Professor Roy Porter of the Wellcome Institute for the History of Medicine and to Dr Aileen Ribeiro, Head of the History of Dress Department at the Courtauld Institute of Art, for their stimulating essays. After its Edinburgh showing, the exhibition will be seen at the National Portrait Gallery, London.

An exhibition of this scale and ambition can only be made possible through the help of many people. This is particularly the case with our colleagues at the National Portrait Gallery in London, especially the Director, Charles Saumarez Smith, as well as Carole Patey, Kathleen Soriano and Jacob Simon. Within the National Galleries of Scotland, we are most grateful to John Dick, Keeper of Conservation, and his team, for the treatment of a number of items. We would also like to thank those owners who agreed to having their works conserved. Likewise, thanks are due to Antonia Reeve who has photographed most of the exhibits in Scotland.

Our greatest debt is to those owners who have lent works to the exhibition, thereby depleting their own collections for many months. We can only hope to repay their generosity by means of the pleasure and enlightenment we feel sure the exhibition will give to a wide public in the two capital cities. Special thanks for their assistance in various ways are due to Maureen V. Attrill, James Austin, Mark Baily, Gerald Barnett, Alan Bell, Susan Bennett, Philippe Bordes, Hugh Brigstocke, Geremy Butler, Gywneth Campling, Michael Clarke, Katherine Coombs, Jane Cunningham, the Hon. Ashley Dawson-Damer, Peter Day, Helen Dorey, Godfrey Evans, Tim Faulkner, Alexandra Fennell, Kate Fielden, Tino Gipponi, Mariella Goffredo de Robertis, Antony Griffiths, Robin Hamlyn, Kate Hannah, Karen Hearn, Simon Jervis, David Lavender, Christopher Lloyd, Valerio Manfrini, Theresa-Mary Morton, Kirsten Aschengreen Piacenti, Jane Rick, the Hon. Jane Roberts, A. J. Stirling, the Countess of Wemyss and March, Henry Wemyss, Baroness Willoughby de Eresby, John Winter, Robert Wood, Stephen Wood and Aroldo Zevi.

Stephen Lloyd's proposal to mount an exhibition on the Cosways seemed attractive in light of the Merchant Ivory Productions film, *Jefferson in Paris*, which was released on both sides of the Atlantic earlier this year. The film concerns the romance of Maria Cosway with Thomas Jefferson in 1786 (starring Greta Scacchi as Maria Cosway, with Simon Callow as Richard Cosway). Ismail Merchant's suggestion that we include two of the costumes used in the film was most gratefully accepted. We also owe a debt of gratitude to John Bright and Jenny Beavan who designed and made the costumes, and thanks are due to Cosprop Limited for making the two costumes available and for assisting with their installation.

Finally, we must thank our sponsors, Mobil North Sea Limited. We regard them as rather special sponsors, having had a very productive and happy relationship with them over a number of years, and we are grateful to Chris Patey and Lloyd Slater for their early commitment and enthusiasm for this project. We are also very grateful to the Dunard Fund, who supported the exhibition at a critical juncture by facilitating the American loans.

TIMOTHY CLIFFORD
Director, National Galleries of Scotland

DUNCAN THOMSON
Keeper, Scottish National Portrait Gallery

LENDERS TO THE EXHIBITION

AUSTRIA

Graphische Sammlung Albertina, Vienna

FRANCE

Musée de la Révolution française, Vizille

IRELAND

National Gallery of Ireland, Dublin

ITALY

Museo degli Argenti, Florence

Museo Nazionale del Bargello, Florence

Galleria degli Uffizi, Florence

Fondazione Cosway, Lodi

Biblioteca Nazionale Braidense, Milan

SWITZERLAND

Dario Zendralli, Lugano

UNITED KINGDOM

Her Majesty The Queen

Trustees of the 10th Duke of Argyll

Cecil Higgins Art Gallery, Bedford

Attingham Park, The Berwick Collection (The National Trust)

Commander Gerald Barnett, RN (retd)

Birmingham Museums and Art Gallery

His Grace the Duke of Buccleuch and Queensberry, KT

Towneley Hall Art Gallery and Museums, Burnley Borough Council

Syndics of the Fitzwilliam Museum, Cambridge

Lord Courtenay

The Duke of Devonshire and the Chatsworth Settlement Trustees

National Gallery of Scotland, Edinburgh

Scottish National Portrait Gallery, Edinburgh

Andrew Edmunds

The Rt Hon. the Earl of Elgin and Kincardine, KT

Glasgow University Library

Grimsthorpe and Drummond Castle Trust

His Grace the Duke of Hamilton and Brandon, KT

Lt-Col. R.L. Jenkins

Beryl Kendall

The Hon. Christopher Lennox-Boyd

Trustees of the British Museum, London

Courtauld Institute Galleries, London

Garrick Club, London

Library of Hertford House, London

London Library

Trustees of the National Gallery, London

Trustees of the National Portrait Gallery, London

Royal Academy of Arts, London

Royal Society for the encouragement of Arts, Manufactures and Commerce, London

Trustees of the Sir John Soane's Museum, London

Tate Gallery, London

The Board of Trustees of the Victoria and Albert Museum, London

Wellcome Institute for the History of Medicine, London

Thomas Williams, London

His Grace the Duke of Marlborough

Whitworth Art Gallery, University of Manchester

Visitors of the Ashmolean Museum, Oxford

Bodleian Library, Oxford

City of Plymouth Museums and Art Gallery

The Rt Hon. the Earl of Shelburne

The Rt Hon. the Earl of Wemyss and March, KT

UNITED STATES

Yale Center for British Art, New Haven

Yale University Art Gallery, New Haven

The Metropolitan Museum of Art, New York

New York Public Library

Henry E. Huntington Library and Art Gallery, San Marino

Worcester Art Museum

AND MANY OWNERS WHO WISH TO REMAIN ANONYMOUS

The following works are exhibited in Edinburgh only: 10, 44, 146, 148, 150, 160, 161, 195, 257, 262

The following works are exhibited in London only: 147, 149, 194, 261

ACKNOWLEDGEMENTS

This exhibition is founded on my doctoral research on Richard Cosway undertaken at St Cross College, Oxford University. The research has been supported by various funds, including a W. Keck Foundation Fellowship which enabled me to spend a month at the Henry E. Huntington Library and Art Gallery in San Marino; a travel scholarship from the British School at Rome, which provided the opportunity to spend four weeks at the Fondazione Cosway in Lodi; and a substantial subsidy from the Paul Mellon Centre for Studies in British Art for a photographic campaign in Italy.

My journey began at the Huntington in California, where I was – and remain – extremely indebted to Bob Wark and Shelley Bennett, both for encouraging my early interest in the Cosways and for allowing me access to the papers of the late Diana Wilson, whose discoveries and unpublished research at Lodi in the 1970s represented such a breakthrough in the serious study of both artists. On my visits to the beautiful and tranquil Lombard town of Lodi I have always been welcomed with the utmost hospitality by Elena Cazzulani, Tino Gipponi, Valerio Manfrini, Monsignor G. B. Pettinari and Angelo Stroppa. Another exhibition and publication on the archives and collections in Lodi is being prepared by the Fondazione Cosway. Further archival documentation will be published in a forthcoming volume of *The Walpole Society*.

The Paul Mellon Centre for Studies in British Art, based in London, has been a source of constant encouragement, and I would like to thank in particular Brian Allen, Michael Kitson, Clare Lloyd-Jacob, Evelyn Newby, Elizabeth Powis, Kim Sloan and Douglas Smith. I have been warmly received by private owners and museum curators across Europe and America, and I would like to express my gratitude to them all. The staff of various libraries have been most helpful, in particular those working in the *fototece* of the National Portrait Gallery, the Courtauld and Warburg Institutes in London; the Yale Center for British Art, New Haven; the Frick Art Reference Library, New York; the Department of the History of Art and the Department of Western Art of the Ashmolean Museum, Oxford; and the Provenance Index and Library at the Getty Center, Santa Monica, where I was able to advance my research significantly in the initial stages.

Over the long period of research I have benefited from being able to discuss my findings with my attentive and patient supervisors, Francis Haskell and Nicholas Penny, as well as a number of colleagues, fellow enthusiasts and friends, among them Julia Armstrong, Malcolm Baker, G. E. Bentley Jr, Ilaria Bignamini, Philippe Bordes, Edward Chaney, Andrew Clayton-Payne, Jane Cunningham, William Drummond, Judy Egerton, Pat Fara, Alexandra Fennell, Daphne Foskett, Burton Fredericksen, Paul Gwynne, Ben Halliday, Sir Hew Hamilton-Dalrymple, Derek Johns, Julia King, Bob Maccubbin, Adam Maclean, Elizabeth McGrath, Robert Oresko, Daphne Ottaway and other members of the Ottaway family, Michael Phillips, Adam Potkay, Pierre Rosenberg, Wendy Wassing Roworth, Nick Savage, Marsha Keith Schuchard, Gianni Carlo Sciolla, Susan Sontag, Lindsay Stainton, Yuri Stoyanov, Claire Tomalin, Frances Vivian, Clive Wainwright, Richard Walker, Aidan Weston-Lewis, Catherine Whistler, Selby Whittingham, Haydn Williams, Elizabeth Witts, Jeremy Wood, Andrew Wyld and others whom I have unwittingly forgotten. The late Jim Murrell and Robert Bayne-Powell generously shared with me their deep knowledge of the portrait miniature. My grandmother Anne Woodroffe first set off my interest in the Cosways, while Lisa Clothier was a constant support and companion throughout the research. I thank them all, as well as the many others who generously offered me pieces of information, which, however seemingly small, were always significant.

This exhibition would not have happened without the enlightened financial sponsorship of Mobil North Sea Limited and support from the Dunard Fund. I am grateful to Timothy Clifford, Charles Saumarez Smith and especially Duncan Thomson for their combined vision and enthusiasm which helped foster the idea of the exhibition, as well as to Michael Clarke and Julius Bryant who gave the project their support at key moments. Colleagues at the National Portrait Gallery in London have been ready with advice and assistance, including Peter Funnell, Sarah Kemp, Jacob Simon, Kai Kin Yung and in particular Kathleen Soriano. At the National Galleries of Scotland many colleagues have played vital roles in making the exhibition a reality, in particular Anne-Marie Wagener who has handled the press and information, Liz Smith who has processed the loan data, and Janice Slater who has co-ordinated the complex transport arrangements. The preparation of the exhibition has coincided with the making and release of Merchant Ivory's film *Jefferson in Paris*, which is distributed by Buena Vista. I am very grateful to Daniel Battsek, Paul Bradley, Simon Callow, Ismail Merchant, Siân Perry and Greta Scacchi for their encouraging support of the exhibition. I imagine that the interest created through this unique synergy and fortunate timing between the exhibition and film would have been greatly to the liking of Richard and Maria Cosway.

Stephen Lloyd
Assistant Keeper, Scottish National Portrait Gallery

Throughout this publication figures in **bold** type within square brackets refer to catalogue numbers.
All works illustrated are by Richard Cosway unless otherwise stated.

INTRODUCTION

$\mathcal{R}$ICHARD and Maria Cosway were one of the most remarkable artist couples active in Europe in the late eighteenth and early nineteenth century. As Thomas Jefferson was to write, they were 'indeed ... of the greatest merit possessing good sense, good humour, honest hearts, honest manners, and eminence in a lovely art'.[1]

They bear comparison with Angelica Kauffman and her husband and manager Antonio Zucchi, as well as with Elisabeth Vigée-Lebrun and her husband, the art dealer Jean-Baptiste-Pierre Lebrun, although in both these instances the woman's reputation was – and has remained – greater than that of her partner.[2] In contrast, Richard Cosway (1742–1821) has always been considered one of the outstanding portrait miniaturists of his generation, overshadowing the various significant achievements of Maria Cosway (1760–1838), which stem from her varied career and complex personality. Their artistic biographies and reputations, when studied both separately and in conjunction, shed considerable light on the manners and taste of fashionable society during the period, as well as on some of its most famous and influential figures.

Richard Cosway, on his arrival in London in 1754 as a twelve-year-old boy, was fortunate to be taken under the wing of *William Shipley* [**1**], one of the most influential figures in the development of the arts in London during the mid-century, who founded a drawing school and the Society for the Encouragement of Arts, Manufactures and Commerce. By 1767 Cosway's miniature of *Mrs Draper* was being rapturously admired in *The Journal to Eliza* by Laurence Sterne, the famous author of *Tristram Shandy*; and a few years later Cosway painted a fine oil portrait of her [**6**]. In the early 1770s the artist's friendship with Charles Townley, the important collector of classical sculpture, gave rise to the commissioning of a genial but revealing conversation piece [**5**]. Confirmation of Richard Cosway's rise as a fashionable and versatile portrait painter, both in oils and miniatures, was sealed by his election in 1771 as a Royal Academician.

Maria Hadfield was born in 1760 in Florence, where she enjoyed a remarkable upbringing. Her mother and father managed a group of three inns, which were mainly frequented by British visitors on the Grand Tour. She studied music and copied paintings in the Gallery of the Uffizi and the Pitti Palace, taking lessons from a variety of resident and visiting artists. In 1778 she was elected a member of the Florentine Accademia del Disegno. Later that year she visited Rome and Naples in the company of some of the younger British artists. After the death of her father Charles in 1776, her mother Isabella decided to move the whole family to London, where they arrived in 1779.

Richard Cosway was nearly forty and a well-established artist when he met Maria Hadfield, eighteen years younger, and who was already trained as an artist and musician. They were married in London in January 1781. The following decade was to prove one of great artistic and social success for both of the Cosways. Together they made a considerable impact on their contemporaries. They established an extremely fashionable studio and *salon*, first at their home in Berkeley Street, and then from 1784 at Schomberg House in Pall Mall [fig. 1]. The regular concerts that Maria Cosway hosted – and performed in – became some of the most sought-after social events in the London calendar. As the *Library of Fine Arts* reminisced in 1832, the Cosways 'kept house in style, in a sort of co-partnership of so novel a character, as to surprise their new neighbours, astonish their old friends, and furnish wonderment for the table-talk of the town ...' William Blake at this date enviously noted the extraordinary lifestyle and social success that the couple enjoyed.[3]

Richard Cosway was admired in his lifetime – and has been ever since – for the beauty and elegance with which he transformed the sitters in his portrait miniatures. These representations, which are both glamorous and intimate, can be seen as the mirror in which fashionable Regency society saw itself reflected. As was noted by the essayist William Hazlitt, who was the artist's most sensitive critic, these miniatures 'were not fashionable – they were fashion itself'. However, Cosway's artistic achievement was considerably greater. Until recently the wide-ranging nature of Cosway's identity as an artist has been given little serious attention by art historians.

His miniatures were complemented by equally fashionable – and similarly priced – portrait drawings, a genre which the artist did much to transform. Both the miniatures and drawings were vigorously promoted throughout Cosway's career by their reproduction as prints, in particular as fashionable stipples by engravers of the calibre of Bartolozzi, Cardon and the Condé brothers. Over a hundred and sixty of Cosway's portraits were reproduced in this way over the sixty-year duration of his career, although this figure also includes a number of mezzotints, etchings and line engravings. The mezzotints were especially appropriate for reproducing Cosway's hitherto little-known oil paintings, mainly portraits, but also a few subject pictures, which he executed throughout his career and exhibited with varying degrees of success at the Royal Academy. Another fifty of Cosway's numerous subject compositions, which were mainly drawings on classical, mythological, literary, fanciful and religious themes, were also engraved, mainly for the flourishing decorative print market. By mid-career the artist's status – as well as the popularity of his fashionable prints – can be seen from a printseller's advertisement in a newspaper of 1788, where engravings were available after various foreign and English artists, numbering 'Guido, Rembrandt, L. de Vinci, Raphael, S. Rosa, Claude, Sir J. Reynolds, Bunbury, Cipriani, Gainsborough, [and] Cosway'.[4]

Critical to a broader understanding of Cosway's reputation as an artist and man of taste is that he was one of the most significant artists active as a collector and *virtuoso* – or connoisseur – in late Georgian and early Regency society. There had been a long and established tradition, both abroad and at home, of successful artists taking on this status and being involved in the art market, as can be seen for example in the careers of Rubens, Van Dyck, Rembrandt and Lely during the seventeenth century. Among Cosway's contemporaries, most of the artists were collectors, principally of Old Master pictures, drawings and prints. The most notable of these artist-collectors, who were usually portraitists, were the Richardsons (father and son), Hudson, Reynolds, West and Lawrence. The paintings were often sold on for profit to clients, while the drawings and prints were retained as prized sources for the study of the Old Masters. Richard Cosway was on a par with these collectors, and he can now be recognised as one of the most important artist-collectors and connoisseurs of the period.[5]

Once artists had established themselves as collectors and connoisseurs, they were thus able to advise their wealthy clients on the merits of particular purchases of Old Master pictures, drawings and other *objets d'art*. Cosway was an artist who was notably successful in setting himself up as a fashionable arbiter of taste. Not only did he portray his royal, aristocratic and wealthy clientele in an array of stylish poses and a variety of fashionable media, but he also advised his clients on purchases of Old Master pictures which were so highly sought after throughout the period.

His main influence was on the Prince of Wales, eldest son of George III, and who was later to become Prince Regent and eventually George IV. After first portraying the Prince in 1780 at the age of eighteen, Cosway became the favourite artist of the brilliant but dissolute heir to the throne. The Prince has been described sympathetically as 'glowing with charm, bursting with life and wildly extravagant', although his excessive appetites made him a regular target of the caricaturists, in particular Gillray [**139**]. Yet the Prince was the most committed royal patron of the arts since Charles I in the second quarter of the seventeenth century. Cosway enjoyed his patronage from 1780 to 1808, being entitled to use the phrase *Primarius Pictor*, or 'Principal Painter', as part of his signature from

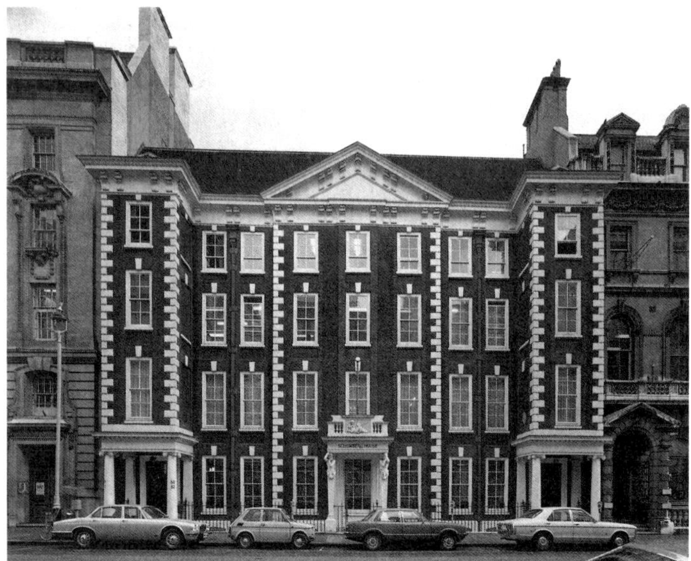

Fig. 1 *Schomberg House, 80–82 Pall Mall, London* 1698

1785 until his death. Cosway was also the main adviser to the Prince on all matters artistic, and more specifically on the painted decoration for the spectacular interiors at Carlton House [figs 2 & 3].[6] Undoubtedly this royal connection partially propelled Richard Cosway to such social success – the marriage to Maria being the other key event – as the *Library of Fine Arts* noted in 1832:

> *It was, however, the gay Prince of Wales who made Richard Cosway. The patronage of this* arbiter elegantiarum *of the fashionables, at once rendered the favoured painter – all the fashion. He* painted *the miniatures of the lovely Mrs. Fitzherbert, and made even* her, *more beautiful than she was. The Prince was charmed, the fair sitter was delighted, Cosway was eulogised, caressed, courted, had the secret* entré *at Carlton House, and at once was set afloat by royalty on the full tide of good fortune.*[7]

Even within their lifetimes both Richard and Maria Cosway were much envied for their success and affectations, and were also the targets of lampoons on account of their high social profile. After his death in 1821, Richard Cosway's reputation languished throughout the middle of the century, with Victorian commentators holding him up as an instance of Regency decadence. However, a reassessment of his reputation as a miniaturist facilitated an astonishing rise in interest in him in the late nineteenth century. By contrast, Maria Cosway's work has hardly been seen in public since she last exhibited paintings at the Royal Academy in 1801. Her name and reputation have until recently been subsumed under those of her husband. Richard Cosway always suffered criticism from his contemporaries, mainly on account of envy from fellow artists and critics, but also from his deserved reputation as a narcissist. The artist cultivated a highly fashionable personal appearance as a *macaroni* or dandy, which expressed both his highly extrovert personality and also may have been an attempt to conceal his physical shortcomings, both in terms of his lack of height and his pronounced facial features. Throughout his career Cosway had to put up with satires, caricatures and abuse about his supposed resemblance to a monkey. Despite this hostility Cosway seems to have actively courted and even enjoyed notoriety, at one stage early in his career owning a pet baboon, which later bit him in the leg and had to be put down.[8]

After Cosway's death, late Regency and early Victorian commentators continued a scurrilous and arch vein of criticism, which concentrated on attacking his notorious ostentatiousness. From 1865, when the huge exhibition of portrait miniatures was held at the South Kensington Museum, up until the famous sale of J. Pierpont Morgan's great collection of miniatures at Christie's in 1935, there was exceptional competition by collectors for Richard Cosway's work as a portrait miniaturist and to a lesser extent for his portrait drawings, and continually high prices were paid for his work.[9] The period of greatest interest in Cosway's work occurred in late Victorian and Edwardian times – between 1890 and 1910 – when a series of publications, auctions and exhibitions was devoted to him and in particular to the miniatures. In 1890 a catalogue raisonné of the reproductive prints after his work was published by the dealer Frederick Daniell. The only previous biography on the Cosways was written by George C. Williamson, which was published in 1897 with a second edition following in 1905. This concentrated on his reputation as a miniaturist as well as his social notoriety, although it included a valuable documentation on Maria Cosway's later life in Italy. Williamson also curated the only exhibition previously devoted to the Cosways, held at Moncorvo House in London in 1895, and which concentrated to a great extent on the miniatures.[10]

These were much sought after by private collectors, members of the royal family and by wealthy American collectors. A key player was Joseph Duveen, the highly influential dealer who helped create the taste for Georgian portraiture among American collectors. In 1926 and 1927 he sold about a hundred portrait miniatures, of which sixty were attributed to Cosway, to the Californian railroad baron, Henry E. Huntington, for the huge price of almost half a million dollars. These were purchased by Huntington at the same time as he was acquiring the famous oil portraits such as *The Blue Boy* by Gainsborough and *Mrs Siddons as the Tragic Muse* by Reynolds. One of the reasons why Huntington made such a major acquisition was probably that he felt he was in competition with another American industrialist, J. Pierpont Morgan, who around the turn of the century had amassed an outstanding collection of miniatures in which works by Cosway comprised a major element. The author of Morgan's great four-volume catalogue was the same George C. Williamson, who, apart from writing the biography of the Cosways, had also produced books on many of his contemporaries such as John Downman, George Engleheart, Ozias Humphry, Angelica Kauffman, Andrew Plimer, John Russell and Johann Zoffany.[11]

The culmination of this surge of interest in Richard Cosway came with the decision to include a statue of him on the façade of the new building designed by Aston Webb for the Victoria and Albert Museum on Cromwell Road. This was carved by Ernest George Gillick in 1906. It may seem surprising to us that Richard Cosway was included in this array of artists, architects and designers, who represent the Edwardian pantheon of the visual arts. Equally interesting is the fact that the statue of Richard Cosway was placed in the position of honour to the right of the monarch Edward VII, immediately to the west of the main entrance. Thus Richard Cosway was situated ahead of the other eighteenth-century artists represented, namely Romney, Reynolds, Gainsborough and Hogarth, who both before and since have remained key figures in the canon of British artists of that century.

High prices continued to be paid for Richard Cosway's miniatures up until the outbreak of the Second World War. This was notably the case when J. Pierpont Morgan's great collection of portrait miniatures was sold at auction in 1935. The highest sum paid was £892 10s for a portrait of *Mrs Parsons*, and substantial prices were paid for other important miniatures such as £189 for *An unknown lady* [121] signed and dated 1794, £336 for *Lady Elizabeth Foster* and £672 for the portrait of *Madame du Barry*.[12] However it was exactly this mixture of brilliance and flattery, combined with flamboyant personality, which so successfully reflected and evoked the Regency and its social élite, that caused Richard Cosway's critical downfall after the Second World War, when the American taste for British eighteenth-century portraits, so skilfully created and sustained by Duveen, then declined so dramatically. After the War, even art historians such as Basil Long and Carl Winter, who made a special study of the portrait miniature, while acknowledging Richard Cosway's technical and fashionable accomplishment, were essentially unsympathetic to what they saw as the artist's 'sprightly sentimentality'. However, it was Ellis Waterhouse, another influential historian of British art, who, despite doing so much to revive the serious study of eighteenth-century portraiture, suffered the most extreme reaction to Richard Cosway, even suspending his critical judgement, commenting on the work as 'over-poignant' and his style as 'one which fits in very well with the affectations of the Regency period and with the cult of the bijou; but for all its technical accomplishment, it is very difficult to judge it at all by any serious standards'. This was written in 1947 in a time of considerable austerity, which provides some context for his later damning comparison of miniatures by Samuel Cooper and Richard Cosway, as well as censure of the periods they epitomised, 'which show a certain similarity with one another in the corruption of their manners and the prodigality of their wealth'. Yet, despite this antipathy, Waterhouse surprisingly did rate Cosway as an oil painter, commenting that the portraits – as with those of the Courtenay family [93, 151] at Powderham Castle, or those commissioned by the Marquis of Blandford, and now at Blenheim Palace [94, 149] – could be

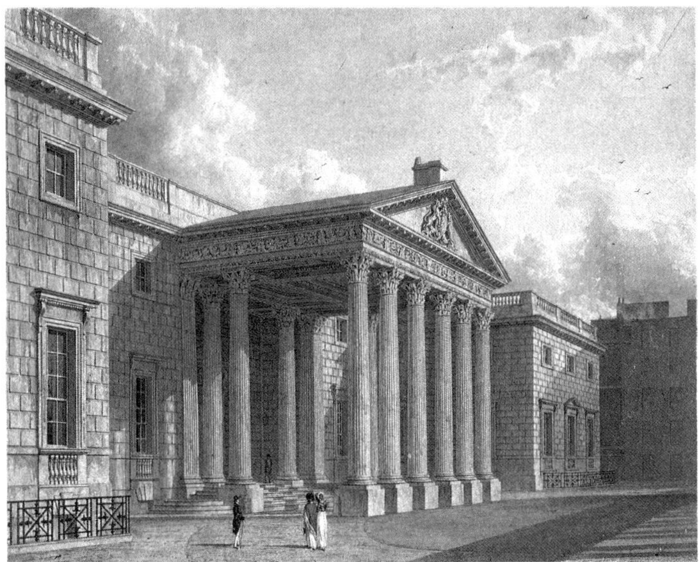

Fig. 2. *The North Front, Carlton House, London, c.*1819, by William Westall (The Royal Library, Windsor Castle)

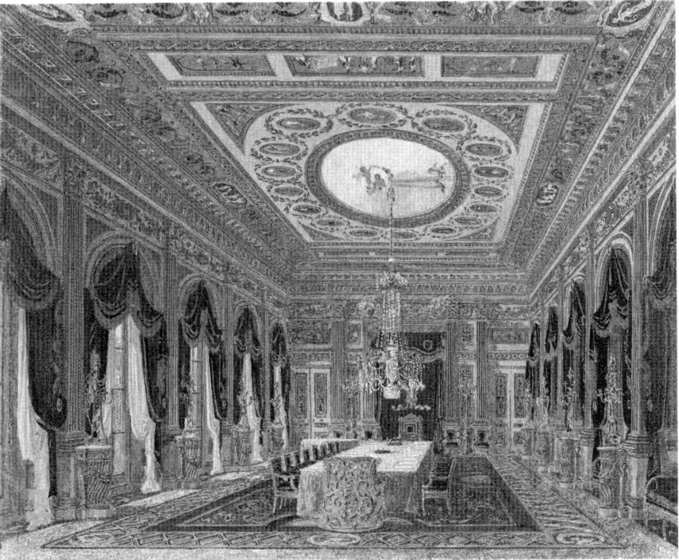

Fig. 3 *The Throne Room, Carlton House, London, c.*1818, by Charles Wild (The Royal Library, Windsor Castle)

remarkable, although he accurately described the oils as in general being 'smart and somewhat mannered but solid and not evanescent' unlike the miniatures.

Another reason why Cosway's reputation sank so low after 1945 was that, with his most distinctive medium being miniatures, he has suffered from the way in which this genre of portraiture has been studied separately from the more mainstream areas of oil painting and landscape watercolours. The art historical literature on portrait miniatures – and even more so on the portrait drawings with their related engravings – has, with few exceptions, tended to be rather isolated, and works in these media have made little impact on recent general exhibitions and more wide-ranging studies on the nature of portraiture.[13]

Maria Cosway's reputation has suffered to an even greater extent than Richard Cosway's, and she has been seen merely as an accompaniment to the artistic reputation and social notoriety of her husband. Hampered in her own lifetime by the obstacles placed in the way of talented women, as she admitted, she failed to sustain the quality of her work despite its ambition, variety and imagination. Only a small number of her works have survived, and even fewer have been studied or exhibited. While Richard Cosway's achievement as an artist has alternately benefited and suffered from the changing taste of succeeding generations, his miniatures have always been admired and collected. However, when his prolific and varied artistic production is revealed and re-examined in light of his highly extrovert personality, it can be seen that he was both one of the most significant artists and arbiters of taste during the later Georgian and early Regency period, and that his life and art shed considerable light on the sensibility of this intensely fashion conscious social élite.

If Richard Cosway's reputation has fluctuated wildly with the vicissitudes of taste, then Maria Cosway's remarkable life and achievements have been almost completely forgotten and unjustly ignored by posterity. Indeed this neglect may well have been because of the very breadth of her artistic achievement. In this respect, a balanced estimation of her production as an artist may have been hampered by the fact she was often referred to as 'accomplished', a term used to describe talented women in this period.[14]

Her reputation has also suffered from the fact that her career developed in three countries, Italy, Britain and France. An Anglo-Florentine, Maria Cosway was essentially Italian in her outlook, but her artistic career mainly happened in London, where she was never entirely happy, while the most extraordinary social episodes of her life took place in Paris. As with Elisabeth Vigée-Lebrun and Angelica Kauffman, it is this European aspect of her life that marks out Maria Cosway's enterprising activity as an artist and as a woman.

Despite being disappointed as an artist, and suffering considerable unhappiness as a wife and mother, Maria Cosway did find fulfilment in later life, reflecting in 1830: 'my elevated and happy station could but produce envy, malice and enemies, these I pass over unworthy of a thought – proofs will be one day in the hands of my friends to make me as worthy of their friendship'. When fully studied, Maria's extensive correspondence will provide the foundation of a fuller assessment of her life and career. However, despite her pessimism, her artistic production also deserves to be studied in greater depth. The assessment of its quality raises questions about the difficulties faced in the late eighteenth and early nineteenth century by talented women in acquiring professional status, especially within the confines of a marriage to another artist. It is perhaps inevitable that this artistic side of Maria Cosway will be overshadowed by her remarkable life, which sheds new light on many of her most famous contemporaries. Whether studied as a 'muse', an artist, musician or educationalist, it is important that all aspects of her life be considered within her unusual status both as a versatile semi-professional woman and as an Anglo-Italian. As she wrote in old age in her autobiographical letter of 1830, 'while Mr. C[osway's] memoirs' would be short, her own 'would be perhaps too long, but very full of interesting matters'.

While both Richard and Maria Cosway deserve to be studied and re-assessed in their own right as artists, it would be a mistake not to consider the influence they had on each other, both artistically and in terms of their social reputation. Not only were they one of the most extraordinary couples of the period, but their status as fashionable artists – and the great range of work they produced – also reveals much about the *mentalité* of the society in which they starred.

RICHARD & MARIA COSWAY
REGENCY ARTISTS OF TASTE AND FASHION

STEPHEN LLOYD

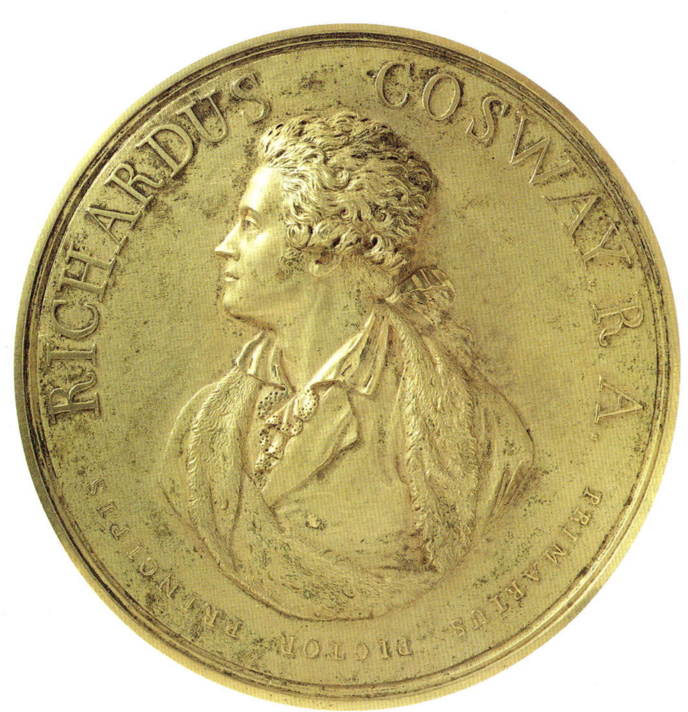

Unknown Medallist *Richardus Cosway RA c.*1790 [146]

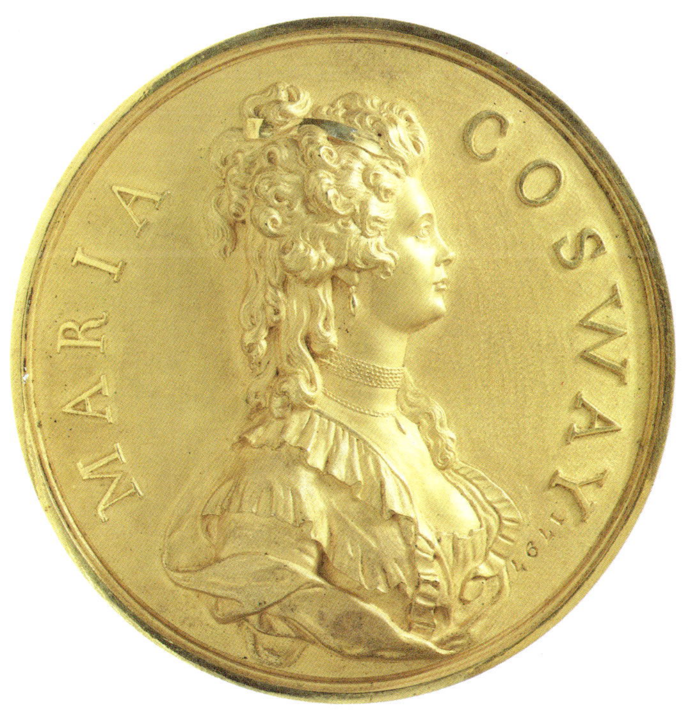

Unknown Medallist *Maria Cosway* 1797 [148]

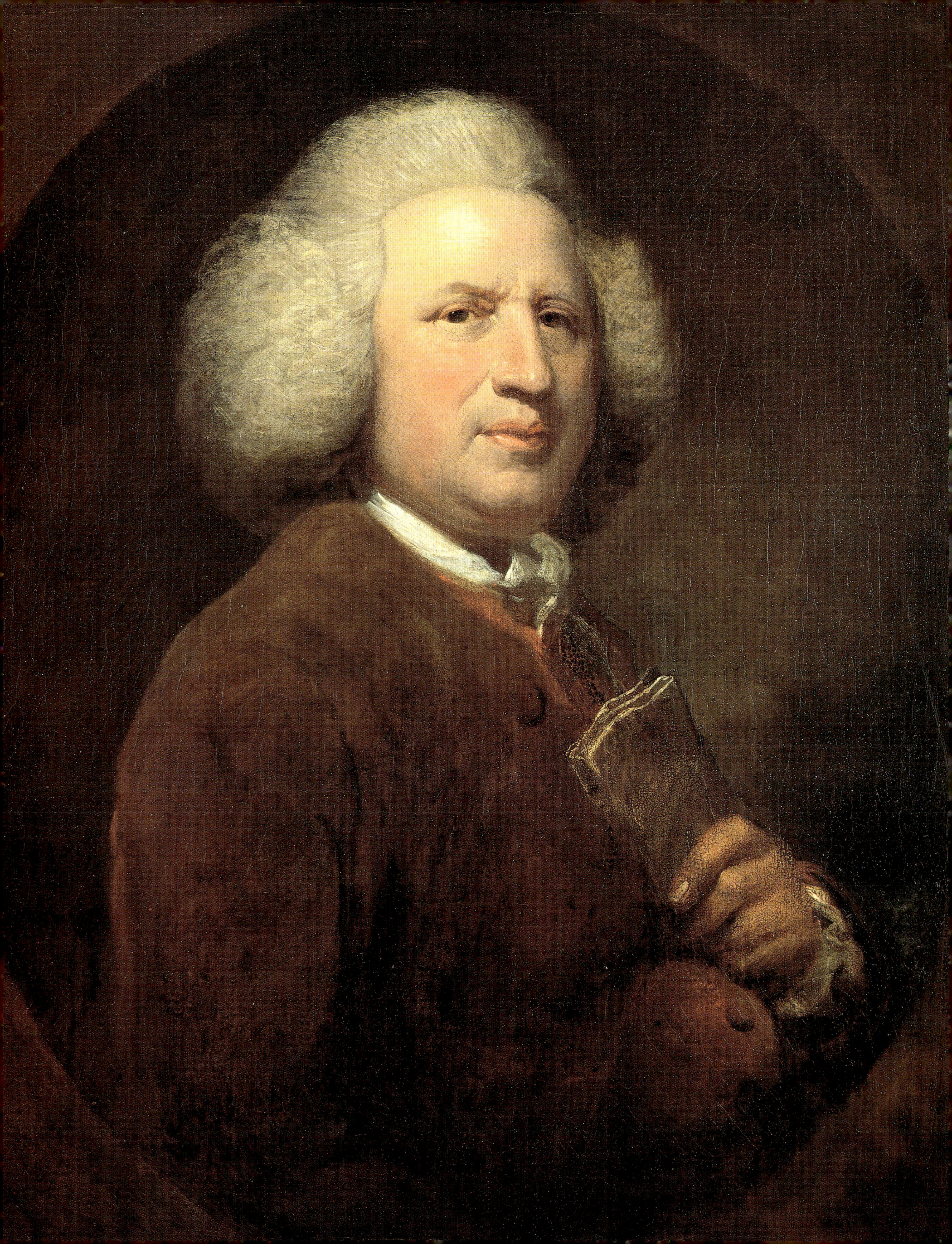

RICHARD COSWAY
EARLY LIFE AND CAREER IN DEVON AND LONDON
1742–70

*F*ROM the money he gained, and the gaiety of the company he kept he rose from one of the dirtiest boys, to one of the smartest of men.'[1] Little is known about Richard Cosway's early life as 'one of the dirtiest boys'. Even the exact date of his birth has not been established. His christening took place in the parish church of Oakford, near Tiverton in Devon, on 5 November 1742. His parents were named as Richard and Mary, but nothing else has yet been found of the immediate family circumstances. It does not appear that he had any brothers or sisters.[2]

There has been some confusion over Cosway's exact date of birth, it often being stated that he was born two years before the christening, in 1740. Indeed it appears that the artist himself was either forgetful or mischievous concerning the truth about his age. The year before his death he was reported as repeatedly informing one of his executors, Sir John Carr, that he was eighty-four. After Cosway's actual death in 1821, the sculptor Richard Westmacott announced to his fellow Academicians that he had obtained a certificate from the parish register where he had been born, which indicated that Cosway was in his eighty-second year. This was also the age noted on his burial certificate. However, it is much more likely that 1742 was the correct year of birth. He was described as being twelve years old when he won first prize in the inaugural drawing competition at the Society of Arts in 1755. This was also confirmed by the miniaturist John Smart, who was one of Cosway's earliest friends in London, and who was well aware of his rival's vanity regarding his age. Interestingly, a hint of Cosway's attitude to his age can be seen in his self-portraits, a remarkable series which Cosway executed throughout his life. A recurrent feature, particularly in the late examples which show him in middle to old age, is the artist's marked tendency towards idealisation of himself as a perpetually young man [103].[3]

The name Cosway seems to have been fairly common in the Tiverton area during the eighteenth century, but little is known about the origins of the name or the wider family. However, Richard Cosway was the only person with that surname recorded as being born in Oakford at that period. This small hamlet is situated in the upper valley of the River Exe, about twenty miles north of Exeter, and around eight miles north of the prosperous wool town of Tiverton. Cosway's mother and father may have been living in Oakford at that time because of a fever that ravaged Tiverton in 1741, forcing many families to find temporary refuge elsewhere.[4]

Further information about the artist's early life and his family's origins was provided not long after Cosway's death in a biographical essay by Allan Cunningham, which was included in his *Lives* of British artists. This was based to a large extent on information provided by a cousin of the artist, *Sir William Richard Cosway* [184], a naval officer who had been Collingwood's secretary at the Battle of Trafalgar. He corresponded with Maria Cosway and her major autobiographical letter to him was used by Cunningham in his life of Richard Cosway. However, within this account, which was relayed by Sir William to Cunningham through the agency of another cousin, Sir Andrew Halliday, it is possible to detect the voice of Cosway himself, both in the attempt to enhance the family's status and reputation and especially in the telling reference to his artistic hero Rubens:

The following is the information I have been able to collect of Mr Cosway. His family were settled at Tiverton in Devonshire in the reign of Queen Elizabeth, their patrimonial estate of Coombe Willis being about 5 miles from that town and they are supposed to have emigrated from the Low Countries during the time of the Duke of Alva's persecution bringing to Tiverton the woollen manufactory, which his family were engaged in until the French Revolutionary War. As this family connection with the woollen trade kept up a communication with Holland, some of his family preserved pictures of the Flemish School and of Rubens, the admiration of which probably had an influence on the taste of our young Author. His father was master of the school at Tiverton and at 7 years of age he was punished for neglecting his lessons and being always 'idly engaged in drawing' his passion so entirely absorbed him that in a few years after his Uncle who was the Mayor of Tiverton and Mr Oliver Peard the leading Merchant of the then principal woollen manufacturing Town in England, determined to give him a fair chance of cultivating his talent, and sent him to London where he studied under Hudson with great success and was much sought after in Society where his wit and conversational talents placed him high.[5]

This account is important, since, with the absence of any direct autobiographical materials by Cosway, it represents the traditional view of his early life and training. It does seem likely that Cosway's father was a teacher, and he may have kept his own school. Certainly there is no evidence that either father or son taught or attended Blundell's, which was the major school in Tiverton. It is worth noting that Sir Joshua Reynolds, who was then emerging as one of the leading portraitists in London, was also from Devon, and that his father had similarly been a schoolmaster in Plympton. Likewise, the established society painter Thomas Hudson, who taught Reynolds and possibly Cosway for a short while too, was also a Devonian. As soon as the young Cosway began to show promise as a draughtsman it is very probable that he would have been made well aware of these two highly successful Devon-born artists. Any early indication of Cosway's skill in work on a small scale would also have encouraged comparison with another famous Devonian, Nicholas Hilliard, the quintessential Elizabethan and Jacobean miniaturist.[6]

Of the other key mentors to whom Sir William Cosway refers in his letter, the uncle who was Mayor of Tiverton must have been *Thomas Cosway* [12], who held that office in 1758. Cosway portrayed him and his second wife *Katharine* (née Proby) [13], whom he married in 1761, in two of his earliest miniatures, which were probably commissioned to commemorate their marriage. The importance of Thomas Cosway to the young artist is also indicated by the fact that his earliest extant signed and dated miniature, which was painted a year earlier, also represents his uncle.[7] In what is a highly precocious technical performance, the sitter is shown half length within an ambitious composition, resting on an anchor, with cliffs and a ship at sea depicted in the background. In addition, a bust-length oil portrait from this date by Cosway of his uncle survives in a private collection. It is possible that this series of portraits may have been painted by Cosway to mark the beginning of his professional career in 1760, when he first exhibited publicly in London, and it may also have been intended as an important act of early patronage and support for the young artist.

A second key figure from Cosway's early life in Tiverton was Oliver Peard, a wealthy local businessman and another sometime Mayor of Tiverton in 1743 and 1753, who may well have been godfather to the young boy. Peard is likely to have encouraged Cosway's father to send his son to London to train as an artist, and also offered to maintain him there. A third local figure who appears to have been of influence over Cosway's future career was a Dr Newte, under whose patronage and auspices, the satirist Anthony Pasquin noted, Cosway 'made the first development of his ability'. This may have been Dr Samuel Newte, who was a member of a local family that was known for its benefactions to the parish church of St Peter's in Tiverton.[8]

Clearly Cosway was showing enough early signs of promise in his drawing that his family and mentors decided to send him at the very young age of twelve to London to train as an artist. They must have seen or heard of an advertisement published by *William Shipley* [1], a drawing master and portraitist recently established in London, who was announcing his newly founded Society for the Encouragement of Arts, Manufactures and Commerce through a competition with premiums for 'the best Drawings, by Boys and Girls, under the age of 14 years, and Proof of their abilities, on or before the 15th day of January, 1755'. The circumstances of Cosway's arrival in the capital at the end of the previous year were recorded in the Society's minutes by Shipley. On 27 November the committee of the Society, which comprised Shipley, Lord Romney, the surgeon Husband Messiter and the wealthy linen draper John Goodchild, met and the minutes recorded that: 'Several Specimens of Drawings done by Richard Cosway of Tiverton were produced, it was thought prop[r]. his parents be writ to think what will be the expense of his coming to town'.

A few weeks later, at another meeting on 18 December, Shipley stated 'that he had a note' of the boy's imminent arrival. As the journey from Exeter to London then took about three days by stage-coach, it is likely that Cosway would have arrived in the capital before Christmas. Certainly it was the case that the young boy was taken very much under the wing of Shipley. It appears that Cosway became one of his most favoured pupils, and lodged with the drawing master in his various homes over the next five years until Shipley's retirement from the Society in 1760.[9]

As to the drawing competition, Cosway was immediately successful, winning the first prize of five pounds in the under fourteen-year-old category for a chalk drawing showing the *Head of one of the Vertues expressing compassion*, which would almost certainly have been copied from a print. This practice was the first stage of artistic training, and prints represented a vitally important body of visual material for the development of an artist's *oeuvre*. The most important such drawing by Cosway to have survived is his large copy after a print of Guido Reni's renowned fresco in Rome of *Aurora and the Chariot of Apollo*, the drawing later being acquired by Sir John Soane.[10] The fact that Cosway won this competition was also significant in that his work would have been noted by the jury, which was made up of some of the most established artists of the day, including the sculptor Henry Cheere, the antiquarian and royal librarian Richard Dalton, as well as the engravers Robert Strange and Jacob Bonneau. Another influential figure in Cosway's development was Viscount Folkestone [22], later the 1st Earl of Radnor, who was not only President of the Society, but also a major collector and connoisseur. His son Jacob – later the 2nd Earl – was to become one of Cosway's most important patrons both in terms of commissions and in the purchase of Old Master pictures from the artist.

Thus Cosway was immediately brought into contact with some of the key figures of the thriving London art world and market, which was still dominated by a taste for foreign – and notably Italian – art, whether in patronage, connoisseurship or collecting. The struggle towards a self-respecting national school during the course of the century was led by Hogarth, and helped by the creation of various art academies and institutions in London. The founding of the Society of Arts was a key event in this process, which eventually culminated in the establishment of the Royal Academy in 1768.[11] This climate of artistic improvement was reflected in the text of the certificate for the first competition that Cosway won in 1755:

But as to an ingenious Mind, Reputation and Esteem are more desirable than any pecuniary Gratuity; this Certificate is likewise given, as a farther Encouragement, for the said Richard Cosway to exert his utmost Endeavours for the improving himself in this useful Art, and for the rendring his Improvements therein as much as possible beneficial to the Public.

William Shipley was one of the most important figures in the development of the arts during the eighteenth century. The son of a London stationer, he made a living as a minor painter and drawing master in Northampton before returning to the capital to establish the Society of Arts. His purpose was 'to embolden enterprise, to enlarge Science, to refine Art, to improve our Manufactures and extend our Commerce'. The patriotic agenda of this scheme was reinforced by his proposal 'to render Great Britain the school of instruction, as it is already the centre of traffic to the greatest part of the known world'.

In parallel to his foundation of the Society of Arts, Shipley established a drawing school to train potential young artists with a view to their contributing to 'such manufactures as require Fancy and Ornament, and for which the knowledge of Drawing is absolutely necessary', as he announced in a newspaper advertisement. Clearly Shipley's intention was to improve the standard of draughtsmanship in the field of fashion and design. To this end he was concerned that 'the Society would not be misunderstood to aim at raising numbers of what are usually called Painters'. However, many of his pupils went on to become established artists and professional painters, including Cosway himself.[12]

Another important aspect of Shipley's school for Cosway was that he was surrounded by a new generation of young art students, who were to make a substantial contribution to the increasingly confident artistic climate both in London and across the country during the second half of the eighteenth century. The second placed prizewinner to Cosway in 1755 was *John Smart* [**137**], who was to rival Cosway's pre-eminent position as a portrait miniaturist during the next half-century. Other students who were to become successful artists included the miniaturists Ozias Humphry and *Richard Crosse* [**24**], a fellow Devonian who was a deaf-mute, the landscape painter William Hodges, the portraitist and genre painter Francis Wheatley, the portraitist William Pars, the history painter John Hamilton Mortimer, the mezzotint engraver Richard Earlom, and the sculptor Joseph Nollekens. From within this peer group Cosway later made friendships, engaged in competitive rivalry, established professional relationships and forged his distinctive artistic style and persona.[13]

After his initial prizewinning success Cosway was awarded premiums on four more occasions up to 1760, when he set himself up as an independent artist. In 1757 he won second prize, worth four guineas, 'for the most ingenious and best fancied Designs ... proper for Weavers, Embroiderers or Calico-Printers drawn by Boys under the Age of 17'. In the following year he again came second, this time to John Smart, in the category 'for the best drawings of an Human Figure in plaster by Boys and Girls under the Age of 18', the cast being the *Dancing Faun*. The importance of the study of the forms of classical sculpture was emphasised by a similar competition held in the following year for 'the best Drawings of an Human Figure or Figures, or Basso Relievos, from Models or Casts in Plaster, the Princi-

pal Figure not under Twelve inches'. Cosway won fourth prize behind Nollekens for his copy of *The Fighting Gladiator* [fig. 4]. This was copied from a cast at the Duke of Richmond's Gallery in Whitehall, which had been opened to students in March 1758. Under the direction of the painter Giovanni Battista Cipriani and the sculptor Joseph Wilton, this was an influential but short-lived school. Its importance and purpose can be gauged from a contemporary account: '... the study of these most exact copies from antiques may greatly contribute toward giving young beginners of genius an early taste and idea of beauty and proportion; which when thoroughly acquired will in time appear in their several performances'.[14]

The exposure to classical sculpture was of great importance for the formation of Cosway's style and his aesthetic response. This was especially the case in light of his not undertaking a visit to Italy, unlike so many of his artistic contemporaries and potential aristocratic patrons. However, much of his later artistic output, in particular the portrait and subject drawings, was infused with a deep understanding of classical forms and types, as in the drawing of *Anthony and Cleopatra* [**11**]. Cunningham was well aware of this aspect in Cosway's work:

> *He had, however, other claims to public notice; his drawings from the antique were graceful and accurate; to copy with the pencil the fine flowing outline of a Grecian statue, and catch the true proportions, require a fine eye and a skilful hand; and Cosway seems to have had both. This sort of practice he acquired in the Duke of Richmond's gallery. His outlines caught the eye of Bartolozzi, who with Cipriani, pronounced them admirable.*

The support and encouragement of these two émigré Italians, the latter a highly fashionable designer and the former a stipple engraver, who was to reproduce many of Cosway's most graceful miniatures and drawings, would also have been critical at this period. Cunningham noted that Cosway 'introduced a touch of the antique into his fashionable miniatures' – as can be seen in *Miss Elliot in the character of Pallas* [**17**] – and that this benefited the development of his early career. Another unidentified friend of Cosway perceptively remarked of the artist's whole style that 'he inclined more to the neat, the graceful, and the lovely, than towards the serene, the dignified, and the stern; and though his admiration of the antique was great, this was modified by his continual studying of living nature, and from a taste for whatever was soft and elegant'.[15]

The year 1760 was the last year in which Cosway entered the Society of Arts' competitions. He won the first prize, worth ten guineas, in the section 'for the best Drawings of an Human Figure after Life drawn at the Academy for Painting, etc., in St. Martin's Lane, by Youths under the Age of 24'. Like other pupils at Shipley's school Cosway had been able to study from the life at the St Martin's Lane Academy, an important precursor to the foundation of the Royal Academy. Also in 1760 Cosway exhibited a work publicly for the first time, the oil portrait of his mentor *William Shipley* [**1**]. This was shown at the inaugural exhibition held by the Society of Arts, in the year of Shipley's retirement from his official duties. Not only is this portrait a tribute by pupil to master, but it also marks Cosway's public arrival on the consciousness of the London art world.

Cosway's portrait of Shipley was shown at the landmark exhibition of works of living British artists, which was organised by the Society of Arts. The first such public exhibition, consisting of a hundred and thirty works by sixty-nine artists, it was an enormous

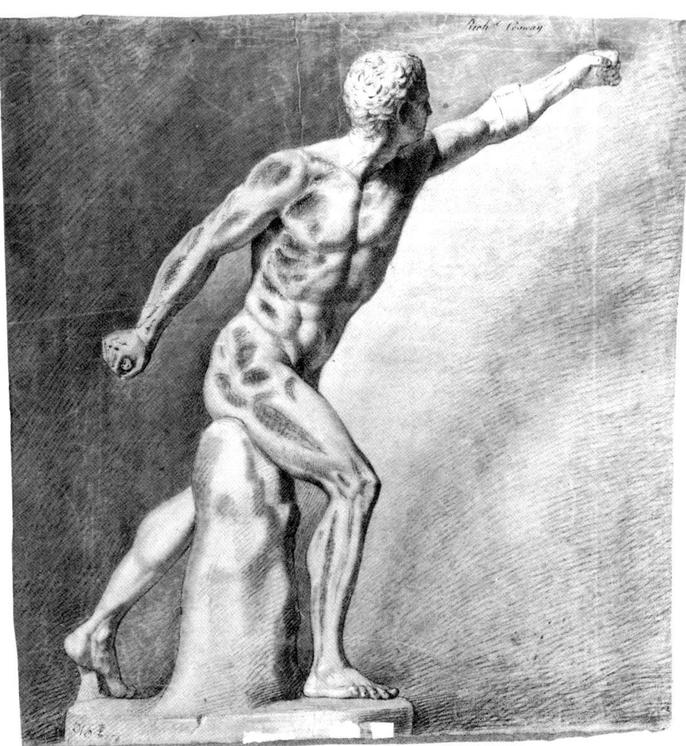

Fig. 4 *The Fighting Gladiator, c.*1758–9 (Royal Society of Arts, London)

success, being seen by 20,000 visitors in the two weeks of its duration, and so crowded that there were scenes of public disorder. Cosway's picture betrays the influence of two highly successful fellow Devonian artists, Thomas Hudson, with whom he may have trained, and Sir Joshua Reynolds. Here Cosway has adopted Reynolds's use of strong characterisation, warm chiaroscuro and distinctive impasto for the facial highlights – all of which traits could be seen in the work of Rembrandt, whose paintings were greatly admired by artists, patrons and collectors in the eighteenth century.

In this sensitive portrayal Cosway has caught both the taciturn determination and the benevolent mind of this remarkable teacher and philanthropist. The painting was clearly of great importance to Cosway as he retained it in his collection until 1785, when he presented it to the Society. In thanking the artist for his generosity, the Society described the portrait as 'so striking a Resemblance of the parent of their Institution'. In 1787 it was placed over the chimney in the Committee Room at the Society's Room in the Adelphi, with a new frame and inscription stating that 'his public spirit gave rise to this Society'.

The success of Cosway's portrayal of Shipley may be judged by the description of the sitter in an account of him written towards the end of his life: 'He was a man grave in his deportment, slow, and sometimes hesitating, in his speech, not from defects, but from consideration; and had, especially when sitting, something of the heavy appearance of the late Dr. Johnson, yet under this unpromising aspect, he possessed a most benevolent heart, joined to an inquisitive, intelligent, and highly cultivated mind …' Cosway also successfully defined Shipley's well-known taciturnity. The calm concentration of the gaze is reinforced by the sitter's firm hand gesture.[16]

The circumstances of Cosway's training as an oil painter are unclear. Traditionally he is supposed to have studied for a while with Thomas Hudson, who ran a very successful portrait practice in London during the mid-eighteenth century. A number of artists were apprenticed to Hudson, notably Mortimer and Joseph Wright of Derby during the 1750s. However there is no specific evidence that Cosway trained with Hudson: it is clear that Cosway was in fact apprenticed to Shipley in 1755, and that it was from him that he would have learned the basic elements of oil painting.[17]

During the 1760s it seems that Cosway was involved in the teaching of drawing skills. In the year after Shipley retired, he handed over the running of his school, which was now established on the south side of the Strand in Beaufort House, to Henry and William Pars. Cosway was likely to have taught at the school, especially since he had lodgings there, and also used that address when exhibiting his work in 1763. Four years later he established his house and studio in Orchard Street, off Portman Square, in the fashionable West End. In the following year Cosway moved to an even more desirable address at 4 Berkeley Street just off Piccadilly, where he lived until his move to Schomberg House in Pall Mall seventeen years later. The previous occupant of this house had been the late John Shackleton. For a socially ambitious artist such as Cosway, it would have been advantageous to move into premises that had formerly belonged to a court artist who had been Principal Painter in Ordinary to George II. Both this fact and the central location of the house demonstrated the extent to which Cosway's career had progressed during this decade.[18]

Indeed, throughout the 1760s Cosway exhibited publicly at the Free Society of Artists, first from 1761 to 1764 and then two years later, while from 1767 to 1769 he returned to the Society of Artists. He exhibited a wide variety of work, including paintings, miniatures and drawings. There were many different formats for the portraiture in oils, whether bust-length portraits, half-lengths, three-quarter-lengths, small full-lengths or conversation pieces, as well as watercolours, and miniatures in watercolour or on enamel. Apart from 'in character' portrayals that included Cupid, Pallas [17] and Sigismunda, Cosway also exhibited a few subject pictures such as a Magdalen, both in a miniature and as an oil, a miniature of the Madonna, and a 'tinged' drawing of Venus and Adonis. Of all the works that Cosway exhibited during this decade only the portrait in oils of *William Shipley* [1] and the large miniature of *Miss Elliot in the character of Pallas* [17] at Lodi have survived.

The combination of versatility and ambition shown by Cosway at this date was to continue throughout his career. He was unique among his peers for sustaining a successful output in all three media of oils, drawings and miniatures. He was therefore justified in being described in Thomas Mortimer's invaluable trade directory *The Universal Director* (1763) as a 'Portrait Painter', as opposed to a miniaturist. By contrast some of Cosway's major rivals were described as follows: John Smart as a 'Miniature Painter'; Nathaniel Hone and Gervase Spencer both as 'Portrait Painter in enamel'; Samuel Cotes and Jeremiah Meyer both as 'Enamel and Miniature Painter'; while only Richard Crosse used the same description as Cosway. With respect to the portraits in oils, Cosway would have been well aware of the profusion of competitors in this market, which was dominated by Ramsay, Hudson, Reynolds and Cotes, while the demand for conversation pieces was supplied by artists of the calibre of Zoffany, Wheatley and Mortimer. In light of this fierce competition Cosway diversified the output of his portraiture, which, combined with his artistic facility and anticipation of changing fashions, helped sustain the momentum of his career.[19]

It is not known with whom Cosway trained as a miniaturist, but it is very improbable that it was with either Hudson or Shipley. His first securely signed and dated miniature was that of Thomas Cosway, painted in 1760. In the previous year he had produced a small portrait of *Edward Goldney* [25], a printer from Bristol and an author of religious tracts. This engaging, but rather awkward portrait, in which the sitter's head is too large for the body, was engraved by T. Chambars, and is both the earliest extant portrait by Cosway and the first work of his to be reproduced as an engraving. The artist's uneven development as a portraitist in oils is evident, and contrasts with the sureness of his portrait miniatures from the following years [12–16]. The densely worked handling of these portraits is close to the style of Nathaniel Hone and Gervase Spencer. They were two of the most prominent exponents of what has been aptly called the 'modest' school of portrait miniaturists working in a very small scale from about 1740 to 1770. Either Hone or Spencer might be considered as Cosway's possible master for miniatures in the techniques of both watercolour on ivory and in enamels on copper.[20]

Miniatures were becoming an increasingly popular type of portraiture during the course of the eighteenth century. This is indicated by the publication in 1752 of the sixth English edition of Claude Boutet's *The Art of Painting in Miniature*, the original of which had been published in numerous editions in France in the late seventeenth and early eighteenth century. The accessibility of this art form was indicated by the title page of the 1752 edition, which claimed that the volume would teach 'the speedy and perfect Acquisition of that Art without a Master. By rules so easy, and in a Method so natural as to render this charming Accomplishment universally attainable ...'[21] In light of the popularity of this book, which made the craft of miniature painting accessible to the amateur, the possibility should be considered that Cosway may have been self-taught, and just transferred his training as a draughtsman and oil painter to the practice of miniature painting.

His early activity as a miniaturist included his being 'employed to make drawings of heads for the shops, as well as fancy miniatures and free subjects for snuff-boxes for the jewellers, mostly from ladies he knew'. Very few of Cosway's erotic miniatures have survived, a notable exception being *An unknown lady* [46] painted *c*.1780, shown lifting a veil to reveal the upper half of her naked body. Two snuff-boxes inset with erotic scenes showing Leda and the swan were later treasured by Maria Cosway and coveted by Sir Thomas Lawrence. In a letter of 1830 from Maria Cosway to Sir John Soane, she stated as a postscript: 'Sir T. Lawrence's death has broken a hope I had of placing well that famous snuf[f] boxs of Mr: C[osway], with beautifull Leda & another on the same subject. He wished much to possess them & we were in Correspondence about them for they are subjects that was I to die & be found would no doubt go in the fire'.[22]

Further evidence that Cosway painted erotic miniatures is found in Ozias Humphry's manuscript biography of George Stubbs, where the origin of the latter's technique of painting in enamel is being discussed: 'His [Stubbs's] determination was thus begun to make experiments & improvements in Enamel Painting – Mr. Cosway had receivd some commissions to paint loose & amorous Subjects from abroad – & in discoursing together it was he who first suggested to him the first Idea of attempting subjects in this Line of Enamel which after having considered the matter he willingly acquiesced ...' As Stubbs's first dated painting in enamel was made in 1769, Cosway's encouragement probably occurred in the late 1760s, although none of Cosway's enamels or items from this specific commission have yet been identified. Nonetheless, this statement is evidence both of Cosway's willingness to discuss technical experimentation and to share such knowledge with fellow artists. A few years later, in 1775, Stubbs painted a portrait of Cosway's pet dog, of the Spanish or Papillon breed – on account of the shape of its ears and face – shown appropriately chasing a butterfly [194]. It has been plausibly suggested that this picture, which is considered the most engaging of Stubbs's canine portraits, was commissioned as a gesture of friendship between the two artists.[23]

Relatively few miniatures painted during the 1760s can be confidently identified as being from Cosway's hand. Between the signed and dated Thomas Cosway of 1760 and the *Miss Elliot in the character of Pallas* [17] exhibited in 1769, there are only three signed examples.[24] One of these is the double portrait of *Henry, 3rd Duke of Buccleuch, and his brother the Hon. Campbell Scott* [15], which is

signed and dated 1764, and is a partial copy after a painting by Reynolds of the two boys in 'Vandyke' fancy dress. The technique and style of Cosway's early miniatures have been described by the contemporary art historian Patrick Noon as:

... typically small in scale but painted with a surplus of paint that can be dark and heavily impasted in his backgrounds. Inspired by contemporary portraiture in oil, he aimed in such works at creating a dramatic ambience for his sitters that would intimate a complex and noble personality. His characteristic method of modelling the face with vigorous hatchings and large dots of water-colour is already in evidence in his first essays, and like a number of his contemporaries, he initially favoured a greyish-brown tint for shading.

Another contemporary commentator Graham Reynolds, describing the early phase of Cosway's miniatures, rightly made particular reference to the unsigned portrait of *Lady Sarah Bunbury* [16], datable to *c*.1765–70, and compared it with the later development of Cosway's mature style of miniature painting:

... [it] already has the softness of touch and firmness of modelling of Cosway's later manner, but the head is small in size and the whole miniature modest in conception. The pose and ornamental background imitate the mannerisms of Reynolds's official portraiture, and it is his way of treating the background above all which reveals that Cosway has not yet discovered, as he was shortly to, that the way to profit to the full from the luminosity of his ivory surface was to use transparent pigment and leave the ground to tell as much as possible.[25]

The culmination of Cosway's miniature painting at this date was his portrait of the actress *Miss Elliot in the character of Pallas* [17], which was exhibited at the Society of Artists in 1769. This is a notably large portrait miniature in which Cosway has shown the sitter in a suitably theatrical pose. Dressed *all'antica* with flowing robes, Miss Elliot wears a plumed helmet, a breastplate adorned with the Medusa's head, and she rests her hands on a shield, all set against a dark and dramatic sky. An ambitious portrait, it was no doubt intended to make an impression while on public display, and would have been compared to Samuel Cotes's similarly styled miniature of *Mrs Yates as Electra in Voltaire's 'Orestes'*, which was shown in the opening exhibition at the newly founded Royal Academy.

Cosway's increasing success as a miniaturist during this decade was noted by Laurence Sterne who repeatedly praised a portrait miniature by Cosway of his beloved *Mrs Draper* [6], for whom he wrote *The Journal to Eliza* (1767). In this intense lover's journal, written in the last year of Sterne's life, the miniature stands in for his Eliza who is away in India. The writer uses the portrait to invoke all his affection for his loved one, and it thus becomes a symbol and conduit for the great intimacy he feels for his Muse. The miniature soothes Sterne when he is dejected; he kisses it over and over again; he looks at it for hour upon hour; he passes it around the dinner table, and he confesses: '... I verily think my Eliza I shall get this Picture set so as to wear it, as If first purposed – about my neck – I do not like the place tis in – it shall be nearer my heart – Thou art ever in its centre ...'[26]

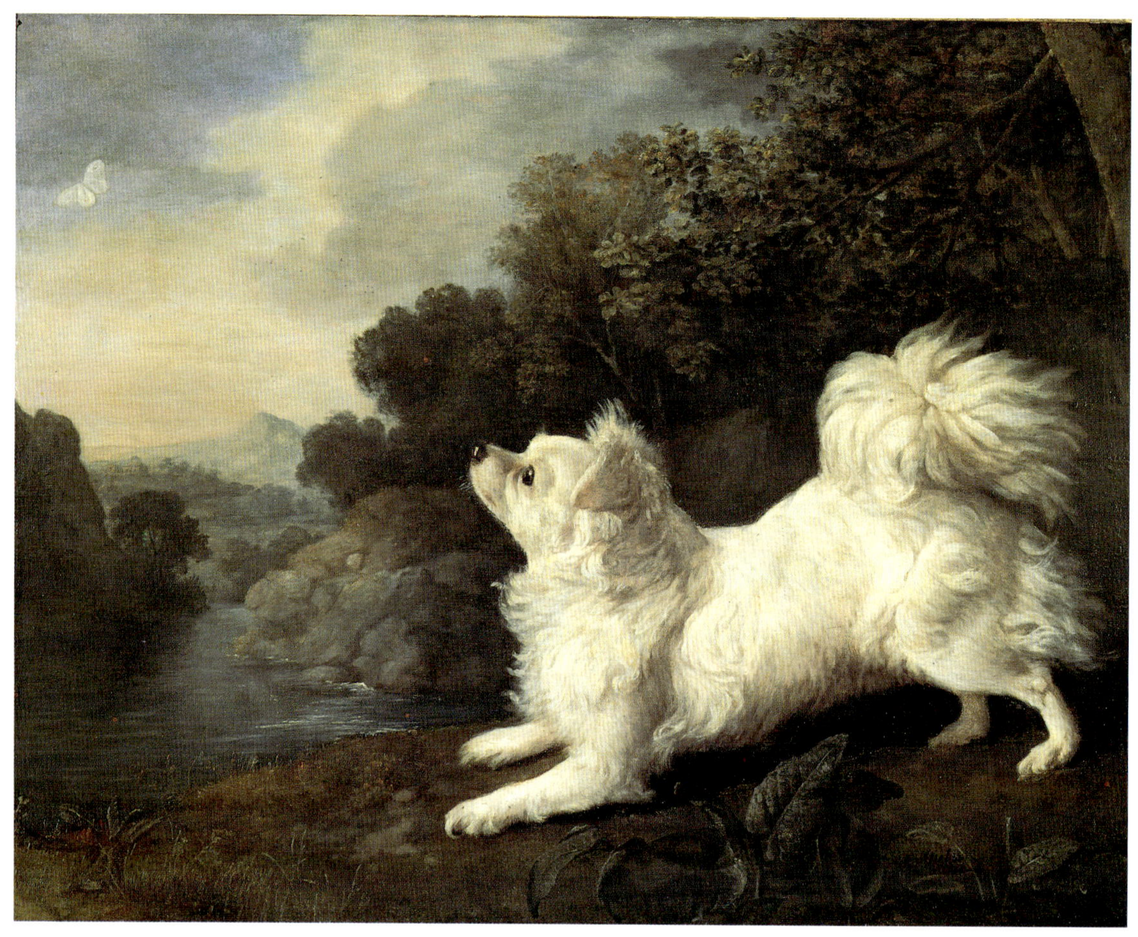

Plate 2   George Stubbs *Portrait of a Spanish dog belonging to Mr Cosway* 1774–5 [**194**]

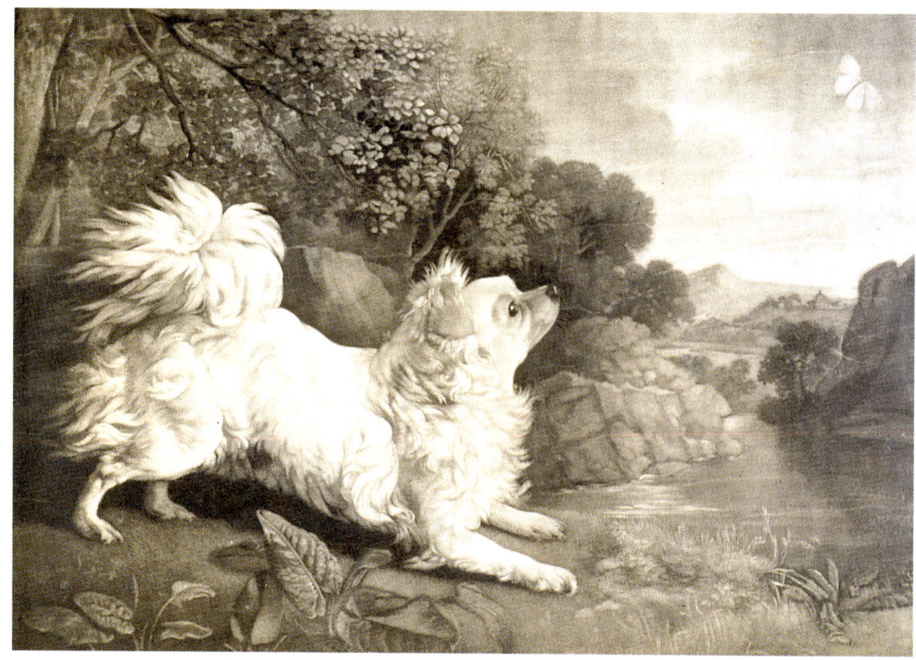

Plate 3   E. Fisher after George Stubbs *Mr Cosway's dog* 1782 [**195**]

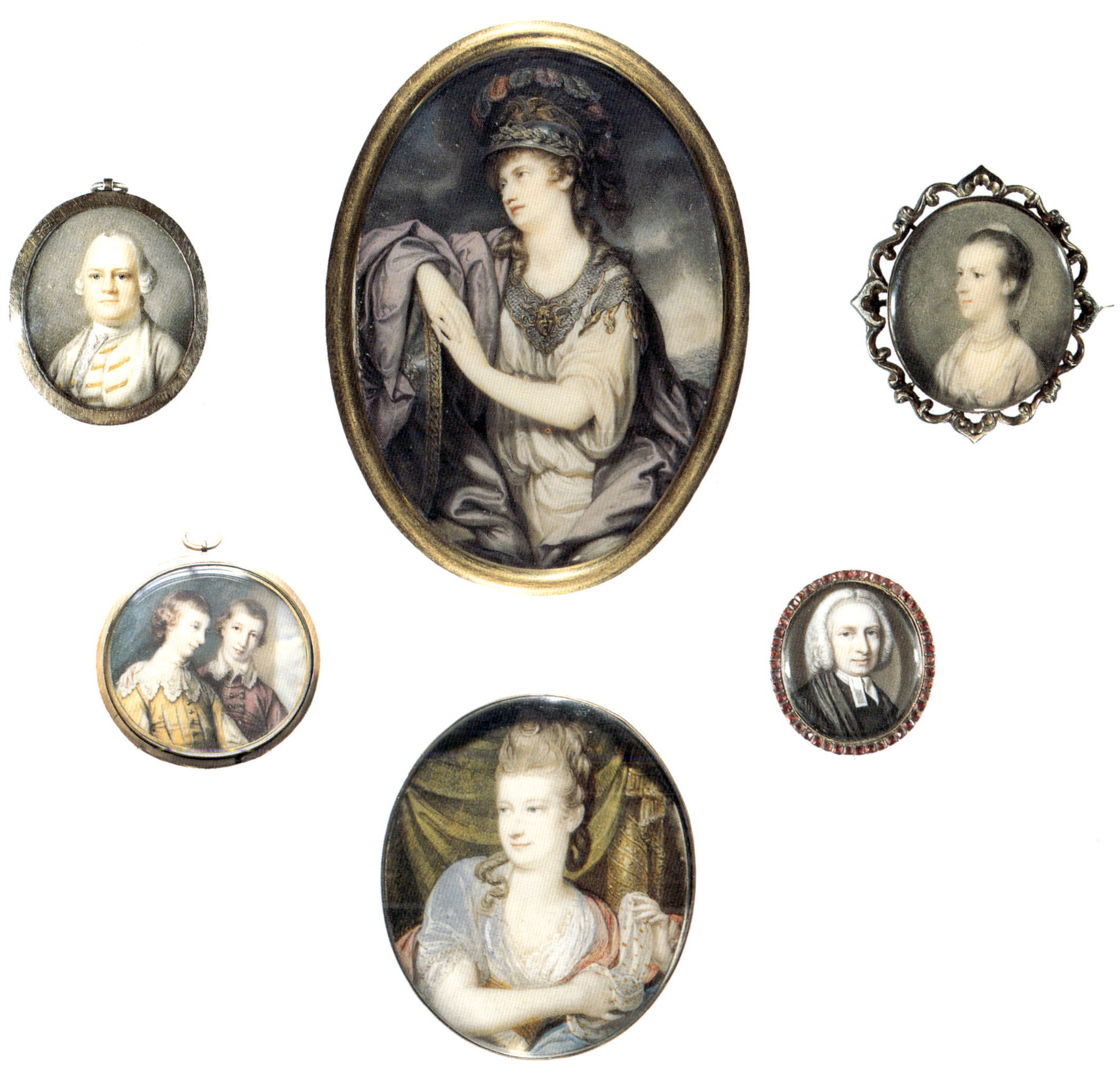

TOP LEFT Plate 4 *Thomas Cosway c.1761* [12]
TOP CENTRE Plate 5 *Miss Elliot in the character of Pallas* 1769 [17]
TOP RIGHT Plate 6 *Katharine Cosway c.1761* [13]
MIDDLE LEFT Plate 7 Richard Cosway after Sir Joshua Reynolds, *Henry, 3rd Duke of Buccleuch, and his brother the Hon. Campbell Scott* 1764 [15]
MIDDLE RIGHT Plate 8 *An unknown divine c.1760–70* [14]
BOTTOM Plate 9 *Lady Sarah Bunbury c.1765–70* [16]

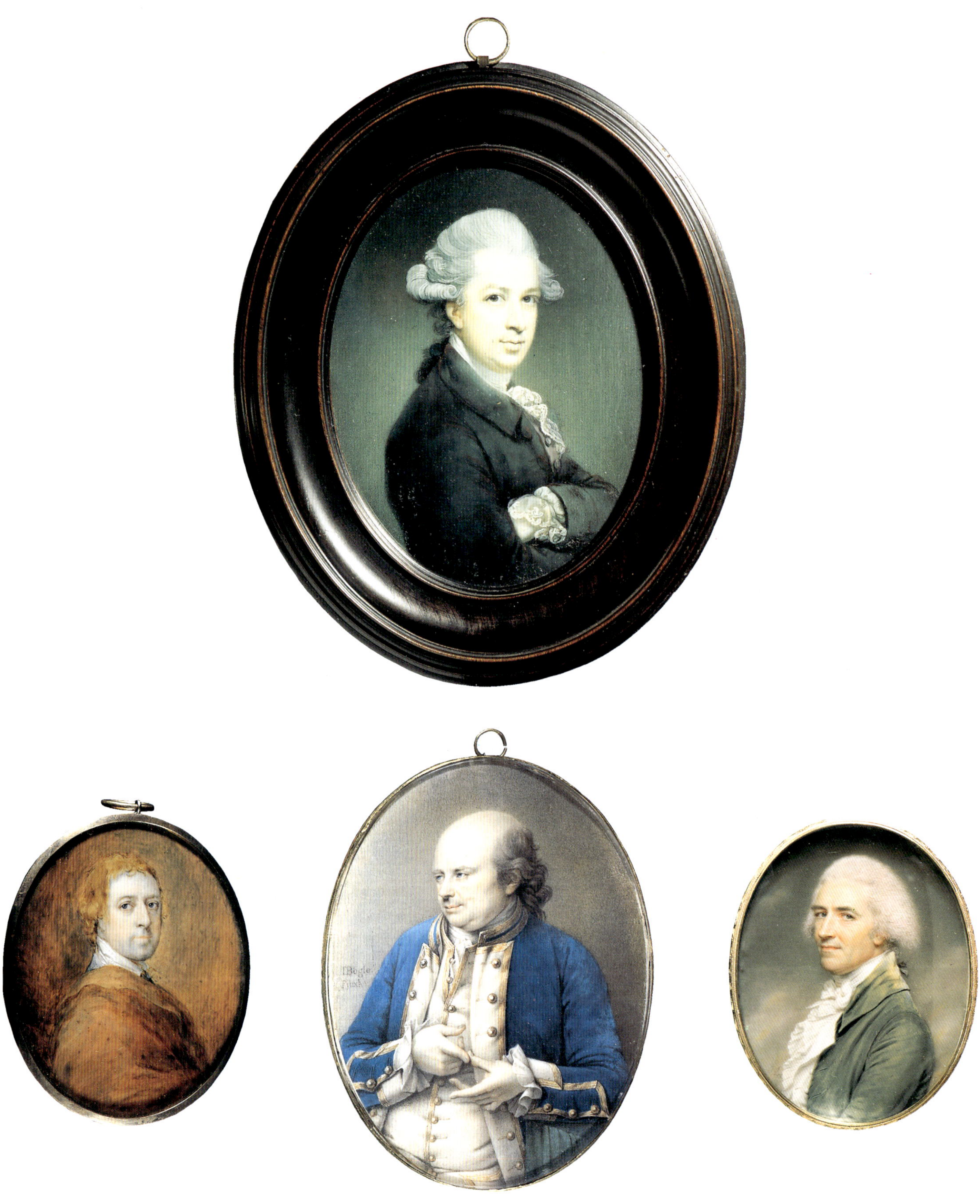

TOP Plate 10   Richard Crosse, *Self-portrait c.*1780 [**24**]
BOTTOM LEFT Plate 11   Richard Cosway after Thomas Gainsborough, *William, 2nd Viscount Folkestone and 1st Earl of Radnor* 1812 [**22**]
BOTTOM CENTRE Plate 12   John Bogle *Commodore George Johnstone c.*1767–74 [**23**]
BOTTOM RIGHT Plate 13   John Smart *Self-portrait* 1797 [**137**]

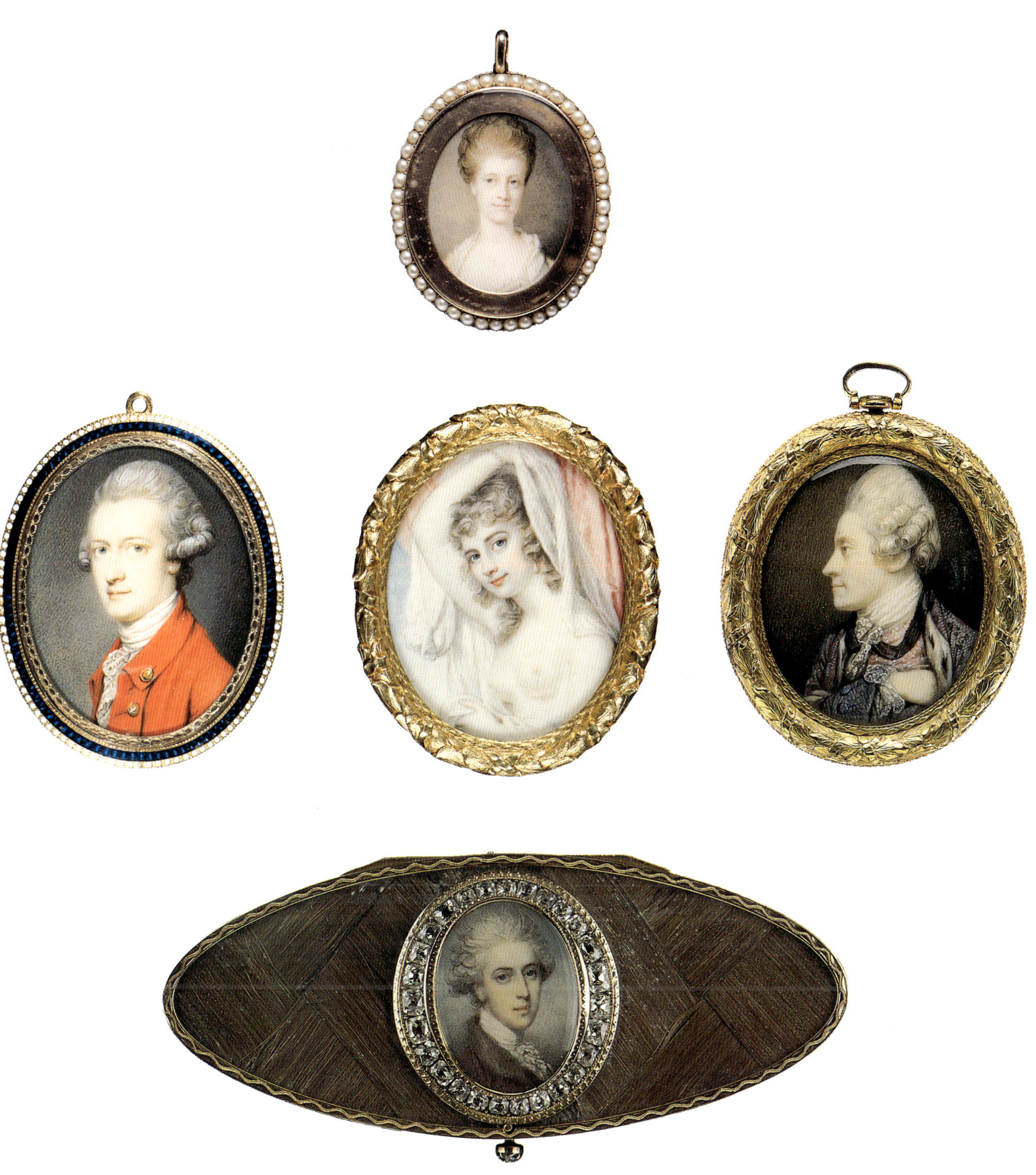

TOP Plate 14 *Anne, Countess Winterton c.1775–80* [**19**]
MIDDLE LEFT Plate 15 *Thomas, 2nd Lord Lyttleton c.1775–9* [**20**]
MIDDLE CENTRE Plate 16 *An unknown lady c.1780* [46]
MIDDLE RIGHT Plate 17 *Self-portrait c.1770* [**18**]
BOTTOM Plate 18 *Robert, 4th Duke of Ancaster and Kesteven c.1775–9* [**21**]

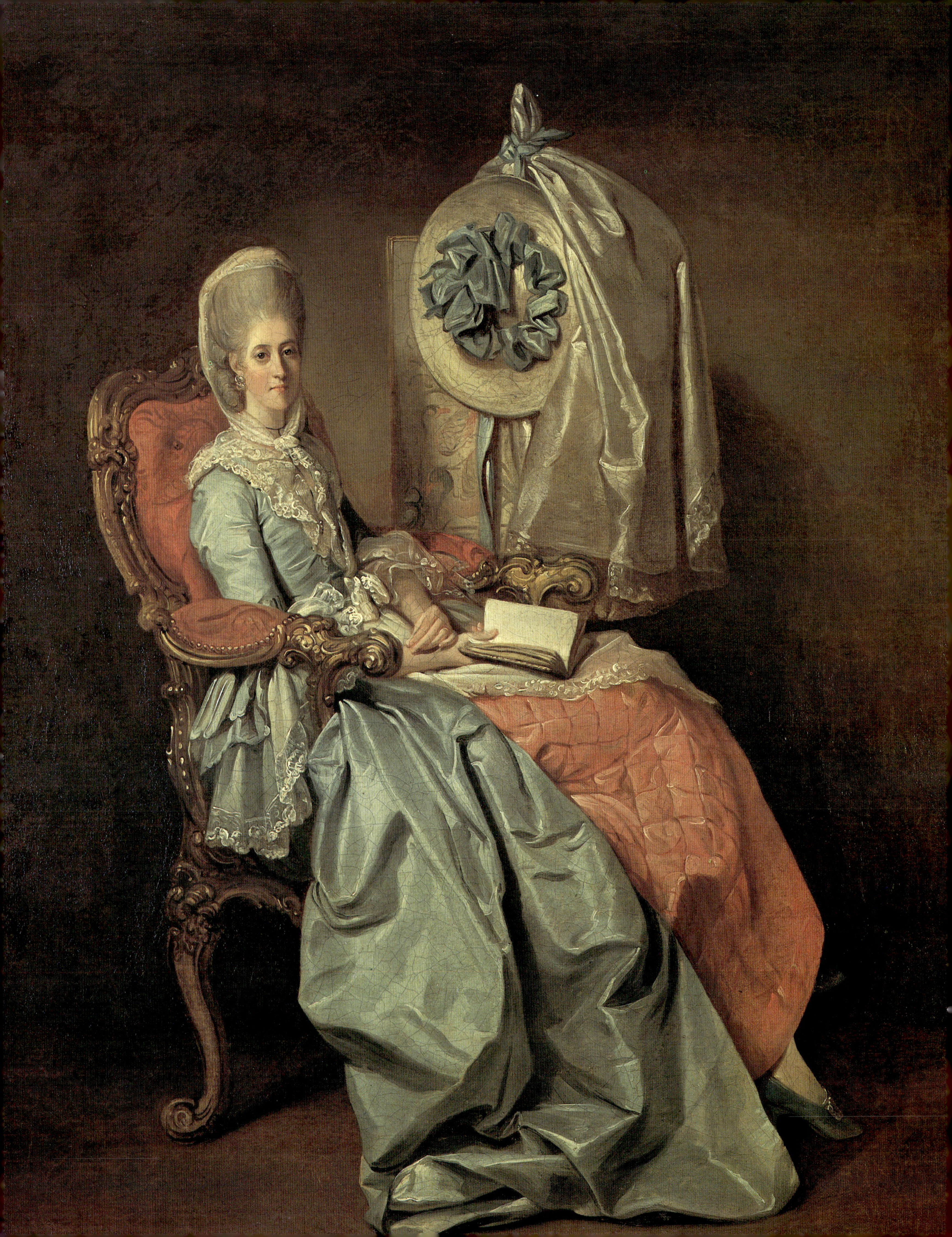

RICHARD COSWAY
ROYAL ACADEMICIAN
1770–80

*C*osway's increasing status in the 1770s was closely linked to his membership of the newly founded Royal Academy and his regular exhibition of paintings at its annual summer exhibitions. While not a founder member, in 1769 he was admitted as a student to the Academy's schools, which was a prerequisite for

later membership. The programme of teaching was carefully prescribed, and its main components included drawing from plaster casts after the antique and also from the 'living model'. These two linchpins of the teaching programme can be seen clearly depicted in Zoffany's famous group portrait of *The Royal Academicians,* which was painted in 1771–2 for the King and Queen [fig. 5]. Within a year of enrolling in the schools, Cosway had been put forward for election as an Associate Academician. Having exhibited three oil paintings in 1770, he was elected a full Academician in the following year. His original diploma certificate is still preserved at the Fondazione Cosway in Lodi. His diploma work presented to the Academy was a small octagonal oil painting of *Venus and Cupid,* notable for a marked eroticism and mannerist composition.[1] The fact that Cosway was making a reputation for himself as an ambitious oil painter as well as a miniaturist may have had some bearing on his rapid elevation into full membership of the Academy. Among the founder members there was only one miniature specialist, Jeremiah Meyer, who enjoyed the patronage of George III. Very few other portrait miniaturists were elected to the Academy, so it can be seen that Cosway's oil paintings were especially significant at this date to the promotion of his career.

Cosway's new-found status among his fellow Academicians is clearly revealed in Zoffany's group portrait. He is shown prominently as the second standing figure at the far right of the painting, elegantly posed and dressed, with chin thrust forward. Various accessories may be noted: he rests on a prominently extended cane, his hat is tucked under his arm, he wears a waistcoat decorated with gold braid, and he sports a sword, the only Academician to do so apart from the President, Sir Joshua Reynolds. The whole pose of the body with the outstretched arm and the turning head imitates that of the *Apollo Belvedere,* then one of the most famous statues that had survived from antiquity. This ostentatious reference can also be seen as appropriate for an artist who used forms and subjects from both classical art and literature throughout his career. It is notable that Cosway was the only Academician to adopt such a self-consciously classical pose, with the others all assuming relaxed poses more reminiscent of the nude model.

However, Zoffany has added a counterpoint to Cosway's classical pose by having him rest his cane on the lower belly of a plaster cast of a *Venus* lying on the floor. This detail is especially noteworthy within the context of the all-male group. The two women artists Angelica Kauffman and Mary Moser, who were founding members of the Academy, were not permitted to attend the life classes, and were thus represented *in absentia* through paintings hung on the wall. Zoffany can perhaps also be seen as commenting on Cosway's highly-sexed nature. Further light on this sexually assertive pose is shed by comparison with Cosway's own contemporaneous painting, the conversation piece of his friend *Charles Townley with a group of connoisseurs* [5] seen admiring pieces of female statuary from the antiquarian's collection. The artist's promiscuous attitude to women at this point in his life is revealed in his remarkably frank correspondence with Townley during the painting of the group portrait. In a letter written in 1772 to the collector who was then in Italy, Cosway boasted: 'Italy for ever say I – if the Italian women fuck as well in Italy as they do here, you must be happy indeed – I am such a zealot for them, that I'll be damned if ever I fuck an English woman again (if I can help it)'.[2]

In this revealing portrait Zoffany also records Cosway's supreme self-confidence, which was widely perceived as verging on the arrogant. Some of these qualities were noticed by the caricaturists. As early as 1761 Cosway's reputation as the dandy and the monkey may well have provided the inspiration for a satire by Hogarth published as a tailpiece to the catalogue of the Society of Artists' exhibition that year [fig. 6]. After Cosway's death an unknown essayist, writing in the *Library of Fine Arts,* noted that 'Hogarth designed another beau for his frontispiece to the first exhibition catalogue, as a quiz upon connoisseurs; everyone but Cosway recognised the similitude …' In this image a monkey, dressed as a fashionable connoisseur, is shown watering three dead trees described as 'exoticks'. This was an attack on the amount of attention given by connoisseurs to paintings by the Old Masters, who were foreign, at the expense of the national school of art. This critique was especially pertinent within the context of one of the earliest public exhibitions in Britain devoted to living painters.[3]

From early in his career Cosway was known for his connoisseurship and his foppish appearance, which included the anachronistic wearing of a sword. Peter Pindar recorded a witty lampoon of Cosway as a monkey, which had been stuck on his front door after he had moved in 1791 into the imposing Adam-style townhouse on Oxford Street at Stratford Place:

> *When a man to fair for a show brings a lion,*
> *'Tis usual a monkey the sign-pole to tie on!*
> *But here the old custom reversed is seen,*
> *For the lion's without and the monkey's within.*

The criticism was said to have hurt Cosway to such an extent that he moved two houses up into Stratford Place, to number 20, away from the exposed position on Oxford Street. Cosway was also much derided by his artistic peers, but was clearly adept at parrying such barbs. A description of an Academicians' meeting at the Turk's Head public house in Gerrard Street in the early 1770s is revealing of Cosway's status among his peers, as for instance when he was confronted by the physically imposing painter Francis Hayman and the landscapist Richard Wilson:

> ... Cosway ... who had been at court attended in all the gay costume of the drawing-room, with pink heels to his shoes, &c., but the room was so full he could not find a place. 'What', said Frank Hayman, 'can nobody make room for the little monkey?' Wilson laughed, and exclaimed, 'Good G-d! how times and circumstances are changed; sure, the world is turned topsy-turvy, — formerly, the monkey rode the bear, but here we have the bear upon the monkey.' This set the table in a roar, in which Hayman joined heartily, and rising, shook hands with Cosway, who received him with the greatest familiarity and politeness, and instantly every chair in the room was set at his service.[4]

Clearly the artist was quite capable of deflecting such criticism through his manners, wit and confidence in his social position. He obviously relished attention and deliberately attracted notoriety. Despite the barbs aimed at what was considered to be his facial similarity to a monkey, Cosway actually owned such an animal at this period. When he was working on the Townley conversation piece [5], his delivery of the painting was delayed as John Towneley wrote to his nephew in Rome in August 1773:

> I have called several times upon Cosway, but get no performance of his Promise; I mean about finishing and putting up your conversation Piece. The last time I called I found him laid on a Soffa in his night gown — and the calf of one of his legs bundled up; on my enquiring the cause he acquainted me, that his monkey or Baboon had tore a great Piece out of his leg; and that he was under Dr. Hunter's hand for a cure; the Poor animal has been put out of its pain, by the same hand, and the Dr. had the pleasure of Disecting him, and put him in spirits in terrors to all Monkeys.[5]

Inevitably Cosway was the target of caricatures, such as Matthew Darly's *The miniature macaroni* [26] of 1772, which was one of a whole series on the *macaronis* or young men wearing the latest fashions from Italy. Here the diminutive Cosway was shown in fashionable tight-fitting dress, with particular prominence being given to his wig, cane, sword and handkerchief. In the same year Cosway was lampooned by Philip Dawe in the caricature titled *The macaroni painter, or Billy Dimple sitting for his picture* [27]. The early critical tradition identifies the fashionable painter in this image as Cosway, who was very active as an oil painter in this decade.[6]

The public profile of the artist was heightened not only by these caricatures, but also through a continual stream of self-portraits. The latter practice was a useful element in the fashionable portraitist's strategy to retain a successful portrait business. In an untraced early etching from 1760 he drew attention to himself wearing a chain and medal, an overt reference to both his vanity and his earlier prizewinning at Shipley's drawing school.[7] Similarly in the miniature *Self-portrait in profile* [18], painted around 1770, Cosway used the more intimate format to exhibit his sartorial elegance, sporting a luxurious fur-lined coat. The three-quarter-length *Self-portrait in Vandyke dress* [4], from about the same date, is a confident demonstration by the artist of his artistic and social pretensions. This portrait reveals the most distinctive elements of Cosway's portraiture: a fascination with masquerade dress and his profound study of the seventeenth-century Old Masters, notably Rubens and Van Dyck.[8]

Cosway was undoubtedly the most fashion-conscious artist of his generation, with a marked streak of vanity. Apart from the numerous self-portraits, caricatures and portrayals by other artists, there are various contemporaneous accounts that testify to his remarkable appearance. His presence at the auction houses was noted by J.T. Smith: 'I have often seen Mr. Cosway at the Elder Christie's Picture-sales, full-dressed in his sword and bag; with a small three-cornered hat on the top of his powdered toupee, and a mulberry-silk coat, profusely embroidered with scarlet strawberries.'

Another commentator, Cunningham, later added: 'such was the dress of those whom princes delighted to honour'.[9] Certainly the

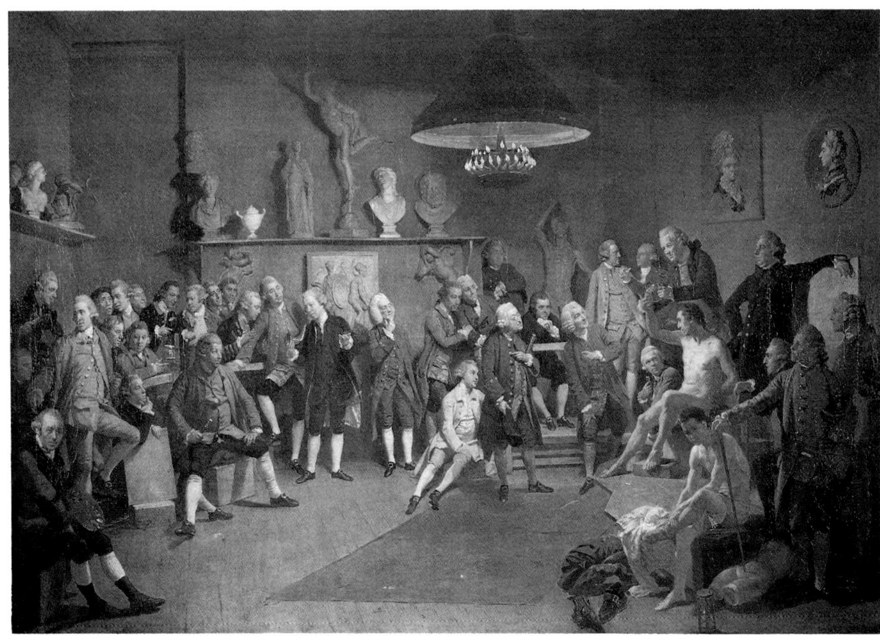

Fig.5 *The Royal Academicians*, 1771–2, by Johann Zoffany (The Royal Collection)

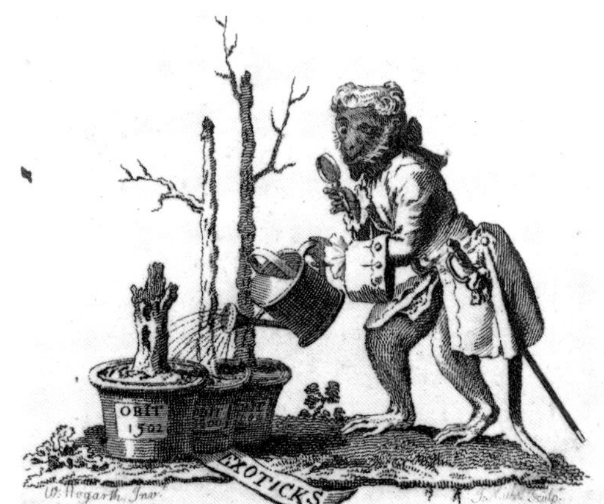

Fig.6 *Tailpiece of Catalogue of Pictures exhibited in Spring Gardens*, 1761, by William Hogarth (The British Museum, London)

artist's acute fashion sense would have attracted the attention of the young Prince of Wales. The marked contrast as to how the King and his heir viewed Cosway's ostentatious manner is shown in a revealing and amusing passage, probably dating from the late 1780s, written by one of the artist's contemporaries, Henry Angelo, which deserves to be quoted in full:

The Royal Family were not regardless of this prying spirit of the great painter in little, and frequently enjoyed a laugh at his expense, on their return from these visits to the Royal Academy exhibition.

His present majesty, who in his meridian gaiety, honoured Cosway with more than common patronage, according to the on dits *of the day, is said to have been much amused with the superlative politeness and courtier-like address of this celebrated miniature painter; and on one particular occasion, to have enjoyed a hearty laugh at his expense.*

Cosway was certainly the greatest fop of all who ever were dubbed R.A. and esquire, by the royal sign manual.

It happened, that his present Majesty, then Prince of Wales, in consequence of the indisposition of his royal sire, paid the royal academicians a visit on the day of the private view of the King. The president of the academy being at this time confined by a fit of the gout, Cosway, on the important occasion, acted as locum tenens.

Determined to pay all due honour to the royal visitor, and his suite, he received the Prince at the gate of the Royal Academy, attired in a dove-coloured, silver-embroidered court dress, with the concomitants – sword, bag, and chapeau bras.

He followed his royal highness through all the apartments, uttered a hundred high-flown compliments, and strutted, on his scarlet heels, as important in his own estimation, as any newly created lord, making his way through a vista of gazers in the passage to the court.

When the Prince retired, the grand little man attended his royal highness to the carriage, and in the presence of the huzzaing crowd, retreated backwards, with measured steps, making at each step a profound obeisance. The mischievous fates, looked on, *and the Prince looked* out *of the carriage; his royal highness could not refrain, – for the representative of the Royal Academy bent himself with such magnificent circumflexion of his little body, that, his sword getting between his legs, tripped him up, and he was suddenly prostrate in the mud. – 'Just as I had anticipated, ye gods!' exclaimed the Prince: when the royal carriage flew away, as on the wings of the wind.*

Poor Tiny Cosmetic! *as the satirist dubbed him; the giant porter carried him into the Royal Academy, in his arms; the great doors were closed upon the laughing rabble, and the motherly housekeeper tenderly wiped away his misfortune, with a scented damask napkin.*

My old friend Cosway, though a distinguished artist, and a very intelligent, loquacious, entertaining little man, was certainly a mighty macaroni, *which rendered him the more remarkable among his old colleagues at Somerset-house; for though cynics may aver, that every society can muster its* quota *of coxcombs, the King [George III] himself used to say, 'Among* my *painters, there are no fops'; and the King knew them well, royal academicians and associates, even to a man.*

Reynolds, for example, the first president of the Royal Academy, was not even a courtier. It is not likely then, that he was either a macaroni, *a fribble, or a fop.*[10]

Angelo describes Cosway in much the same way as he appears in Zoffany's painted portrait, clearly standing out from his more sober Academicians, notably Reynolds. As Cosway's social status increased through the 1770s and into the following decade with the patronage of the Prince of Wales, so his highly fashionable profile burgeoned – and similarly the envy of other artists and commentators. The critic Allan Cunningham later concluded sourly that Cosway's astonishing rise to success was based on the profitability of his portrait miniature business: 'to rise from indigence to affluence, and step out of the company of indifferent daubers into that of lords and ladies of high degree, could not be accomplished, Cosway imagined, without putting on airs of superiority, and a dress rivalling that of an eastern ambassador. His affectation was not unobserved by his brethren: his fine clothes, splendid house, and black servant, were offences after their kind'.[11] Yet Cosway's social success was based on his versatility as an artist. At the core were his portrait miniatures, but he was also experimenting as a draughtsman, and through his collections developing his role as a connoisseur. He also exhibited a wide variety of oils at the Academy, which were critical for demonstrating the range of his production to a fashionable clientele.

The *Self-portrait in Vandyke dress* [4] is a bravura essay in self-promotion which deliberately interprets the style and appearance of a seventeenth-century Baroque artist. Cosway wears the so-called 'Vandyke' dress which was enormously popular in the second half of the eighteenth century both for masquerade parties and for portrait sittings. Here the young artist refers to the masquerade by incorporating a mask, which is placed on a table adjacent to his palette and brushes. Apart from the dress where the cloak, collar and sword are prominent features, Cosway has also adopted a standard pose from Van Dyck's repertoire. He rests his right hand on his hip, with the elbow jutting towards the viewer, while the left hand is supported either by a portfolio or a small painting. The whole image, despite some awkwardness in handling the composition on a larger scale, is a highly revealing statement of Cosway's artistic and social aspirations.

Around 1770, and close in date to his *Self-portrait in Vandyke dress*, Cosway painted a portrait of *Lancelot 'Capability' Brown* [3], who was the most influential landscape gardener of his generation. This portrait has also been attributed to Nathaniel Dance, and it closely resembles the portrait of 'Capability' Brown from a similar date by Dance on loan to the National Portrait Gallery in London. The distinctive use of chiaroscuro and strong characterisation is typical of Cosway's early oil paintings, as can be seen in the portraits of *William Shipley* [1] and *Charles Townley with a group of connoisseurs* [5].[12]

In 1770 Cosway completed the ambitious group portrait of *The Witts family* [2], which was painted to commemorate the premature death of Broome Witts, a successful linen draper in the City of London. He is represented posthumously as Fortitude in the centre of the painting, shown introducing his sister Sarah Witts as Hope, as a companion to his wife, Elizabeth, née London, depicted as Distress. The three figures are shown in classical styles of dress with attributes that allude to their allegorical personifications. Fortitude is dressed as a Roman soldier and stands in front of a column on top of which is a figure of Minerva concealed in shadow; Hope rests on her anchor and points upwards; while the figure of Distress sits barefoot with hair and clothes in disarray. Beside her a snake is caught in a thicket. The melancholy mood of the composition is reflected in the desolate and rocky setting by the sea. In contrast with the muted colouring of the background are the stronger colours for the costumes and the notably delicate handling of the faces.

The Witts family reveals a keen awareness by Cosway of contemporary debates on history painting and attempts to raise the status of portraiture. The composition alludes to the subject of 'The Choice of Hercules', in which the classical hero stands between the female figures of Virtue and Vice, and which the artist drew in a watercolour sketch from this date. As *The Witts family* was one of the first oil paintings Cosway exhibited at the Academy, he was no doubt attempting to impress his audience – and responding to Reynolds's ambitious programme being set forth in the annual lectures later known as the *Discourses* – by combining the modest genre of the conversation piece with the ambitions of grand manner portraiture.[13]

Not all of Cosway's early oil paintings were exhibited at the Academy, and one of the most significant not to be shown there was the group portrait of *Charles Townley with a group of connoisseurs* [5]. This intimate conversation piece, which is so revealing of contemporary male attitudes to connoisseurship, is the most fully documented of all Cosway's oil paintings. For much of this century it was considered to have been painted by Zoffany, with the correct attribution being made only in 1969. It precedes by a decade the much better-known painting by Zoffany of Charles Townley in his library at Park Street, London, painted from 1781 to 1783 (Towneley Hall Art Gallery and Museums, Burnley).

Charles Townley was one of the most notable collectors of classical sculpture in the second half of the eighteenth century. Many of the works in his collection were acquired as Greek originals during his visits to Italy (1767–8 and 1771–4), where he was advised by the artist and dealer Gavin Hamilton, among others. The collection was sold after his death to the British Museum. However, with the arrival of the Elgin marbles in London it was soon realised that Townley's collection was mainly comprised of Roman copies.[14]

The commissioning of this portrait arose from Cosway's close friendship with Townley, as the artist's extremely frank letters to the collector written at this date testify. The initial idea for the composition of the portrait was explicitly bawdy, as is revealed in a preparatory drawing, in which the six connoisseurs are seen sexually arousing themselves while watching a seventh man fondle one of the marble Venuses.[15] In the finished painting this sexual element was toned down, although the voyeurism remains clear. From Cosway's correspondence with Townley we know that one of the potential sitters, the Hon. Charles Dillon (1745–1813) of Ditchley, was excluded from the group. The six connoisseurs eventually included were, standing from left to right, Richard Oliver (d.1784), Charles Townley, Dr Verdun, Richard Holt, Captain Wynn (b.1734), while Chase Price (d.1777) is shown seated in Cosway's sitter's chair [216]. Oliver was a politician connected with John Wilkes, Verdun was Townley's librarian and curator, and Price was a minor collector of classical antiquities.[16]

Among the sculptures the *dilettanti* are shown admiring, at least

three can be identified from the Townley marbles in the British Museum. The altar, or sepulchral cippus, was purchased from the Burioni Collection in Rome in 1768, the right-hand Venus was acquired from the restorer and dealer Cavaceppi, and the Muse playing the lyre came from the Palazzo Barberini also in Rome. Neither the altar in the background nor the statue of Venus closest to the viewer has been traced.[17] It is worth noting that Cosway enlarged the sculptures to create a more satisfactory compositional balance with the connoisseurs.

From the Townley papers much is known about the slow progress of the painting of the group portrait. As Townley himself was in Italy from 1771 to 1774, he must have sat to the artist before his departure. In 1773 John Towneley was reporting to his nephew in Rome on the conversation picture's progress, but this had been delayed because of Cosway's being attacked by his pet monkey. In fact the artist was not paid for the picture until 14 October 1775, when Charles Townley noted in his account book that he had paid 'to Mr. Cosway at various times for his picture with 6 portraits – £100'.[18]

Townley and Cosway remained close friends, and the artist copied at least one of the collector's sculptures, a *Triform Diana*. It may also be surmised that Townley played a key role in the matchmaking of Richard Cosway and Maria Hadfield during 1780. Townley knew Maria's father, Charles, in Florence, and he was reputed to have given Maria away at her wedding, her father having died a few years earlier. In an unpublished letter, written after Townley's death, Cosway also recalled that he had painted Townley in another painting (untraced) which he described as a 'Head of Him which I painted at one sitting five & Twenty Years ago, it is to me invaluable – as it is most strikingly like – & brings to my recollection a thousand extraordinary *mirthfull scenes* we were jointly concern'd in – in those days of *Jollity*'.[19]

Another important portrait in oils not shown publicly is that depicting *Mrs Draper* [6], painted in 1775. Better known as Laurence Sterne's 'Immortal Eliza', she was the daughter of Mr Whitehill, who worked for the East India Company, and of May Sclater who was from an old Gloucestershire family. Elizabeth Whitehill was born at Anjengo on the Malabar coast in India. After attending a boarding school in England she returned to India at the age of thirteen, to be married in the following year to Daniel Draper, another of the Company's officials. In 1765 the family returned to England, and it was two years later that Eliza met Sterne at the Gerrard Street house of William James and his wife Anne. Eliza presented Sterne with a miniature locket of herself which she tied around his neck with her own hands. This was certainly painted by Cosway, whom Sterne mentions in *The Journal to Eliza* as being the best painter of her likeness: 'I must wait – till the first evening I'm with You – when I shall present You with – them as a better Picture of me, than Cosway Could do for You'.[20] In fact, throughout *The Journal* the miniature of Eliza by Cosway acts as a medium through which Sterne is able to transmit his emotions and thoughts for his beloved ('constantly communing with her picture') after she had returned to India in April 1767. Sterne died later that year, and this famous miniature has remained untraced.

On returning to London in 1775, Mrs Draper published ten letters under the title *Letters from Yorick to Eliza*. It was in this year that she sat to Cosway for this oil portrait.[21] She is shown virtually enveloped in the ornate sitter's chair [216] and the profusion of her fashionable dress. She wears a blue silk taffeta gown, with a quilted satin coral underskirt, and white lace sleeves, which have double, scalloped flounces with lace-edged ruffles. Her hair is dressed fashionably high, and is draped with a white lace fichu tied loosely under the chin. A handkerchief of fine needlepoint lace is placed around her neck and shoulders. From an Oriental screen at her side hangs her lace-edged silk cloak, and a blue-ribboned straw hat. Her shoes have high French heels, pointed toes and large buckles. Tied around her neck is a black silk necklace from which a jewelled ornament is hung. An open book rests in her lap. Yet despite the extreme awareness of fashion in this portrait on both the part of the sitter and the artist, even to the extent that Mrs Draper's portrait appears overwhelmed by the profusion of textures, Cosway still caught a marked sense of melancholy in the sitter's features.[22]

Cosway's slightly later portrait of *Marianne Dorothy Harland, later Mrs Dalrymple* [7], a fashionably dressed woman playing the harp in a domestic interior, can be identified as the portrait exhibited at the Academy in 1779. This is not only on account of the style of painting and dress being appropriate for the date, but also in the light of the critique offered by *The St. James Chronicle*, which felt that the detail in Cosway's painting distracted from the whole: 'The Portraits of this Artist are drawn with Precision, and finished with a painful and minute Attention to little Circumstances. By these Means a Bouquet of Flowers, or a Lady's Ruffles, become the principal Object; and his Productions acquire a concomical and ridiculous Air'.[23] Despite such criticism, Cosway shows that in the 1770s in this portrait, together with those such as *Charles Townley with a group of connoisseurs* [5] and *Mrs Draper* [6], he was determined to compete in the fashionable but competitive market for precisely painted conversation pieces, a genre which was dominated by Zoffany and other artists such as Mortimer and Wheatley.

The small oil of *Rinaldo and Armida* [9], which has been recently discovered, is a rare surviving example of Cosway's subject paintings. The subject was taken from Tasso's popular Renaissance epic poem *Gerusalemme Liberata*, a number of copies of which belonged to Richard and Maria Cosway. The artist chose to depict one of the most popular episodes, which had been commonly treated by seventeenth-century Italian and French artists, most notably Poussin. The Crusader hero Rinaldo had rescued his companions from the beautiful Satanic witch Armida. Seeking revenge she abducted Rinaldo and carried him to her magical kingdom. Cosway depicted the lovers there beside a lake with Armida's palace in the background, in front of which two of Rinaldo's warriors search for him. Rinaldo looks up at his reflection in Armida's eyes, while she gazes at her own image in the upheld mirror. The lovers are surrounded by six playful putti, one of whom mischievously commands the viewer to silence so as not to distract the lovers. The painting was praised by the contemporary critic 'A.B.' in the *Middlesex Journal*:[24]

> *Rinaldo is in a recumbent posture, and appears to be dissolved in an extacy of pleasure. Armida hangs over him with an inexpressible fondness, having a glass in her hand, in which she views herself. Cupid looks as he always does when his arrows have had the desired effect. The colours are thought by some to be too glaring; but it ought to be considered that Armida is every where represented as a flaming beauty, or a beauty somewhat supernatural. The piece has certainly great merit.*

However, Cosway was also criticised for freely interpreting the original text, in as much as Rinaldo should have held the mirror up himself, but the reviewer concluded: 'Painters any more than Poets, are not historians: they represent, not what is true, but what is agreeable'. Certainly, with its rich colouring and profusion of detail, this is one of Cosway's most memorable essays in idyllic eroticism.

Closely related to this oil painting is an ambitious finished watercolour of *Rinaldo and Armida* [10]. The style of the drawing is typical of the rare examples that survive from the 1770s, where the compositions are drawn in prior to the broad application of watercolour. This can be seen in the *Choice of Hercules*, as well as in *Anthony and Cleopatra* [11].[25] In the watercolour of *Rinaldo and Armida* Cosway has interpreted the subject slightly differently from the painting, adding two *putti* to the right of the composition, in place of the two warriors and pair of doves shown in the painting. Armida is shown with an exposed right leg and without the bracelet on her upper right arm. The sense of eroticism in the watercolour is also increased by Cosway's depiction of Rinaldo stretching his right arm out towards Armida and gesticulating to his heart with the left hand. This fine watercolour can be seen as an early demonstration of Cosway's skills as draughtsman, which he was to develop to the full in the following decades, initially with the 'stained' or 'tinted' portraits, and later with the astonishingly varied subject drawings.

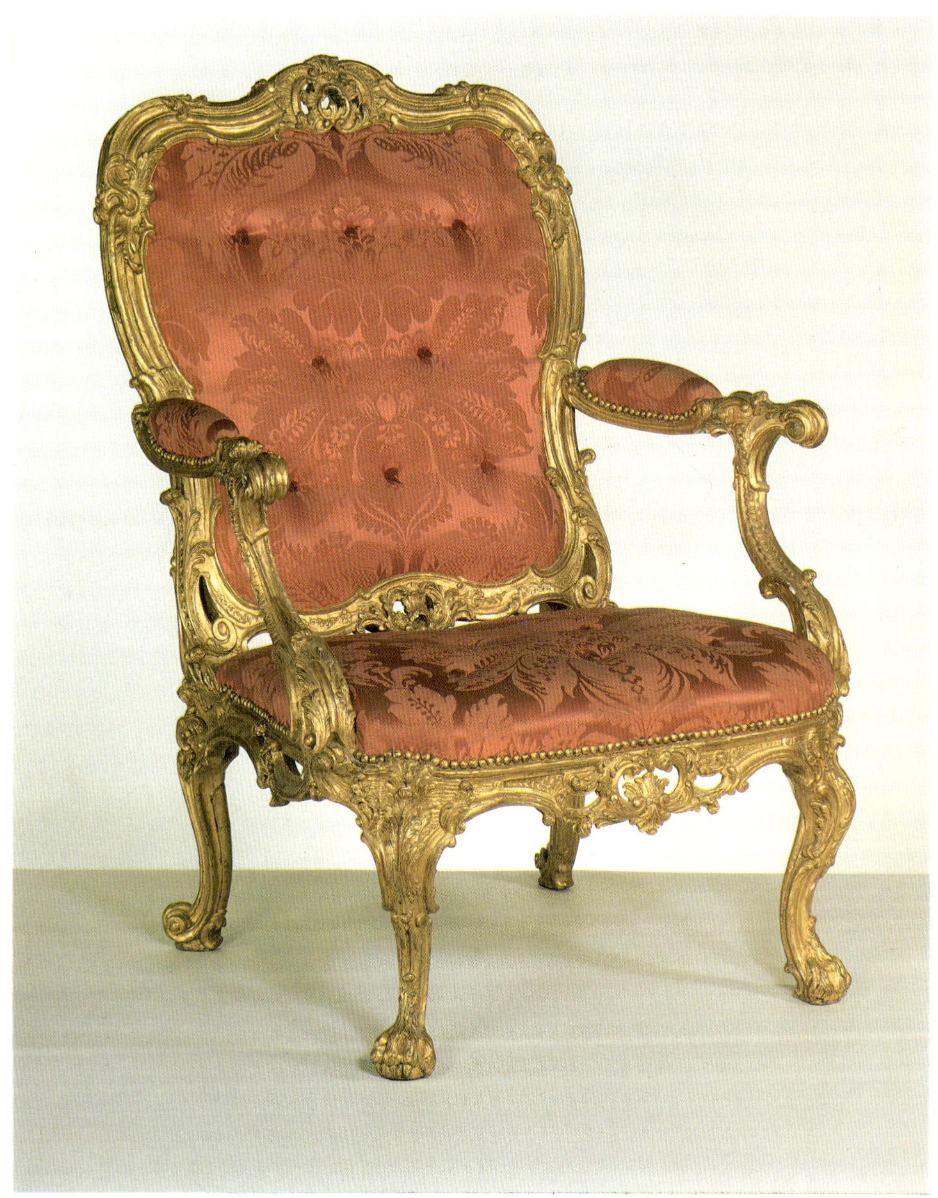

Plate 20 Matthias Lock *Cosway's sitter's chair c.*1755–60 [**216**]

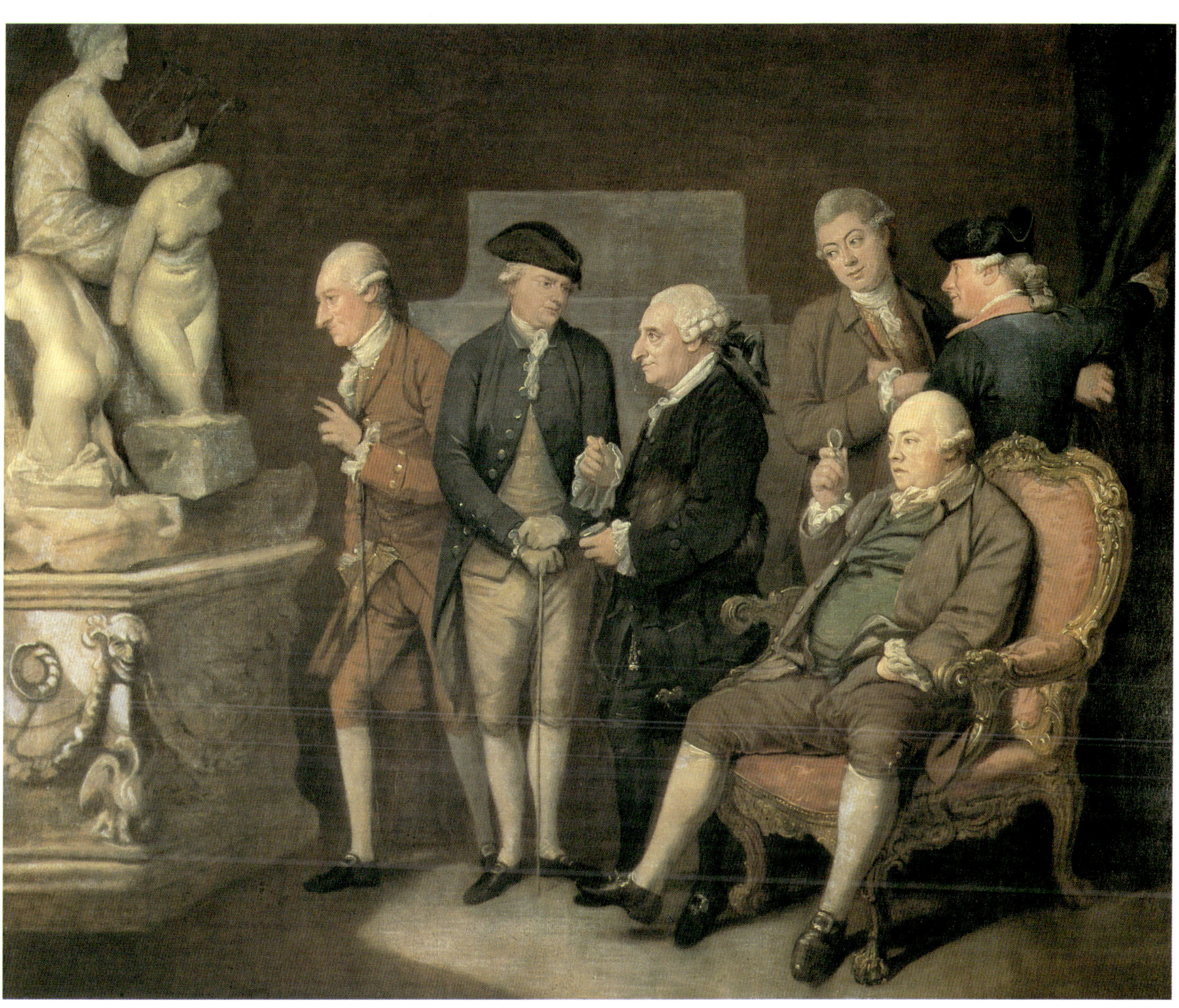

Plate 21 *Charles Townley with a group of connoisseurs* 1771–5 [**5**]

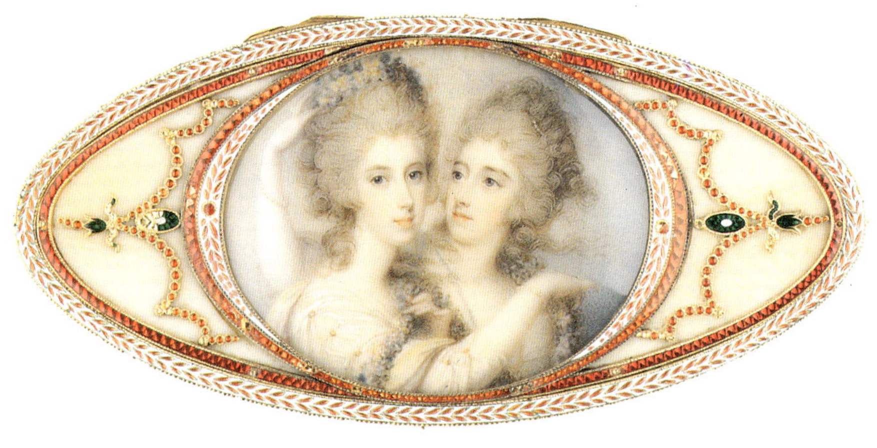

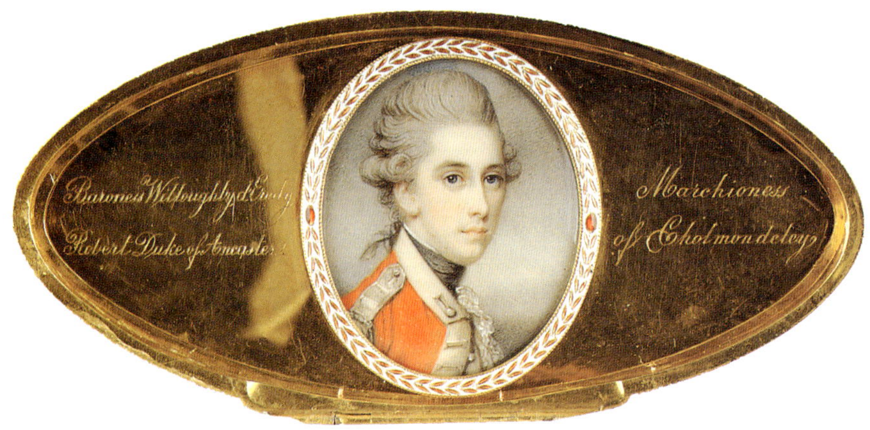

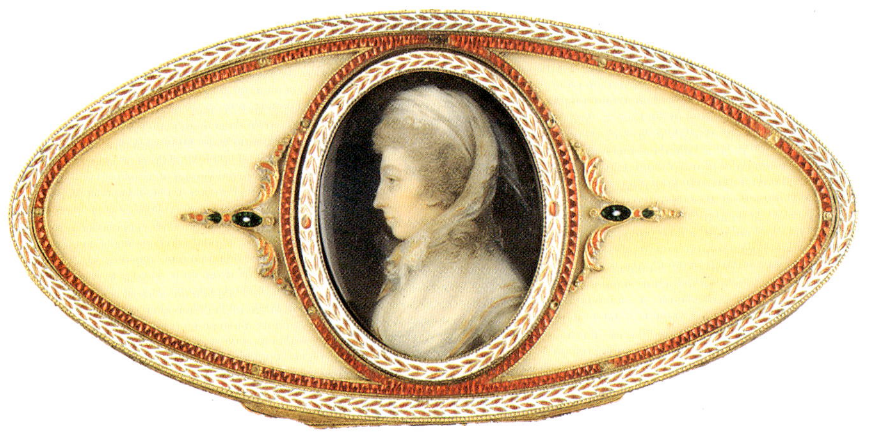

TOP Plate 22a *The Ladies Priscilla and Georgiana Bertie (top of 'The Ancaster Box') c.1780* [47]

MIDDLE Plate 22b Unknown Artist after Richard Cosway *Robert, 4th Duke of Ancaster (inside lid of 'The Ancaster Box') c.1780* [47]

BOTTOM Plate 22c Unknown Artist *Mary Panton, Duchess of Ancaster (base of 'The Ancaster box') c.1780* [47]

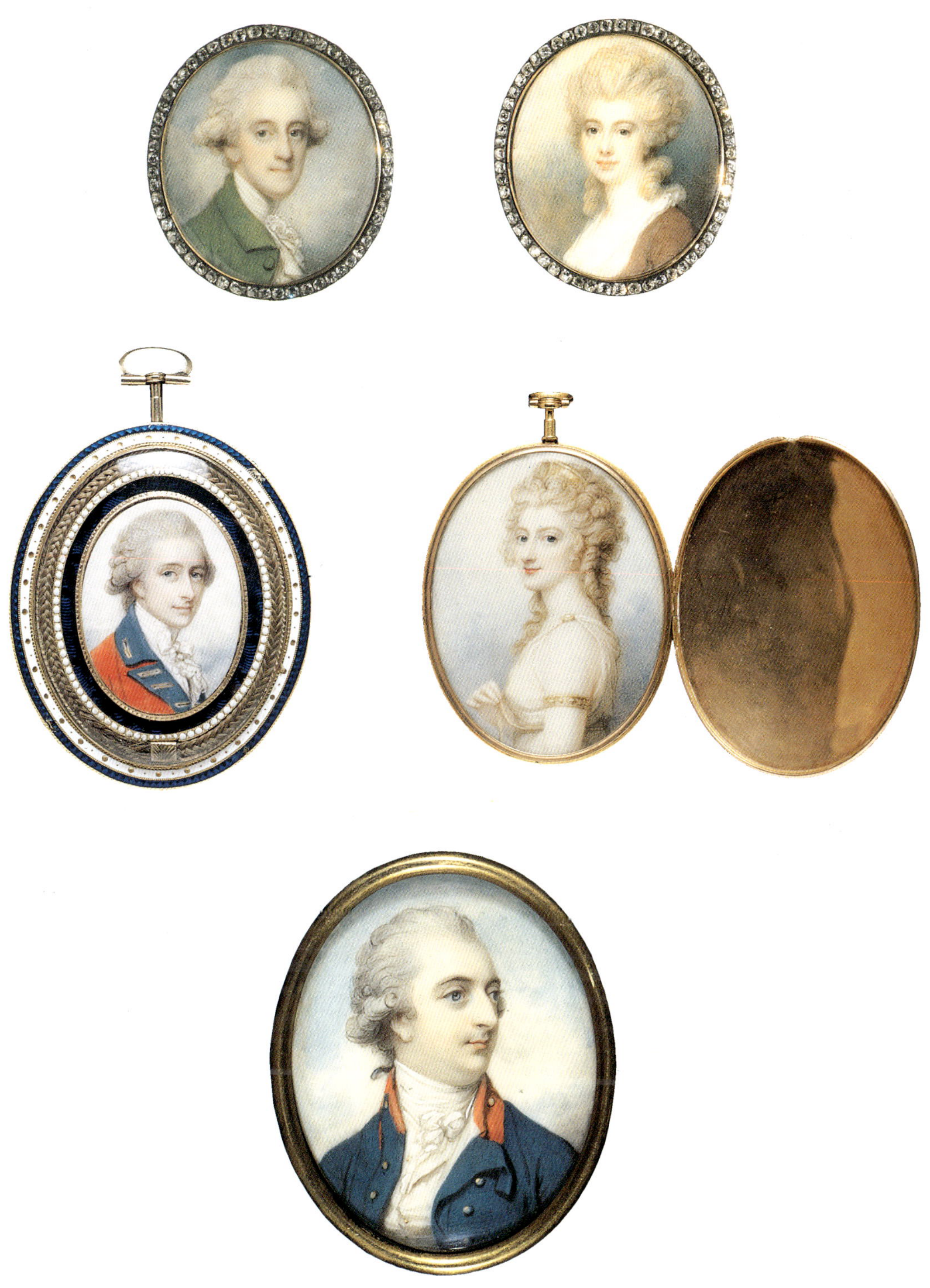

TOP LEFT Plate 23 *Frederick, 3rd Earl of Bessborough c.1780* [**50**]

TOP RIGHT Plate 24 *Henrietta Frances, Countess of Bessborough c.1780* [**51**]

MIDDLE LEFT Plate 25 *An unknown officer c.1780–90* [**48**]

MIDDLE RIGHT Plate 26 *An unknown lady of the Sotheby or Isted Family c.1780–5* [**52**]

BOTTOM Plate 27 *Thomas, Viscount Wentworth of Wellesborough c.1780–5* [**53**]

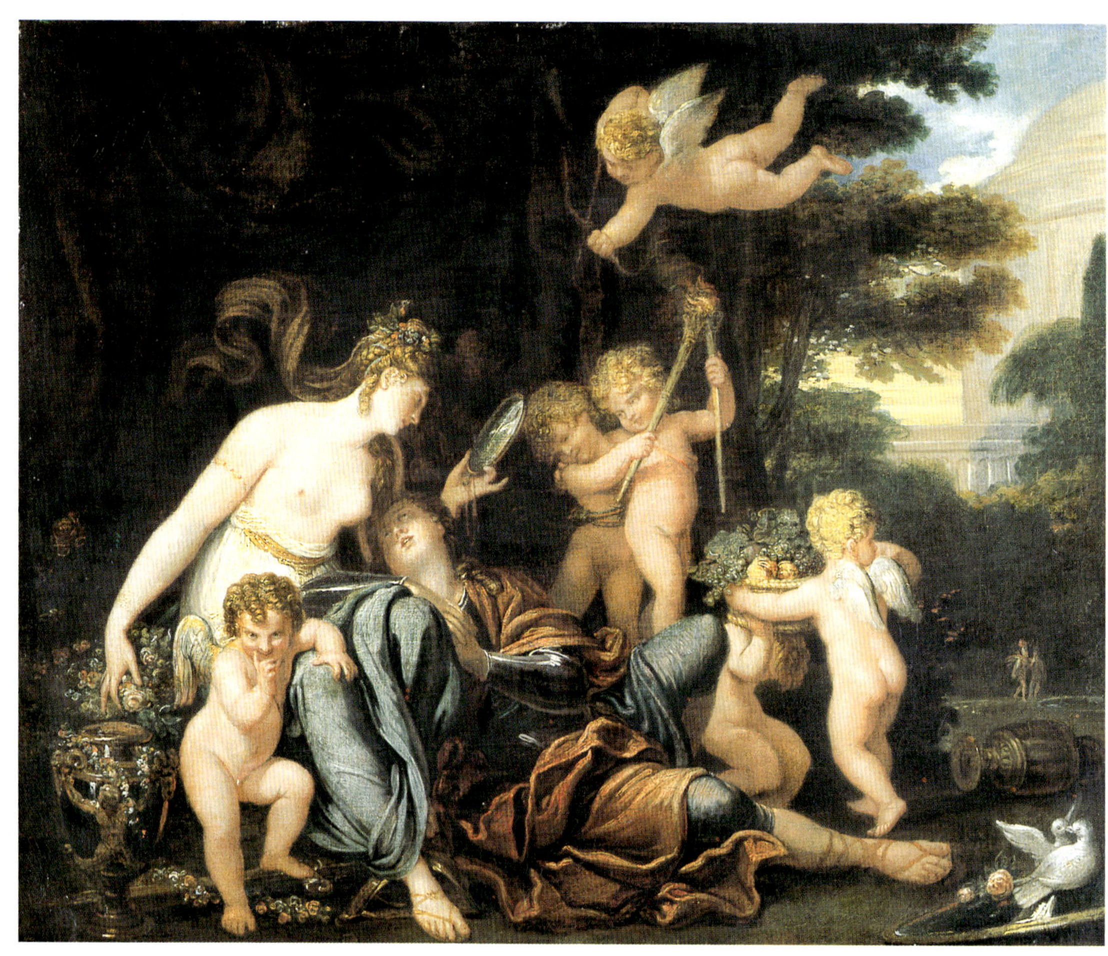

Plate 28   *Rinaldo and Armida* 1772 [**9**]

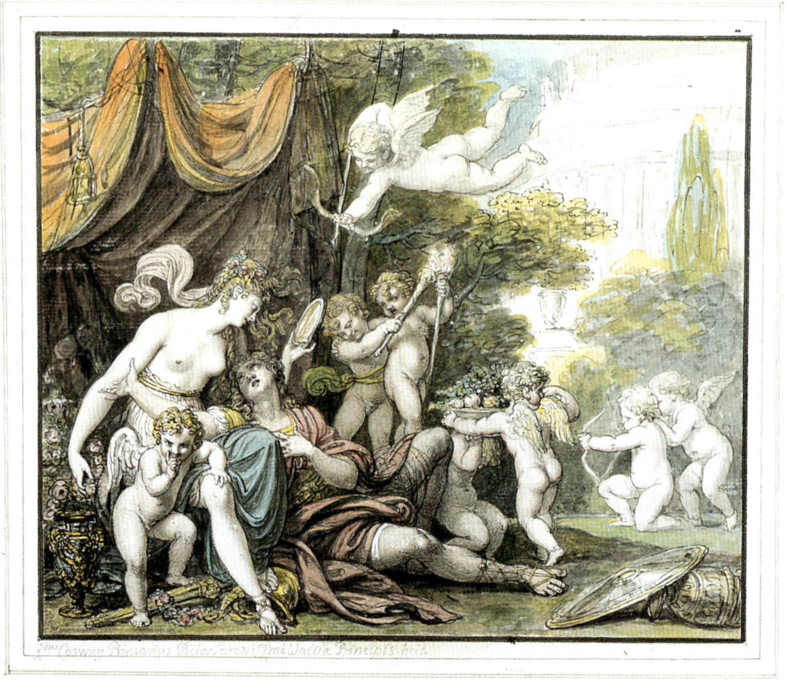

Plate 29   *Rinaldo and Armida* c.1772 [**10**]

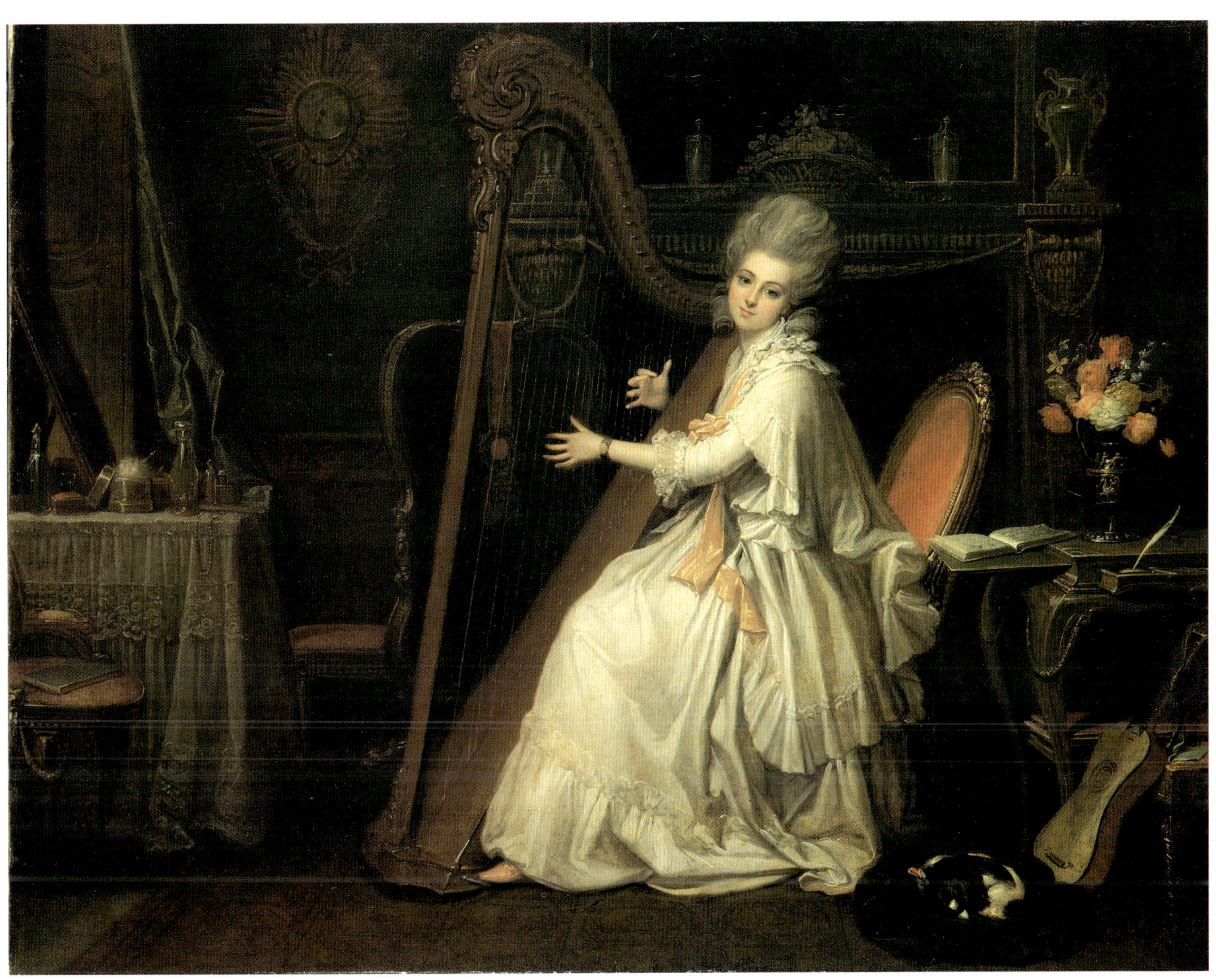

Plate 30   *Marianne Dorothy Harland, later Mrs Dalrymple* 1779 [7]

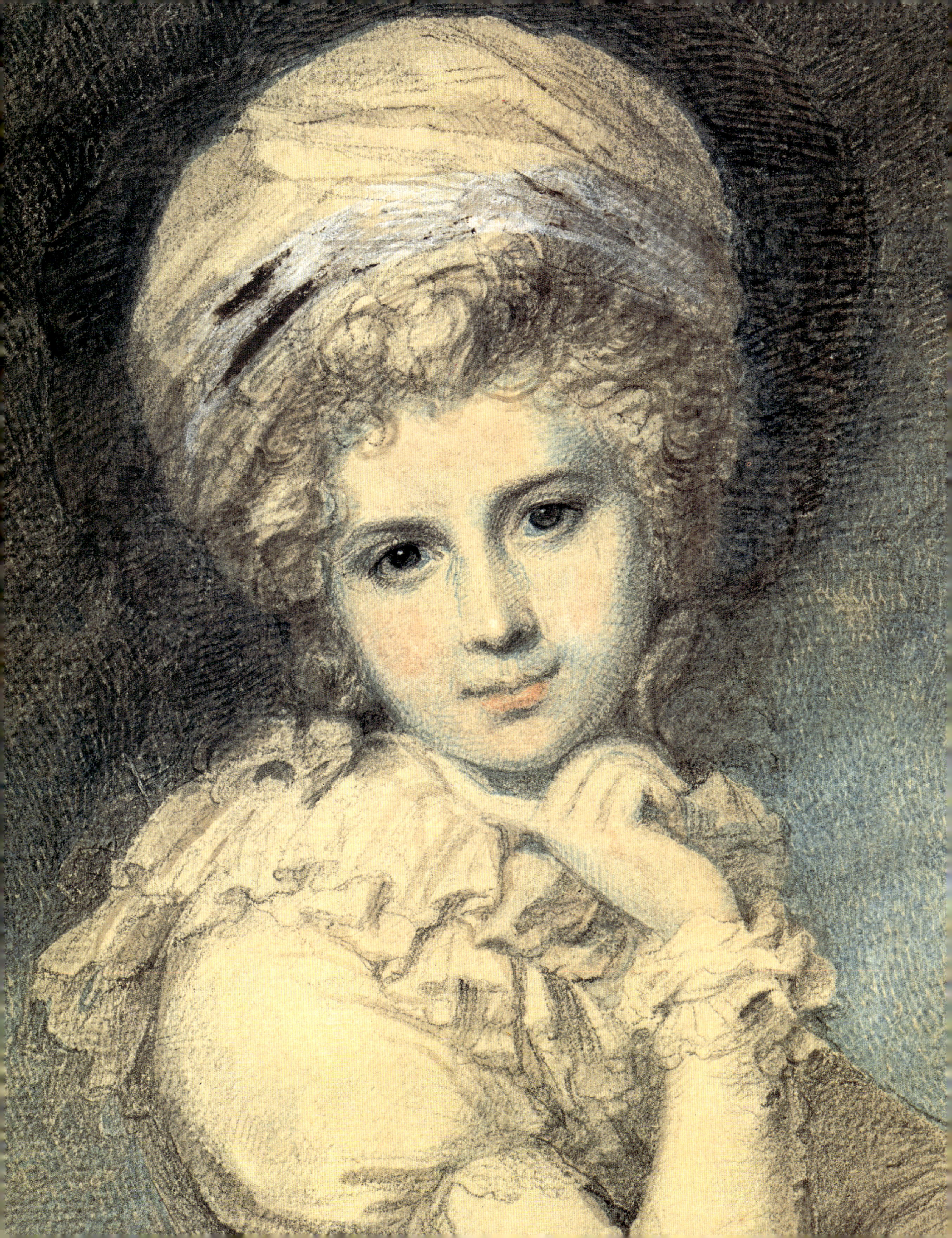

MARIA HADFIELD
ANGLO-FLORENTINE
1760–80

*M*ARIA Cosway enjoyed a remarkable upbringing in Florence within the milieu of the Grand Tour. She was 'not unhandsome, endowed with considerable talents, and with a form extremely delicate and a pleasing manner of the utmost simplicity. But she was withal, active, ambitious, proud, and restless ...'[1] Although the birthdate of Maria Louisa Caterina Cecilia Hadfield[2] has traditionally been considered as 1759, Northcote's statement that 'when she first came to Rome, about the year 1778, she was just eighteen years of age,' as well as the fact that she was termed a minor on the special licence for her marriage in January 1781, point strongly to her being born in 1760. Her parents Charles and Isabella ran a number of inns, which were mainly patronised by visitors from Britain. Maria, whose first language was probably Italian, recalled her family's origins as well as her early life in the autobiographical letter of 1830 to Sir William Cosway:

> *My father, Charles Hadfield, was from Manchester of very rich merchants and manufacturers. I took particular informations and was told no one existed but an old rich lady who lived in the country, the last of the name died very rich but had no family, and no one could say who had been his heir. My father travelling thro Italy found very bad accomodations for travellers particularly the English, this induced him to take a large house and fitted it up quite in the English manner, this brought all the English, and was induced to take two more houses for the same people. Sir, [in] the one on the Arno I was born.*

There was a further description of the inns contained in *A Brief Account of the Roads of Italy* (1775), a guidebook for English-speaking travellers, which mentioned that Hadfield had been running his business in Florence since the late 1740s: 'The Inns are at Carlo's one Charles hadfield who has kept it these twenty and eight years and where most of the English Nobility and Gentry have lodg'd, who have been abroad in that time. It is and has always been a house in very great Esteem in a genteel part [of] town a few doors from the English Envoy. and near the Palace and gardens of great Duke. he has three houses (one of them situated on the river arno) quite near each other'.[3] The particular inn where Maria was born was almost certainly that on the Lungarno Guicciardini (then Capponi) on the corner of the Via dei Gaggi, which was on the left bank of the Arno opposite the Palazzo Corsini. The historian Gibbon recorded in his diary his impressions of a visit to the inn on 19 March 1764: 'We descended on a certain Charles Hatfield, an Innkeeper who is very well known among the English Travellers and who speak highly of him. Judging by our supper, it would appear that he merits this praise'. In the diary entry for a later visit on 19 June of the same year, Gibbon gave more details of the arrangements and also referred to a second set of lodgings which were very close by: 'The price of living at this house we found to be six pauls [*paoli*] (per day) a head for eating, and five for an apartment, the Servants Room included. We indeed were obliged to pay six pauls a day for our apartement, as it was very large, and towards the River. – We lay to night in a ground apartment in another house he has. the opposite side of the street. In the two houses he can lodge above twenty people; most of the apartments very good & pretty cool in Summer'. Gibbon also described another property belonging to 'Charles', a country house about a mile and a half outside Florence, where on at least two occasions he and some companions enjoyed supper and the cleaner air.[4]

Charles Hadfield himself must have been something of a *bon viveur*, and this side of his character is brought out in the friendly caricature known as *The Punch Party* painted in oils by Thomas Patch in 1760, where he is portrayed serving British guests at one of his inns in Florence. The popularity of his inns is attested to by the presence of the complete gamut of Grand Tourists including royalty, members of the aristocracy, writers, connoisseurs and artists. Among the known visitors were Karl Friedrich, the Margravine and Elector (May 1750), Mrs George Craster (*c*.1761–2), Dr John Morgan (1764), James Martin (December 1764), James Boswell (July 1765), a member of the Farington family (March 1765), Sir Lucas Pepys (December 1767), Sir William Watkins-Wynn (October 1768), Charles Townley (January 1772 and December 1773) who corresponded with Charles Hadfield in 1768 over the negotiations for the purchase of pictures and sculptures, a member of the Winchelsea family (December 1772), Patrick Home (August 1776 to April 1777), the landscape painter Thomas Jones (November 1776), the Duke and Duchess of Gloucester (April 1777), T.G. Caulet (1778), Joseph Mercer (November 1778), and the noted travel writer Henry Swinburne (May 1779). It is also worth noting that Prince Charles Edward Stewart, the Young Pretender, was prevented from staying at Carlo's in August 1770 through the action of Sir Horace Mann, the British envoy in Florence. Encounters with such an extraordinary range of people during her childhood must have had a considerable influence on the formation of Maria Hadfield's character.[5]

In her autobiographical letter of 1830 Maria went on to describe a series of extremely disturbing events, in which a number of her elder siblings were killed by a deranged nurse:

> *I may relate a Circumstance at my birth, as extraordinary as unheard of. – four or five children were born before me; put to nurse out of town. My mother used to go frequently, found the child well, and to her great surprise the next day the Nurse Came and the Child had died in the Night. Changed Nurse, Changed place, the same happened thro' four Children. At my birth My father resolved to take a nurse and the Child. One day one a Maid Servant went in the Nursery, took me in her Arms, and said pretty little Creature, I have sent four in heaven and I hope*

to send you also; the governess struck at this extraordinary speech ran to my father, proper enquiries were made, the woman said she thought it doing a good act, and was confined for life. — from that in short my father said I should be brought up a Catholic and all his Children were also. When four years Old I was put into a Convent, under the protection of the Grand Duke and the grand Duchess of Tuscany.

This episode was probably formative on Maria Hadfield's intense religious outlook as well as on the direction of her later career as an educationalist. Yet, despite this family trauma, she soon began to show her artistic and musical talents to such a degree that she was considered a youthful prodigy. She received encouragement from her father and training from a number of artists, as she continued to relate in her letter of 1830:

Being perceived I had natural dispositions I was immediately put to learn music and at six and at ten years of age did what I since have thought extraordinary. At eight years I began drawing, having seen a young lady draw I took a passion for it more than I had for Music. I was taken home and put under the care of an old Celebrated lady, whos[e] portrait is in the Gallery. I had a number of Masters but painting had my preference. This lady soon found I could go further than she could instruct me, and Mr. Zofani being at florence my father ask'd him to give me some instructions. I went to study in the Gallery of the Palazzo Pitti, and Copied many of the finest pictures.

Maria Hadfield was initially made a pupil of Violante Cerroti, and it is known that she copied actively in the Florentine galleries between 1773 and 1778. Among the pictures she made copies of were works by Trevisani, Reynolds, Van Meiris and Correggio, the copy of the Correggio being made under Zoffany's supervision. She also painted in the company of the English miniaturist Ozias Humphry on at least one occasion. Two of these copies survive at Lodi, including versions of Raphael's *Large Cowper Madonna* and Rubens's *Four Philosophers*. Both of these paintings can be seen in Zoffany's famous painting from the 1770s of British visitors shown admiring art works in *The Tribuna of the Uffizi*.[6] Interestingly, Maria Hadfield brought both of these copies with her when she first came to London in 1779, probably in part to demonstrate the level of skill she had attained in Florence. In the previous year, at the age of eighteen, she was elected a member of the Florentine Accademia del Disegno, being described as a *pittrice Inglese*, or English paintress. The culmination of her artistic training came with a visit to Rome and Naples from 1778 to 1779, where she made further contact with many of the artists either resident in or passing through Italy, as she goes on to relate in her letter to Sir William Cosway:[7]

Wright of darby passed only few days at florence and Noticing my assiduity and talent for the art, sprang me to the higher branch of it. My father had a great taste and knowledge of the Arts and Sciences therefore in every way contrived to furnish my mind. He meant to go to England with all his family. As he wished I should see Rome, Mrs. Gore the Mother of Lady Cowper took me with her. There I had an oportunity of knowing all the first living Artists intimately; Battoni, Mengs, Maron, and many English Artists. Fusely with his extraordinary visions struck my fancy. I made no regular study, but for one year and half only went to see all that was high in painting and sculpture, [and] made sketches.

While in Rome and Naples, Maria Hadfield spent much of her time with British artists, on whom she made a great impression. She stayed with the sculptor Thomas Banks and his wife who were then resident in Rome, and took a great interest in the musical scene there. The English painter James Northcote, who was also then in Rome, described her talents and predicted that she would follow in the footsteps of Angelica Kauffman. In 1779 Northcote joined a party of expatriate artists and others who travelled south, as he put it: 'In the month of April following I went to Naples in the company of friends (artists), amongst whom were Maria Hadfield, Thomas Banks, the sculptor, Prince Hoare, Henry Tresham, Alexander Day, the miniature painter and dealer in paintings. Mrs. Banks, and others. After tarrying about a month and seeing whatever was curious in that country, I returned again to Rome.'[8]

Maria also kept up a correspondence with the miniaturist Ozias Humphry, who was studying in Rome in the mid-1770s. Her letters are comprised mainly of gossip about artists, musicians and visitors to Florence, who included Charles Townley, as well as the painters Zoffany, Edwards and Tresham. Among these letters is one of early 1777 from the musician William Parsons to Isabella Hadfield, requesting the hand of Maria. From Isabella's stern letter to her daughter, which is preserved among Humphry's correspondence, it is clear that Parsons was dissuaded from this course. Another young artist, Prince Hoare, who was studying in Rome at this time, had also fallen in love with Maria Hadfield. In a letter of 1781 which Northcote – then in Plymouth – had written to Hoare soon after his return to London from Italy, he states that as Hadfield was about to marry Cosway, Hoare had been so pitied by his friends that it had been arranged for Banks to break the news to him gently. This episode sheds considerable light on the extent to which Maria Hadfield had captured the hearts of this circle of artists – and similarly their envy of Richard Cosway's later good fortune.[9]

However, this period was also one of great emotional confusion for Maria Hadfield, bringing out in her, as she later recalled, strong religious yearnings: 'my mother recalled me [from Rome] to Florence to go with her to England. My inclination from a child had been to be a Nun. I wished therefore to return to my Convent, but my mother was miserable about it and I was persuaded to accompany her'. The exact reason for Isabella Hadfield's decision to end the family business in Florence is not known, but her husband had died in November 1776. It was probable that she was tired after running the inns on her own for two and a half years and may also have been looking to make a suitable match for her talented eldest daughter, as well as advance her career as an artist and musician. Maria and the rest of the Hadfield family travelled to London in the summer of 1779, accompanied by Thomas Banks and his wife. In June that year the Hadfields – Isabella and four of her children, Maria, George, Charlotte and Isabella – had been issued with passports in Florence. Another brother William may also have travelled with the family, as in July 1779 he wrote to Prince Hoare, still in Florence, giving him Maria's temporary address in Paris. It is likely that the Hadfields arrived in London before the end of that year. As Maria later recalled, she was confident about her entry into London society as she 'had letters of introduction from Lady Rivers for all the first people of fas[h]ion Sir J. Reynolds, Cipriani, Bartolozzi [and] Angelica Kauffman'.[10]

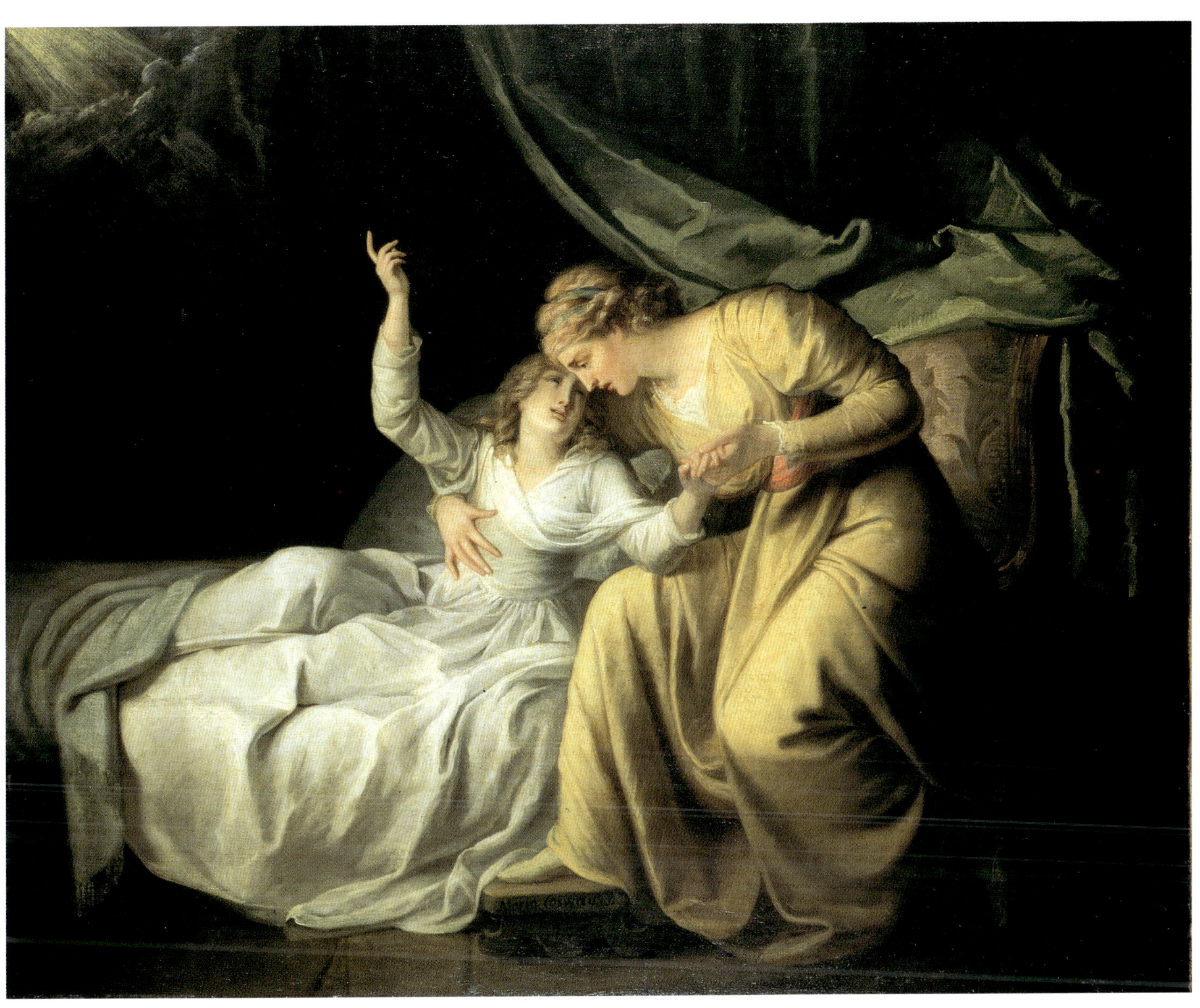

Plate 32   Maria Cosway *The death of Miss Gardiner* 1789 [**224**]

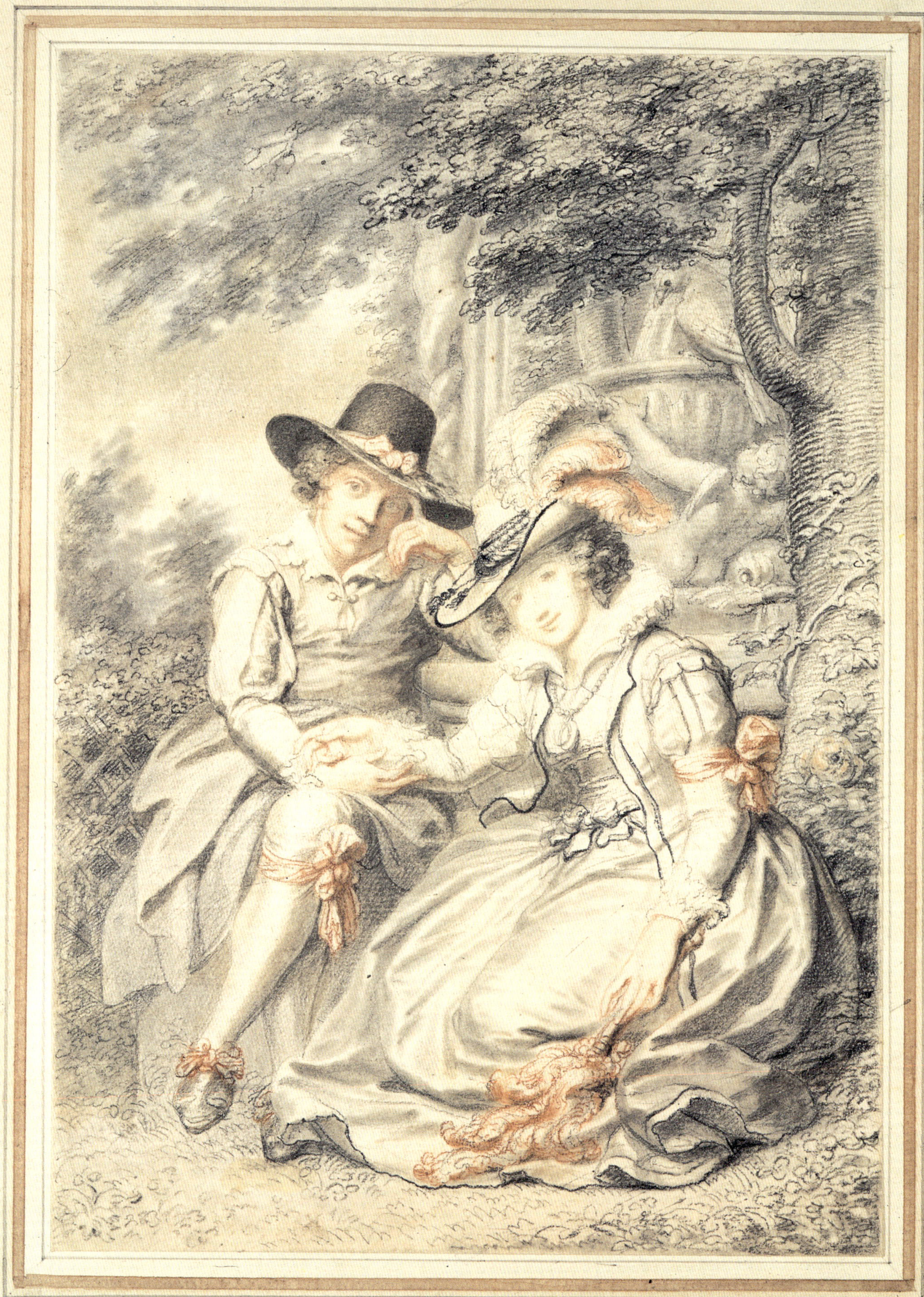

MR AND MRS COSWAY
LONDON AND PARIS
1780–90

*M*ARIA *was filled with the highest expectations of being the wonder of the nation like another Angelica Kauff-mann. But alas! these expectations failed; the money which the father had gained in Florence was quickly spent in England, and the family were soon in some degree of distress. This change, to her so very great, she bore with remarkable fortitude and magnanimity, but in the end, after having refused better offers in her better days, she from necessity married Cosway the miniature painter ...*

Northcote's account of the circumstances surrounding Maria Hadfield's marriage to Richard Cosway indicates that it was to some degree arranged. Certainly it caused considerable astonishment and envy among her admirers, many of whom were Cosway's artistic contemporaries. It is very likely that Maria's mother Isabella was looking to arrange a generous marriage settlement for her precocious elder daughter. As Maria herself put it: 'I became acquainted with Mr. Cosway, his offer was Accepted, my mothers wishes gratified, and I married tho' under Age'. It is very likely that Richard settled the sum of £2800 on Maria, which gives an indication of his prosperity at that time. The couple were married at the fashionable church of St George's, Hanover Square, on 18 January 1781. In the absence of her father Maria was almost certainly given away by Charles Townley [6]. The register was signed by Maria's mother Isabella Hadfield, and also by their friend, the sculptor Thomas Banks, who was likely to have been Cosway's best man.[1]

Throughout the first decade of their marriage up until 1790, when their only child Louisa was born, the Cosways both enjoyed great artistic and social success as well as considerable public attention. Despite their differences in age, they were similar in their temperament and outlook, which was artistic, highly sociable and inclined towards the spiritual. There can be little doubt that it was this alliance of two such creative and assertive personalities which enhanced both their careers and led to such public attention. Richard Cosway rapidly became one of the most fashionable portraitists working in London, while Maria established herself as an artist, musician and *salon* hostess.

In the course of exhibiting every year from 1781 to 1789, Maria Cosway showed over thirty history paintings and portraits in oil at the Royal Academy. This was the major part of her public career as an artist, although she did exhibit further groups of pictures at the Academy in 1796, 1800 and 1801. After the departure of Angelica Kauffman for Italy in 1781, Maria, together with friends Anne Damer and Mary Moser, became one of the foremost women artists exhibiting publicly in London in the 1780s. However, any assessment of her work is hampered by the fact that very few of her paintings have survived, although many are known through prints. Her style is highly eclectic but the formative influence is from her study of the Old Masters of the Renaissance and Baroque, whom she copied so assiduously during the 1770s. One can also detect the influence of her older contemporaries, Reynolds, Fuseli and Kauffman,

in terms of style, handling and the range of subject matter. Maria Cosway's interest in spiritual iconography was part of an increasing trend during the 1780s that was dominated by Fuseli, but which received a mixed critical response. Horace Walpole recorded in his Royal Academy catalogue of 1783 that 'of late Barry, Romney, Fuseli, Mrs Cosway, and others, have attempted to paint deities, visions, witchcrafts, etc., but have only been in bombast and without true dignity'.[2]

Just over a third of her oeuvre from the 1780s was comprised of portraits, many of which were 'in character' and often highly ambitious, such as the full-length of *Georgiana, Duchess of Devonshire,* of 1782 [fig. 28], which is based on Spenser's *Faerie Queene.* The painting, which is now at Chatsworth, was reproduced in a mezzotint engraving by Valentine Green and was published the following year [**229**]. This dramatic full-length shows the Duchess flying through the night sky directly towards the viewer. One critic praised the 'elegant compliment' paid to the sitter, noting the painting's originality and delicacy.[3] This viewer also asserted that Maria Cosway was 'the first of female painters' and among the male sex only inferior to her husband and Reynolds. Other untraced paintings such as *Eolus raising a storm* (1782), *Samson* (1784), *The Deluge* (1785) and *A Vision* (1786) were stylistically influenced by Fuseli, and as such were generally considered failures by the reviewers and critics. It is notable that all four of these compositions were included in the caricature etching of Maria Cosway, titled *Maria Costive at her studies* [**86**]. More successful was the painting of *The Hours* of 1783, which was engraved in stipple [**232**] by Bartolozzi for Thomas Macklin's *British Poets* series. An impression of the print was sent to Jacques-Louis David, who, in a letter to Maria Cosway of early 1788, praised both the composition and its author very warmly:

Je ne vous parlerai que de vous et du plaisir que m'a fait une gravure faite d'après vous représentant les Heures au sein de l'aurore et qui vont insensiblement se précipiter dans celui de la nuit. On ne peut pas faire une poësie plus ingénieuse et plus naturelle. Courage Madame Cosway, à la gloire, à la gloire, sans génie on est rien et avec du génie on est ce que vous êtes. Je regrette de vous avoir connue, car j'aurais voulu ne vous connaitre que pour ne plus vous quitter et nous amuser à raisonner notre art ensemble.[4]

[I will only speak about you and the pleasure I have had from an engraving made after your painting of the Hours at the bosom of dawn, and who carelessly throw themselves into that of night. One couldn't conceive a painted poem more ingenious or more

natural. Take courage Madame Cosway, on to glory, on to glory, without genius one is nothing, and with genius one is what you are. I regret having met you, for I would have wished only to get to know you so that I might never leave you and that we might amuse ourselves discussing our art.]

The Cosways had met David on their visit to Paris in 1786 and Maria had renewed their friendship in 1787. At this date the anglophile David was planning a visit to London, with the intention of showing his 1787 painting of *The Death of Socrates* at the Royal Academy, although eventually nothing came of the projected visit.

David's influence can be seen in the arrangement of figures and the prominent use of gesture in one of Maria Cosway's most significant extant paintings, namely the unusual subject of *The death of Miss Gardiner* [**224**]. Stylistically this reveals the handling, pictorial organisation and lighting characteristic of Reynolds and Kauffman. One of the few signed and dated works by Maria Cosway to survive, this is also probably her finest extant painting. The meaning of this painting has recently been explored. Despite the unusual subject matter it is typical of sentimental taste across Europe, and reflects Maria Cosway's spiritual interests. Miss Gardiner, who is shown dying while being supported by her aunt Lady Townshend, had a vision of her deceased mother, and had expressed a desire to join her in heaven. This work can be seen as offering a specifically feminine vision of death, where emotional expressiveness is contained within a private space and may be contrasted with the more public masculine stoic heroism, which Maria Cosway would have seen demonstrated in David's famous painting *Death of Socrates* (1787).[5]

Many of Maria Cosway's paintings were comprised of subject pictures drawn from the Bible, mythology and literature. As with some of the 'in character' portraits the sources on which she drew were various, and ranged from Virgil and Diodorus Siculus to Spenser and Shakespeare. She also made use of James Macpherson's highly popular *Works of Ossian* for a painting of *Althan* exhibited in 1783. Generally Maria Cosway's oil paintings received very mixed reviews, as did those of her husband. Her paintings were known to a wider audience due to that fact that about a third of the exhibited works were reproduced as prints, mainly by the leading stipple and mezzotint engravers such as Valentine Green and Francesco Bartolozzi.

The course of Maria Cosway's career as a painter was affected by the attitude of her husband, who was fully professional and highly successful. He would have encouraged her both to exhibit at the Academy and to make her work better known through engravings. However, it is clear that she was frustrated in her ambitions as an independent painter, as she herself noted in later life when recalling her earlier career:

I kept very retired for two months until I became acquainted with the society I should form, the effect of the exhibition, the taste and character of the Nation. Mr: Cosway's wish was I should occupy myself as hitherto done in the Arts, & so I did. The first pictures I exhibited made my reputation. The novelty and my age contributed more than the real merit. The portrait of the duchess of Devonshire then the reining beauty & fasion, in the caracter of Cynthia from Spencer, seem'd to strike & other historical subjects from Shakspear, *Virgil & Homer ... encouraged but never proud, I follow'd intirely the impulse of my*

imagination; had Mr: C. permitted me to paint professionally, I should have made a better painter but left to myself by degrees, instead of improving, I lost what I had brought from Italy of my early studies.

The critic Cunningham also reflected that Richard Cosway was too proud to permit Maria to paint professionally, adding that 'this no doubt was in favour of domestic happiness, but much against her success in art'.[6]

However much Richard Cosway limited his wife's potential as a professional artist, he compensated for this by helping to promote her image and by providing – at Berkeley Street and then at Schomberg House in Pall Mall – a luxurious setting for her artistic and musical talents. Judging by his intimate and fashionable portraits of Maria, which were painted or drawn and then often reproduced as prints throughout the 1780s, Cosway clearly loved and idealised his wife. In his earliest portrait of her leaning on a table [**33**], a drawing with watercolour, dating to the first couple of years of their marriage, she is shown three-quarter length, already wearing her characteristic turban, and adopting the engaging pose of resting her chin on her hand. A similarly posed portrait drawing of Maria Cosway was engraved in stipple by Schiavonetti and published in 1791 [**140**]. Richard Cosway also created a series of fashionable images of Maria seated on the ground in a park setting, which was engraved in stipple by Bartolozzi in 1785 [**85**]. This composition was modelled on Rubens's portraits of his first wife, Isabella Brant.

The most original of these images was Cosway's painting – since untraced – of Maria seated at the open window on the third floor of Schomberg House, looking out over St James's Park towards Westminster Abbey and beyond to Surrey. This remarkably romantic conception, for which the landscape was painted by William Hodges, was engraved in stipple by W. Birch in 1787 with the title *A View from Mr Cosway's breakfast-room, Pall Mall, with the portrait of Mrs Cosway* [**90**]. Here the portrait of Maria Cosway is not only of lesser significance within the composition but also within the title of the print itself, where she is subordinated to the fact that this a view from *his* house.

In an etching of *Mr and Mrs Cosway* [**82**], for which the finished preparatory drawing survives in a private collection, Richard Cosway shows himself together with Maria seated in the garden of Schomberg House. It was probably executed to mark the couple's move there in 1784. Richard Cosway composed a personal image that is not only idealised and idyllic, but that was also deliberately intended to evoke an association with his great hero, Rubens. He presents himself and Maria almost as if they are paying tribute to the painting by Rubens of himself and his second wife Hélène Fourment walking in their garden, which was adorned with statues and peacocks. They are both fashionably dressed in fanciful seventeenth-century costume.

The black servant offering the Cosways grapes from a vine is also dressed in a similarly fashionable outfit. It is known that the Cosways employed a black servant at Schomberg House, this having been noted enviously by William Blake in his unpublished satirical play *An Island in the Moon* (*c*.1784). This African-born servant was called Quobna Ottobah Cugoano, and also known as John Steuart or Stewart.[7] As part of a group of black men known as the Sons of Africa, he pursued a vigorous campaign against slavery, writing letters to the Prince of Wales and other prominent politicians. In

1787 he published a treatise titled *Thoughts and Sentiments on the Evil and Wicked Traffic of the Slavery and Commerce of the Human Species, Humbly Submitted to the Inhabitants of Great-Britain by Ottobah Cugoano, a Native of Africa*. However, in this self-portrait with his wife Cosway has not drawn attention to his servant's political agitation, but includes him in the composition both to indicate his social status, and as a reference to black servants who appeared in seventeenth-century portraits by Rubens and Van Dyck.

In contrast to Richard Cosway's idealised portraits of his wife can be set Maria's own self-portraits. Three of these paintings were most probably exhibited at the Academy in 1783, 1785 and 1787, one of which was engraved in mezzotint by Valentine Green and published with the title *Mrs. Cosway* [231]. In this highly assertive and self-confident image Maria presents herself three-quarter length, seated upright and alert against a background of sea and night sky with dawn breaking. The pose she has adopted is notable for the crossed arms. While acting as a neat device to conceal one of the hands – often difficult to represent in a self-portrait – this gesture also lends an air of forthright determination to the image. Maria turns her head to face the viewer with a gaze of wide-eyed intensity and unaffected seriousness. The strength of her presence is achieved, without any references to her skills as an artist or musician, and also without distraction from her fashionable appearance. Notable is her puffed and powdered hair with the characteristic turban. She also depicts herself wearing a dark ribbon choker round her neck which is joined at the front with a heart-shaped locket, from which hangs more ribbon ending in a cross at her breast. While this was a fashionable accessory, Maria Cosway presents here a very strong reference to her Catholic faith, which was of such importance to many aspects of her art and life.

Richard Cosway's individual portraits of Maria were complemented by a group of his self-portraits as a fashionable courtier, again with some of the key images being engraved. Prominent was the *Self-portrait in Spanish dress* [43], which was engraved in stipple by J. Clarke. Shown half length and in profile, Cosway wears a prominent ruff around the neck and an exuberant hat with feather. This print was reissued in 1832 to accompany the essay on Cosway published in the *Library of Fine Arts*. Equally widely circulated was the self-portrait drawing which was engraved in stipple by M. Bova with the title *Rdus. Cosway Armiger R.A.* [83], which referred to his right to bear arms at the Academy. Here the artist presents himself seated on some steps. Sporting a wide-brimmed hat with a prominent ostrich feather, he is enveloped in a cloak, which is a clear reference to Marcantonio Raimondi's portrait engraving of Raphael. This stipple was published in 1786. This was a pair to the Bartolozzi stipple engraving of Maria Cosway seated on the ground [85]. These two portraits were cruelly satirised in a pair of caricatures published later that year, titled *Dicky Causway* [84] and *Maria Costive* [86]. He was presented as a wretched beggar or a failed Dick Whittington – reference no doubt to what were perceived as his humble origins in the West Country, while she was shown as a maddened artist in gaol or an asylum, painting history pictures from her husband's palette.[8]

However, the importance to Richard Cosway of his relationship with Maria Cosway was emphasised by the number of portraits he produced during the 1780s where he presented himself together with his wife. The fact that he was so clearly inspired by the example of Rubens is demonstrated in the drawing in chalks at Lodi of himself and Maria seated in a landscape [34]. The pair of detailed pen and ink drawings of himself and Maria at Lodi from the end of the decade reveal his convincing persona as a connoisseur and courtier [36], while he presents Maria in equally fashionable and extravagant dress, but with full reference to her activities as an artist and musician [37].

The apogee of Richard Cosway's self-promotion with Maria can be seen in the stipple engraved by Robert Thew and published in 1789 as *Abelard and Eloisa* [91] and in a second state with some minor alterations as *Mr and Mrs Cosway* [92]. This remarkably fanciful image is based on a close study of Van Dyck's double portraits and Rubens's domestic scenes. Richard Cosway shows himself as if presenting Maria to the viewer. Attired in seventeenth-century-style fancy dress, he conceals his lack of height by placing himself a step below Maria. She stands calmly, holding a prayer book, with a cross hanging from a string of pearls at her waist. The emphasis given to these details, and part of the intention behind the creation of this image are revealed in the full inscription of the print's rare first state: *Abelard and Eloisa in the gardens of Fulbert's country residence at Corbeil*. The effect was completed by the artist showing himself with an elegant moustache, a detail which was removed from the second state of the print.

The romantic and tragic legend of the medieval lovers was sustained by the publication and translation of their correspondence. Numerous editions of the *Letters of Abélard and Héloïse* were brought out in Britain during the eighteenth century, reaching a peak in the 1780s, when five editions were published. That of 1781 had a frontispiece of Abélard and Héloïse holding hands in Fulbert's garden, where they used to meet secretly.[9] Richard Cosway would certainly have known of this traditional iconography of the lovers and used it accordingly. The identification with Abélard and Héloïse was also relevant for the Cosways in that they professed to own relics of the tragic lovers. In 1797 the diarist Joseph Farington recorded his fellow artist James Northcote's account of an incident when he had asked to borrow a skull belonging to the Cosways: 'Traits of Cosway & Mrs. Cosway were shewn on the occasion. Mrs Cosway sent to desire Northcote would take care of the Skull as "it reminded her of immortality". Cosway expressed a similar wish because it was "the Skull of Abelard".' The critic William Hazlitt, after a visit to Stratford Place at the end of Cosway's life, also noted that among the numerous relics, curiosities and talismans, the artists owned 'the crucifix that Abelard prayed to' and a 'lock of Eloisa's hair'. In this double portrait Cosway's emphasis on the religious elements may be seen as significant for interpreting the way in which the couple saw themselves, especially in the light of Maria's ostentatious Catholicism and his profound involvement with Christian mysticism.[10]

Through such fashionable and fanciful 'in character' images Cosway was drawing attention to the novelty of a successful artistic couple. However, this self-promotion inevitably attracted criticism in the form of gossip and satirical comment. The Cosways were represented in Anthony Pasquin's scurrilous and hilarious satire of 1786, *The Royal Academicians, a farce*. They were also victims of further caricatures, as in 1782 where in *A smuggling machine* [81], a diminutive Richard Cosway is seen using the fame of Maria for the purposes of his social advancement.

The Cosways also attracted considerable criticism on account of their high profile in society. The *salon* they held at Schomberg House drew particular comment: '[Mr.] and Mrs Cosway kept house in style, in a sort of co-partnership, of so novel a character, as to surprise their new neighbours, astonish their old friends, and furnish wonderment for the table-talk of the town'. At these fashionable concerts and soirées Maria was the centre of attention and they provided an ideal environment for her talents as a musician and *salon* hostess. Initially the Cosways had entertained at 4 Berkeley Street, where Richard Cosway had been living since 1768, and then after 1784 in the central section of Schomberg House. This grand townhouse had already gained a reputation as a residence for successful artists, with Gainsborough occupying the west wing from 1774 until his death in 1788. Prior to the Cosways' tenancy the central part of the house had been occupied by the notorious quack doctor and sex therapist, James Graham, who for three years lectured on 'the Grand Celestial Bed', which was the centrepiece of his 'Temple of Health and Hymen'.[11]

William Blake in his unpublished play *An Island in the Moon*, a sharp satire on London society of the mid-1780s, enviously noted the Cosways' ostentatious lifestyle after their move to Pall Mall. He caricatured them as 'Mr. and Mrs. Jacko', in reference to a famous monkey then performing in Astley's circus by Westminster Bridge. This was another reference to Richard Cosway's reputation for resembling a monkey. Blake (alias 'Quid') had another character, the gossipy 'Miss Gittipin', describe all the comings and goings:

> *And I hardly know what a coach is, except when I go to Mr. Jacko's. He knows what riding is [& he does not (deleted)] & his wife is the most agreeable woman. You hardly know she has a tongue in her head, and he is the funniest fellow, & I do not believe he'll go into partnership with his master, & they have black servants lodge at their house. I never saw such a place in my life. He says he has six & twenty rooms in his house, and I believe it, & he is not such a liar as Quid thinks he is [but he always Envying (deleted)].*

Blake's details were correct. Cosway owned a coach, which was unusual for an artist, and he often gave artists lifts to and from the Academy, as Farington noted in his diary. The Cosways' house was very likely to have had twenty-six rooms, which could have been contained within the four main floors of the central portion of Schomberg House, as well as in the attic and basement levels. The 'master', about whom Blake speculated, was almost certainly the Prince of Wales, who was about to appoint Cosway his *Primarius Pictor*, or Principal Painter, in 1785.[12]

At the concerts she organised Maria Cosway held court both socially and musically as she would either sing, or play the harp and various keyboard instruments. Among the musicians appearing were top Italian professionals such as Rubinelli, Tenducci and the male soprano Luigi Marchesi.[13] As Maria later recalled in her autobiographical letter of 1830, 'my exercise in Music made my evenings very agreeable'. She also remembered the many ladies of fashion who attended, as well as other notable visitors: 'General Paoli, the Foreign Ministers, the distinguished foreigners, Lord Sands, Mr. Erskine ... until they became great concerts of the first professors. H.R.H. the Prince of Wales honoured [them] constantly'. The London *bon ton* flocked to Maria Cosway's *salon* and concerts. Those attending included younger members of the royal family, as well as nobility in the circle of the Prince of Wales, and also members of the Whig party. They were joined by artists, musicians, writers, scientists and the curious. Foreigners were welcome, whether royalty, diplomats or *émigrés*. The tenor of these occasions can be gathered from some of the contemporary accounts. The scientist Tiberius Cavallo, writing to the artist Prince Hoare in 1788, described one evening, referring in particular to the recent health fashion for Animal Magnetism – or Mesmerism – of which both the Cosways were devotees:

> *Mrs. Cosway, alias Mary Cosway, alias Lady Mary Cosway, alias the Goddess of Pall-Mall, alias la decima Musa, alias the Magnetic Muse, and sister Charlotte were very glad to hear something of you, and desire their compliments. – Magnetism is, at least apparently, out of fashion there. Two evenings in the week, viz: on monday and thursday, Mary the great sits in state;*

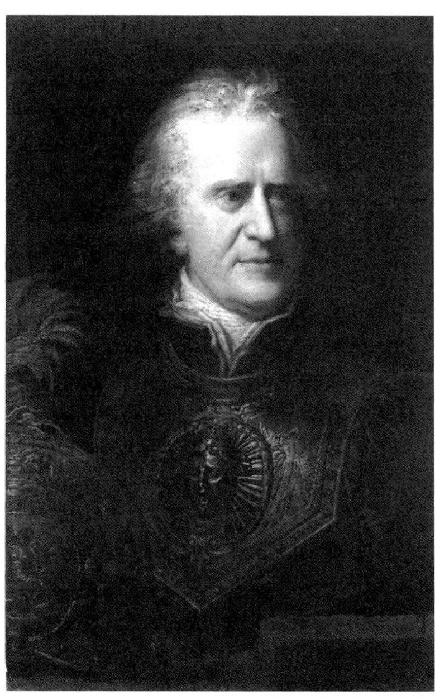

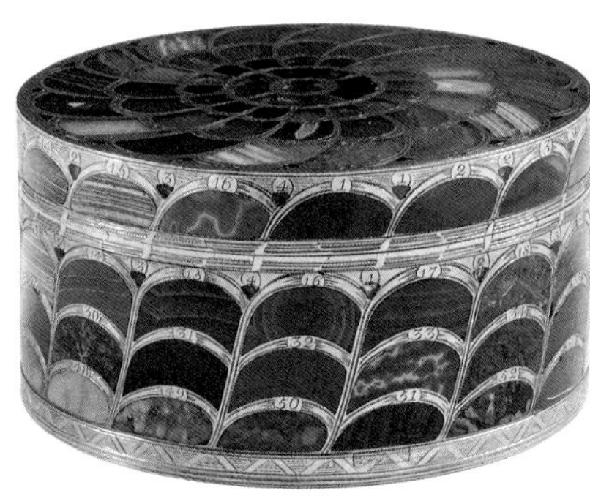

Fig. 7 *General Pasquale Paoli*, 1798 (Galleria degli Uffizi, Florence)

Fig. 8 *Snuff-box*, 1774, by Christian-Gottlieb Stiehl [**257**]

Fig. 9 *The children of Louis-Philippe, Duc d'Orléans*, 1786 (Musée Condé, Chantilly)

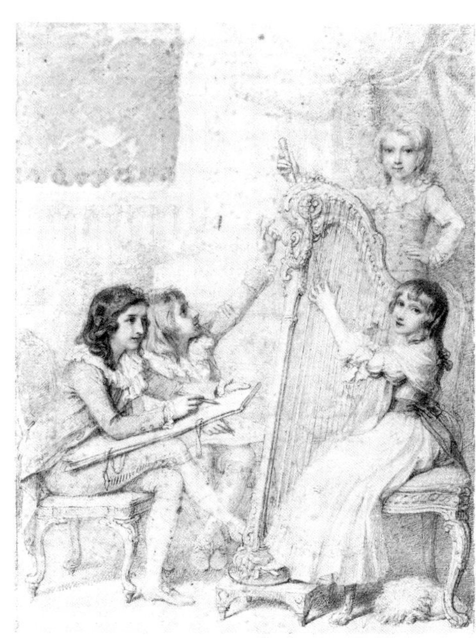

but at the other time[s] she is not at home. On Monday last amongst a great variety of people she had Mr. de Calogne and the French Ambassador, persons peculiarly remarkable for being in one room at the same time. The performance in these stated evenings consists of music, flattery, scraping, bowing, puffing, shamming, back biting, sneering, drinking tea, &c. &c.[14]

A year later, in 1789, Gouverneur Morris, the American envoy in London and a frequent visitor to Schomberg House, was struck by the formality of these occasions, as he noted in his diary:

Visit by Appointment at Mrs. Cosway's; a genteel Company, Dutchess Dowager of Bedford among them. Music very good. The arrangement of the Company however is stiff and formal. There must be in all this as in all other Countries the Ways and Means of bringing People together even to Intimacy, but it seems at first Aspect to be rather difficult.[15]

The connoisseur and collector Horace Walpole, who was another regular visitor over the years from 1786 to 1791, left some of the most interesting accounts of these evenings. He was not especially close to either of the Cosways, but he did show them round his famous neo-Gothic villa, Strawberry Hill, in 1784. He was a rather reluctant visitor to the concerts, which he once described to Mary Berry as like 'Charon's boat', and where, in a letter from a few years earlier, he warned Lady Lyttelton to expect 'a babel of compliments, that will be made to you on y[our] [goo]d looks by the representatives of all the princes in Europe at Mrs Cosway's Diet'. Yet even Walpole could not resist the opportunity of watching the activities of the various foreigners and *émigrés* at play. In a letter of May 1786 to Sir Horace Mann, the British envoy in Florence, Walpole described meeting the Florentine resident Earl Cowper at the Cosways, and then went on to describe both him and the concert in unflattering terms:

Well! you may find I have seen your principled Earl. Curiosity carried me to a great concert at Mrs Cosway's t'other night – not to hear Rubinelli, who sung one song at the extravagant price of ten guineas, and whom for as many shillings I have heard sing half a dozen at the opera house: no, but I was anxious to see an English Earl who had passed thirty years at Florence.[16]

A few months earlier, in January 1786, Walpole wrote to Lady Ossory about another memorable evening, where he encountered Richard Cosway's friend *Mademoiselle La Chevalière d'Eon de Beaumont* [87], a former French diplomat and spy in London, as well as a notorious transvestite and freemason, who also gave fencing displays. Walpole continued his letter with an account of other eminent personalities he met that evening:

Nor was this all my entertainment this evening. As Mlle Common of Two reserve is a little subsided, there were other persons present, as three foreign ministers besides Barthélemy, Lord Camarthen, Count Oghinski, Wilkes and his daughter, and the chief of the Moravians. I could not help thinking how posterity would wish to have been in my situation, at once with three such historic personages, as D'Eon, Wilkes, and Oghinski, who has so great a share in the revolution of Poland, and was king of it for four-and-twenty hours.[17]

The diarist James Boswell was also drawn to Schomberg House in the later part of his life, on one visit in 1787 noting in his diary that he 'drank tea at Cosway's placidly' with the scientist Tiberius Cavallo. Yet Boswell's numerous visits between 1785 and 1787 were

less likely to have been on account of the Cosways than his desire to be in the company of his hero, the exiled Corsican patriot, General Pasquale Paoli. However, Boswell was forced to share his close friendship with Paoli with Maria Cosway, whom the diarist was not beyond flirting with himself. In a letter to her written in 1785, mainly in Italian, Boswell asked Maria Cosway – successfully – to accompany him to the fashionable circus of performing animals run by Astley: '... chi, tutto contrario a li, da alle cane un simiglianza umana, mentre che lei (per servirmi del linguaggio d'Inghilterra) treat men like dogs ...'[18]

Of a considerably more complex nature was Maria Cosway's long and close relationship with Paoli himself, who had been exiled in England since 1769. Pasquale Paoli (1725–1807) had driven the Genoese out of the major part of Corsica, only to find his island annexed by the French in 1768. A considerable celebrity during his first exile in England, Paoli returned to Corsica at the onset of the French Revolution. He returned to England in 1795, where he eventually died in exile. Perhaps the finest portrait of the General was that painted on panel by Cosway, which was exhibited at the Academy in 1798 [fig.7]. He portrayed Paoli in a heroic Titianesque mood, as Renaissance warrior, with glittering armour – a helmet and a breastplate adorned with the Medusa's head. It has been aptly described as an image full of 'high character and grandeur in air and manner, revealing a man of emotional intensity, dignity and claim to power'. The portrait may well have been painted specifically for Maria Cosway, as it hung in her room at Stratford Place. A treasured possession at the Collegio in Lodi, it was bequeathed by her to the Galleria of the Uffizi in Florence, and today hangs in the Pitti Palace in the same city.[19]

It seems likely that General Paoli and Maria Cosway were introduced some time in 1783, possibly at the Cosway *salon*. Immediate common ground was the fact that both were exiles from the Mediterranean. In particular, Maria Cosway disliked the cold and wet climate in London which she found depressing, and she repeatedly tried to encourage her husband to visit Italy, something which he often promised to do, but in fact never accomplished. Maria was clearly comforted by Paoli's company. He was witty, sympathetic and understood the deeply pious and melancholy nature beneath her gay exterior. There is no doubt that, like so many of her male admirers, Paoli was captivated by the combination of her appearance, personality and talent. Clearly there was deep affection between the two. When the Cosways' only child was born in 1790, they gave her the middle name of Paolina, in honour of her godfather. Her first name was Louisa after her godmother, Louisa of Stolberg (1753–1824), who was the wife of Prince Charles Edward Stewart, and who later lived with the writer and poet Count Vittorio Alfieri. In the years after Louisa's christening Paoli and Maria Cosway addressed each other in their letters as 'compare' and 'comare', affectionate terms for godfather and godmother. The extensive correspondence in Italian from Paoli to Maria, dating from 1784 to 1803, attests to their mutual attraction. In 1789, prior to his departure for Corsica, General Paoli gave Maria Cosway a most precious gold snuff-box inset with *pietre dure* [fig.8], made by Christian-Gottlieb Stiehl, which in turn had been presented to Paoli in 1774 by the Elector of Saxony, Frederick Augustus III. This gift of the snuff-box by Paoli to Maria Cosway was a mark of the great esteem and fondness in which he held her.[20]

Maria Cosway, who spoke fluent Italian, French and English, moved at ease among the European cultural and political élite, whether in London, Paris or Italy. She was not only drawn to powerful personalities of either sex, but had the ability to attract their attention, often establishing close relations and friendships. In her autobiographical letter of 1830 among her 'most intimate friends' she only reveals the names of women, including the sculptress Mrs Damer, as well as English aristocrats, such as Lady Lyttelton, the Countess of Ailesbury and the Marchioness of Townshend. She was also close to Louisa of Stolberg, Countess of Albany; she enjoyed the confidence of Letizia Ramolino, the mother of Napoleon, known as 'Madame Mère'. She also portrayed *Giulia Beccaria* [**226**], the mother of the great novelist *Alessandro Manzoni* [**227**], and she corresponded with Isabella Teotochi Albrizzi, one of the most notable society hostesses in Italy, the friend and biographer of Canova.[21]

However, Maria Cosway's most famous relationship was the romance she had with Thomas Jefferson, when he was the American ambassador in Paris, later to become the third President of the United States. Maria met Jefferson in Paris in 1786, when she visited with her husband, who had been invited to execute portraits of the children [fig.9] of Louis-Philippe, Duc d'Orléans [**89**]. Later during the Revolution he was to be known as Philippe-Égalité, and earlier in the 1780s he had been a great companion of the Prince of Wales. It was John Trumbull, the American painter, who first introduced Maria and Jefferson, and who then later acted as a courier for many of their letters between London and Paris. Mysteriously there is a gap of almost three weeks from Trumbull's detailed diary, which would have described the period when Jefferson and Maria were spending much time together. At the end of his life Trumbull tried to account for the missing pages which cover the period from 19 August to 9 September 1786:[22]

Here my Manuscript fails me; I presume that one if not two sheets, have perished entirely. Of the next fragment, one half of four pages are consumed vertically; that is half of each line remains. This begins with the 10th of September, commencing my journey to Frankfort. I very much regret the loss of these twenty days; for after fifty years, memory unaided, can do little to restore the chasm. I distinctly recollect, however, that this time was occupied with the same industry in examining and reviewing whatever relates to the arts, and that Mr. Jefferson joined our party almost daily; and here commenced his acquaintance with Mrs. Cosway, of whom very respectful mention is made in his published correspondence.[23]

Richard Cosway was fully aware of the amount of time that Maria spent with Jefferson; and indeed he accompanied them on outings to various sights and pleasure gardens, including those at St Germain and the Desert de Retz at Marly. On one trip that Jefferson and Maria Cosway made together alone, Jefferson broke his wrist in an accident whose cause is still unexplained. Shortly afterwards, on 3 October 1786, the Cosways left Paris for Flanders. After bidding them farewell and when he had dropped off the Baron d'Hancarville, who was another admirer of Maria Cosway, Jefferson returned to his residence at the Hôtel de Langeac. In great physical discomfort and emotional turmoil he wrote his since famous letter to Maria Cosway, which was composed as a dialogue between his head and his heart.[24]

There has been considerable speculation about the exact nature of the relationship between Thomas Jefferson and Maria Cosway, but this should be balanced by recalling Jefferson's words written to her in a later letter of 21 May 1789: 'Adieu my very dear friend. Be our affections unchangeable, and if our little history is to last beyond the grave, be the longest chapter in it which shall record their purity, warmth and duration'. Maria Cosway had returned to Paris on her own in the second half of 1787, but she and Jefferson failed to rekindle the intensity of their relationship from the previous year. In 1788 Trumbull painted a small oil portrait of *Thomas Jefferson* [fig.10], specifically at the request of Maria Cosway. However, they continued writing to each other up until his death in 1826, towards the end of which they exchanged information on their educational projects, namely her Collegio at Lodi and his University in Virginia.[25]

While in Paris in 1787 Maria Cosway renewed her friendship with Jacques-Louis David and the antiquarian, Baron d'Hancarville. Highly imaginative and somewhat disreputable, d'Hancarville – who had produced the publication of Sir William Hamilton's collec-

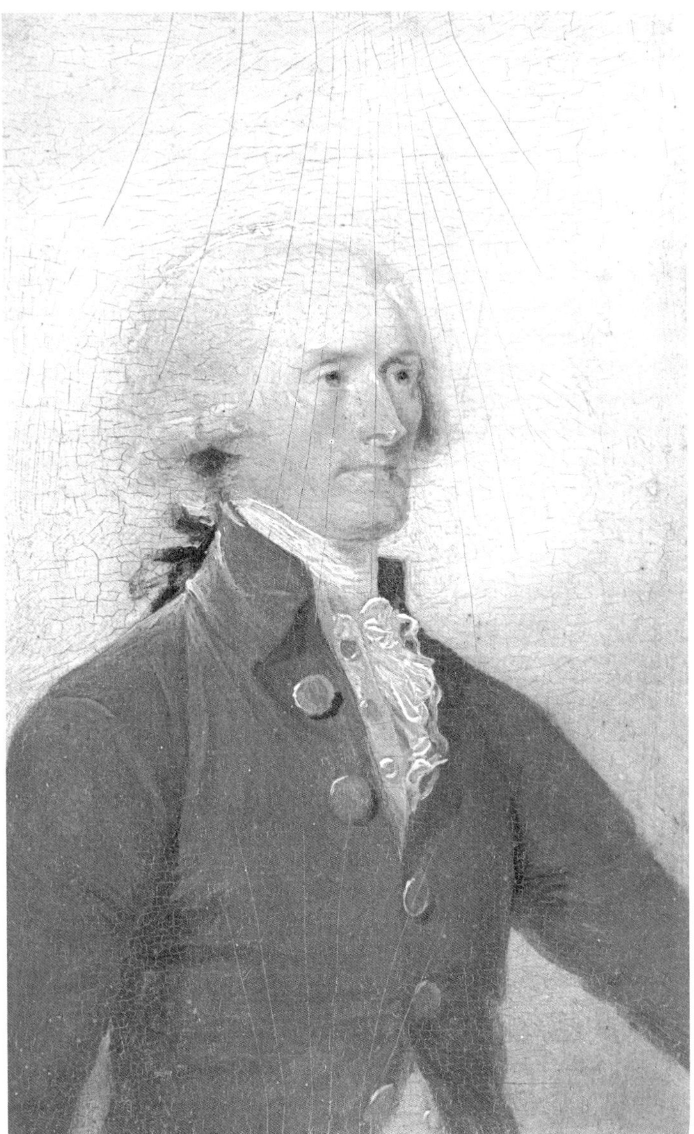

Fig.10. *Thomas Jefferson*, 1788, by John Trumbull (The White House, Washington DC; on loan to the National Portrait Gallery, Smithsonian Institution)

tion of vases, worked as a librarian for Charles Townley, and published his own notorious *Recherches* on fertility cults in antiquity during 1785 – became entranced by Maria, addressing her flatteringly as 'ma très obligeante, ma très obligeante, ma très interessante amie'. His letters to Maria Cosway are not only a mine of information on Parisian cultural circles in the years leading up to the Revolution, but also reveal the crucial role he played in promoting the Cosways' reputations in Paris both during and after their visits.[26] D'Hancarville reported the comments made by leading Parisian artists, led by David, praising Richard Cosway's magnanimous gift to Louis XVI of four huge tapestry cartoons then considered to be by Raphael and Giulio Romano. The anglophile Jacques-Louis David had welcomed both the Cosways, who played a significant role in his projected but unfulfilled 1788 visit to London. Two letters written by David to Maria Cosway in that year attest to their close relations. Greetings and introductions for visiting friends, artists and relatives were exchanged, while prints and draw-

ings were sent back and forth. David praised Richard Cosway's gift of the 1787 stipple engraving by Sailliar of the *Prince of Wales* [**88**], which he had specially framed and hung in his *salon* where it was greatly admired by visitors. David also lavished praise on Maria Cosway's gift of an impression of her composition *The Hours* [**232**], which was engraved in stipple by Bartolozzi in 1788.[27] Maria Cosway's relations with David and his work continued for at least another thirty-five years. She claimed that she had witnessed his attempts to call a halt to the slaughter during the Terror in 1793. She also received close instruction from him on her own painting during her visit to Paris from 1801 to 1803, but was critical of his slavery to the model. Further comments on David's pictorial style came in a letter of 1823 to the antiquarian Francis Douce, who had been one of Richard Cosway's two executors, where she was critical of his late style. However David was rare among Maria Cosway's male friends and admirers in taking a serious and sustained interest in her activity as an artist.[28]

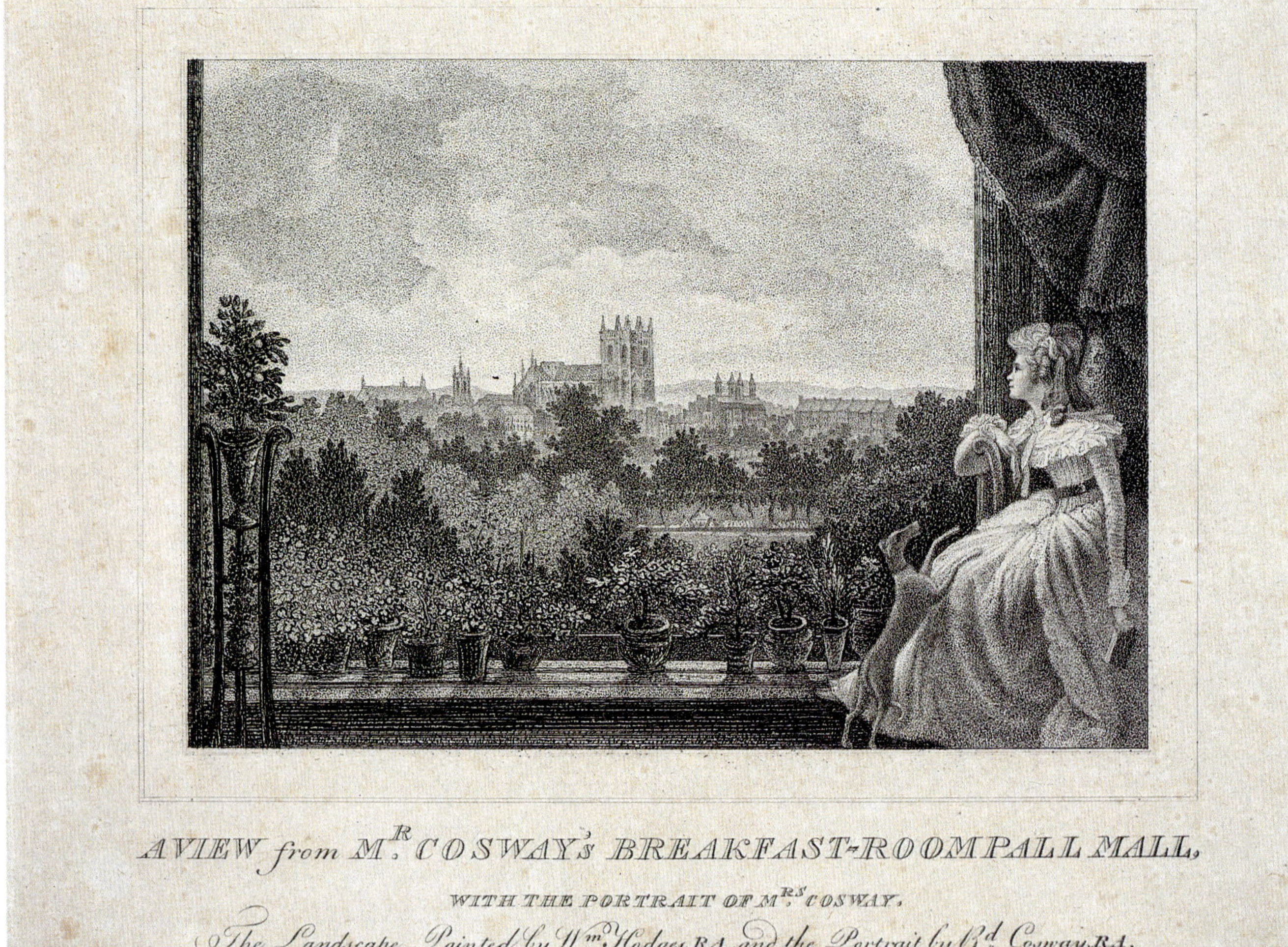

Plate 34   W. Birch after William Hodges and Richard Cosway
A view from Mr Cosway's breakfast-room, Pall Mall, with the portrait of Mrs Cosway 1789 [**90**]

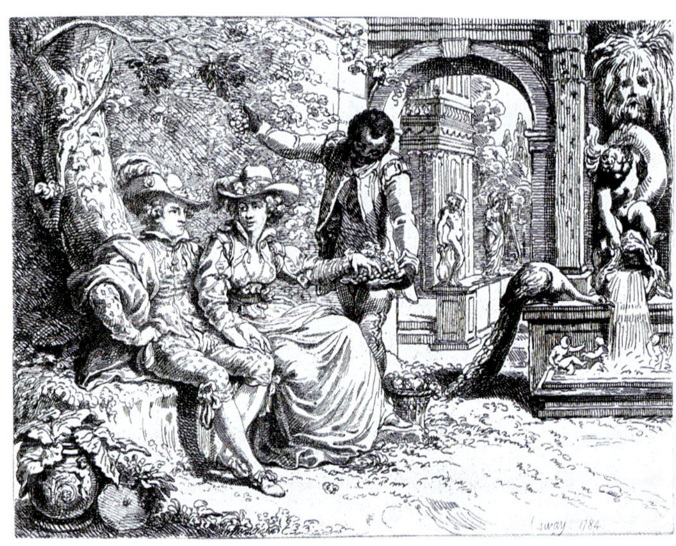

Plate 35   *Mr and Mrs Cosway* 1784 [**82**]

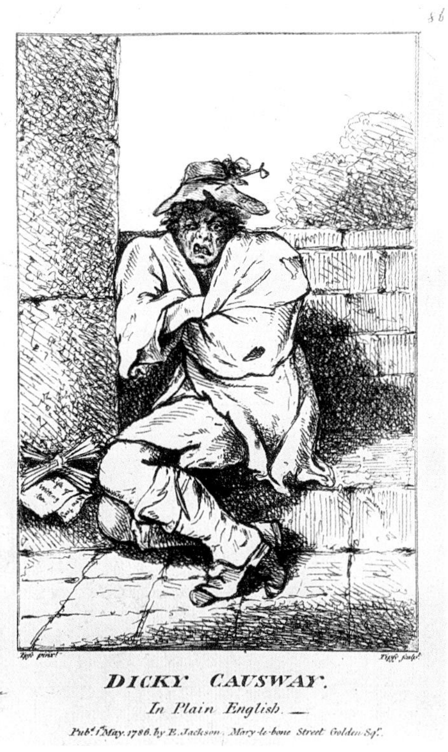

Plate 36   Unknown Artist
Dicky Causway. In Plain English. 1786 [**84**]

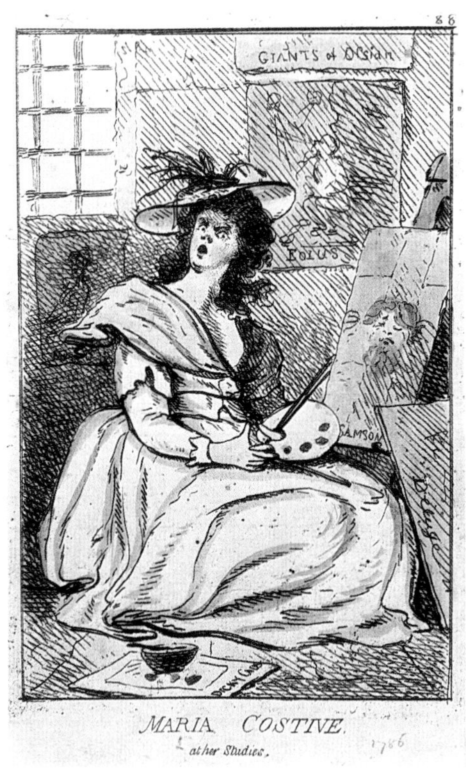

Plate 37   Unknown Artist
Maria Costive at her studies. 1786 [**86**]

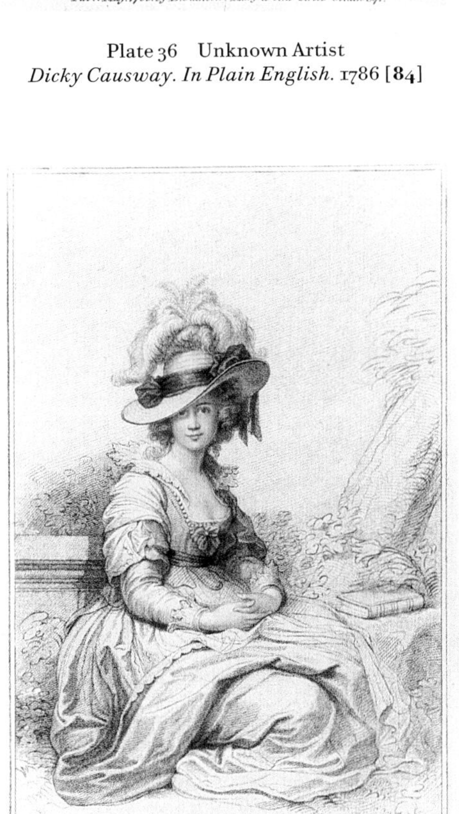

Plate 38   F. Bartolozzi after Richard Cosway
Maria Cosway 1785 [**85**]

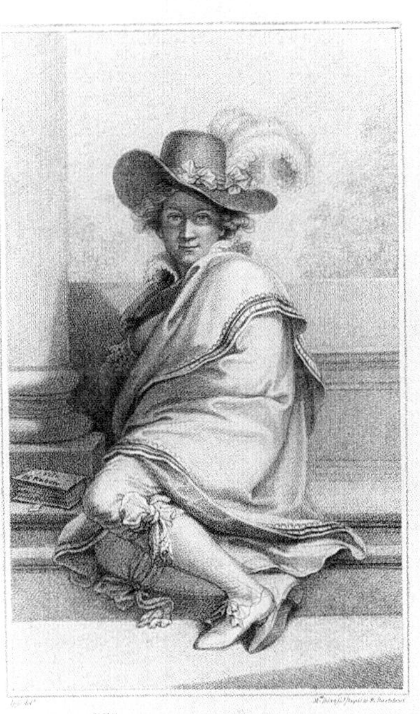

Plate 39   M. Bova after Richard Cosway
*Rdus Cosway Armiger R.A. Primarius Pictor
Serenissimi Walliae Principis* 1786 [**83**]

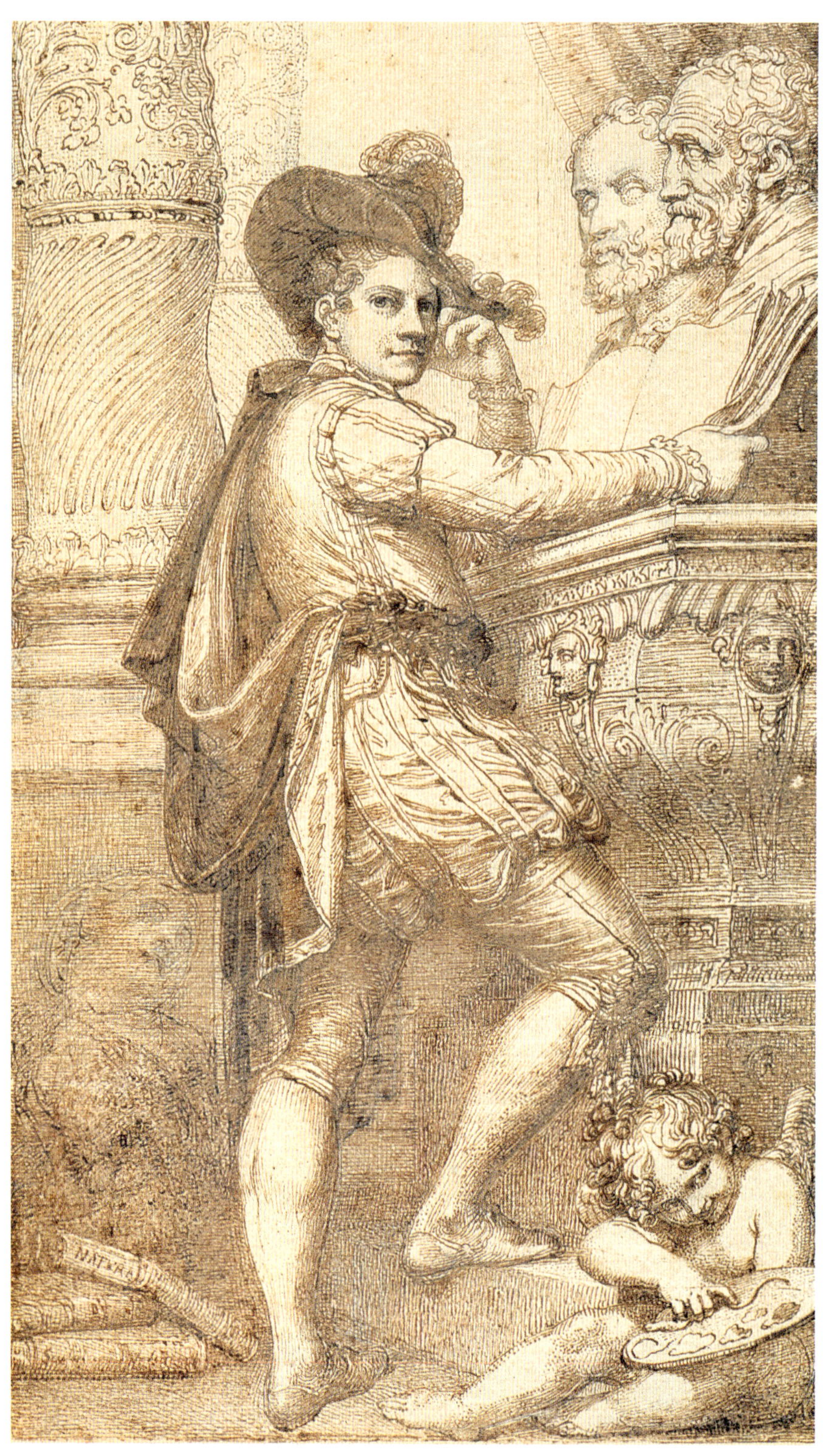

Plate 40   *Self-portrait with busts of Michelangelo and Rubens c.*1789 [**36**]

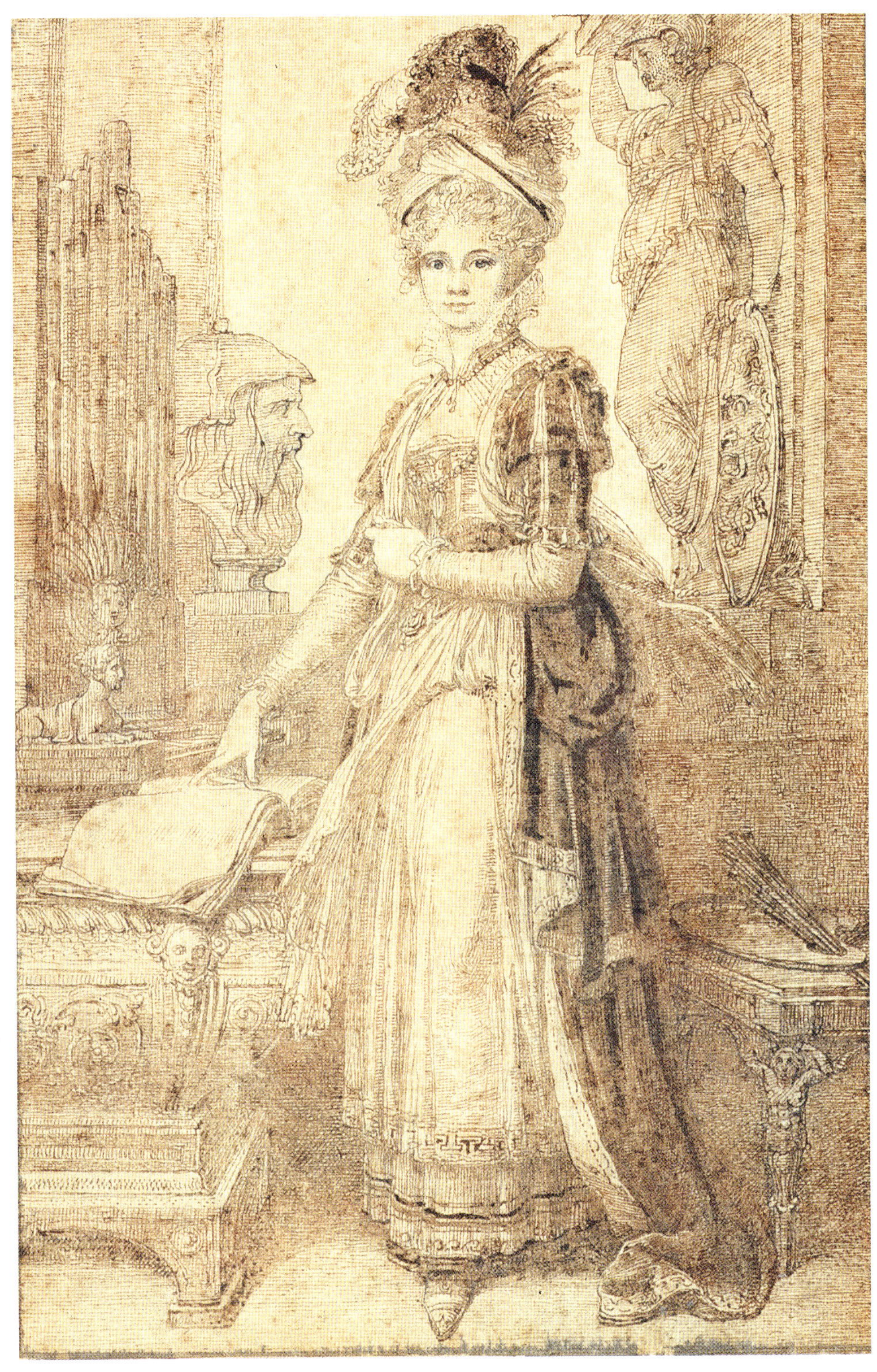

Plate 41　*Maria Cosway with a bust of Leonardo c.*1789 [37]

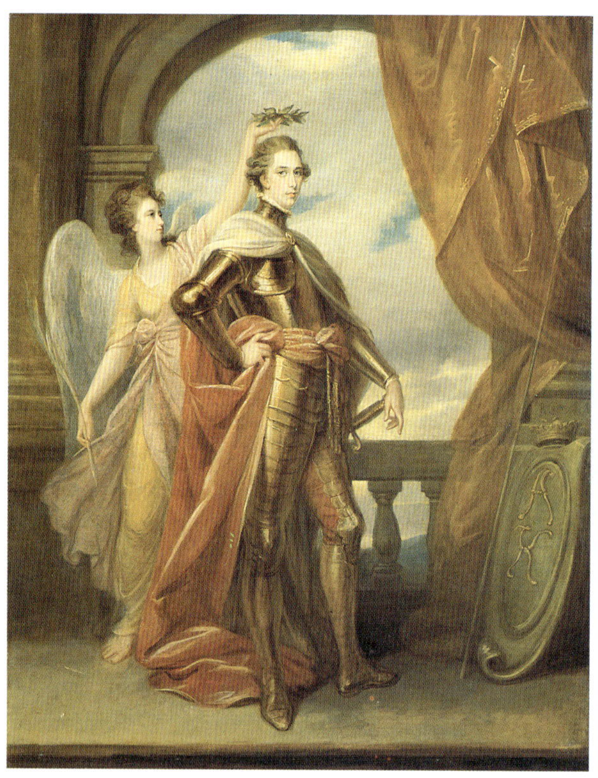

Plate 42   *Robert, 4th Duke of Ancaster and Kesteven, with his sister Lady Georgiana Bertie c.*1779–80 [**8**]

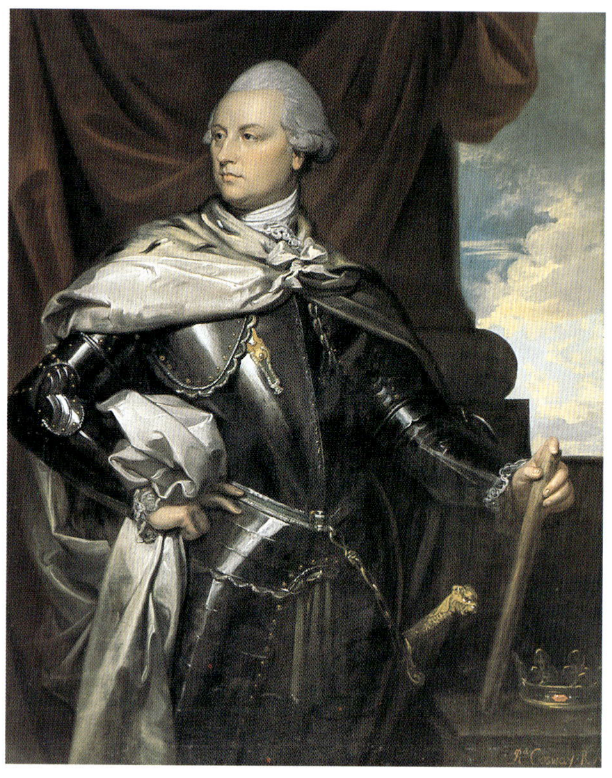

Plate 43   *John, 5th Duke of Argyll c.*1780–5 [**29**]

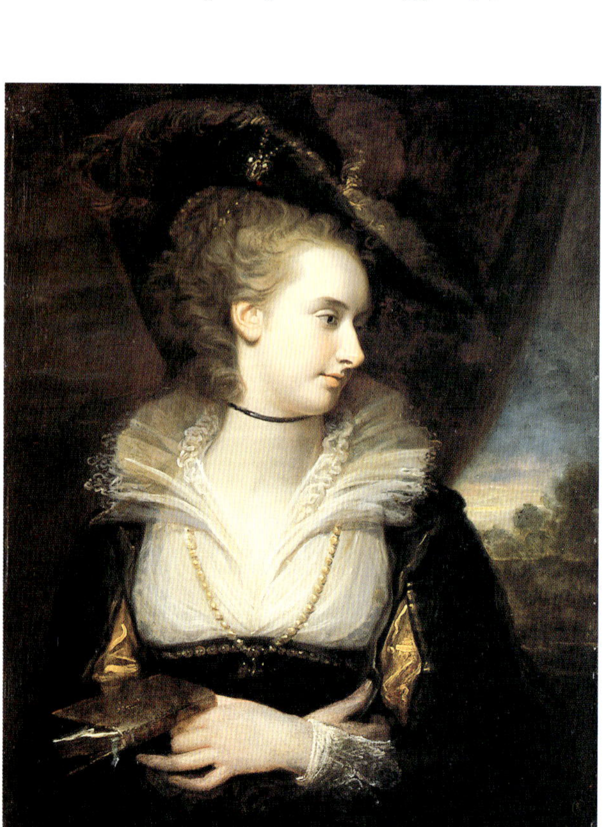

Plate 44   *Elizabeth Milbanke, Viscountess Melbourne* 1784 [**30**]

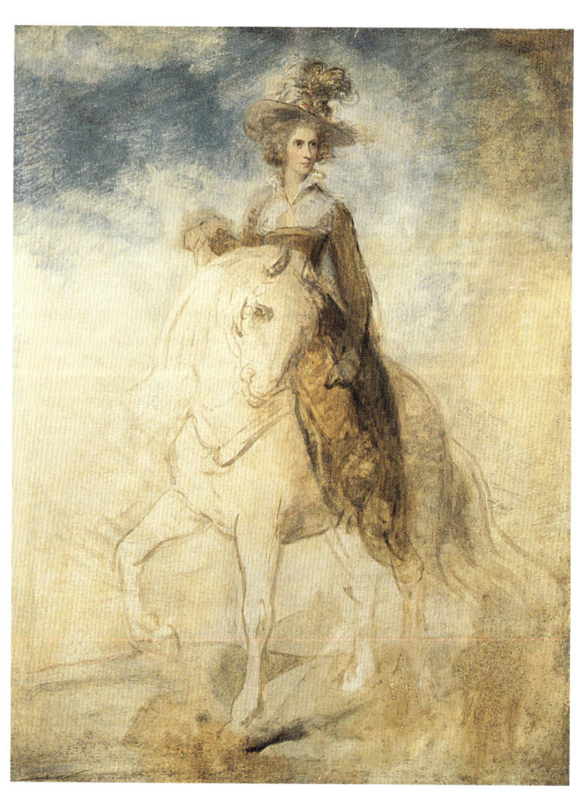

Plate 45   *An unknown lady on horseback c.*1788 [**31**]

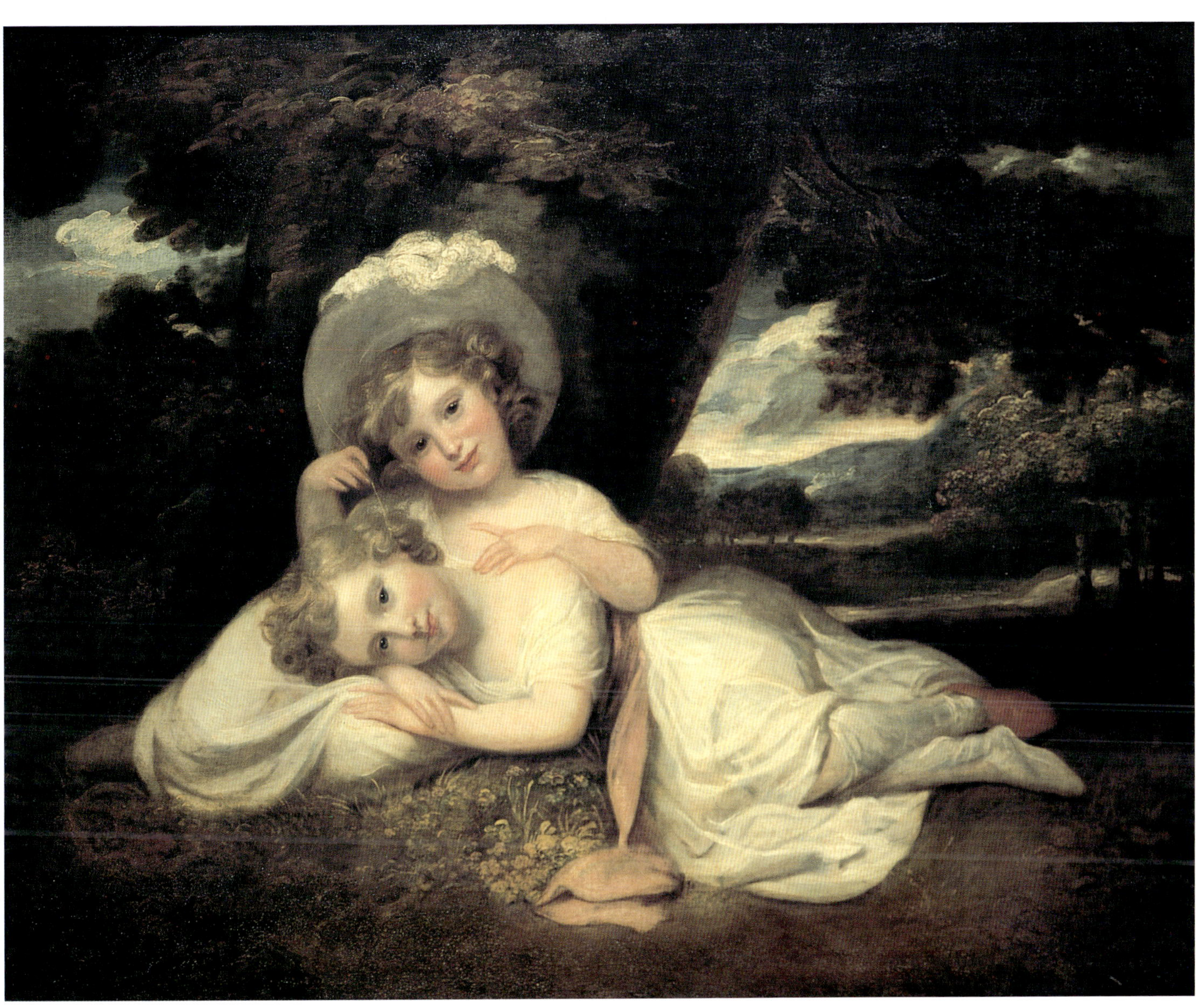

Plate 46   *William, 3rd Earl of Radnor, with his sister the Hon. Mary Anne Pleydell-Bouverie* 1785 [**32**]

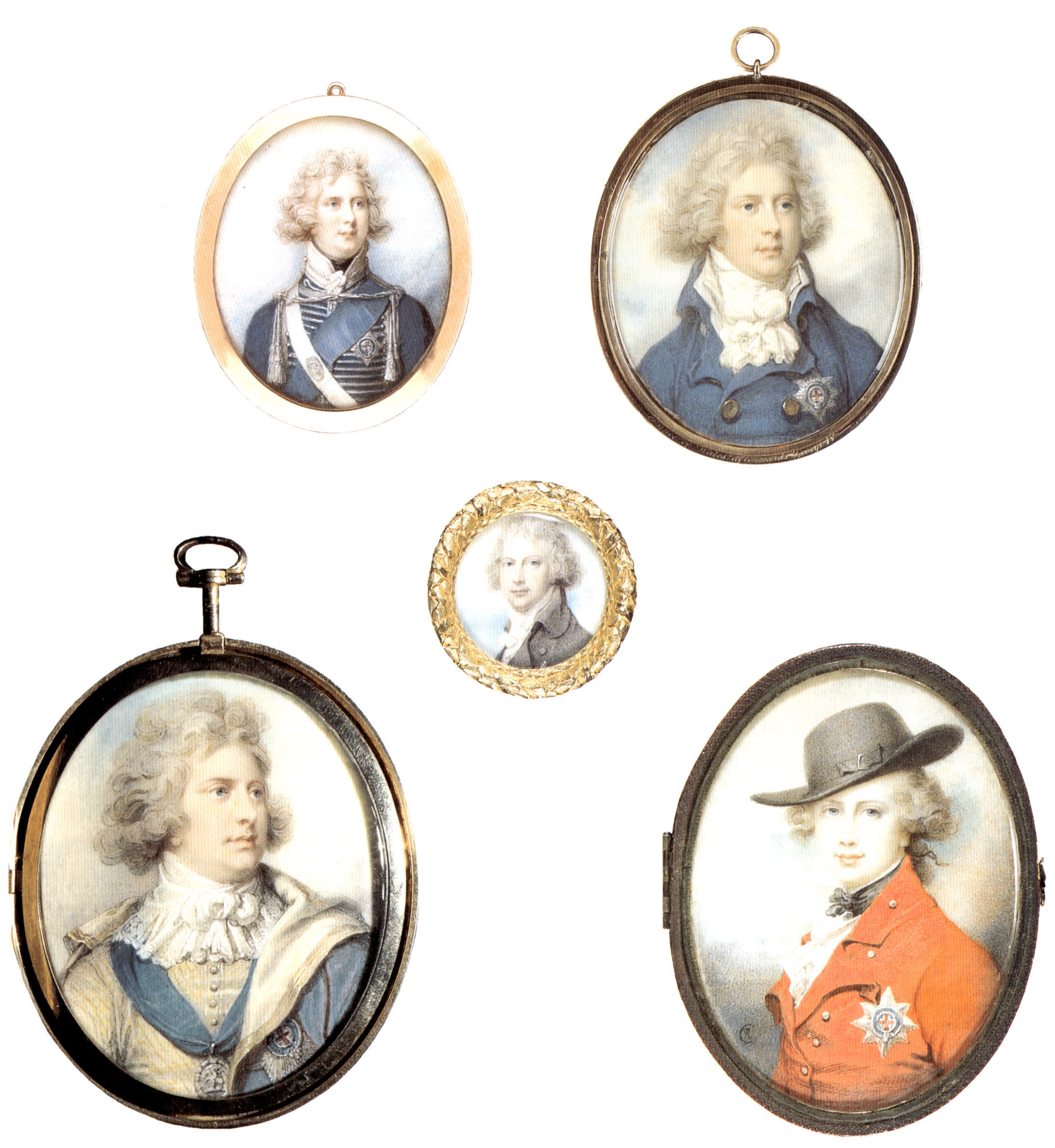

TOP LEFT Plate 47   *The Prince of Wales, later George IV* 1795 [**128**]
TOP RIGHT Plate 48   *The Prince of Wales, later George IV* c.1792 [**122**]
MIDDLE Plate 49   *The Prince of Wales, later George IV* c.1782–3 [**55**]
BOTTOM LEFT Plate 50   *The Prince of Wales, later George IV* 1792 [**118**]
BOTTOM RIGHT Plate 51   *The Prince of Wales, later George IV* c.1780–2 [**49**]

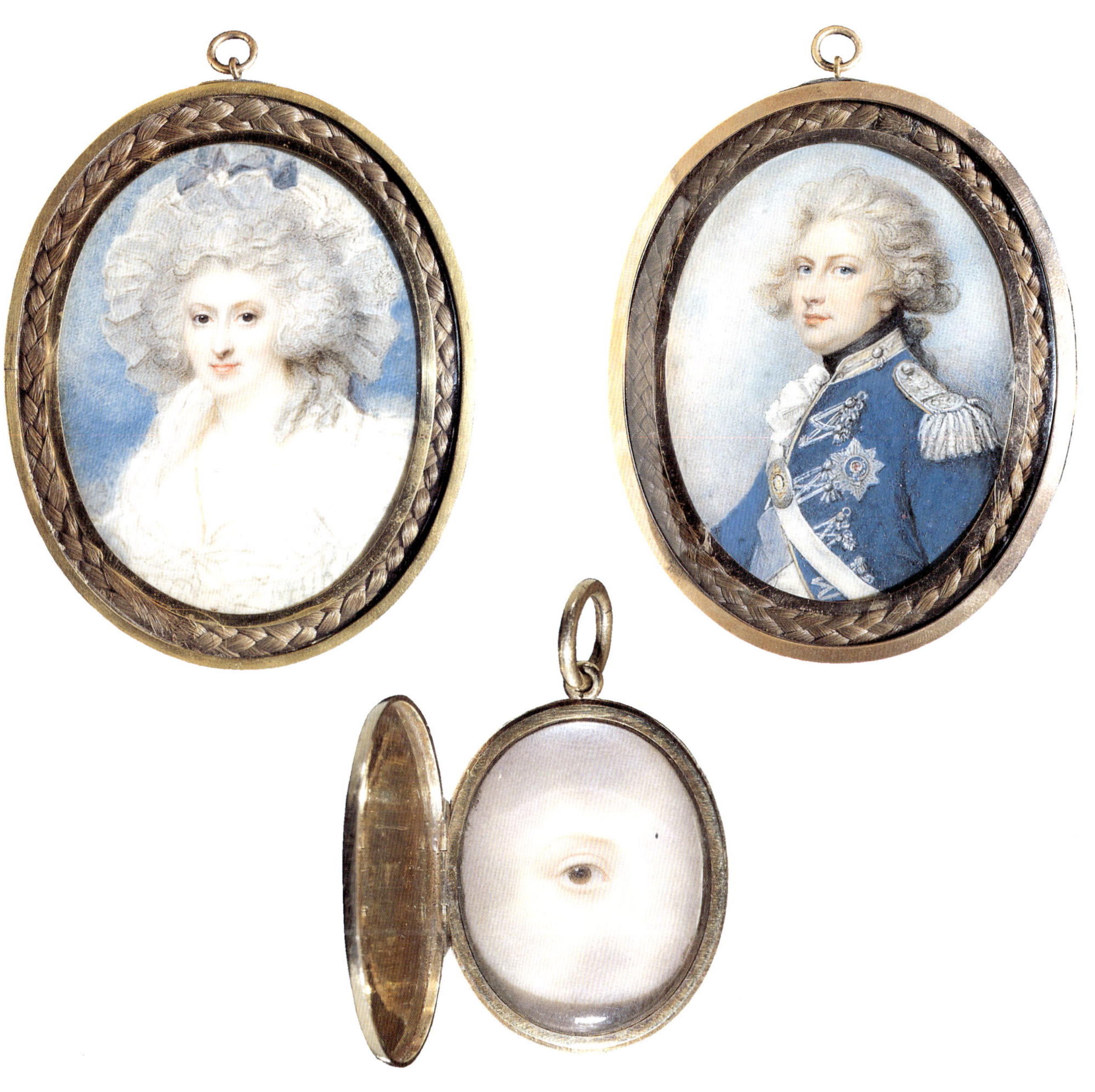

TOP LEFT   Plate 52   *Mrs Fitzherbert c.1785–6* [**59**]
TOP RIGHT   Plate 53   *The Prince of Wales, later George IV c.1785–90* [**58**]
BOTTOM   Plate 54   *Mrs Fitzherbert's Eye* 1786 [**60**]

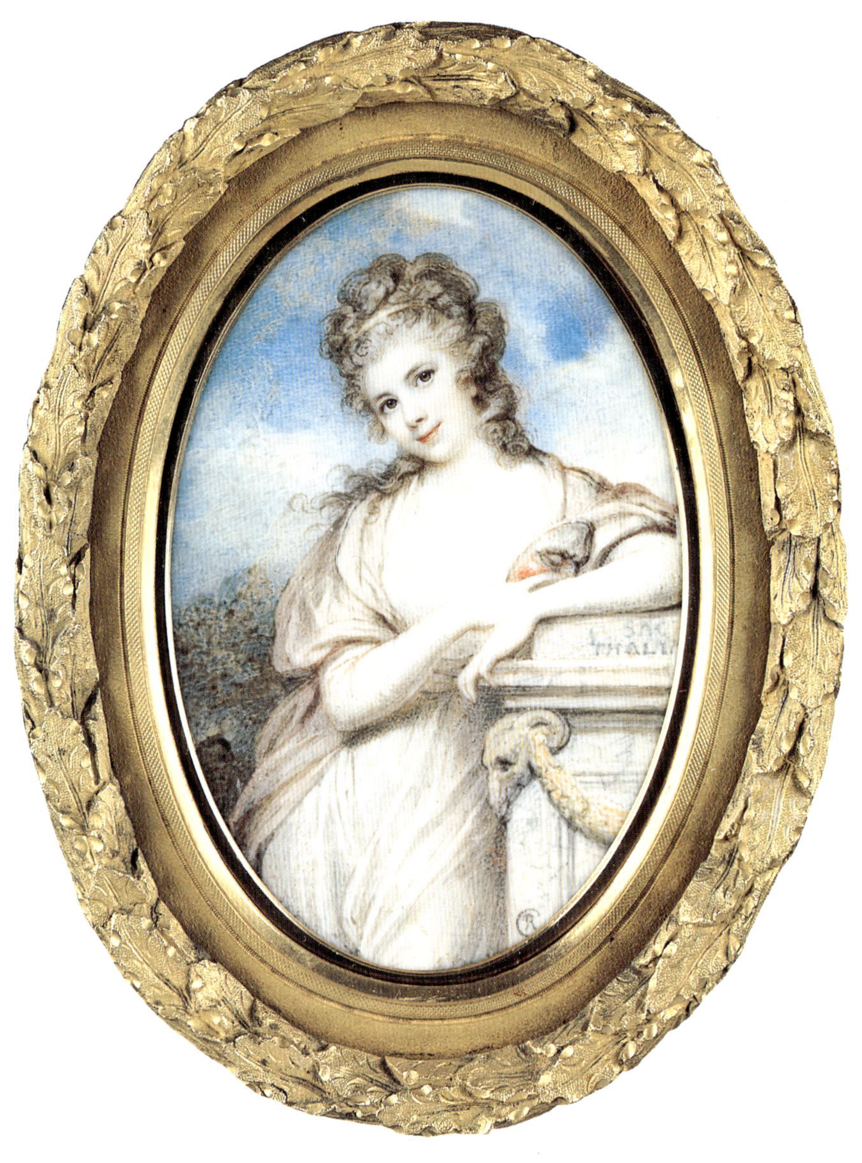

Plate 55 *Mrs Abington as the Comic Muse c.*1783 [**56**]

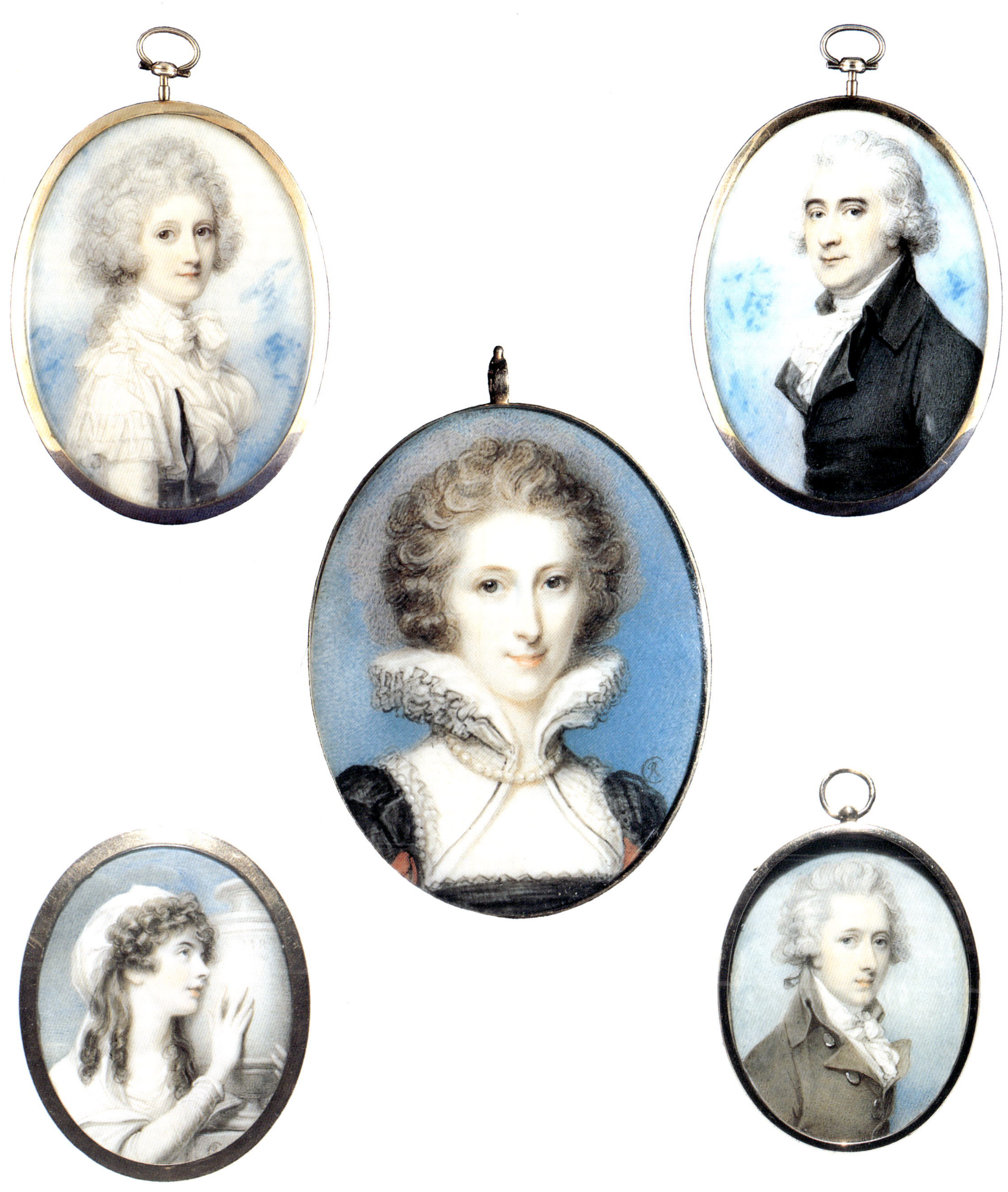

TOP LEFT Plate 56   *Elizabeth, Countess of Hopetoun* 1789 [**68**]
TOP RIGHT Plate 57   *James, 3rd Earl of Hopetoun* 1789 [**67**]
MIDDLE Plate 58   *Anne Damer* 1785 [**57**]
BOTTOM LEFT Plate 59   *Mary Russell, later Mrs Domvile* 1787 [**63**]
BOTTOM RIGHT Plate 60   *Sir Thomas Stepney* 1787 [**64**]

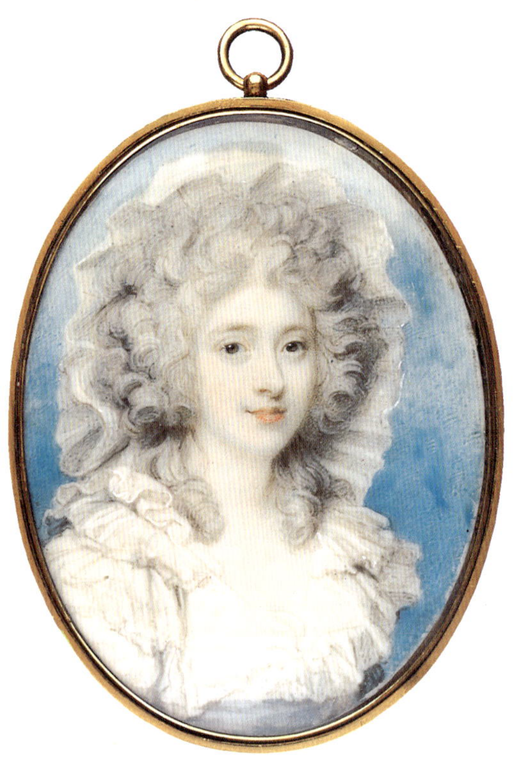

Plate 61   *Georgiana, Duchess of Devonshire* 1786 [**76**]

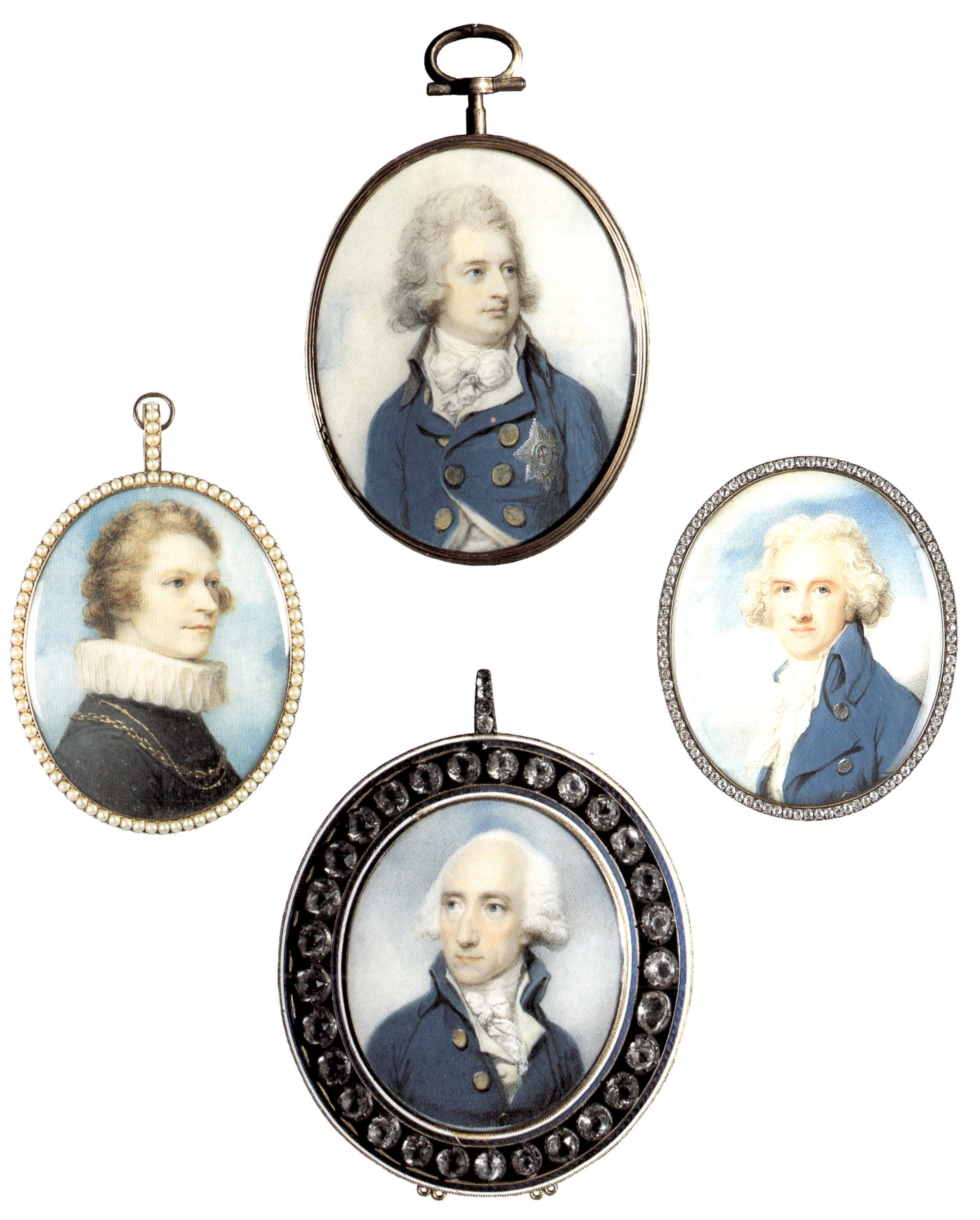

TOP Plate 62   *The Duke of Clarence, later William IV* 1789 [**69**]
MIDDLE LEFT Plate 63   *Self-portrait in Elizabethan costume c.*1785–90 [**71**]
MIDDLE RIGHT Plate 64   *Henry, 2nd Earl of Carrick c.*1785–90 [**74**]
BOTTOM Plate 65   *Warren Hastings* 1787 [**65**]

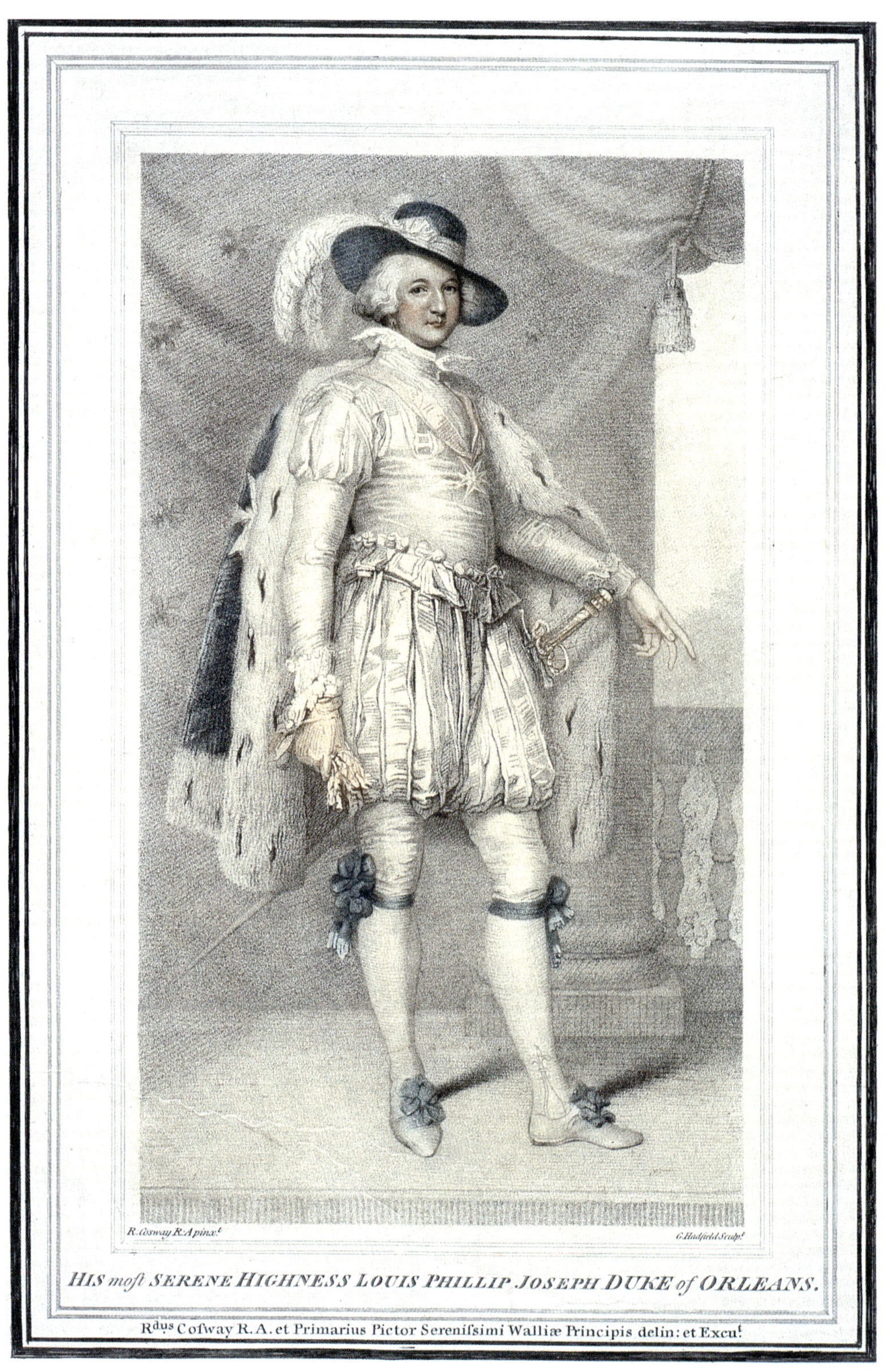

Plate 66   G. Hadfield after Richard Cosway
His Most Serene Highness Louis Phillip Joseph Duke of Orleans 1788 [**89**]

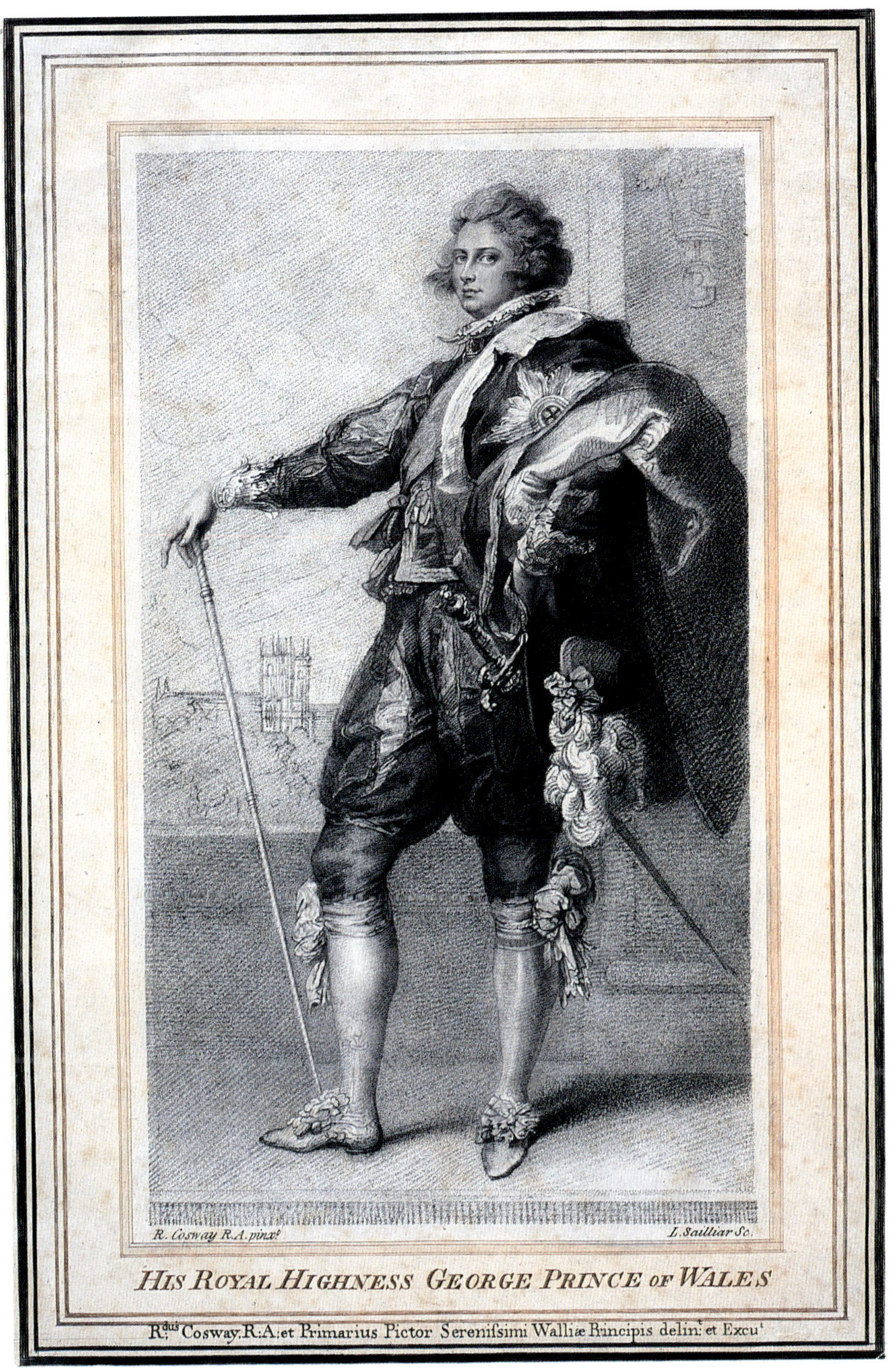

Plate 67   L. Sailliar after Richard Cosway *His Royal Highness George, Prince of Wales* 1787 [**88**]

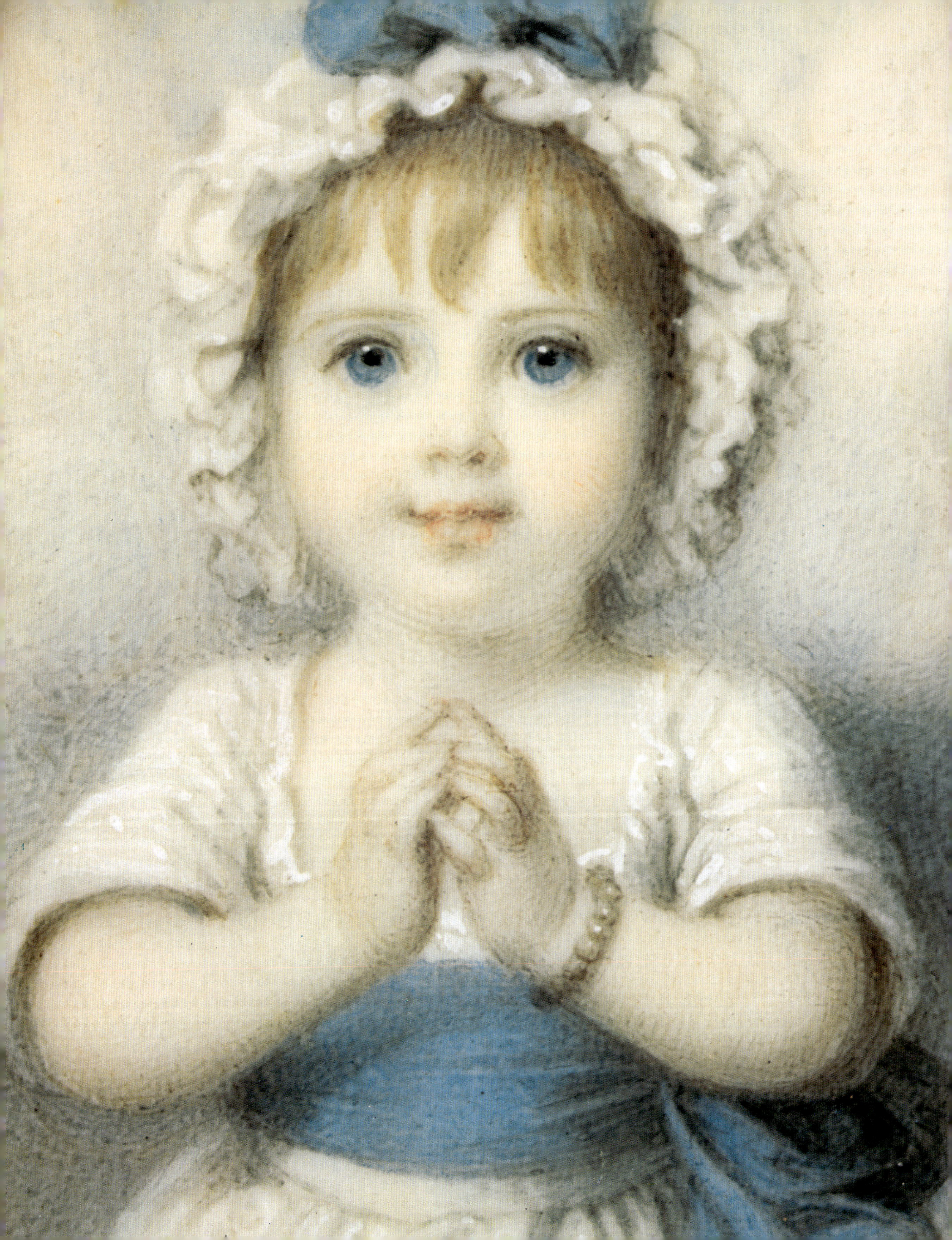

MARIA COSWAY
ITALY AND LONDON
1790–1801

𝓘 HAD *only one child, a little girl. I had [a] bad time & a worse confinement, so that my life was in danger[.] The Physicians agreed change of air[.] Lady Wright was going to Italy for the health of her son. My brother George Hadfield had gained the Gold Medal & sent by the Academy to Rome. M*r*: Cosway bought me a Carriage. With*

*my Maid & my brother we travelled with Lady Wright, but my health [was] so bad I could not go to Rome. As soon as [I] recoverd[,] I wrote to M*r*: C.[.] I was ready to return [.] he kept me from spring to autumn for almost three years as he meant to return himself. But being sudenly taken ill I travelled night & day in the midst of war & dangers in the month of November[,] got home safe & had the happiness of finding M*r*: C. recoverd, and a fine little [girl] to engage all my cares and occupation. All my friends saw me again with infinite pleasure, For two years I had the happiness of seeing my child grow & profit of my education. She was seized by a sore throat & in the sixth year of her life we lost her. Our grief was great. I returnd to painting & painted several large pictures for Chappels.*

As Maria Cosway revealed in her autobiographical letter, the 1790s was a decade marked by great joy, as well as by turmoil, illness and tragedy for herself and Richard Cosway. After suffering an extremely difficult confinement, Maria gave birth to her only child Louisa Paolina Angelica on 4 May 1790. A few weeks later she travelled out to Italy, without Louisa or Richard, in order to recuperate. She was accompanied by Lady Wright, as well as one of her younger brothers, George Hadfield (1763–1826). He had won the gold medal for architecture at the Royal Academy, and was later to design government buildings in Washington under Jefferson's patronage. Maria Cosway's sudden departure from London caused some comment, as typified by Horace Walpole in a letter to Mary Berry: 'surely it is odd to drop a child and her husband all in a breath'. Maria did not return to London for another four and a half years. She explained the circumstances in her autobiographical letter of 1830, first having lamented that 'the climate did not agree with [me]' and that 'in the midst of so much happiness [I] never enjoyed health', while the promised voyage together to Italy never materialised. However, it may be surmised that Maria was suffering from a serious case of post-natal depression. Little is known of Maria Cosway's activity on her first return visit to Italy, except that in 1791 she was in Venice making watercolour copies of paintings by Titian and Tintoretto, and that she later spent time in a convent in Genoa.[1]

Two rare letters from Maria Cosway to her husband survive at Lodi from this period, one from Venice in 1791 and the second from Genoa in 1793, both of which shed considerable light on relations between the Cosways. In the first she opened the letter by referring to Louisa and to her mother: 'I am happy to hear the child has two teeth without pain, & still more glad that you are so fond of her. My mother tells me you are very good to her, & was very kind when she was so ill[.] I thank you much for it.' After mentioning how unwell

she herself had been, Maria wondered whether de Loutherbourg, the artist and faith-healer, and a great friend of her husband's, might be able to assist. She went on to describe some colours and varnishes that she had found in Venice, but hoped that he would come out for them. She ended the letter 'I kiss Louisa a thousand times' and signed herself 'M.C.'.

In the second longer letter sent from Genoa two years later, Maria Cosway clearly revealed some of the emotional and religious turmoil, as well as practical difficulties, that she was undergoing. This letter was delivered to Richard Cosway by Madison, Maria's maid, who must have returned to London from Italy at this time. The letter opened:

You will receive this letter by Madison who will give you an exact account of me from the first moment I left England[,] as she has been a constant witness[,] having never been from me One Moment, to the time she sees me enter into the Convent. May you receive these informations that may please you, & have some satisfaction about me. Whatever I may have done to displease I again ask your forgiveness as I have done before in one of my letters to which I have had no answer. I shall say no more, & trust only to God who hears & sees all, who receives all, & has mercy for all.

Maria Cosway was clearly in some distress, not having heard from her husband for some time. She went on to describe the difficulties she had encountered in trying to enter a convent. The nuns had been reluctant to admit her as she was married to a Protestant who was also a stranger, and who had failed to write to support her application for admission. Maria Cosway continued by thanking her husband for sending out £80 and wanted to know whether the £60 that he allowed her a year would be included in the new sum. She also asked him to send some kind of credential that might prove that her husband was 'a man of some property for their thinking me the wife of a painter is certainly a poor credit as painters are in these Countries'. Maria then went on to discuss Louisa's education and religious upbringing, where there had clearly been some considerable disagreement with her daughter's father:

... the child is my only wish & thought, & my fears only for her religion. From the first impressions depends her sentiments of the true faith, let me repeat you to take care they are of the pure catholick. May it please the Almighty to enlighten you & show you the blind errors in which you are not only unhappily fallen into but more unfortunatly persist in them ...

Maria Cosway finally mentioned that she was sending various letters for friends, as well as several books for her husband on the different places she had visited, especially those with descriptions of pictures, which she had marked according to their degree of merit. She ended the letter with the statement: 'I hope the child is well, may God protect her, believe me / Your dutifull Wife M. Cosway'.[2] The long separation from her child must have been particularly difficult to bear, but Richard Cosway was clearly devoted to his daughter. Two sensitive portraits of Louisa Paolina Angelica Cosway survive, a miniature in which her hands are held together as if at play [**127**] and a full-length portrait of her aged five, a stipple engraving [**143**] by Anthony Cardon taken from an untraced drawing.

In November 1794 Maria Cosway had returned to London to live with her husband in his new residence in Stratford Place [fig. 11]. Only one and a half years later, on 29 July 1796, Louisa Cosway died at the age of six after catching a sore throat. Richard Cosway then drew her lying peacefully on her deathbed [**99**] in an unbearably poignant image. This tragic event had a devastating effect on both parents. Maria Cosway confined herself to her room, while Richard Cosway commissioned their friend Thomas Banks to sculpt a sarcophagus for the embalmed body of the child, which was then installed in the back drawing room. Maria's Catholicism became even more overt. She had an Italian confessor, and attended Mass regularly, sometimes at the Portuguese chapel in London, and often in the company of General Paoli. In addition she made plans to set up her first school for girls in Knightsbridge to be run on religious lines. Religion and education were increasingly to dominate the rest of her life.[3]

Maria Cosway continued her artistic career throughout the 1790s, although on a greatly reduced level of activity. Among her compositions that survive from this decade, a number show women grieving or prostrate, seated on seashores and by rivers, as well as fleeing from unspecified dangers – images which may relate to the artist's distressed psychological state. The first of these images is the dissolving wood-nymph *Lodona* [**233**], taken from Pope's poem *Windsor Forest*, which was engraved in stipple by Bartolozzi and published in 1792.[4] This was based on an untraced oil painted for Thomas Macklin's *Poets' Gallery*. Maria Cosway exhibited only one painting at the Academy during the course of the decade: the untraced picture of *An Hebrew Woman carrying her offering to the Temple* in 1796. Towards the end of the decade Maria Cosway resumed her painting, executing a number of religious subjects. In 1799 she completed a huge altarpiece representing *The Exultation of the Virgin Mary, or the salvation of mankind, purchased by the death of Jesus Christ*, which was exhibited under that title at the Academy in 1801. A smaller version survives at the Fondazione Cosway in Lodi, while a year earlier the composition was engraved in mezzotint by Valentine Green as *The Descent from the Cross* [**235**]. The intensely emotional treatment of this subject – with its vivid colouring and broad handling – places particular emphasis on the Virgin, who is shown raising both her arms in triumph. This painting heralded a surge of painting and other artistic projects from Maria Cosway during the first four years of the nineteenth century, and which to all intents mark the end of her career as an artist.

In 1800 she exhibited seven paintings at the Academy, with three more being shown in the following year. The most significant work was *The Birth of the Thames*, which was engraved by P.W. Tomkins in 1802 [**237**]. In this highly unusual subject and its original treatment, Maria Cosway imagined the River Thames as a baby being raised above the bull-rushes by a chorus of water-nymphs and a swan. The print was published by Rudolph Ackermann from his influential printselling business, the *Repository of Arts*.[5] Ackermann went on to publish many more of Maria Cosway's works. Among these projects were a drawing book of her etchings after a selection of Richard Cosway's sketches, titled *Imitations in Chalk* (1800); two series of illustrations depicting moral stories known as *A Progress of Female Virtue* and *A Progress of Female Dissipation* [**251**], which were engraved by Anthony Cardon; and the series of twelve pen and wash illustrations to Mary 'Perdita' Robinson's pathetic autobiographical poem, *The Winter Day* [**238–49**], which were etched in acquatint by Caroline Watson. The poem and accompanying designs contrast 'the evils of poverty and the ostentatious enjoyment of opulence'. Ackermann in his introduction to the poem and illustrations aptly described Maria Cosway's style as demonstrated in these illustrations, and his criticism can be taken as referring to much of her other work:

Mrs Cosway's designs, it must be admitted, are sometimes eccentric, but it is the eccentricity of genius, and we have seen instances where she has snatched a grace beyond the reach of art. That extravagance carried to excess is an error, cannot be denied, but we prefer the artist who rather overcharges his figure, to him who touches the canvas with a timid feeble pencil, and leaves the imagination of the spectator to express what he cannot or dare not express. We prefer the extravagance of Michelangelo to the highest finishing of a dull Dutch artist. The horse that outstrips his competitors may be curbed; but the animal who is sluggish and incapable of exertion cannot be spurred into speed'.

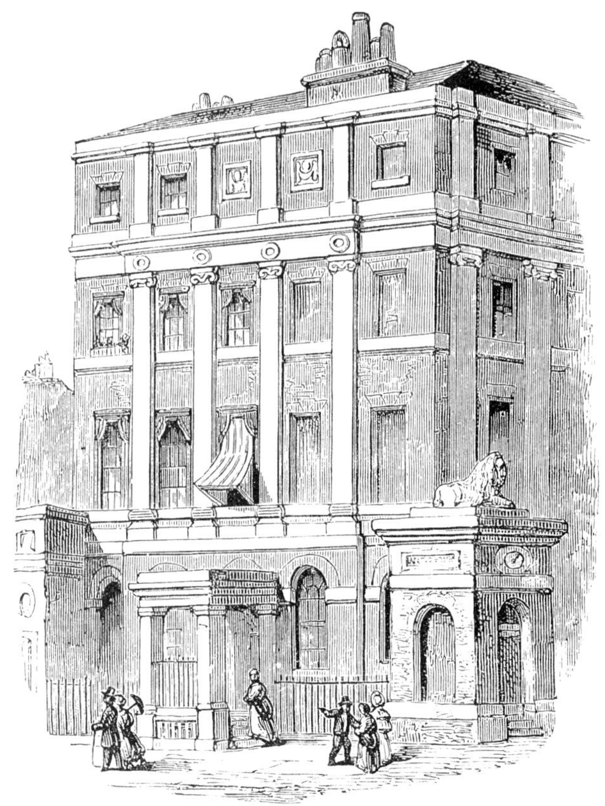

Fig. 11 *22 Stratford Place, Oxford Street, London, c.*1770s

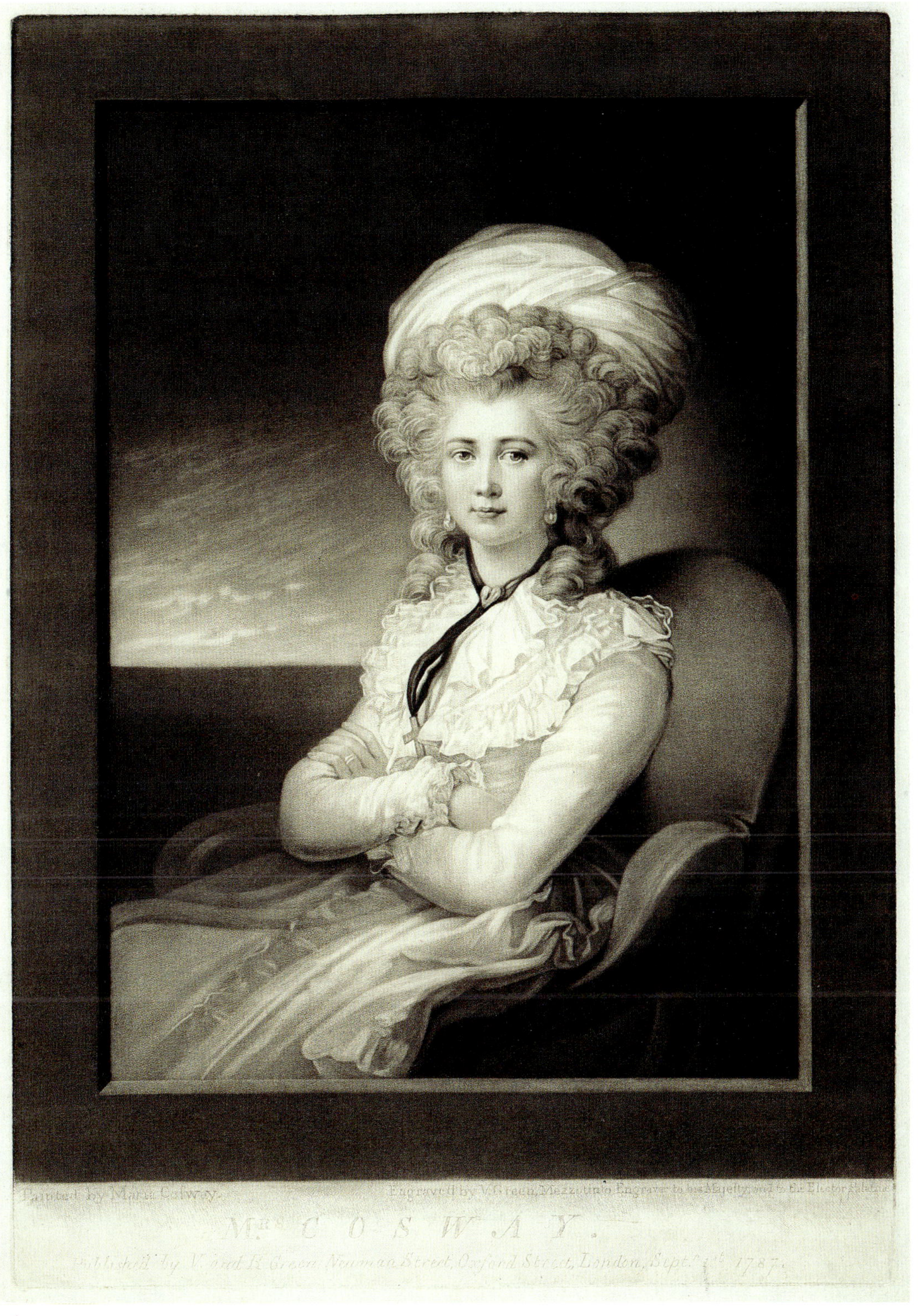

Plate 69   V. Green after Maria Cosway *Mrs Cosway* 1787 [231]

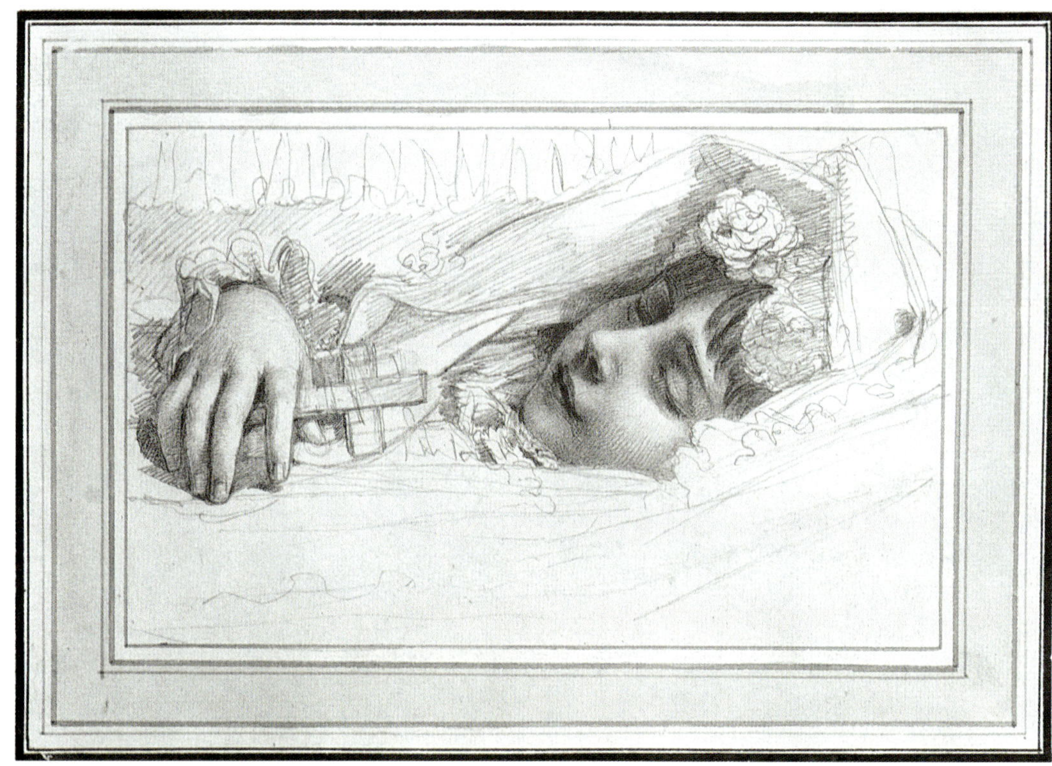

Plate 70   *Louisa Cosway on her deathbed* 1796 **[99]**

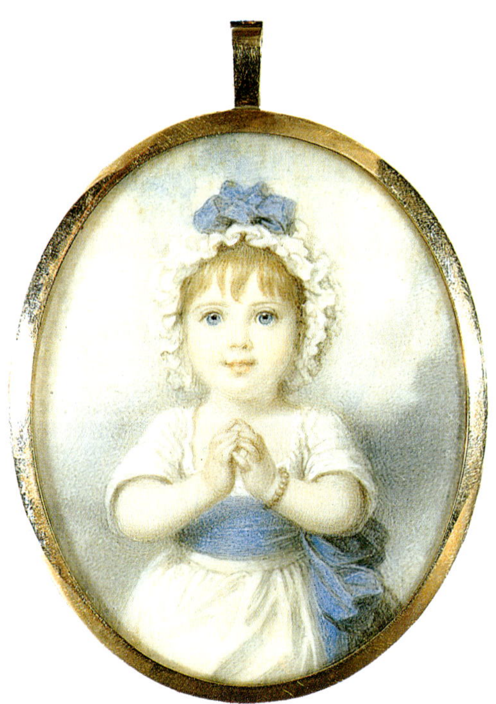

Plate 71   *Louisa Paolina Angelica Cosway c.1795* **[127]**

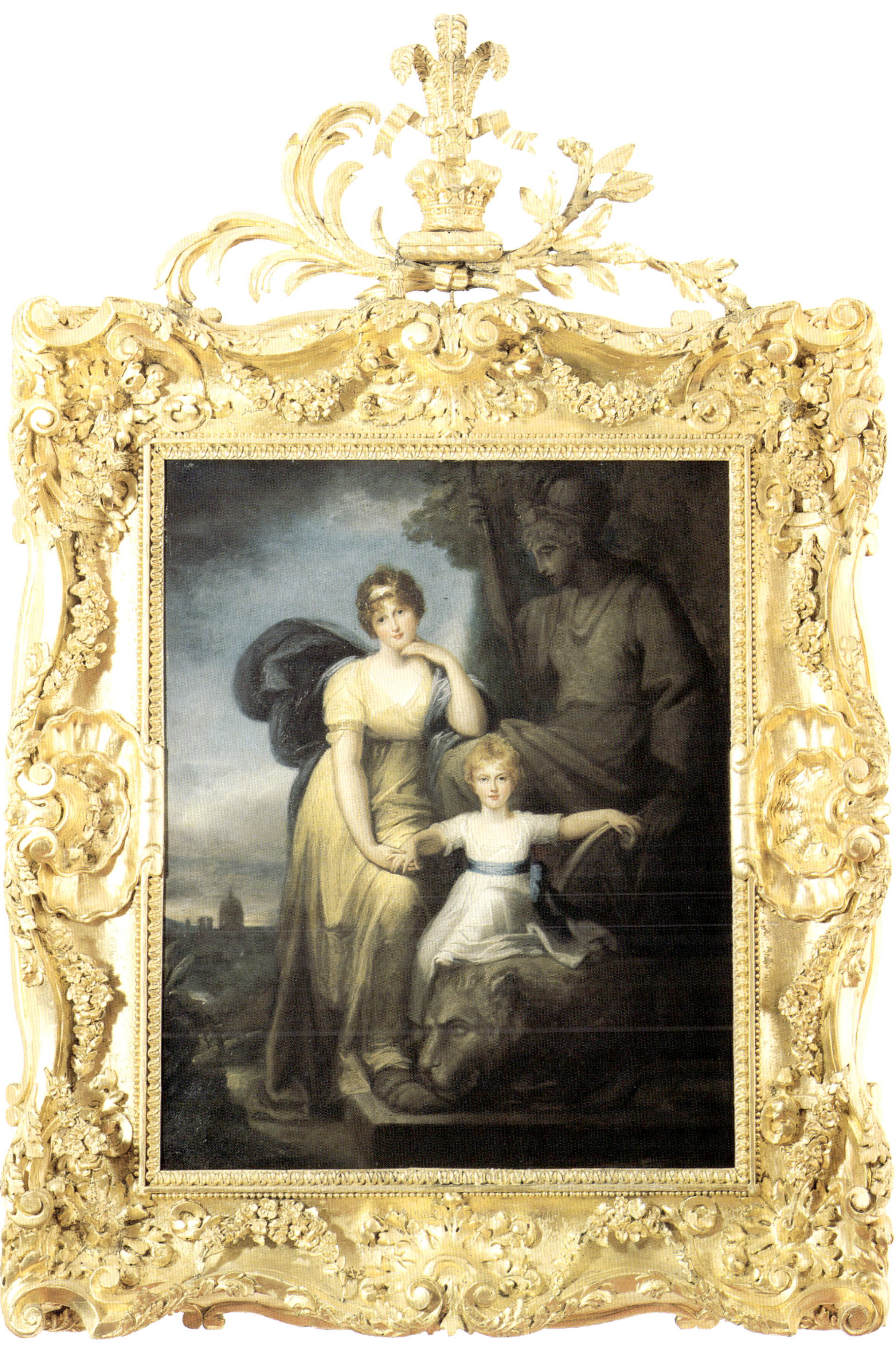

Plate 72   Maria Cosway and Sir Thomas Lawrence *Caroline, Princess of Wales, and Princess Charlotte* 1800–1 [**225**]

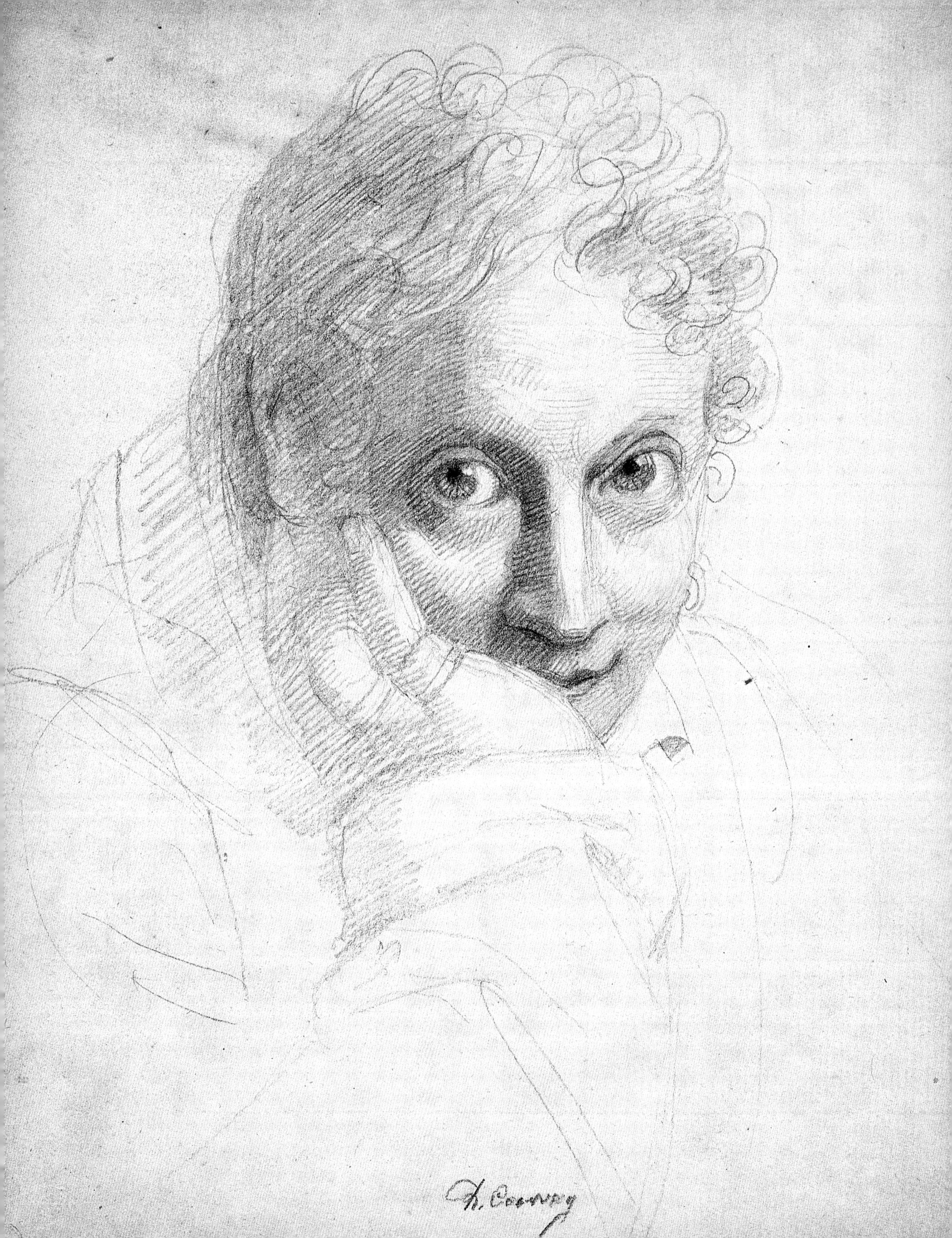

R. Cosway

RICHARD COSWAY
COLLECTOR, CONNOISSEUR
AND VIRTUOSO

I THERE *recollect seeing him stand at the fireside, upon one of Madame Pompadour's rugs, leaning against a chimney-piece, dedicated to the Sun ... His new house he fitted up in so picturesque, and, indeed, so princely a style, that I regret drawings were not made of the general appearance of each apartment; for many of the rooms*

were more like scenes of enchantment, pencilled by a poet's fancy than anything, perhaps, before displayed in a domestic habitation. His furniture consisted of ancient chairs, couches, and conversation-stools, elaborately carved and gilt, and covered with the most costly Genoa velvets; escritoires, of ebony, inlaid with mother-of-pearl; and rich caskets for antique gems, exquisitely enamelled, and adorned with onyxes, opals, rubies, and emeralds. There were also cabinets of ivory, curiously wrought; mosaic-tables, set with jasper, blood-stone, and lapis lazuli, having their feet carved into claws of lions and eagles; screens of old raised oriental Japan; massive musical clocks richly chased with ormolu and tortoise-shell; ottomans, superbly damasked; Persian and other carpets, with corresponding hearthrugs, bordered with ancient family crests, and armorial ensigns in the centre; and rich hangings of English tapestry. The chimney-pieces were carved by Banks, and were further adorned with the choicest bronzes, models in wax and terracotta; the tables covered with old Sèvre, blue, Mandarin, Nankin, and Dresden china: and the cabinets were surmounted with crystal cups adorned with the York and Lancaster roses, which might have graced the splendid banquets of the proud Wolsey. His specimens of armour were truly rich ...

This evocative description by the critic J.T. Smith of Richard Cosway among his remarkable interiors at Stratford Place helps establish the artist as one of the last and most distinctive of the *virtuosi*, or arbiters of taste, of the late eighteenth and early nineteenth century. As well as being a passionate connoisseur of decorative arts, furniture, sculpture, armour and *objets d'art*, he amassed substantial collections of fine Old Master paintings, drawings and prints. Acknowledged and admired as a notable *virtuoso* by contemporaries such as Lawrence, Soane and Hazlitt, Cosway formed his collections and interiors on the basis of his Romantic antiquarianism, eccentricity and imagination.[1]

How the artist saw himself in the context of the profuse decoration described by Smith can be seen from his finished drawing of *c.*1789, the *Self-portrait with busts of Michelangelo and Rubens* [36]. The artist shows himself distracted momentarily from the study of a volume, which we know from a preparatory drawing in a private collection was a life of Rubens. The book rests against the busts of two of his most important mentors. In the background is an interpretation of Rysbrack's portrait of Rubens, while closer to the viewer is the bust of Michelangelo. Another preparatory drawing in a private collection shows Cosway gesticulating towards just one bust. In what amounts to a manifesto of his social and artistic ambitions he

has surrounded himself with objects and props, rich in allusions to his status both real and imagined. The pose and fancy dress self-consciously recall Van Dyck's male figures; the flamboyant hat echoes Rubens's self-portraits; the twisting column brings to mind those reputedly from the Temple of Solomon, preserved at St Peter's in Rome, and intrepreted by Raphael in the tapestry cartoons for the Sistine Chapel; the sculptures and the knowing child genius or putto, who marks with his finger the Hogarthian S-curve of ideal beauty onto the artist's palette, all combine to emphasise Cosway's artistic and aesthetic inheritance. The Old Master painting, the books, the busts and the richly gadrooned chest all refer to differing aspects of his activities as a collector. In this private image Richard Cosway deliberately and grandly stakes claim to his self-made role as a sophisticated courtier-artist, as if presiding in a temple dedicated to art.

It has been plausibly suggested that the bust of Michelangelo, which appears in this *Self-portrait* [36], is the version of the famous bust by Daniele da Volterra [212] that may have been the one recorded in Cosway's collection.[2] There are differences in size and detail of the neck structure between the bust shown in the drawing and that at the Ashmolean. In defence of Cosway's ownership of this particular bust, it might be added that the artist was not beyond reinterpreting the scale and details of objects represented in his compositions, as can be seen in the oil painting of *Charles Townley with a group of connoisseurs* [5], where the classical sculptures are shown enlarged. Clearly a version of this most famous of portraits of Michelangelo acted as a spur to Cosway's admiration of the great Florentine, particularly in the execution of his late religious drawings with their sensitive draughtmanship [170–6].

Little is known of Cosway's activity as a collector in the early part of his life, although it is certain that he was inspired by the very active tradition of the artist-collector. Rubens, Rembrandt and Lely were three of the most influential figures from the seventeenth century, while two of the more significant collections in the third quarter of the eighteenth century were those formed by the successful portraitists Hudson and Reynolds. Cosway's earliest likely acquisition, which was also practical, was the ornate rococo *Sitter's chair* [216] designed by Matthias Lock, which the artist must have taken possession of before 1771, when he began work on the oil painting of *Charles Townley with a group of connoisseurs* [5]. The chair not merely acted as a studio prop but was spectacular enough to be included as a suitable adornment for significant portraits.

The classical forms, compositions and subjects that were at the heart of Cosway's aesthetic were fundamental to his artistic training, but Townley's growing, and increasingly important, collection of classical sculpture would have provided numerous opportunities for further study. Cosway's continuing interest in this collection, as well as in classical sculpture in general, is revealed in a letter he wrote after Townley's death in 1805. There was speculation that the collection would be removed from London to Townley's native Lancashire, of which the fashionable and metropolitan Cosway was deeply critical:

> ... *I dread the Idea of his [Townley's heir] carrying all his* matchless collection *into the interior of Lancashire – where they will (not indeed wash their sweetness in the desert Air – as such* Stone's *do not emit much flavor) but they will be buried, as Townly Castle is at least Ten Miles from any Market Town ...*

After adding that Townley had left £5000 for the construction of a suitable gallery for the sculptures in or near London, Cosway went on to report the arrival of the Elgin marbles in the capital and his early attempts to find them a suitable temporary home:

> ... *I have seen three Hundred* Vases's Columns Bassorelievos &c &c &c &c &c – *transmitted to this Country by Lord Elgin, from* Greece & Egypt, *& which are the most astonishing things ever taken out of that Country* – the carriage alone *has cost ten thousand Pounds – they are now on the premises in Privy – Gardens (at the Duchess Dowg. of Portland) – I have endeavour'd to persuade Lady Elgin to whom the direction of them is now delegated to procure Count Trimdisoff's Gallery in the new Road for their reception, that they may be advantageously seen by the Publick ...*

Cosway's early enthusiasm for the marbles acquired by *Thomas, 7th Earl of Elgin* [**180**] and his desire to see them on display was also noted by Philip Hunt in a letter of 1805 to Lord Upper Ossory: 'Mr. Cosway and some other English artists have engaged Lord Elgin to form them [the marbles] into a public Exhibition at London to be opened in the course of the ensuing summer'. These attempts at public display were unsuccessful, although eventually both the Townley and the Elgin marbles were acquired by the nation for display at the British Museum.[3]

Despite very little being known about Cosway's early acquisitions for his collection, it is likely that he would have been gradually filling his house and studio in Berkeley Street with a conventional range of works of art. This decoration would have become increasingly necessary for the fashionable artist's developing career. However, one piece survives which is highly revealing of Cosway's vision and taste, namely his magnificent *Sitter's chair* [**216**], which has been described 'as an outstanding example of the English rococo style from the point of view of both design and execution'. A detailed description of the chair gives some sense of what must have been one of the most splendid of artists' sitter's chairs used during this period, and which reveals so much about Cosway's love of rich and sinuous decoration: '... the moulded and pierced frame to the cartouche-shaped back is carved with acanthus scrolls and flower sprays and is fitted with an upholstered panel. The seat frame is decorated in a similar manner with fish-scale panels, framing the open cartouche and is supported on cabriole legs, which have acanthus foliage on the knees and terminate in lion paw feet'. The designer's drawing for this armchair survives in the Victoria and Albert Museum.[4] The chair is also important in that it is the only surviving piece of furniture known to have been made from a design

by Matthias Lock (*c*.1710–65) who was one of the foremost designers of ornament and makers of carved furniture in London in the mid-eighteenth century.

Cosway either purchased – or more likely commissioned – the chair directly from Lock's workshop. Little is known of Lock's life, except that he was associated with Thomas Chippendale, and that between 1740 and 1752 he published influential designs of ornamental motifs and carved furniture in the rococo style. His reputation later in life can be gauged from the comments made by the cabinet-maker James Cullen in a postscript to a letter dated January 1768 to Lord Linlithgow, for whom he was working at Hopetoun House. Lock was mentioned as 'a very Eminent carver and Gilder' and the enclosed drawings were described as 'valuable being designed and drawn by the famous Mr. Matt. Lock lately deceased who was reputed the best Draftsman in that way that had ever been in England'.

Cosway probably acquired the chair in about 1770, a few years after he had settled in Berkeley Street. He was particularly concerned to establish himself as a socially visible portrait painter working in miniatures and in oils. To this end both a fashionable personal appearance and an appropriately decorated studio were critical for attracting an upmarket clientèle. Cosway, who was a great collector of furniture – as is made clear from the auction of his *Virtù* collection in 1821 – and often included details of such pieces in his portrait drawings, took such delight in the chair that he included it in a number of portraits. Most notably, it appears in the painting of *Charles Townley with a group of connoisseurs* [**5**] and the portrait of *Mrs Draper* [**6**]. However, it also occurs in portrait drawings of *Mrs Delany* (*c*.1770–5), *Frederick, 5th Earl of Carlisle* (*c*.1785–90), and of *Hyacinthe Gabrielle Roland, later Countess of Mornington and Marchioness Wellesley*, signed and dated 1787.[5] In all of these representations of the chair Cosway lovingly dwells on the 'serpentine design with its "raffle" leaf ornament and scrolling curves', which is related to Hogarth's Line of Beauty. As the putto makes clear in Cosway's drawn *Self-portrait with busts of Michelangelo and Rubens* [**36**] by tracing this famous mark on the artist's palette, the core of the artist's style was dependent on this sinuous yet elegant line. The armchair – in everyday use by his sitters – would have been the single most important piece of furniture in his remarkable interiors, which were so full of ornament. Thus the chair, which would have constantly stimulated the artist during the act of portraiture, was at the very centre of Cosway's artistic vision.

In 1780 two significant events occurred which were to change Richard Cosway's life and bring further opportunities for augmenting his collections as well as emphasising his burgeoning role as a connoisseur. The first was his meeting with Maria Hadfield, his future wife. The second was his portrayal of the Prince of Wales, who was to become his main patron. In view of the concerts organised by Maria Cosway and the growing royal and aristocratic patronage, there was increasing need for even more sumptuous interiors. Eventually this led to the Cosways' move in 1784 to Schomberg House.

In his role as *Primarius Pictor* or Principal Painter to the Prince of Wales, a title which he was entitled to use from 1785, Cosway was able to consolidate his position as the main portraitist to the Prince and his circle of family, mistresses and courtiers. Cosway was highly paid as the principal painter, who probably organised the painted decorations of the rooms at Carlton House, indeed contributing a ceiling himself for the Grand Saloon. He also enjoyed the position of artistic adviser and factotum to his royal patron and acted as surveyor of his burgeoning picture collection. This entailed various responsibilities, including the recommendation of purchases, controlling access to the pictures and having the condition of the paintings assessed. For instance, in 1795 Cosway 'ascertained' a large bill for the cleaning of the Prince's pictures, which had been submitted by George Simpson.[6]

Cosway played a key role in advising the Prince on the formation of his first picture collection, which was assembled before 1800. These works were mainly military scenes and portraits, as well as paintings by sixteenth- and seventeenth-century Italian Old Masters. There were also later French, Dutch and Flemish paintings, including the work of Rubens and his pupils. Works from the latter three schools laid the foundations for the second collection of pictures, which was essentially formed after 1806.

As well as offering advice on acquisitions, Cosway purchased a number of works on the Prince of Wales's behalf. These included a portrait of *Frederick, Prince of Wales, with his hunt* by Charles Phillips, bought for ten guineas in 1784; an unidentified picture by Watteau for ten guineas in 1792; *The Duet* by Carel de Moor for fifteen guineas at Baron Nagel's sale in 1795; a picture from the Chalon sale for seven guineas, also in 1795; and *The Funeral of Louis XIV*, then attributed to Van der Meulen, for fifteen guineas in 1796 or 1799.[7]

It is also likely that Cosway placed pictures from his own collection on approval for purchase by his patron. A work that the Prince may have rejected was one of the most unusual works in Cosway's collection, namely *The Mass of St Giles* [fig. 12] painted around 1500 by the eponymous master. The panel was attributed to 'John de Mabuse' by Cosway in his 1791 private contract catalogue of pictures [**219**], and it was described by the artist in the following terms, which provides considerable insight into his connoisseurship:

St Thomas Aquinas performing mass in the abbey of St Denis, to Louis IX King of France. — The finishing of this picture is so minute, that the application of magnifying glasses only render its perfection more visible — and, notwithstanding its minuteness, the effect of the whole together, at a distance, is broad, simple, and grand. — The characters of the heads, which are all portraits, are full of expression, and the figures are composed with dignified simplicity. — The perspective, both aerial and lineal, is perfect — and though there are apparently scarce any shadows, yet, from the artful management of the local colours, the picture has all the force of Rembrandt.

Despite the historical inaccuracies in this account – in fact it shows St Giles offering Mass before Charles Martel – as well as the unlikely comparison with Rembrandt, it is easy to see how this painting, with its glittering light effects and ecclesiastical setting, would have appealed to Cosway's visual imagination and antiquarianism, although it was perhaps too unusual for the taste of the Prince of Wales.[8]

However, Cosway's greatest contribution to the Prince's collection complemented his patron's rapidly growing group of French decorative arts. In 1789 the artist made a spectacular gift to the Prince of four Gobelins tapestries from Coypel's *Don Quixote* series [fig. 13]. The London press noted this largesse, *The World* reporting on 12 April 1789 that 'The Tapestry, so sumptuous as to be princely, Mr. *Cosway* has therefore very properly presented to the PRINCE'. As William Combe, brother-in-law to Maria Cosway, noted, these tapestries were soon to 'form one of the principal embellishments of Carlton House'. If the generosity involved in an artist's presentation was notable, then so was the manner in which Cosway had received the tapestries. He had been given these on 18 July 1788 by Louis XVI, a type of gift which was normally reserved for foreign royalty and ambassadors. Cosway also received a Savonnerie carpet which he retained for his own use.[9]

The reason that the artist was the recipient of such extraordinary

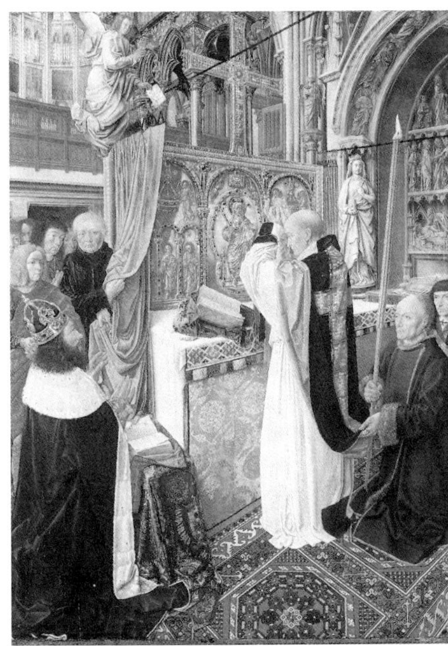

Fig. 12 *The Mass of St Giles, c.*1500, by the Master of St Giles (The National Gallery, London)

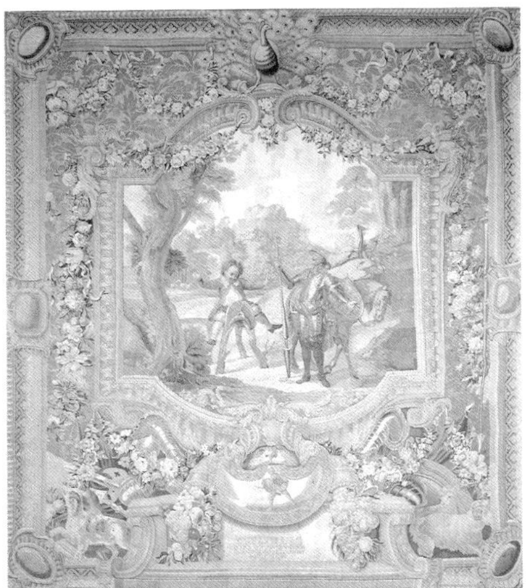

Fig. 13 *Don Quixote and Sancho Panza* (from the *Don Quixote* Gobelins tapestry series), *c.*1780, after C. A. Coypel (The Royal Collection)

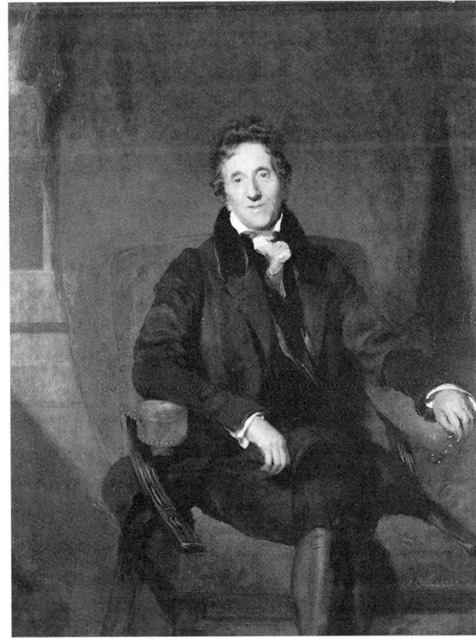

Fig. 14 *Sir John Soane*, 1828, by Sir Thomas Lawrence (Sir John Soane's Museum, London)

and unprecedented royal largesse was on account of his own gift in 1786 to the French King of four huge tapestry cartoons from Schomberg House, which he intended to adorn the empty spaces of the Grand Galerie at the Palais du Louvre. These cartoons were then attributed to the hand of Raphael and Giulio Romano, and were considered by Cosway to represent the *Triumph of Camillus*. Still preserved in the Louvre, although not on display, they are now considered to be from the studio of Giulio Romano, with three scenes from the *Fructus Belli* series and the fourth illustrating a scene from the *History of Scipio* cycle of tapestries.[10]

There is no clear evidence as to the reasons why Cosway was prepared to make this magnanimous gift of the cartoons as opposed to a sale. The offer was made during the Cosways' visit to Paris in the late summer and early autumn of 1786. While Maria embarked on her affair with Thomas Jefferson, Cosway was occupied with the commission to portray the children [fig. 9] of *Louis-Philippe, Duc d'Orléans* [**89**]. Even if the gift did not have diplomatic connotations, Cosway would have seen the donation of the tapestry cartoons as a further opportunity for the advancement of his social status and reputation as an artist and connoisseur.

A key intermediary in the presentation of the cartoons was the antiquarian Pierre-François Hugues, also known as Baron d'Hancarville, who was a friend of both the Cosways. He had been cataloguing Charles Townley's collection of classical sculpture and had most probably met Richard Cosway through this connection. It was d'Hancarville who introduced Cosway to the Comte d'Angiviller, Director of the King's Works, thus setting the transaction in process. In a letter of 29 August 1786 d'Hancarville assured d'Angiviller of the high esteem in which Cosway was regarded as a collector and connoisseur:

> *Il jouit d'une fortune très-considérable, c'est un très-grand connoisseur, et loin de se deffaire d'aucun tableau, il augmente tous les jours ceux qu'il possède en très-grand nombre et les magnifiques collections d'estampes et de dessins qu'il a rassemblées.*[11]

> [*He enjoys a very considerable fortune, is a very important connoisseur, and far from having to sell any of his pictures, every day he increases his collection substantially, as well as the magnificent collections of prints and drawings which he has assembled.*]

Before the four tapestry cartoons were despatched to France they had been displayed in the Great Saloon at Schomberg House. In their place were hung over a hundred Old Master paintings, a substantial part of Cosway's collection. By the time that Cosway had published his private contract sale catalogue in 1791, he had amassed nearly five hundred paintings, which were displayed in nine apartments or rooms on all four floors of the Pall Mall residence. On the ground floor they were shown in the eating room, the gallery and the great saloon; on the first floor, in the study and the drawing room; on the second floor, in the dressing room and another study; and on the third floor, in the bedroom and the breakfast room. From this last room there was an excellent view over St James's Park, a prospect which was painted by William Hodges, with Cosway adding a portrait of Maria from his own hand [**90**].

The reason for the artist's sale of his picture collection was ostensibly due to the move to a new residence on Stratford Place.[12] However, the artist must have bought paintings for resale at a profit, and

in this sense was acting like a very upmarket dealer, or more correctly a *marchand-amateur*. Among the known buyers in 1791 were the nobility. William, 3rd Viscount Dudley and Ward, apart from paying the considerable sum of £100 for the *Mass of St Giles*, also spent £100 on a Teniers *Landscape*, £50 on a *Boar Hunt* by Rubens and Van Uden, £40 on a *Flemish Farm Yard* by Rubens, £25 on a *Moonlight Scene* by Van der Neer, £20 and £15 for two paintings by Jordaens of *Ulysses* and *Baucis and Philemon*, and £10 for a *Landscape* by Rubens.[13] Another major purchaser was *Jacob, 2nd Earl of Radnor* [**62**], who was an important patron of Cosway. He bought five paintings from the artist in 1791, including a portrait by Otto van Veen of *Prince Albert, Governor of the Low Countries*, a Sassoferrato *Madonna* and a panel by Rubens and Van Uden of *Cupids Harvesting*. However, one of the most significant purchases was a *View of the Escorial* claimed to be by Rubens, though in fact by Verhulst after a sketch by Rubens, which had formerly belonged to King Charles I. In addition he purchased an important three-quarter-length portrait claimed erroneously and romantically by Cosway to be a Raphael and representing his mistress known as 'La Fornarina'. Cosway's comment about this painting, that it had 'all the grandeur of Michael Angelo', was astute in light of the fact that this very fine panel is by Sebastiano del Piombo, the painter Michelangelo most influenced. Cosway's identification of the sitter was optimistic as the portrait is now considered to show an unknown lady.[14]

Other paintings that have been identified from the 1791 catalogue include a portrait by William Dobson, which was thought by Cosway to represent the poet *Nathaniel Lee* [**192**], *The Rape of Ganymede* [**191**] by Rubens and a study of *An old man reading at a window*, then claimed to be by Rembrandt but now considered to be by a seventeenth-century imitator of Rembrandt. Cosway's sensitive description of it reveals his appreciation of the unusual light effects coming from the window 'into which the sun shines through a watery atmosphere. – The shadow of the divisions of the window are on the white wall, which constitutes the eye of the picture. – The effect of which is of the first impression'.[15]

As was expected of the taste in collecting Old Master paintings at this period, Cosway had concentrated his collecting in conventional areas, namely the sixteenth- and seventeenth-century Italian painters, together with the seventeenth-century Dutch and Flemish schools. The latter dominated with almost a quarter of the collection being comprised of paintings and sketches attributed to Rubens and his two main pupils, Van Dyck and Jordaens. The short descriptions of most of the paintings in his collection were almost certainly composed by Cosway, with emphasis on any striking artistic qualities and noteworthy provenances. Works were claimed to have been formerly in the French royal collection, a variety of English aristocratic families, and from a number of Italian palaces such as the Aldobrandini in Rome and the Barbarigo in Venice, as well as from other distinguished artists including Rubens, Lely, Hudson and Reynolds. In addition, many of the paintings came from collections in Flanders, probably acquired during the Cosways' visit there in 1786.

Throughout the 1780s the Cosways entertained regularly, holding salons or highly fashionable musical evenings that were attended by eminent visitors. While the collections of Old Master paintings helped create a fitting atmosphere, they also enabled Richard Cosway to establish his reputation as a connoisseur and *virtuoso*, while at the same time attracting and flattering the clientele for his portraiture business, which was at the root of his prosperity. Similarly, Maria Cosway's concerts would have benefited from these elegant surroundings, with visitors being suitably impressed.

With the birth of their child Louisa in 1790, circumstances changed drastically for the Cosways. Almost immediately Maria travelled to Italy, leaving Richard Cosway to look after Louisa on his own. In 1791 he decided to sell a large part of his picture collection and move to Stratford Place. Cosway lived there for the next thirty years, being rejoined by Maria from 1794 to 1801 and again from 1817 until they moved to a smaller villa on the Edgware Road shortly before Richard's death. If J. T. Smith provided the most evocative description of the way in which the collections were reinstalled in the richly decorated interiors, it was the great literary critic William Hazlitt who left the most memorable description of Cosway at Stratford Place, fully recognising the deeply imaginative, if eccentric, characteristics of the artist's Romantic world:

> *He was Fancy's child. All other collectors are fools to him: they go about with painful anxiety to find out the realities: — he said he had them — and in a moment made them of the breath of his nostrils and the fumes of a lively imagination. His was the crucifix that Abelard prayed to — the original manuscript of the Rape of the Lock — the dagger with which Felton stabbed the Duke of Buckingham — the first finished sketch of the Jocunda — Titian's large colossal portrait of Peter Aretine — a mummy of an Egyptian king — an alligator stuffed. Were the articles authentic? — no matter — his faith in them was true. What a fairy palace was his of specimens of art, antiquarianism, and* virtù *jumbled all together in the richest disorder, dusty, shadowy, obscure, with much left to the imagination (how different from the finical, polished, petty, perfect, modernized air of Fonthill!) and the copies of old masters, cracked and damaged, which he touched and retouched with his own hand, and yet swore they were pure originals! He was gifted with* second-sight *in such matters: he believed whatever was incredible. Happy mortal! Fancy bore sway in him, and so vivid were his impressions that they included the reality in them. The agreeable and the true with him were one.*[16]

Hazlitt published this powerful reminiscence of Cosway twice. The second occasion was in his essay 'On the Old Age of Artists', which was published in *The Plain Speaker* in 1826, and where he added two colourful details, claiming to have seen 'the feather of a Phoenix' and 'a piece of Noah's ark'. The account had been first published four years earlier in his essay 'Fonthill Abbey' for the *London Magazine*. Essentially a damning critique of William Beckford's collections at *Fonthill Abbey* [166] in Wiltshire, a 'desert of magnificence' and a 'cathedral turned into a toy-shop', Hazlitt lamented the absence of even 'one lofty relic of sentiment or imagination'.

However, it is clear that Cosway himself was a great admirer of Beckford, and spent a week at Fonthill Abbey in 1807 with the reclusive collector. In a letter to *Jacob, 2nd Earl of Radnor* [62], Cosway excitedly recorded his impressions of the visit to Wyatt's neo-Gothic extravaganza, where he received the very rare privilege of being shown the fabulous collections by Beckford himself:

> *I found an Invitation from* Mr. B. *to visit the* Abbey, *this opportunity (which I apprehended perhaps might never happen again under such an advantageous circumstance), I could not resist, and such a wonderful accumulation of* Treasures *of every possible description in Books, Manuscripts, Prints, Books of Prints, Gems, Cameos, Carvings in Ivory, Ebony, the most rare Japan, China, &c, &c, &c, &c, &c, of the highest Class and in the purest state of preservation, I believe does not exist in Europe, and which can never be shown but by* Mr. B. *himself, so that instead of three days to which time I had limited my stay from London, I was employ'd* Ten Whole Days *in examining what I believe to be only a* fiftieth *part of the contents of the Abbey and I really think I should have remain'd there to this Hour.*[17]

Cosway's own collections were similar in many ways to those of Beckford. The main differences, apart from the imaginative as already criticised by Hazlitt, were those of size and degree of luxury. Both men were avid book collectors and formed substantial libraries, though of contrasting scale and purpose. Beckford was primarily a bibliophile, searching for rare and luxurious volumes, in particular on travel, history and literature, while Cosway satisfied his spiritual interests, amassing works on divinity and many related subjects including the occult, astrology, magic, witchcraft, alchemy and the cabbala – as seen from the 1821 sale catalogue of his books. As an artist forming a substantial library, Cosway can be compared instructively with Reynolds, Fuseli, Flaxman and Lawrence. As an artist with religious interests he was like de Loutherbourg, a fellow animal magnetist and faith healer.

Despite the lack of visual representations of the interiors at Stratford Place, an accurate idea of the collections and their arrangement can be gleaned from a comprehensive inventory compiled in 1820, the year before the artist's death. Every area of wall space in the house was filled with paintings, both Old Masters and works by the Cosways. Rooms on the three main floors overflowed with furniture, on which there were placed *objets d'art*, china, plate and sculpture. Significant artistic and musical items as well as unusual objects were to be found throughout the house.

On the ground floor were situated the parlour or dining room; the back parlour, where could be found the portfolios of prints and drawings, as well as books of prints; the saloon, also known as the painting room; and the armour closet which contained a small but choice collection.[18] On the first floor were located the drawing room, with a fireplace carved by Thomas Banks, a piano and a Savonnerie carpet, which was presumably the one presented by Louis XVI; the back drawing room, where there was a large sarcophagus, an organ, two miniature painting desks, and a *Colour box* [215], which was claimed to have belonged once to Rubens; a closet, with another desk for painting in miniature; and the library, where there was a skeleton inside a case. On the second floor was the main bedroom and Mrs Cosway's room which was notable for the presence of a harp. The prominent staircase was decorated with pictures, armour and casts, while in the basement was located the plaster room, which contained 'a great number of Heads, Hands and Feet'.[19] The luxurious and diverse nature of Cosway's collections of furniture, sculpture and *objets d'art* is revealed in the sale catalogue listing them in 1821, the title page of which stated:

A CATALOGUE

OF THE VERY CURIOUS AND VALUABLE

Assemblage of Miscellaneous Articles

OF

TASTE AND VIRTÙ,
The Property of that distinguished Artist and Virtuoso,
RICHARD COSWAY, ESQ. R.A.
CONSISTING OF
ANCIENT ARMOUR,
BUHL & INDIA CABINETS,
Antique Bronzes, Marbles, Terra-cottas,
CANDELABRA OF RICH ORMOLU,
SPLENDID CARVED TABLES, TRIPODS AND BRACKETS,
OLD CHINA,
An EGYPTIAN MUMMY *and an* IBIS,
AND NUMEROUS OTHER ARTICLES OF TASTE AND CURIOSITY.[20]

Among the most significant influences on Cosway's Romantic antiquarianism must have been Horace Walpole's collections at Strawberry Hill, his famous neo-Gothic residence on the Thames at Twickenham. In 1787 both Richard and Maria Cosway were given a personal tour of the villa and collections by Walpole himself, and Cosway also owned a copy of Walpole's published *Description of Strawberry Hill*. Walpole's attitude to collecting was in turn derived from earlier eighteenth-century cabinets of curiosities and objects of *virtù*, notably those of Dr Mead, the Earl of Oxford and the Duchess of Portland.[21]

Cosway seems to have been unusual among contemporary artists and architects in that he was a genuine *virtuoso*, collecting objects that were beautiful, rare, precious and of antiquarian interest. The collections of de Loutherbourg and Zoffany, who both acquired armour, were similar to a certain degree, but only that of Sir John Soane [fig. 14] could be truly classed as that of a *virtuoso*.[22] This was beyond the more usual collecting by artists and architects, who, depending on the degree of their success, concentrated on engravings and books of prints, leading on to casts and sculptures, drawings and paintings. Cosway built collections in all these areas, and was almost certainly modelling the totality of his collections and his persona as an artist-collector on seventeenth-century exemplars, such as Rembrandt and even more so Rubens.

Indeed, Cosway owned at least two paintings of Rubens's house in Antwerp, which he would have explored on his visit there in 1786. The inclusion of a bust of the Flemish master in the finished drawing at Lodi, the *Self-portrait with busts of Michelangelo and Rubens* [36], is one of many instances that reveal Cosway's obsession and self-identification with the Flemish artist. The dealer William Buchanan, who used Cosway's talent as a connoisseur to gain the interest of the Marquis of Stafford in the purchasing of Old Master paintings, described in a letter of 1804 to an agent how he intended to retain Cosway's services: 'As for Cosway, I think we may secure his good offices by the Rubens Drawing I have lately got, which is a most masterly sketch as I ever saw and is invaluable to an artist – particularly Cosway who is so wrapt up in Rubens'.

There is considerable other evidence of Cosway's fascination with Rubens. He owned numerous paintings by the Old Master, including the small sketch panel of *The Rape of Ganymede* [191] and the study for the Whitehall ceiling of *King James VI and I uniting the Kingdoms of Scotland and England* [190]. There was also the large collection of 704 prints – as well as books of prints – after Rubens and 92 drawings attributed to the master. The portraits in black chalk of *Pieter van Hecke* [206] and the artist's son *Frans*

Rubens [207], as well as the *Studies after Michelangelo's 'Madonna de' Medici* [205], are good examples of the high quality of works that Cosway was able to acquire. Among the curiosities that Cosway owned was what he claimed to be *The Rubens colour box* [215], which he bought on his visit to Antwerp in 1786. The exact details of how Cosway came into the possession of the colour box are not known, but it may have come from a dealer, private collector or even from Rubens's house. This is not to say that the box actually belonged to Rubens, though this remains a possibility. Current opinion notes that it is mid-seventeenth century in date, and is likely to have been made in the East Indies. It relates to the design of spice boxes, but the rare occurrence of such a colour box indicates that it was constructed with a specific function. The decoration includes elaborate inlaid work, and there are Eastern motifs engraved on the mounts and hinges.[23]

Cosway was clearly in no doubt as to the provenance of the box, and used it for storing his pigments throughout the rest of his career. In the light of his obsessive interest in Rubens, the pleasure Cosway would have gained in acquiring and then using this box can only be imagined. After her husband's death, Maria Cosway presented the colour box in 1822 to her friend Sir Thomas Lawrence, who had been overwhelmed by his visit to Stratford Place, describing it as a true 'Artist's House'.

One of Cosway's main reasons for touring Flanders was undoubtedly to pay homage to Rubens and to take the opportunity to buy art works. In making this visit, Cosway was following in the wake of another important artistic mentor, Reynolds, who in turn recognised Cosway's connoisseurship of Rubens. In an undated letter, probably from the 1780s, Reynolds wrote to Cosway requesting, as 'a great favour', that he be able to borrow for a few days a sketch by Rubens of *Jupiter and Venus*.[24]

Indeed, to gain some idea of what Cosway's interiors at Stratford Place must have been like, one must visit Sir John Soane's Museum in Lincoln Inn's Fields, which was formerly the architect's house, and which still preserves the rich and cluttered effects of Soane's curiosity. It can be argued that the way in which Cosway placed significant objects together to create a resonant effect had an influence on Soane. The architect and his wife were very friendly with Richard and Maria, as is revealed in the surviving correspondence and in Soane's notebooks. The friendship appeared to flourish after 1801, perhaps after Maria had left for Paris. Cosway and Soane, who were both Academicians, regularly called on or dined with each other. On 10 December 1803 Soane noted that he went to Cosway's and 'survey'd his house'. When Maria Cosway returned from Italy in 1817 to nurse her ailing husband Soane was a particularly attentive visitor. After Richard Cosway died in 1821, Soane and Maria sustained an intensive correspondence into old age, and he was her executor for many years.[25]

There were also exchanges of works of art and books. Soane acquired an oil painting by Maria Cosway of *A Persian going to adore the sun*, painted in 1784. Maria presented him with a case of four figurines, two classical bronze statuettes and two Ushabti mummies [258], the former coming from Lodi, and the latter being a gift from Vivant-Denon, the great French archaeologist and organiser of the Louvre. Vivant-Denon had come to know Maria during her stay in Paris from 1801 to 1803, when she was copying the paintings in the Louvre [252]. Soane was in turn a subscriber to the publication of this ambitious project [**253**], and acquired both monochrome and coloured sets of the resulting prints. He later sent her a copy of the published *Description* of his famous house in Lincoln Inn's Fields.

In 1811 Richard Cosway presented Soane with a copy of the 1736 edition of Vignola's famous architectural treatise, *Règles des Cinq Ordres d'Architecture* [**217**]. This volume also bears Cosway's monogram of an R inside a C, which has been tooled in gold onto the leather spine of the book. Like Soane, Cosway was a great book collector. At his Stratford Place residence Cosway had a room converted into a library, which was almost exclusively devoted to works on religion, astrology, magic and the occult. There was also a skeleton preserved in a glass case, and it is highly likely that Cosway's notorious seances, as well as his astrological investigations, took place in this room. The inventory drawn up in 1820 of the contents of his house revealed that he had over 3500 books, about two thirds of which were devoted to religious and spiritual matters. The rest of the collection, which was to be found in bookcases throughout the main reception rooms of the house, was comprised of volumes relating to art, including many books of prints and emblems. More conventional subjects were *belles-lettres*, travel and history. The English, French and Italian books in Maria Cosway's rooms were dominated by accounts of famous women, texts of religious devotion, including over forty different editions in various languages of *The Imitation of Christ* by Thomas à Kempis, and more general works of literature and history.

Further evidence for Soane's friendship with Cosway is revealed by the fact that the architect acquired three drawings by Cosway: the early copy of Guido Reni's *Aurora*, as well as those representing *Andromache and Astyanax* [**45**] and *Venus mourning Adonis* [**167**]. The architect also made a number of diverse purchases for his own collection at the sale of Richard Cosway's 'Miscellaneous Articles of Taste and Virtù' in 1821, which showed his appreciation of the high quality and interest of the objects concerned. Among the more interesting pieces of sculpture that Cosway had owned were a terracotta by Nollekens and twenty-two wax *modelli* by Giambologna, the latter all displayed in the front drawing room on the chimney piece. The sculptures on the fireplace had been carved by Thomas Banks after a design by Cosway himself.[26]

These pieces of sculpture would have been well known to Soane, who eventually bought fifteen lots comprising thirty-two antique, Renaissance and Baroque marbles, bronzes and terracottas:

A pair of marble vases
Three fragments, in terra-cotta — Caryatidae, &c
An oratory, with image of the Virgin, and a Female reclining on emblems of Mortality, both in marble
Two children, in terra-cotta, with escutcheons
A [figure of] Charles, the Second, [in terracotta]
A figure resting on an urn, in T[erra]. C[otta]. [**213**]
Figure of a Gentleman, in T[erra]. C[otta]. trunk of a figure, ditto, and a pedestal
Three antique fragments of marble, carved in bas-relief
A group, Bacchus and 2 Fawns, in marble
Four small bronze figures, Hindu
Small figure of a Gladiator, ditto of Boreas, and one armed
The bull breaking the egg, on a marble stand [**211**]
The triform Diana, on a marble pedestal [**210**]
Antique figures of Mars and Hercules

A pair of Egyptian figures, on small plinths, and a Chinese Female [27]

A number of these pieces have been identified and are preserved in Sir John Soane's Museum; they shed light on Cosway's taste and on how he used his collection as a stimulus for his artistic imagination. The antique bronze statuette of the *Triform Diana* [**210**] shows the goddess of hunting and of the moon in her triple form known as Hecate. The missing attributes which the figures originally held would have been either torches (for the goddess of the moon) or snakes which refer to her role as a guardian to the Underworld. Cosway may have added the base and its decoration, which is notable for the supporting leaves and herm-like figures. He would have found this object interesting from both the religious as well as iconographical and compositional points of view. He copied a 'Triform Diana or Hecate' from Charles Townley's collection.[28] Cosway often sought to explore the complex pose of three women shown together, as in the 1795 drawing of the *Princess Galetzin and her two daughters* [**98**] and the 1805 painting of *The Hons Sophia, Louisa and Mathilda Courtenay* [**151**].

Another of Soane's acquisitions from Cosway was the antique bronze statuette of *The bull breaking the egg* [**211**], which was a subject commonly treated in classical art. This object would have had special resonance for both Cosway and Soane in that its iconography had been discussed as a central element of the influential publication, *Recherches sur l'origine, l'esprit et les progrès des arts de la Grèce ...* (1785) by the self-styled Baron d'Hancarville (1719–1805), who was a highly imaginative if unconventional art historian.[29] He was a sometime curator of Charles Townley's collection of classical sculpture and very friendly with both the Cosways during the 1780s. D'Hancarville, in his syncretic investigation into the origins of religion as a fertility rite, interpreted the bull breaking the egg as symbolic of the regenerative powers of the creative urge.

Soane also acquired from Cosway the terracotta model [**213**] for the statue of the Secretary of State, James Craggs the younger (1686–1721), which was placed on his tomb at Westminster Abbey. The monument as a whole was designed by James Gibbs, but the statue was created by Giovanni Guelfi (*fl.*1714–34), who came to London from Italy under the auspices of Lord Burlington, and later worked at Chiswick and on Burlington House. The sculptor may have been engaged on the Craggs monument through the interest of Alexander Pope, who knew both Craggs and Burlington. Pope took a close interest in the development of the monument and composed the epitaph. Guelfi had difficulties with the actual portrait since he had never met Craggs. This may account for the absence of the original face on the terracotta model, hence the provision of a carved wooden face, probably when it was in the ownership of Cosway or Soane. The cross-legged pose adopted by the sculptor for this statue was one of the earliest to derive from classical Roman sources. It later became one of the most popular poses for standing portraits, whether sculpted or painted, in the eighteenth century, and Cosway made considerable use of it throughout his oeuvre.

Prominent among Soane's acquisitions from Cosway's collection are a pair of marble vases considered be of eighteenth-century Italian origin; a pair of terracottas of children supporting escutcheons, standing high up in the Monk's Parlour; a terracotta statue of *Charles II* by Arnold Quellin; and the plaster model of *Van Dyck* by Rysbrack.[30] The serpentine pose employed by Rysbrack in this statuette, with the weight of the body thrust onto one of the hips, was especially favoured by Cosway in his male portraiture – as in the oil of *William, 3rd Viscount Courtenay* [**93**]. Van Dyck was another artist whom Cosway greatly admired as the ideal courtier-artist, and whose style had an enormous influence on the development of his full-length portrait drawings. These were usually executed in pencil with an 'unfinished' effect for the body, and with watercolour 'tinting' or 'staining' for the faces. The pair of pen and ink drawings at Lodi – the *Self-portrait* [**36**] and that of *Maria Cosway* [**37**] – are exceptional in that they are finished throughout and lack watercolour, although the pose adopted by the artist himself, especially in one of the preparatory sketches, is evidence of his extreme awareness of the repertoire of poses used by Van Dyck in his male portraiture. Cosway, like Reynolds and many other eighteenth-century artists, made frequent use of his collections of paintings and drawings and, in particular, prints, as source material for compositional, formal and decorative motifs in his own work.

While Cosway's collections and the spaces he created for them acted as a constant source of visual material and inspiration, it is less easy to estimate the impact upon his contemporaries of Cosway's taste and activity as a collector. Between 1784 and 1790 the salon and concerts that Maria Cosway presided over at Schomberg House attracted a range of visitors from the *bon ton* of society, including the gossipy Boswell, Walpole and Fanny Burney. In the private contract sale of paintings held in 1791 the artist found a ready market among his aristocratic clientele. After the move to Stratford Place Cosway was visited by friends who seem to have been mainly artists and connoisseurs, such as the sculptor Thomas Banks, the antiquarian and bibliophile Francis Douce – who later became one of Cosway's executors – and picture collectors such as Robert Udney and Caleb Whitefoord. The accounts of the critics Hazlitt and J.T. Smith are eloquent responses to Cosway's sense of Romantic imagination and status as a *virtuoso*. Yet it was probably Soane who learned the most from imbibing the rich and exotic effects of rampant antiquarianism, bizarre curiosity and deep connoisseurship that must have been so overpowering at Stratford Place.

Another major artist and collector of the period, Sir Thomas Lawrence, was profoundly affected by the realisation that Cosway was a true connoisseur and artist. In a highly revealing letter written to the diarist Joseph Farington after an unannounced visit to Stratford Place in 1811, Lawrence felt compelled to review his previously jaundiced opinion of Cosway, while reflecting on his own station as an artist, and the nature of his surroundings at home:

> ... *I have been out ... to see Cosway's Drawings, and I am returned most heavily depressed in spirit from the strong impression of the past dreadful waste of time and improvidence of my Life and Talent ... I have since been to Cosway's, and have seen an* Artist's House, *such a mass of* fit Materials *and so much Talent and Information in its Possessor (tho' not seeing him in Person), as to make me ashamed of the injustice, which prejudice, or say* just *opinion of his positive faults of character as a Man, have led me to commit against the general weight of his estimation as an Artist. – What are Mr. Phillips, and Mr. Owen, and Sir William Beechey, and Mr. Shee's in mere colouring, when compar'd to the knowledge – the familiar acquaintance with, study; and often happy appropriation and even liberal imitation of the Old Masters, the fix'd Landmark of Art, of this*

> *little Being which we have been accustom'd never to think or speak of but with contempt? – I know that the first feeling of your mind on reading this, will be something of surprise at this strange disproportion'd praise of Cosway!! but I know likewise from the ingenuousness of your Nature, that had you been with me, the impression had been mutual – You say of me that I serve my Profession as an amateur, and I seem to come home to the* House *of an amateur; so little of the proper Character of an artistic dwelling does it seem to have – the Bell is ringing, and my paper is fill'd so that I must finish – but destroy instantly, or keep this letter, it expresses the sincere mortification and sincere as bitter regret of your attach'd and oblig'd Friend T.L.*[31]

This was high praise as Lawrence, along with Reynolds, was not only one of the greatest artist-collectors of his generation, but the individual who formed the most outstanding collection of Old Master drawings ever put together in the British Isles, dominated by peerless groups of drawings by Michelangelo and Raphael. Apart from being so unexpectedly forced to confront the reality of a true artist's house, what impressed Lawrence so much at Stratford Place were not only Cosway's own drawings, but also the substantial collection of sheets by the Old Masters. Lawrence was able to buy a major group of these drawings from Cosway's posthumous sale in 1822, including the pen and ink *Design for a bed* [**196**], then thought to be by Raphael but now known to be by Bandinelli; the *Seated angel playing the harp* [**203**] in black chalk, then possibly considered to be by Correggio and now attributed to Lodovico Carracci; and the portrait in chalks of *Frans Rubens* [**207**] drawn by his father.

The catalogue or inventory of the contents at Stratford Place compiled in 1820 reveals much about the location of Cosway's own art works and those that he collected. The Old Master drawings, which numbered about 2500 strong, were grouped together by artist, subject and size in twenty-nine portfolios, books and boxes. Among the groups of drawings by sixteenth-century Italian masters, were: Parmigianino (44 in number) and Correggio (27); Michelangelo and his school (67); Giulio Romano (26) and Raphael '& school' (44); Baccio Bandinelli (52); and Titian (39) and other Venetian masters (14). In addition, the seventeenth-century Dutch and Flemish artists were represented, including a very large book containing works by Rubens (92), Van Dyck (46) and Jordaens (23), as well as a thin portfolio of drawings by Rembrandt (30). About 250 Old Master drawings formerly owned by Cosway, approximately a tenth of his collection, have been traced today. They have been identified by the two variant marks of Cosway's monogram, which were stamped on all the drawings before they were sold in 1822.

Cosway was part of a distinguished tradition of artists with studios in London who collected Old Master drawings, and who left evidence of their ownership by means of these stamped monograms. This began in the mid-seventeenth century with Sir Peter Lely, and continued with Richard Gibson, Jonathan Richardson father and son, Thomas Hudson, Sir Joshua Reynolds, Benjamin West, Nathaniel Hone, Paul Sandby and Thomas Banks, culminating with Sir Thomas Lawrence.[32] Selections of the finest drawings belonging to Cosway and many of his contemporaries, both artists and connoisseurs, were etched for Conrad Martin Metz's luxury volume *Imitations of Ancient and Modern Drawings*, first published in 1789 with a second and revised edition following in 1798. Among the works in Cosway's collection which were illustrated, thus displaying his connoisseurship, were the chalk drawings by Holbein of a *Woman with four children* [**204**] and by Giulio Campi – then thought to be by Giulio Romano – of *Salome carrying the head of St John the Baptist* [**200**].

About seven hundred of Cosway's own drawings, which included unfinished portraits, sketches and historical subjects, were kept together in eight books and portfolios in the back parlour on the ground floor. Only one of these survives intact, the *Sketchbook* now in the British Museum [**188**], which was compiled over a forty-year period from 1770 to 1810. With these was a group of twelve highly finished drawings that were framed and glazed and must have been among the artist's most prized works in this medium. They included 'Mr. Cosway's own portrait whole length' which is almost certainly the *Self-portrait as Esau* [**161**], *Love chaining Time* [**168**], *The Descent from the Cross* [**174**] and one of the two drawings of a *Madonna and Child* [**171**], which was in a 'Japan' or lacquered frame. Other finished drawings included portraits, mythological studies, and *The Death of Leonardo da Vinci* [fig. 15], a highly charged and complex late composition in which Cosway depicted King François I offering comfort to the famous artist in his last moments. This in turn can be seen as a meditation by Cosway on the relationship of artists with monarchs, on which he would have drawn from his long experience with the Prince of Wales, who was soon to become George IV.[33]

Also to be found in the back parlour at Stratford Place was 'A large Book with Prints from Mr. Cosway's Works in number 163', where the artist had collected together all his single portrait and

subject prints that were published throughout his career. Located close by were cases and shelves with over 250 books of prints, a similar number of titles on art, while in 'a cabinet by the door to the dining room' there were fifty books of emblems and another forty small books of prints. In addition there were sixty-six portfolios and books of around 7500 loose prints. The prints were grouped under artist and, as with the Old Master drawings, were mainly comprised of those after artists from the sixteenth-century Italian school. There were also groups of prints representing the seventeenth-century Dutch and Flemish painters, in addition to some devoted to a number of German, French and English masters. Cosway formed a number of portfolios of prints which related to various thematic interests including those after the antique, landscapes and portraits.

As with his own paintings, which were hung throughout the house adjacent to those by the Old Masters, Cosway kept his own prints and drawings in close proximity to the collections representing the earlier artists. His close knowledge of the styles, techniques and compositions of the Old Masters as represented in his collection is especially clear in his subject drawings, although his own work always has a distinctive character of mannerist elegance and eclectic spirit of decorative ornament. Cosway's earlier finished watercolours from the 1770s, such as the *Rinaldo and Armida*, reveal a knowledge of seventeenth-century Italian compositional types that is mediated with a playful French rococo spirit. More literally, by the 1780s Cosway could adapt a specific composition such as the *Andromache and Astyanax* [**45**] from a drawing of a 'Mother and Child' by Raphael. In the 1790s, with his use of highly finished pen and ink in the drawings of *Mars and Venus* [**105**], *Prometheus* [**106**] and *Sextus applying to Erictho* [**107**], Cosway indicates an awareness of the drawings and prints of Goltzius, as well as of his recently deceased contemporary J.H. Mortimer.

So too one can detect that certain Old Master drawings in Cosway's collection may have been particularly useful to the artist for his own compositions. For instance, the drawing currently attributed to Lodovico Carracci of a *Seated angel playing the harp* [**203**], which was traditionally attributed to Correggio when it entered the British Museum, may have been in a group of four chalk drawings of angels in the sale of Cosway's *Drawings and Prints*, and which were among the sixty-three sheets attributed to Correggio and his 'imitators'. Cosway collected numerous drawings of angels, both as compositional resource and no doubt because of his religious inclinations.[34] Over sixty of his surviving drawings at Lodi relate to angels and they appear throughout his oeuvre, even in portraits, as with the drawing of *Elizabeth, Countess of Hopetoun and her daughters Jasmin and Lucy* [**97**]. Cosway was also fascinated by the *contrapposto* figure of the angel playing the harp, lyre or other musical instrument. This was the basis of his composition *Harmonia*, which was engraved in stipple by Anthony Cardon in 1798, as well as of the oil portrait of *Lady Caroline Spencer* at Blenheim Palace.[35] This is just one instance, as Lawrence realised so acutely, of how Cosway was constantly able to refer to the drawings, prints and books he had collected as a source of study, appropriation and imitation for every aspect of his artistic vision and production.

After the death of her husband in 1821, Maria Cosway completed the sales of her husband's collections and after a tour of Scotland returned in the following year to Lodi, where she resumed the direction of a convent school for girls that she had established in 1812.

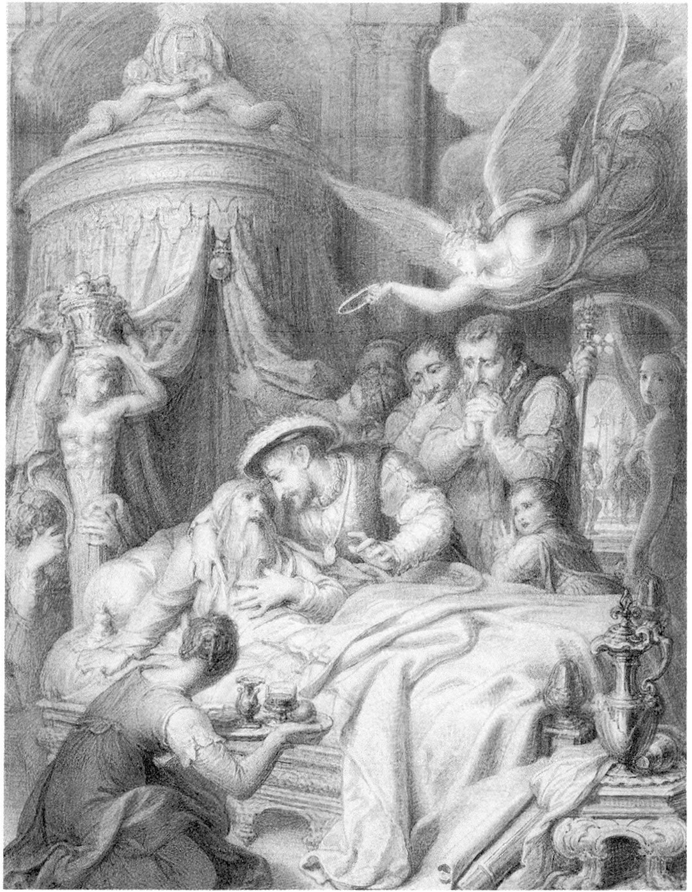

Fig. 15 *The Death of Leonardo da Vinci, c.1815* (A.J. Stirling)

Apart from the proceeds of the sales, she also took to Italy the last intact collection formed by her late husband, that of his own drawings and sketches. These subject drawings, many of them highly finished, were executed in the style and spirit of the Old Masters. That Lawrence was indeed a great admirer of Cosway's own subject drawings is revealed in a letter Maria Cosway wrote to Soane in 1830:

As to my correspondence with Sir T. Lawrence it was very friendly, but he always wished to purchase Mr. Cosway's drawings & these I never can part with. They form all my delightful amusement as well as admiration. I have kept the Collection together that it may be left and always preserved in his family.[36]

In the last years of Richard Cosway's life Maria Cosway remained loyal to her elderly and ailing husband, who was portrayed towards the end of his life in a remarkably frank watercolour, possibly by Thomas Rowlandson. After her husband's death Maria Cosway tirelessly promoted his subject drawings, exhibiting them at Mr Stanley's auction rooms in Old Bond Street, and also sending them down to Brighton for inspection by the new King, who declined the offer to purchase them. However, as she explained in a letter of April 1822 from her correspondence with the antiquarian and bibliophile Francis Douce, she had little success with either initiative: 'M[r]: Cosway's exhibition went off very bad, nobody came and I have made an expence. I don't regret [it] because the intension was honorable to his memory. The King returned *all* I sent. T'was not his fault but those about him'.[37]

This lack of interest from either the public or the King must have been partly because Richard Cosway's subject drawings, which were so influenced by the Old Master tradition, would have seemed outdated in comparison with the more fashionable linear neo-classical style epitomised by Flaxman and Stothard. However, after returning to Italy via Paris later that year, Maria Cosway elicited a more favourable response from abroad, as she noted in a letter to Douce in November:

I had the pleasure of showing M[r]: Cosway's Drawings to the few Artists & Connoisseurs who remained in Town [Paris]. At Turin, Milan, Parma & … they have been very much admired to a degree of Astonishment, they all say that they never saw so beautiful & new a Style, All Coreggio's, Parmigiano's grace with MichelAngiolo['s] knowledge. Poor M[r]: Cosway! how happy and gratified I feel to make his great talent known where the fine Arts had their birth. I have not been able to go to Bologna & Florence but hope to make that tour in the Spring, with the same satisfaction.[38]

In a letter written to Douce a few months later in February 1823, Maria Cosway went even so far as to praise her husband's drawings in comparison with paintings by her old friend David which had recently been exhibited in London, and whose style and practice she criticised: 'I long to hear the result of David's pictures. I never thought his style would please in England, he draws well & composes better, but his colouring is bad, & he follows the model before him too minutely …' She then went on describe David's late painting of *Cupid and Psyche*, which she had seen in Paris the year before: 'I saw in Count Somariva's collection who has all the works of Modern Artists a Cupid & Psyche by david, I never was more astonished Cupid is after a handsome boy … [but] it gives a vulgar tast[e]less appearance. How different from our inimitable Cos:'.[39]

Visitors to the Collegio in Lodi were shown Richard Cosway's drawings and up until her death in 1838 they were a source of great pleasure and pride to Maria Cosway. Today, despite the sale of a large group of drawings at Christie's in London on 1 June 1896, there still remain over six hundred separate drawings by Richard Cosway at the Collegio in Lodi. These cover the full range of his work and include finished sheets, which still retain their original mounts, and unmounted sketches and studies. The drawings were kept in their original portfolios and albums, although they were separated from these in the late 1970s.

Today, apart from the group of larger mounted works the drawings are grouped as follows: portrait studies; figure studies; classical as well as post-classical sources; biblical subjects; maternity; angels; and miscellanea, which include copies, costume studies, animals, landscapes and designs. Two other groups are comprised of sketches and drawings by Maria Cosway, the majority of which were copies relating to her project at the Louvre from 1801 to 1803; and also works by other artists, most of which are unattributed.[40] This large group of drawings remains the most important source for the study of Richard Cosway's artistic achievement, throughout his career from his early academic copies of the 1750s through to the mannerist intrepretations of the standing portrait drawing and the religious compositions of the 1810s. It can be seen that draughtsmanship, whether in chalk, pen and ink, watercolour, wash or in his favourite pencil, was at the very heart of his activity. Studies were frequently undertaken to prepare the compositional arrangements for portraits; figure arrangements were endlessly explored; the sources of classical and Renaissance literature in addition to the Bible were repeatedly interpreted; favourite themes such as the Madonna or mother with child and flying angels or putti were continually rehearsed and explored. The wide variety of his styles, media and subjects can be seen as a response to those of his favoured Italian and Flemish Old Masters. In this context as a draughtsman he sits apart from his more original major contemporaries, whether Fuseli or Romney in their preoccupation with Romantic drama, Flaxman with his austerely linear neo-classicism or Blake with his uniquely mystical vocabulary. The unifying characteristics of Richard Cosway's own drawings are sensitivity, virtuosity and sentiment, while they are also distinguished by Cosway's love of decorative ornament, subtle texture and intense emotion. These drawings, as Lawrence realised, when seen in the context of the Old Masters and when surrounded by the Romantic antiquarianism of the interiors at Stratford Place, are an essential expression of Richard Cosway's response to his artistic inheritance and self-identity as a *virtuoso*.

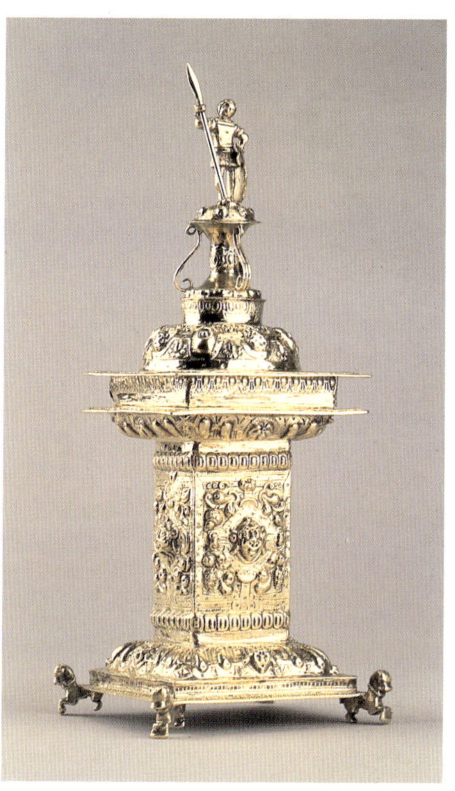

Plate 74   Unknown English Goldsmith
The Cosway salt 1584–5 [**214**]

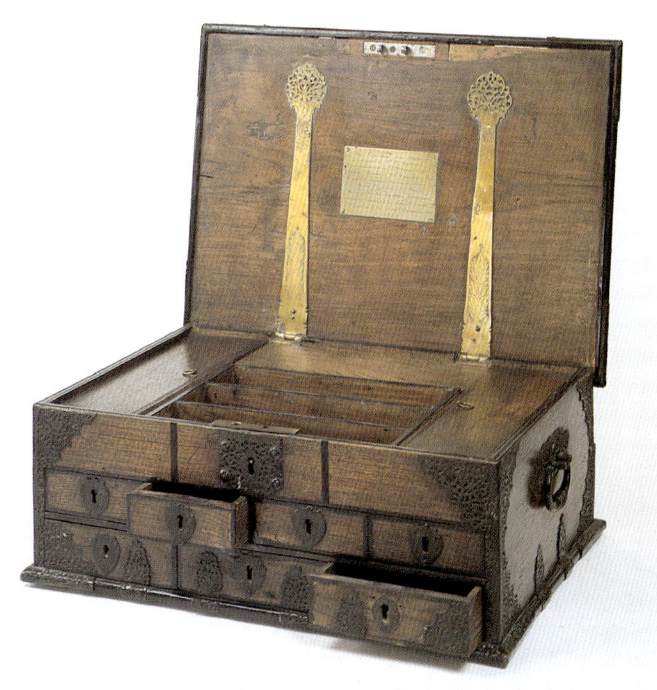

Plate 75   Unknown Cabinet-maker *The Rubens colour box*
mid–17th century [**215**]

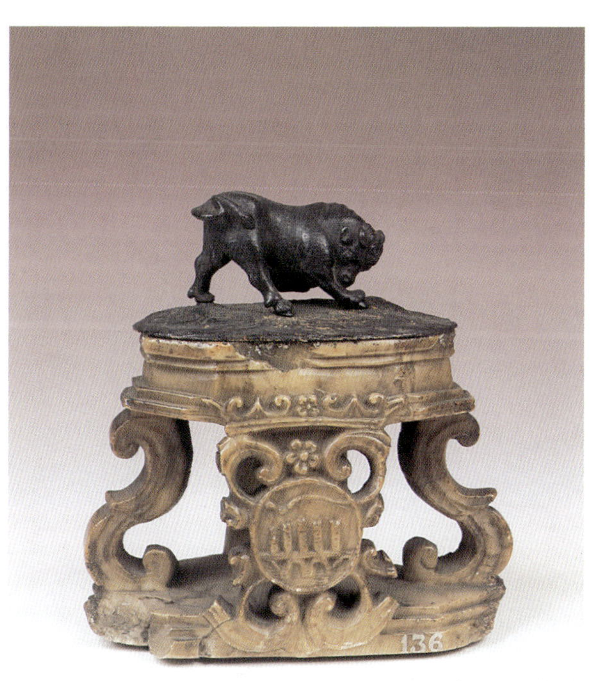

Plate 76   Unknown Artist *The Bull breaking the Egg*
Classical period [**211**]

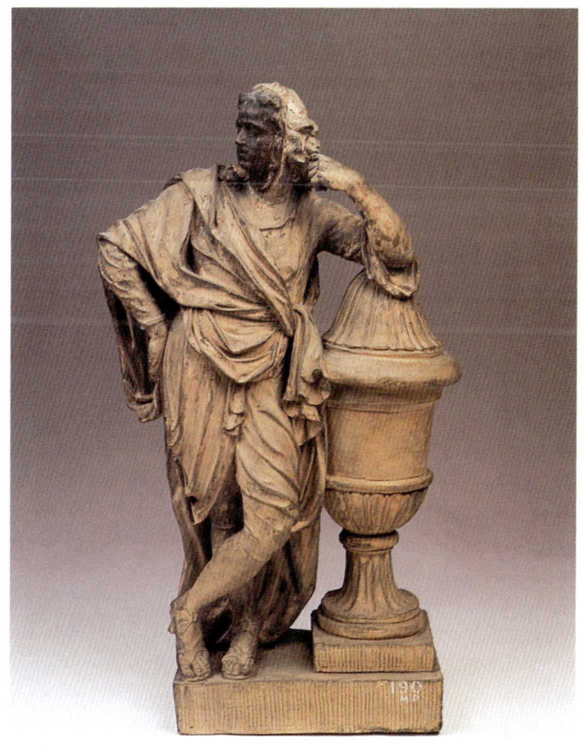

Plate 77   Giovanni Battista Guelfi *Figure for the monument to
James Craggs in Westminster Abbey* c.1727 [**213**]

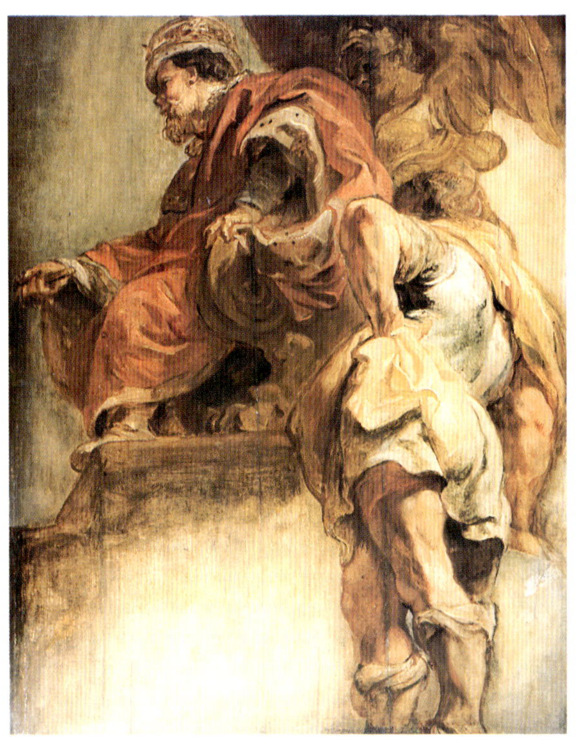

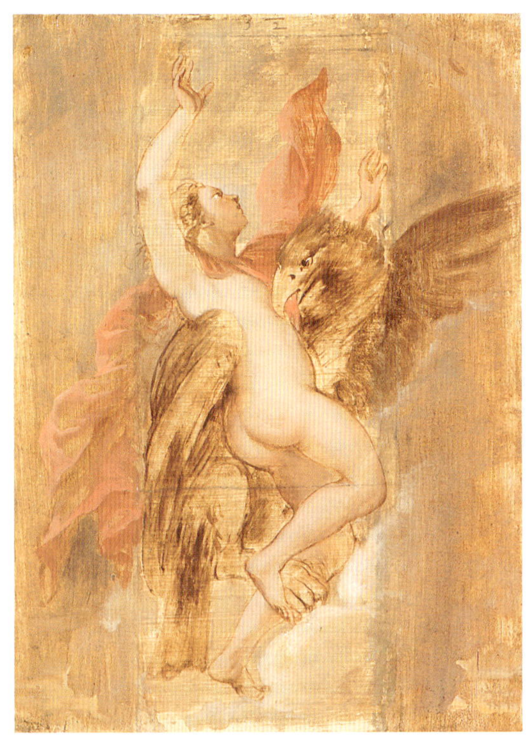

Plate 78   Sir Peter Paul Rubens *King James VI and I uniting the kingdoms of Scotland and England c.*1629 [**190**]

Plate 79   Sir Peter Paul Rubens *The Rape of Ganymede c.*1636–7 [**191**]

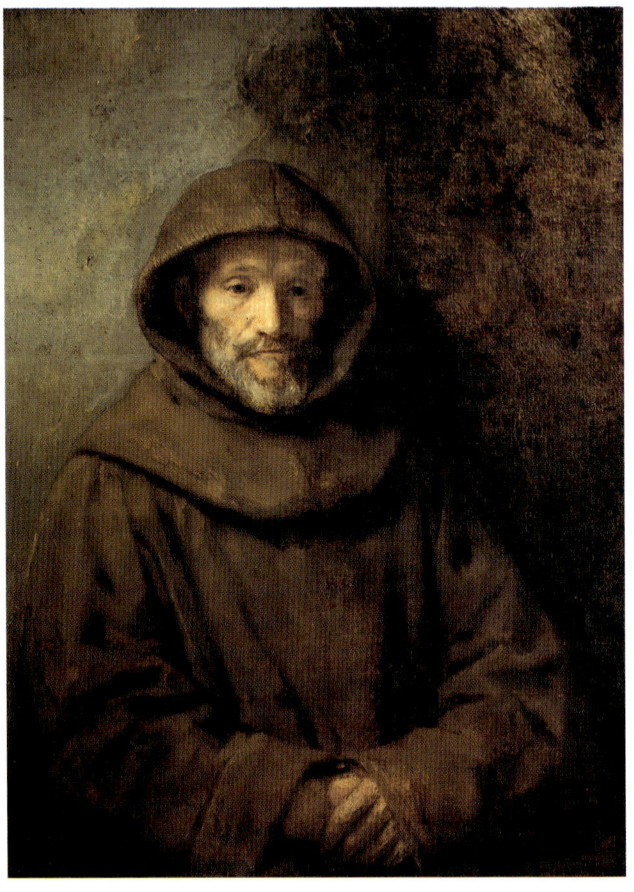

Plate 80   Rembrandt van Rijn *A Franciscan friar c.*1655 [**193**]

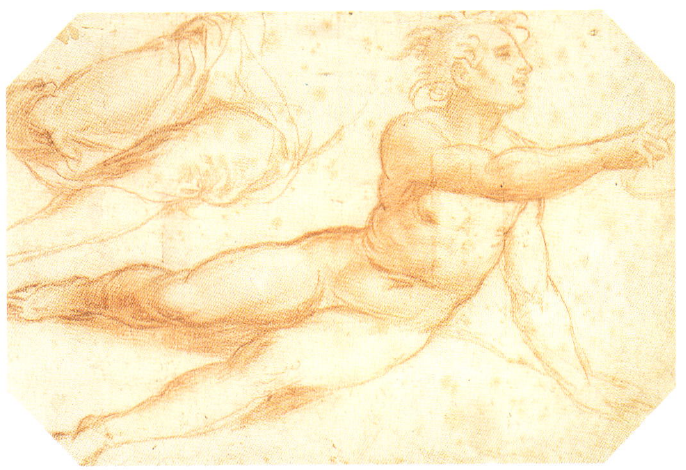

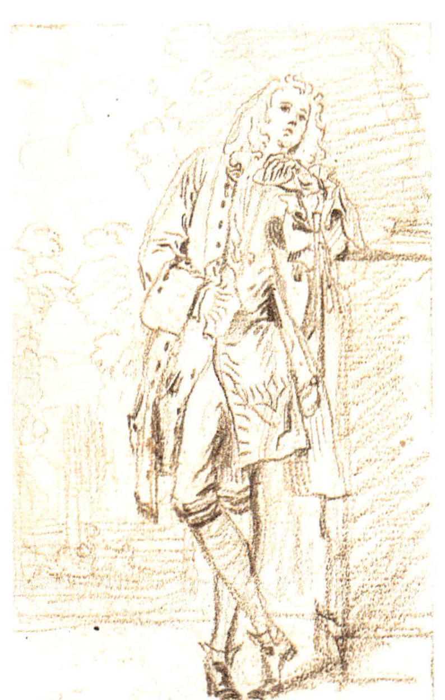

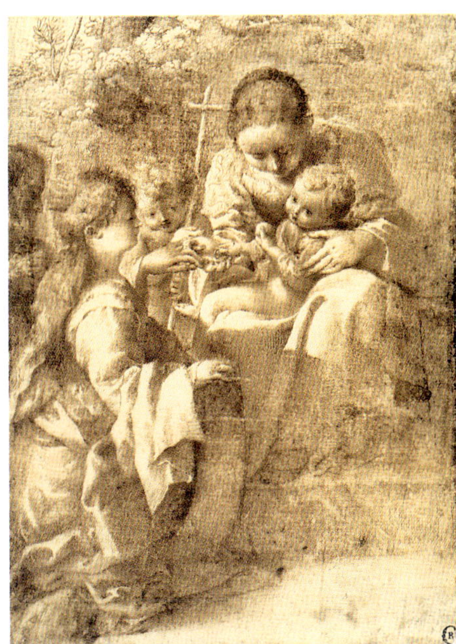

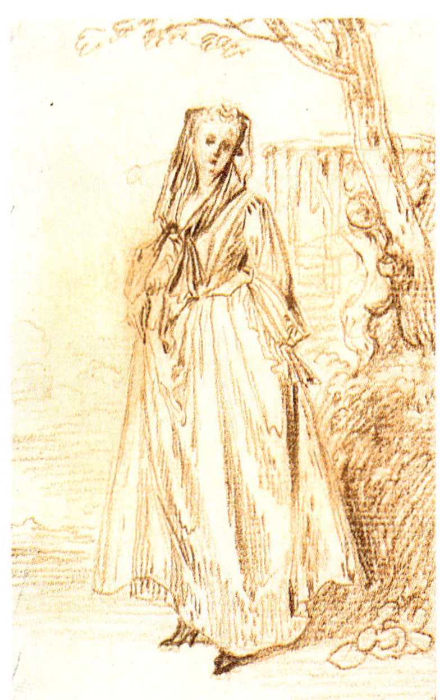

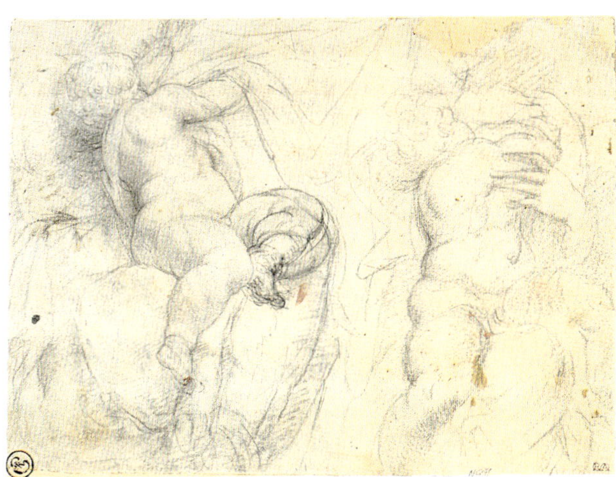

TOP Plate 81 Giovanni Battista Naldini *Study of a reclining nude man c.*1570–80 [**201**]

LEFT Plate 82 Jean-Antoine Watteau *A gentleman standing in a park c.*1710–20 [**208**]

CENTRE Plate 83 Pietro Faccini *The mystic marriage of St Catherine c.*1580–90 [**202**]

RIGHT Plate 84 Jean-Antoine Watteau *A lady standing in a park c.*1710–20 [**209**]

BOTTOM Plate 85 Sir Peter Paul Rubens after Michelangelo Buonarroti *Studies after the 'Madonna de' Medici' c.*1600–10 [**205**]

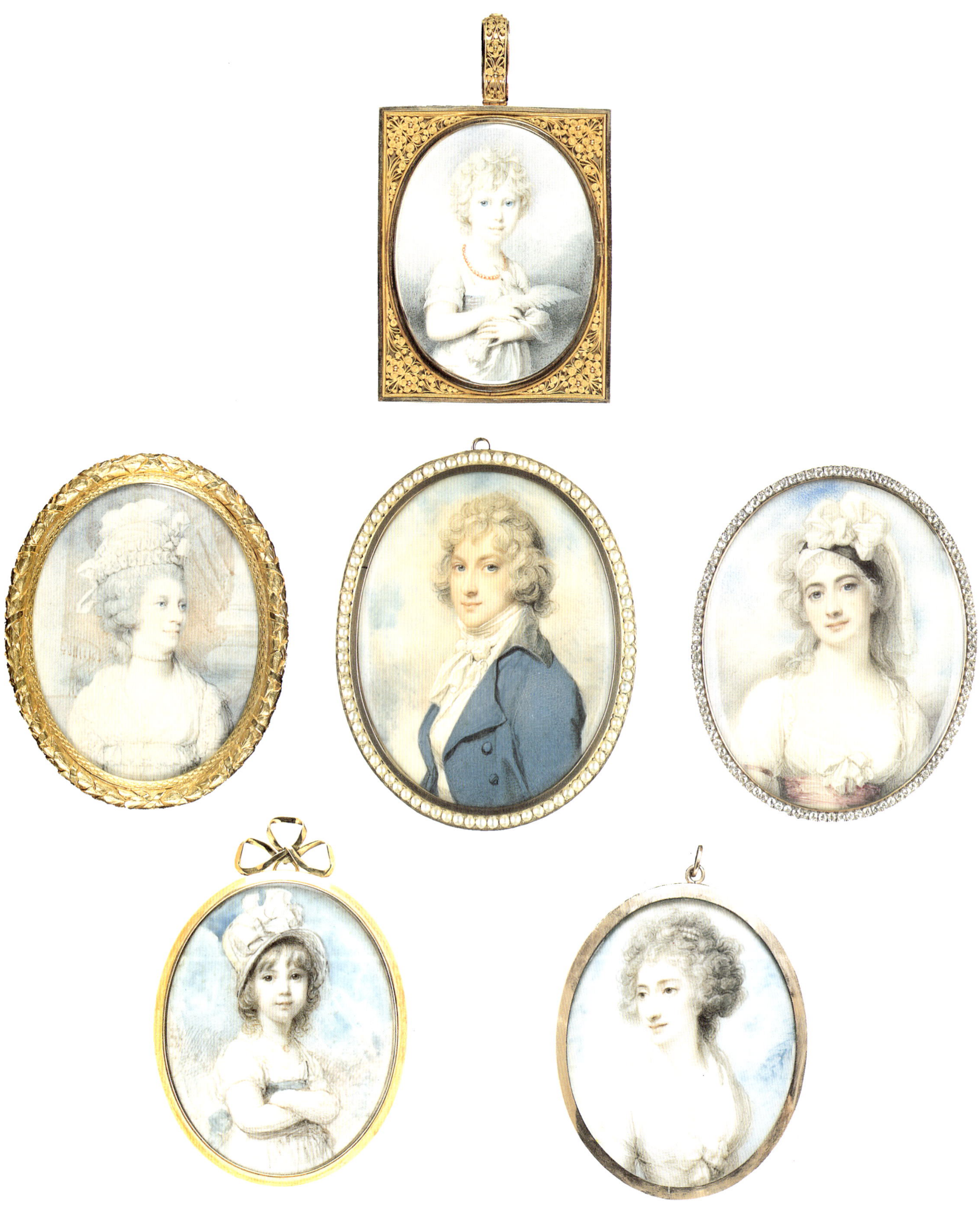

TOP Plate 86   *Princess Charlotte of Wales c.*1799 [**134**]
MIDDLE LEFT Plate 87   *Queen Charlotte* 1795 [**131**]
MIDDLE CENTRE Plate 88   *Miss Sophia Bankes c.*1795 [**125**]
MIDDLE RIGHT Plate 89   *Mrs Fitzgerald* 1794 [**120**]
BOTTOM LEFT Plate 90   *Lady Elizabeth Bingham c.*1790–5 [**124**]
BOTTOM RIGHT Plate 91   *An unknown lady* 1790 [**113**]

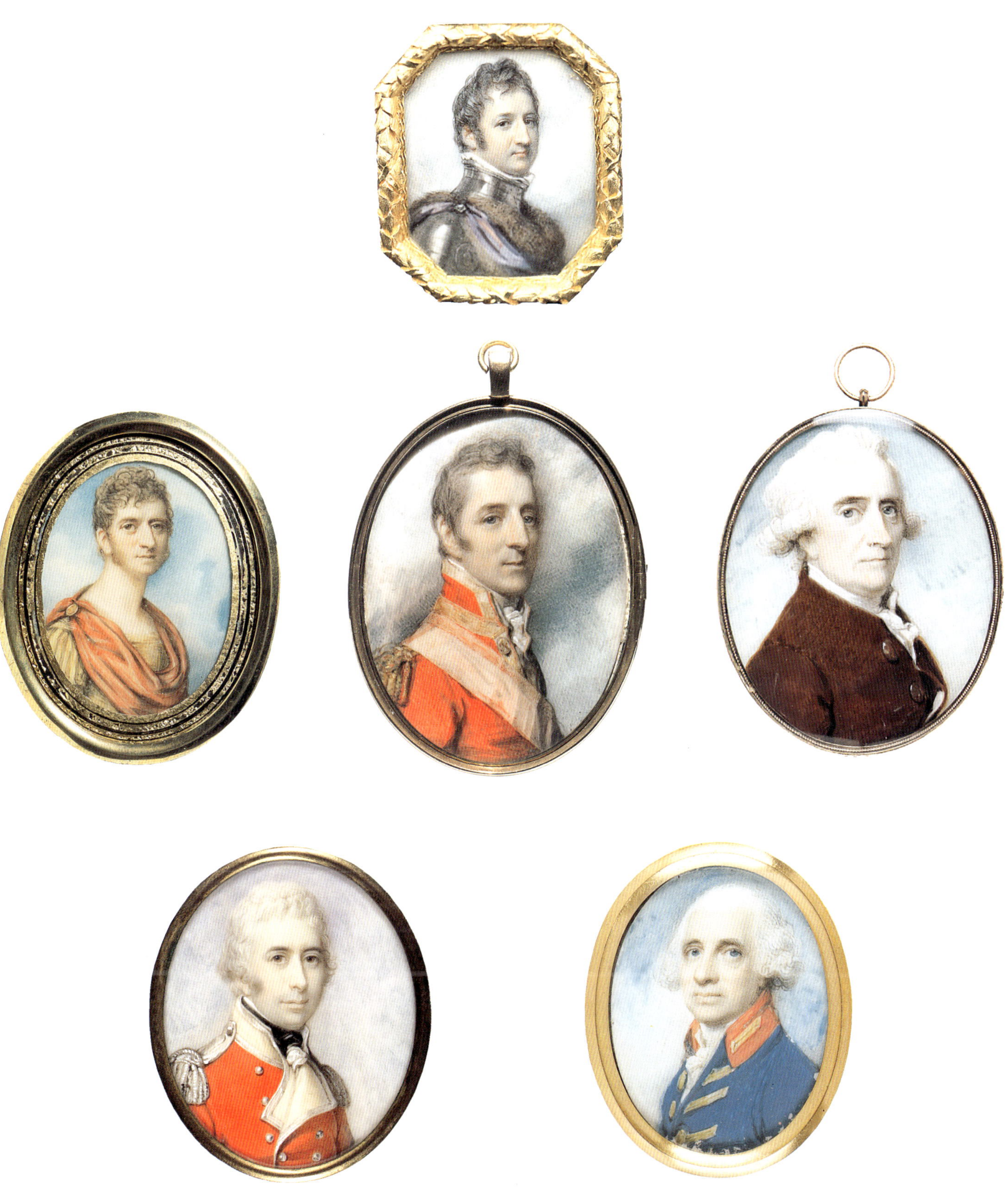

TOP Plate 92   *Louis-Philippe, Duc d'Orléans, later King of France c.1805* [**178**]
MIDDLE LEFT Plate 93   *John Philip Kemble 1795* [**126**]
MIDDLE CENTRE Plate 94   *Arthur Wellesley, later 1st Duke of Wellington 1808* [**181**]
MIDDLE RIGHT Plate 95   *Self-portrait in old age c.1805–10* [**182**]
BOTTOM LEFT Plate 96   *Thomas, 7th Earl of Elgin 1807* [**180**]
BOTTOM RIGHT Plate 97   *Richard, Admiral Earl Howe 1798–9* [**133**]

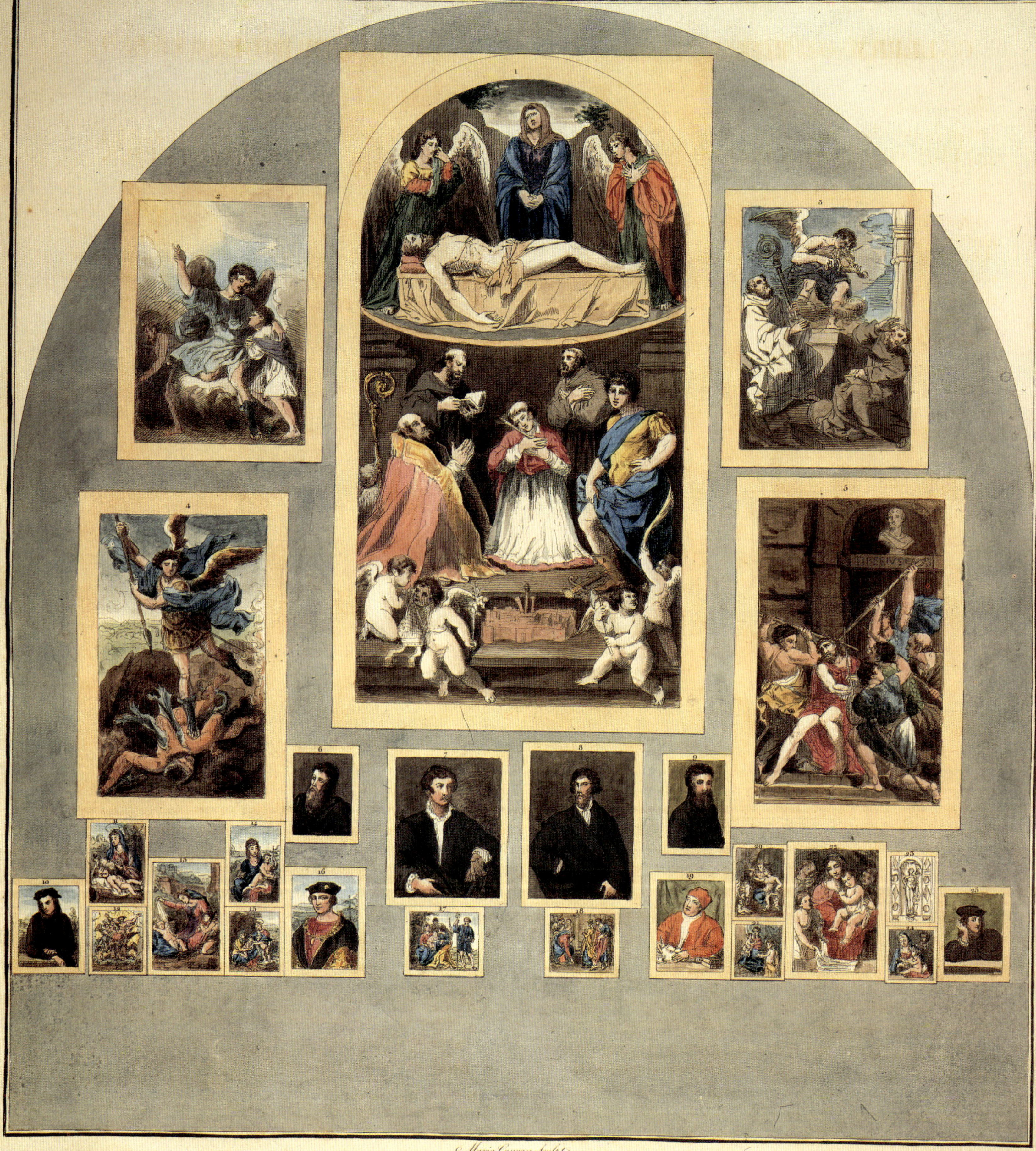

Raffaelle, & N.os 4, 10, 12, 13, 15, 19, 25.
Giulio Romano .... 9, 20, 21, 23, 24.
Tiziano .... 5, 7, 8.
Leonardo da Vinci .... 14, 16.
Paolo Veronese .... 6, 17.
Guido .... 1.

Domenico Feti .... 2.
Sebastiano del Piombo .... 22.
Guercino .... 3.
Baldassar Peruzzi .... 11.
Alessandro Veronese .... 18.

J. Griffiths
Auteur du Texte & Propriétaire de l'Ouvrage.

Déposé à la Bibliothèque Nationale, en Ventose an 10.

MARIA COSWAY
PARIS, LYONS, LONDON AND LODI
1801–38

*O*F ALL the artistic projects Maria Cosway was involved in around the turn of the century, the most ambitious and demanding was the one in Paris from 1801 to 1803, undertaken with the support and encouragement of her husband, who remained in London. She described how this came about in her autobiographical letter:

*The Gallery of the Louvre made a great noise at this time, M*ʳ*: C. could not go as the two Nations were at War, he sent me. I began my great work of all the pictures, and had then an oportunity of knowing intimately all the then reigning family. My work was stop'd but could not get a passport to go home.*

The project involved copying and etching the arrangement of Old Master pictures, as organised by Dominique Vivant-Denon, in the Musée Central based in the Louvre, which was being filled with art works looted by Napoleon's armies. The scheme was a joint venture by Maria Cosway and Julius Griffiths, an entrepreneur who was to write the texts in French and English and publish the plates by subscription, either coloured or in monochrome. The intentions behind the project were outlined in a prospectus of 21 March 1802 titled *Gallery of the Louvre at Paris*, and subscribers in Britain were encouraged to apply to the printseller Colnaghi. The copy of the prospectus sent to Sir John Soane survives in the library of his museum, in which it is clear that the intention was educational and decorative.[1]

The numerous CHEFS D'OEUVRE *of the* Italian, French, Flemish *and* Dutch *Schools, displayed in the* GALLERY OF THE LOUVRE, *present a new and most interesting spectacle, equally calcu-lated for the Refinement and Gratification of Taste.*

The Admirers of the Arts in every Country cannot but wish to have an Opportunity of acquiring some Knowledge of those sublime productions.

An Undertaking has therefore been entered into that will bring a Representation of THE WHOLE COLLECTION *before* THE WORLD, *by which Means every Individual may form* a Museum *within his own Apartments on the plan of the Louvre, and obtain a competent Knowledge of the Subjects and Merits of all the Pictures contained in that wonderful Assemblage.*

The Plan is to publish, by Subscription,
CORRECT ETCHINGS
OF
THE WHOLE COLLECTION
OF THE
PICTURES IN THE GALLERY OF THE LOUVRE AT PARIS,
BY
MRS. COSWAY,
Who is now residing at Paris for the Purpose.
The Work will be delivered IN NUMBERS
Each Number will contain TWO ETCHINGS *on separate Plates.*

Each Plate will represent the Pictures that compose one of the Compartments of the Gallery, *which is at present divided into* fifty-seven.
The work will be continued until the whole Collection shall be completed.
To every Number will be added
AN HISTORICAL ACCOUNT OF EACH PICTURE,
With new and interesting Anecdotes relative to the Artists,
BY
J. GRIFFITHS, ESQ.

After a list of the Old Masters – mainly sixteenth- and seventeenth-century painters – whose works were to be represented in the first number, the prospectus went on to reveal how the plates of the compartments of pictures in the Grand Gallery at the Louvre were to be displayed:

In order to convey the most perfect Idea of each Picture in the Louvre, *the superior Impressions of the Plates will be coloured and tinted up as nearly as possible to* the Effect of the Original – *and as the Plates are formed to correspond with the* Louvre Compartments *(when the Work is finished) the Whole may be disposed in* Domestic Galleries or Drawing Rooms, *so as to resemble* the Museum in the Louvre.

The prospectus ended by listing the prices to be paid for the plates. For subscribers each number with coloured etchings was set at £1. 5s, while those in monochrome were less expensive at 15 shillings. The prices for non-subscribers were higher by about six shillings in each case. It was hoped that following pairs of numbers of the plates were to be issued every month, although this was an optimistic forecast. Eventually eight plates etched by Maria Cosway were published in three parts during 1802 under the title of the *Galerie du Louvre* [**252**], before the scheme was curtailed by the resumption of hostilities between France and Britain. In their unfinished state these little-known etchings remain a very important record of the distribution of pictures within the Grand Gallery of the Louvre, in what was then the world's greatest museum.

Maria Cosway gained support for the project by creating an album [**253**] of her etched and coloured copies of the Old Master paintings which she then showed to prospective subscribers in Paris. This album was titled in French and English, *Musée Central, Ou Galerie du Louvre à Paris* (and *Gallery of the Louvre at Paris*), for the benefit of subscribers from both sides of the Channel. The French side of the album was signed personally by all the leading members of the Bonaparte family including Napoleon (signed

OPPOSITE Plate 98   Maria Cosway after various Old Masters *Galerie du Louvre (Plate 1)* 1802 [**252**]

Bonaparte), his mother (*Bonaparte Mère*), his wife (*Josephine Bonaparte*), his brother (*Lucien Bonaparte*) and his uncle (*Fesch*). Further subscribers based in Paris were then listed, including Francesco Melzi, Vice-President of the Cisalpine Republic, the collector Giovanni Battista Sommariva and Madame Recamier.[2] At the other end of the album the list of British subscribers was headed by 'His Royal Highness The Prince of Wales' and 'His Royal Highness the Prince of Cumberland', and went on to include members of the nobility, politicians, artists and collectors including, 'The most Noble Marchioness Townshend', 'The R.H. Earl Spencer', 'The H. T. Erskine', 'The R.H. Earl Cowper', 'The R.H. Lord A. Hamilton', 'The H. M^rs. Damer', 'W.J.Ottley Esqre.', 'Dr. Burney', 'Sir Francis Burdett', 'M^r. Hope', 'John Soane Esqre.' and 'Lord Egremont'. The presentation album of Maria Cosway's copies after Old Master paintings in the Louvre is not only an invaluable record of the pictures that had arrived there, but it is also a testament to her tenacity as an artist and her extraordinary ability to build on her network of influential friends and supporters.

Maria Cosway noted her progress on the copying project in many of the entries in her diary from June 1802 to May 1803. She was also observed at work in the Louvre by a number of British visitors to Paris at this time during the cessation of hostilities between Britain and France known as the Peace of Amiens. Notable among these was the artist and diarist Joseph Farington. For instance on 20 September he noted a visit to the Louvre on a day it was so crowded that he visited a section of the Gallery not yet open to the public where he found Maria Cosway copying a painting by Titian there alone. Clearly her contacts with the Bonaparte family and the Director of the Louvre, Dominique Vivant-Denon, had given her unparalleled access to the expanding collection. However, Maria Cosway's progress on the project with Griffiths was far from smooth. In September 1803 Farington was informed by a Captain Barclay of the East India Service that Maria Cosway was working for Julius Griffiths on 'the publication of prints representing the arrangement of pictures' in the Louvre. Farington went on describe Griffiths as

> ... the Son of a Hop Merchant who lived in the Borough of Southwark, — that He was a Speculator, a Man of much adventure and had been Master Attendant at a Settlement in the East Indies: That He is about 35 Years of age and is speculating now in various ways in hopes of making a fortune: That He is a Man of abilities, but irregular.

In view of the later problems that Maria Cosway encountered with the completion of the Galerie du Louvre this description of her business partner is revealing. A few weeks later in October, on the day he was leaving Paris for London, Farington called on Maria Cosway to pick up a parcel he had agreed to take back to England. She revealed to him the origins and full history of the copying project, as well as the extent to which she was being exploited by Griffiths:

> She mentioned to me Her situation with Mr. Griffith abt. the publication of the Gallery & *said it was her own scheme and was approved by Mr. Cosway, and that she came to France for that purpose; but Her original Idea was to publish* etchings *of the most remarkable works only. It was in Paris that she communicated Her Scheme to Mr. Griffith who proposed to unite with her in it. A contract was formed and she undertook to supply a Plate of a Compartment one in every Month till the whole shd. be*

> completed: That He was to undertake the expenses of paper, — printing &c & that after all expenses were paid she was to have a third of the profits. Mr Griffith then announced himself Proprietor of the work & extended the Scheme so far by making letterpress descriptions as to render it very expensive. — She has now been twelve months and has not received a shilling on account of the work, & Mr Fitzhugh & Daniell who know Griffith in India have cautioned her against him. I told her He had been represented to me as a Speculator & in a way that caused me to think he should be upon her guard. She said Griffith had now no objection to her quitting the work which He then wd. have executed by better Artists than she was, but it was a favorite work of Mr Cosway's, and of her own, which she did not like to relinquish, though she had so compromising a prospect before her. She had spoken to Mr Erskine on the subject and He had recommended to Her to close Her engagement, but she said it was like advising a person to part with a favorite Child.

Maria Cosway then showed Farington sketches she had made after works by Van Dyck and Albano, which were larger than those which were being published. Her conversation with Farington ended by her asking him to communicate their discussion with her husband.[3]

Just over a week earlier Farington had recorded in his diary an extraordinary public breakfast hosted by Benjamin West at his hotel, at which Maria Cosway had been present immediately beforehand although she did not actually sit at the meal. Farington's diary is remarkable for the fact that he not only recorded the guests but, as was his custom, he also noted down the exact seating plan. Among the British visitors present were the actor John Kemble, while among the French guests were Vivant-Denon, as well as the French artists Houdon, Gerard, Vincent and Vigée-Lebrun. This occasion gives some idea of the artistic milieu in which Maria Cosway found herself in Paris during 1802.[4]

Further light is shed on her activity in Paris from her own diary. She was a frequent visitor to David's studio where she particularly admired his great equestrian portrait of *Napoleon crossing the Alps* now at Malmaison, of which she made a copy, now preserved at Lodi. Based in an apartment at the Hôtel Marigny near the Louvre, as she put it she 'had the opportunity of knowing intimately all the then reigning family'. Maria Cosway was regularly received by Napoleon's mother, Letizia Ramolino, known as 'Madame Mère'. However she was closest to Napoleon's uncle, Joseph Fesch, who was soon to be made Archbishop of Lyons and later Cardinal. He and Maria Cosway developed a particularly close friendship. Fesch presented her work at the Louvre to the First Consul. She in turn regularly showed British visitors around Fesch's great art collection while they were in Paris during the Peace of Amiens.[5]

The friendship between Cardinal Fesch and Maria Cosway led to his promising to pave the way for her 'to found a College for young Ladies' in Lyons, as she described this venture in her autobiographical letter of 1830. With his appointment as Archbishop, this became a reality and she ran an educational establishment there from 1803. However, the reality of this project was beset with difficulties, as is testified by her extensive correspondence with Fesch that was to continue until 1836.[6] Another result of their friendship was that while at Lyons in 1807 Maria Cosway corresponded with Antonio Canova over his making a *gesso* or plaster cast of the marble bust he was carving of Cardinal Fesch, the original of which is now in the Musée Fesch at Ajaccio in Corsica, while the primary plaster *modello* is in the Gipsoteca at Possagno [fig. 17]. Three letters from Maria Cosway to Canova concerning this commission survive in the archive at Bassano, while a letter from Canova to Maria Cosway is preserved at Lodi. It is not known whether the plaster bust of Fesch was ever delivered to Maria Cosway in Lyons or whether it exists to this day.[7] Eventually, due to political difficulties, the school closed down in 1809 and Maria Cosway left Lyons for Lombardy in the following year.

After the closure of the college in Lyons in 1809, Maria Cosway, who was unable to return to London because of the hostilities between France and Britain, looked to found another educational establishment. While staying with her sister Elisabetta Mola at Casalpusterlungo in Lombardy, Maria Cosway was approached by Francesco Melzi d'Eril (1753–1816), Vice-President of the Cisalpine Republic and later Duke of Lodi. The two had met in Paris in 1786, and had renewed their friendship during Maria Cosway's two-year sojourn in Paris after 1801. According to her later autobiographical letter, Melzi who 'was anxious to have in Italy an establishment the same as that formed at Lyons', bought a convent at Lodi – about twenty miles to the southeast of Milan – where she was enabled to set up another convent school for girls aged six to twelve. Melzi's role in the foundation of the Collegio in Lodi is commemorated by the presence there of a fine neo-classical marble bust [fig. 18] attributed to G. B. Comolli. The convent, which formerly housed the Padri Minimi, was attached to the church of Santa Maria delle Grazie, so that the institution was initially known as the Collegio delle Grazie [fig. 19]. Originally established under secular authority, in 1830 it came under the religious order of the Dame Inglesi. Maria wrote that she was 'consolidating the establishment which has the reputation of being the first in Italy', and that she was 'following a vocation' she 'always had, occupied in a good work to the benefit of young ladies'. The prestigious nature of the Collegio attracted visits from the Austrian Emperor Francis I in 1816, the year of Melzi's death, and also from the Empress Maria Carolina in 1825,

with the consequence that Maria Cosway was made a Baroness [256] by Francis I in 1834.[8]

The Collegio was held in particularly high regard throughout Lombardy, with many of the daughters of the social élite being educated there. The most famous pupil was Vittoria, a younger daughter of the great writer, *Alessandro Manzoni* [227], and who was taught there from 1831 to 1835. Her departure from the Collegio was commemorated in the commissioning of a large oil painting by the Brescian painter, Gabriele Rottini, which represented *Baroness Maria Hadfield Cosway listening to Vittoria Manzoni* [228]. Vittoria's attendance at the Collegio was likely to have been recommended by Alessandro Manzoni's mother, *Giulia Beccaria* [226], who was a friend of Maria Cosway. They had met in Paris during the Peace of Amiens, when Maria had portrayed Beccaria in a lively oil sketch.

Despite the educational demands in Lodi, Maria returned to London in 1815 and for a longer visit from 1817 to 1822 to nurse her husband through the delusions and paralytic strokes he suffered in the last years of his life. Despite his last, and very fine, portrait drawings being dated to 1819, for the last two years of his life he seems to have been virtually incapacitated. Maria's main correspondent at this period was Annette Prudon (1794–1867), who is almost certainly the sister depicted in the centre of Rottini's painting [228]. She was a loyal teaching assistant to Maria Cosway, travelling with her from Lyons to Lodi. She later ran the Collegio in Maria's absence, and may have joined Maria in Britain after Richard Cosway's death. Before returning to Italy in 1822, Maria toured Scotland, and a number of travel guides survive at the Fondazione Cosway in Lodi, including those for the cities of Edinburgh and Glasgow.[9]

It is clear that Maria's long periods away from her husband were caused by the breakdown of their relationship. This may have been in large part due to their increasingly divergent religious interests, as well as to the pressures exacerbated by the events surrounding their separations. In the 1780s Richard had shown considerable enthusiasm for the cult of Swedenborgianism, as well as of Animal

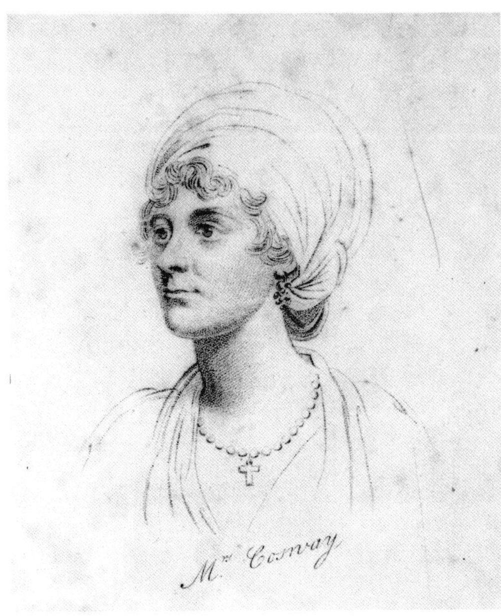

Fig. 16 *Mrs Cosway*, c.1800, by an unknown engraver (Greater London Record Office)

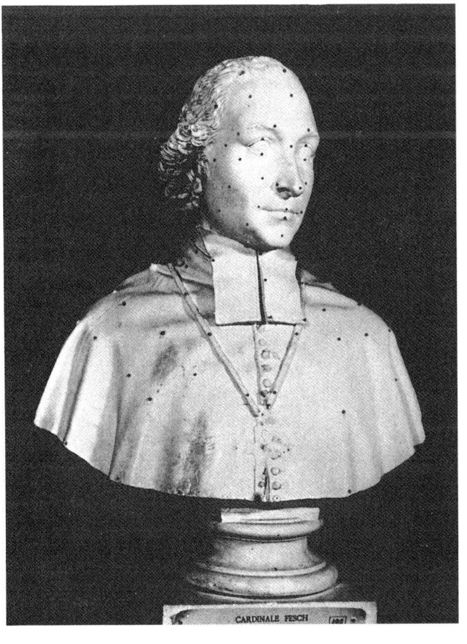

Fig. 17 *Cardinal Joseph Fesch*, 1807, by Antonio Canova (Gipsoteca, Possagno)

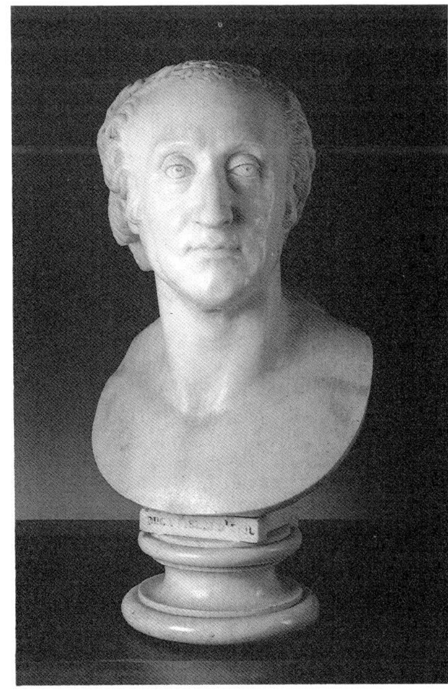

Fig. 18 *Francesco Melzi d'Eril, Duke of Lodi*, c.1802-3, attributed to Giovanni Battista Comolli (Fondazione Cosway, Lodi)

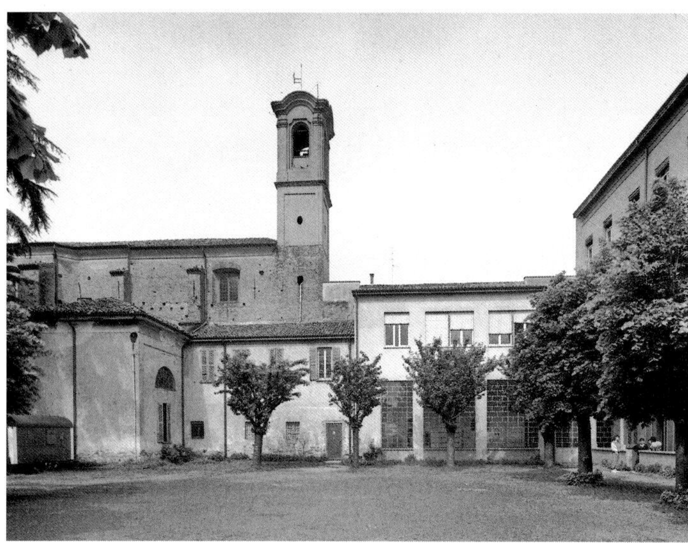

Fig. 19 Santa Maria delle Grazie and the Collegio delle
Dame Inglesi, Lodi

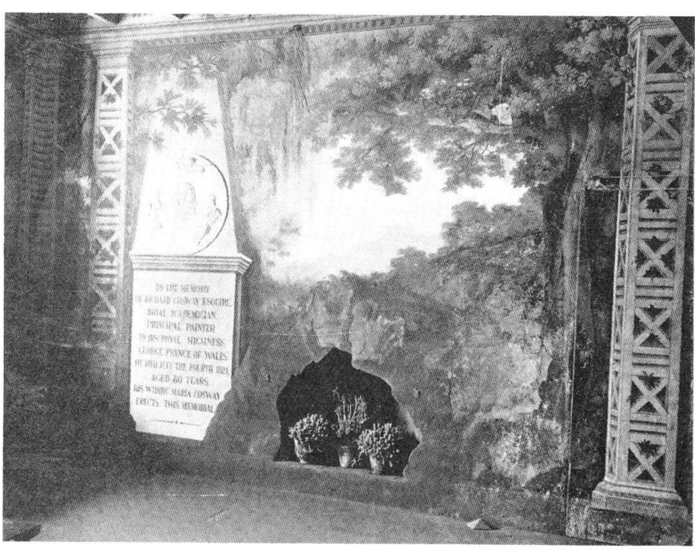

Fig. 20 Memorial to Richard Cosway by Sir Richard Westmacott in the
dining room, Collegio delle Dame Inglesi, Lodi, *c.*1830

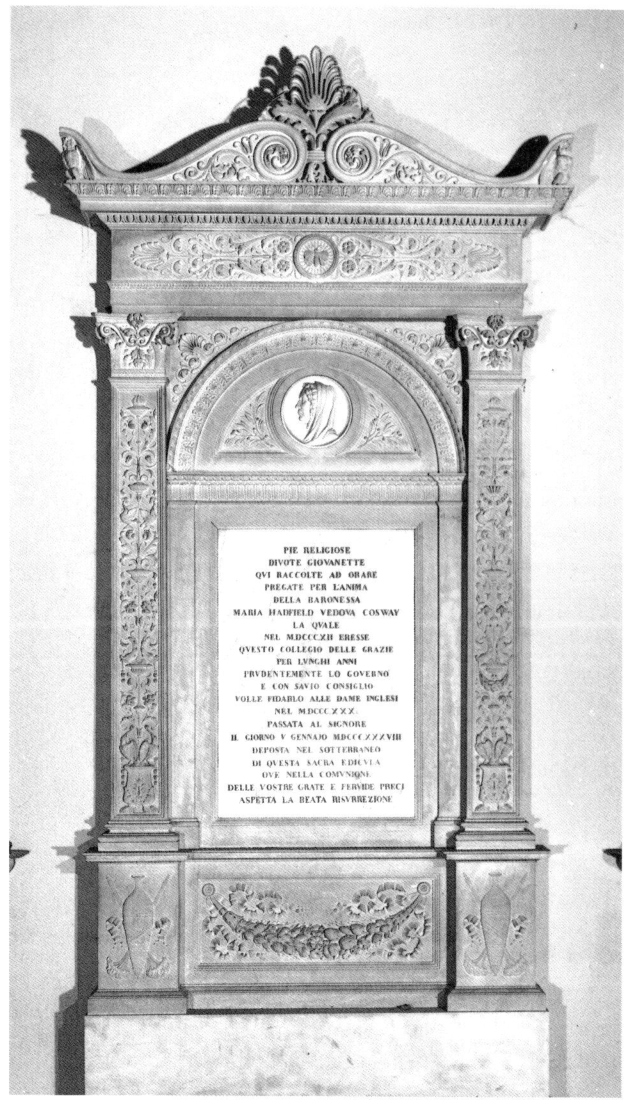

Fig. 21 Tomb of Baroness Maria Hadfield Cosway, 1838
(Santa Maria delle Grazie, Lodi)

Magnetism, the fashionable form of healing, to which Maria also subscribed. However, from the time of Louisa's death in 1796, Richard began to pursue his esoteric and mystical interests more vigorously, while Maria's Catholicism became even more marked. The amateur artist George Cumberland, who was a friend of William Blake and hostile to the Cosways, noted in his Commonplace Book at this time that: 'As to Cosway he is everything or any thing that suits his interest: An alchemist, a Pimp, a Phisionomist, a Christian, an illuminati, a Magician &c &c by turns – he magnetises with Mesmer, strokes with Parkins, conjures with Loutherburge, or Col. Rainsford and talkes baudy with anybody – but he gets business and hurts no one but himself that I can hear of'.

The poet Ugo Foscolo then in London, who had been given a letter of introduction to Maria by Isabella Teotochi Albrizzi in 1817, described Richard Cosway in a letter written in the following year to Louisa of Stolberg, the Countess of Albany. Foscolo compared him with the engraver William Sharp, who was a regular visitor to Stratford Place at that time, as well as a fellow mystic and great friend of Richard Cosway, whom he described as:[10]

> ... un pittore più bizzarro (e gli è tutto dire)
> di esso Sharp, e più fantastico, e più
> profetico, però sono amicissimi, e fanno tra
> loro spesso certe Astrologie e Teologie, e
> predizioni di finimondi.[11]
> [... a painter more bizarre – and everyone
> says the same – than even Sharp, and more
> fantastic, and more prophetic; however they
> are great friends, and are deeply wrapped
> up in Astrology, Theology and predicting
> the end of the world.]

Before and after her husband's death in 1821 Maria Cosway arranged – through the auctioneer George Stanley, and with the help of Thomas Lawrence, John Soane and the antiquarian Francis Douce – a series of five sales of her husband's extensive and curious collections: Old Master pictures, prints and drawings, objects of taste and *virtù*, as well as the extensive library. The auctions raised about £12,000, at least a third of which Maria used to endow the Collegio.[12]

Maria's care for her husband in his last years, and then after his death, the preservation of his memory, were carried out with great sincerity. She made the arrangements for a magnificent funeral, for which the bill of £183 still survives, and which most of the senior Royal Academicians attended. She commissioned a memorial from Westmacott [fig. 20] – the design of which was engraved [**259**] – for St Marylebone New Church, where he was buried. Maria also replicated the monument in a memorial at the Collegio in Lodi, of which only the original

plaster portrait medallion survives, having been given to her by the sculptor. The relief is comprised of a portrait bust of Richard Cosway surrounded by three putti. They are described in the accompanying verses, composed by Maria's brother-in-law, William Coombe, the creator of *Dr Syntax*:

> *Art weeps, taste mourns, and genius drops the tear*
> *o'er him so long they lov'd, who slumbers here.*
> *While colours last, and time allows to give*
> *The all-resembling grace, his name shall live.*[13]

Maria also attempted, unsuccessfully, to leave in Britain the great collection of Richard Cosway's own finished subject drawings, first sending them to King George IV at Brighton. She later organised an exhibition of them at George Stanley's salerooms in Bond Street during April 1822. Later Sir Thomas Lawrence offered to purchase them, but Maria found his offer unsatisfactory.[14] Taking the collection of her late husband's drawings back to Italy in 1823, she promoted them tirelessly, having fifteen of the compositions engraved in Florence by Paolo Lasinio. She also transferred a number of the Old Master paintings to Lodi, which had originally been collected by Richard, including works by Richard Wilson, de Loutherbourg and one of Hercules Seghers' most important landscapes, which had been owned and retouched by Rembrandt. These, together with a few of his paintings and some of her own, were seen by visitors to Lodi and the Collegio. With many of the books that she had collected throughout her life – as well as a few of Richard's – she established the core of the Collegio's library.[15]

Maria Cosway died at Lodi on 5 January 1838, and she was widely mourned in Lombardy.[16] In a final portrait Gabriele Rottini drew the Baroness on her deathbed, holding a crucifix, an image which was then reproduced as a lithograph [**260**]. She was buried in the south transept of the church of Santa Marie delle Grazie, and a monument in the Renaissance style was erected there to her memory [fig. 21]. A monument with a marble bust, based on the late portraits by Rottini, was commissioned and installed in the Collegio [fig. 22]. Meanwhile in Britain Maria Cosway had been virtually forgotten, having outlived almost all of her friends, correspondents and even both her executors, Sir John Soane and Prince Hoare. Two years after her death a protracted and expensive lawsuit was fought by the Collegio in the London courts, to secure Maria Cosway's endowment from a later unscrupulous executor of her will.[17] The Collegio continued as a girls' school – under various administrations – until its final closure in 1978. However, to this day the buildings are still used for a range of educational purposes.[18]

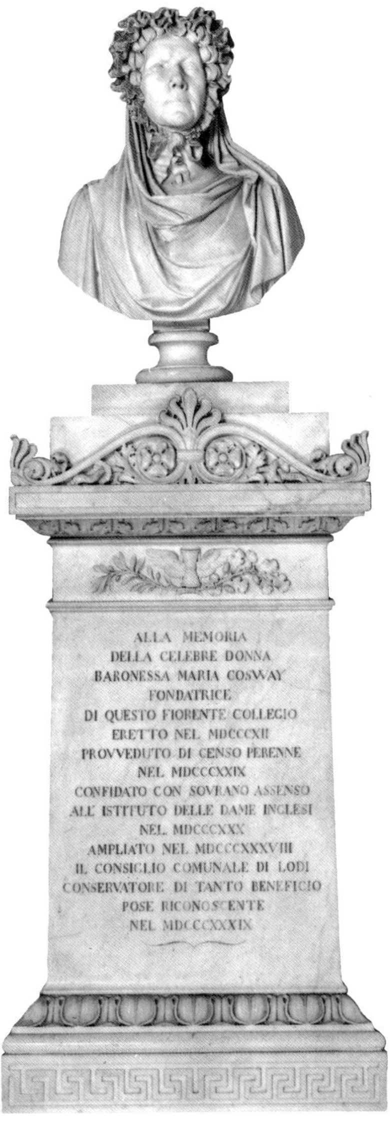

Fig. 22 Monument to Baroness Maria Hadfield Cosway, 1839
(Fondazione Cosway, Lodi)

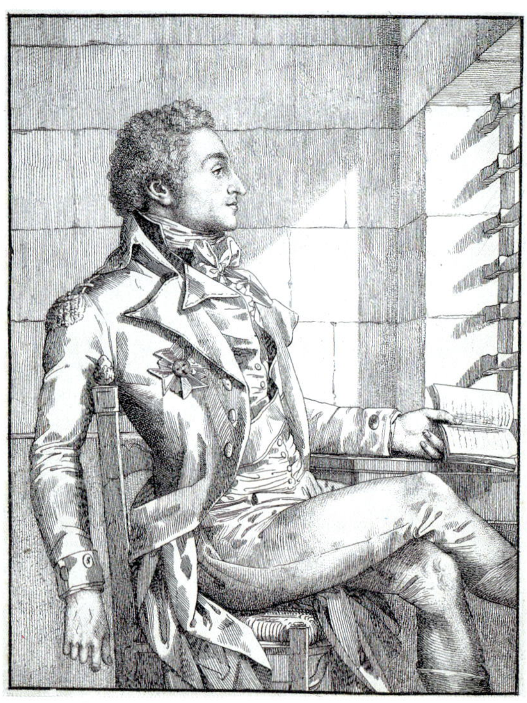

Plate 99   Maria Cosway after Philippe-Auguste
Hennequin *Sir Sidney Smith* 1797 [**234**]

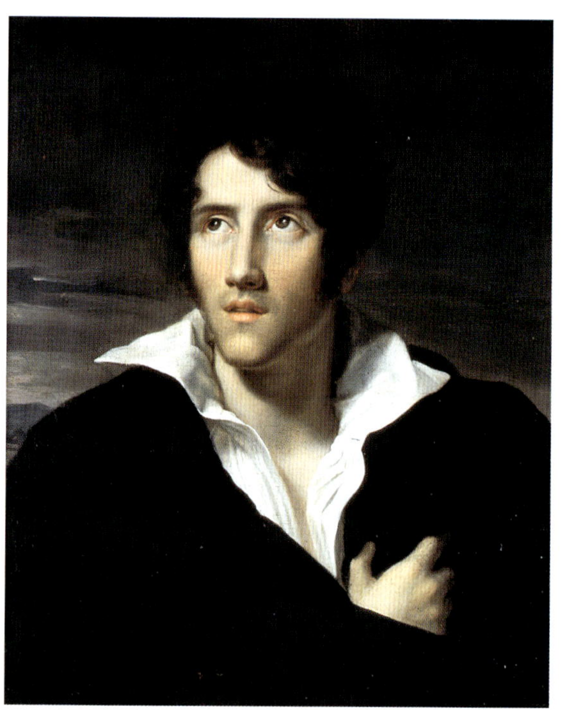

Plate 100   Unknown Artist
*Alessandro Manzoni c.*1805 [**227**]

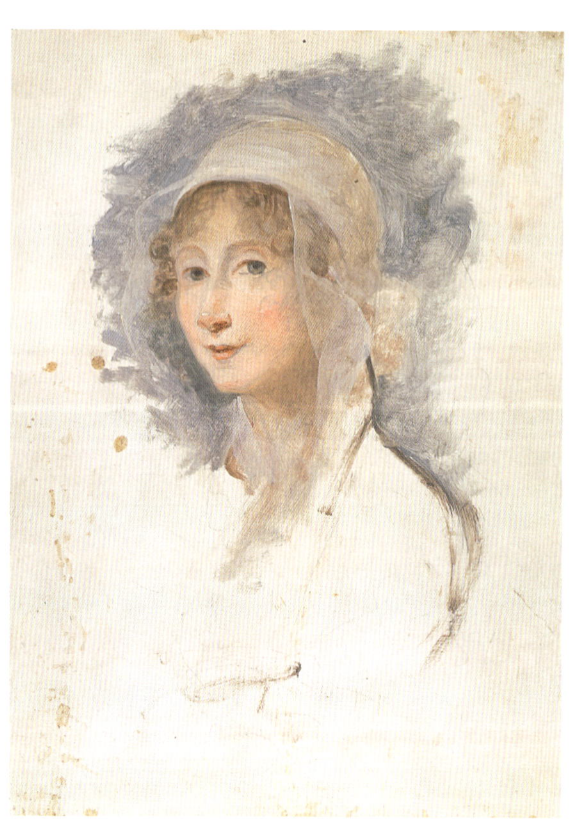

Plate 101   Maria Cosway
*Giulia Beccaria c.*1802–3 [**226**]

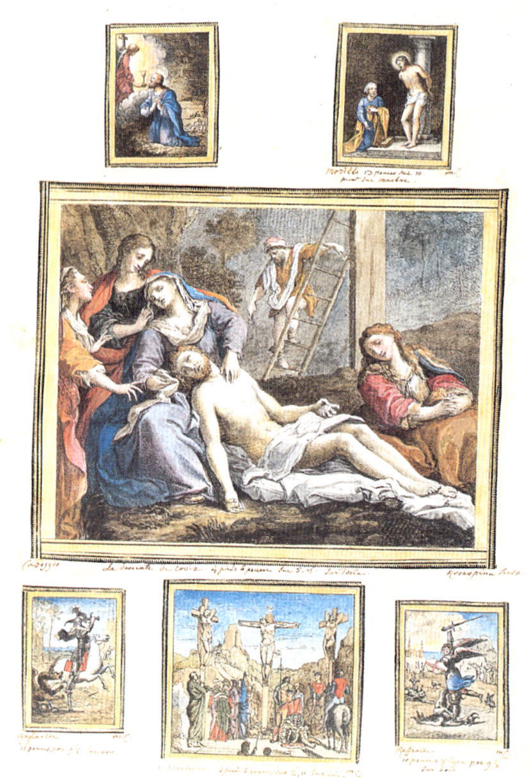

Plate 102   Maria Cosway after various Old Masters
*Musée Central, Ou Galerie du Louvre à Paris
(3rd illuminated fol.)* 1801–3 [**253**]

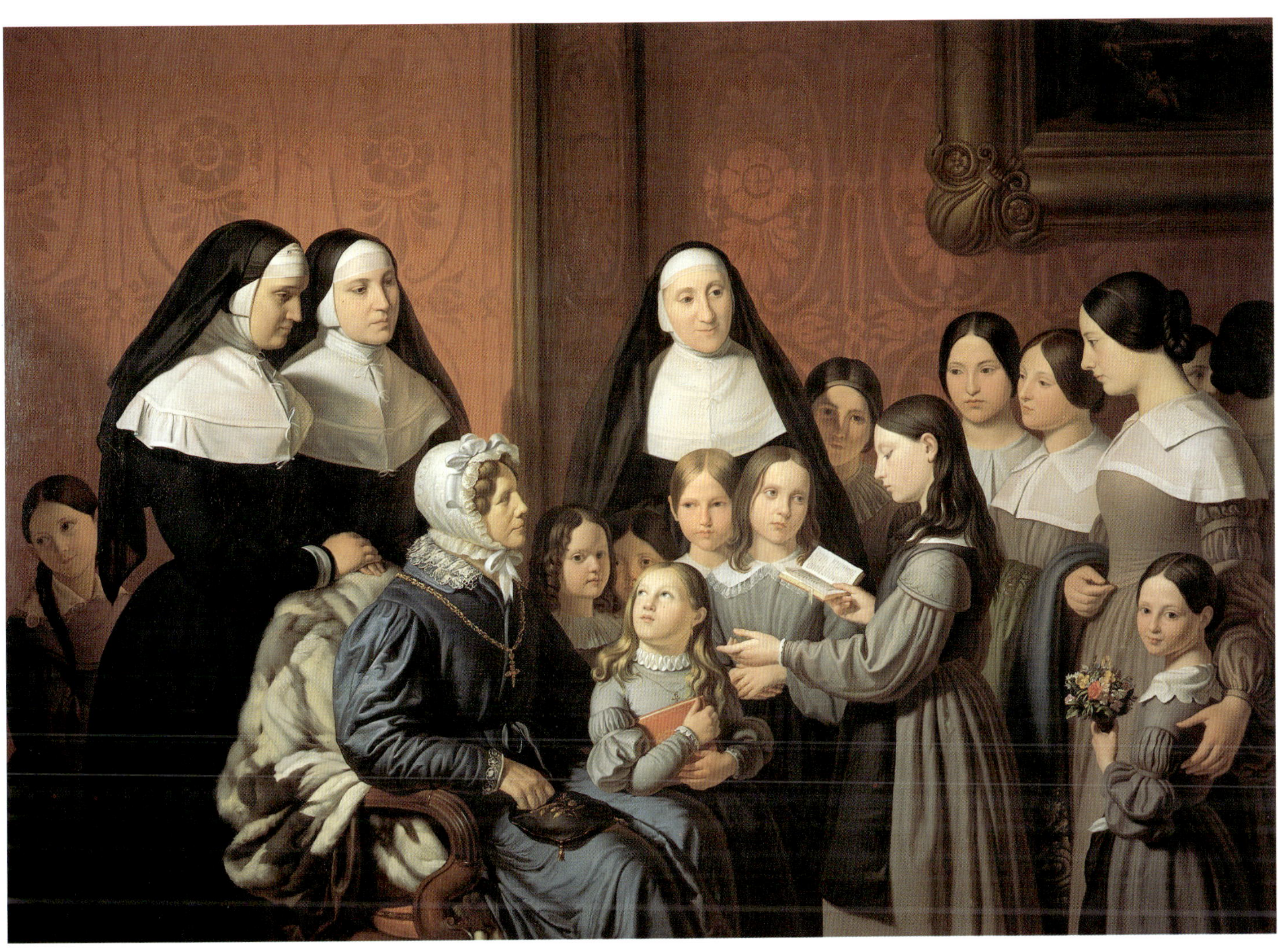

Plate 103 Gabriele Rottini *Baroness Maria Hadfield Cosway listening to Vittoria Manzoni c.*1835 **[228]**

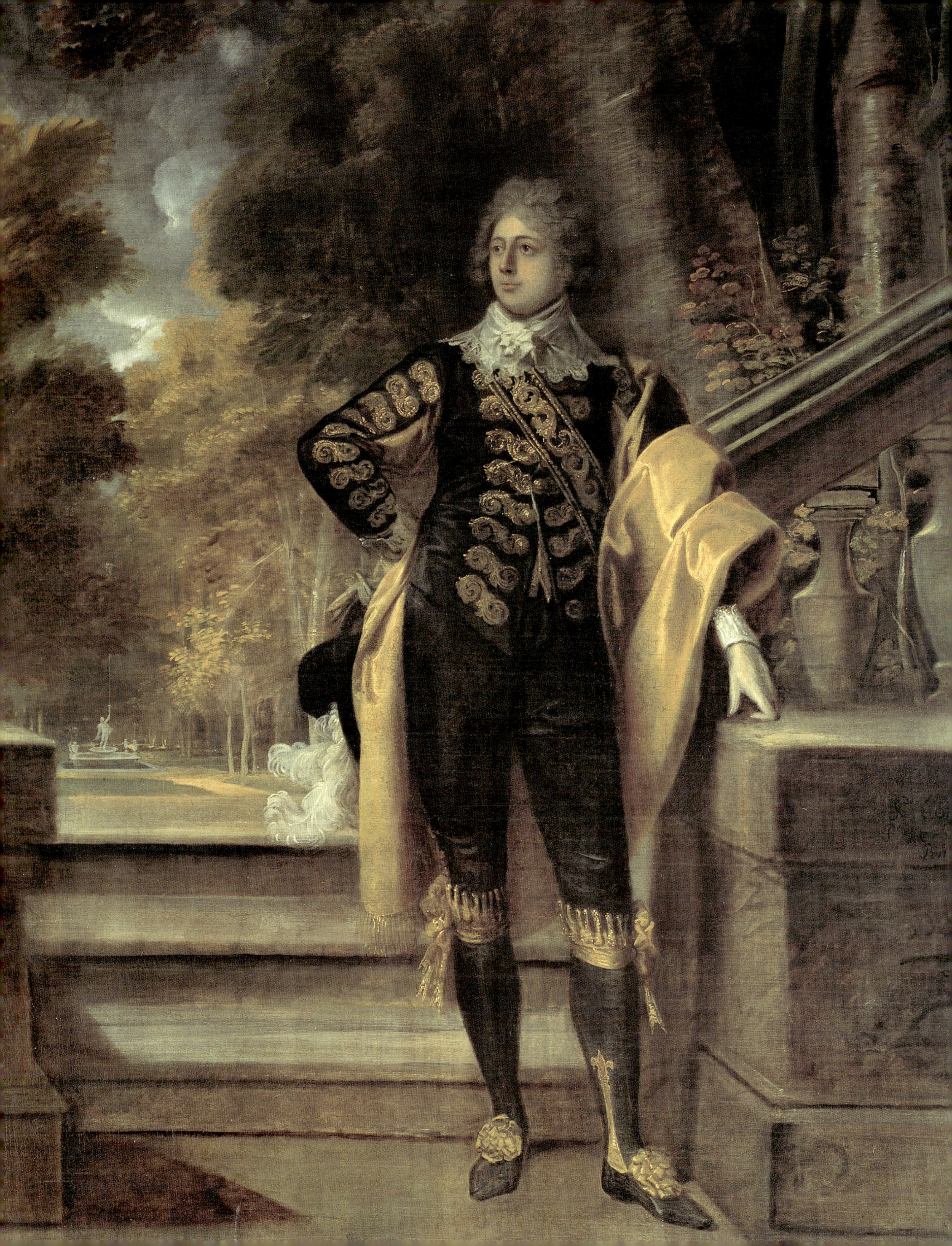

ROY PORTER

THE COSWAYS' LONDON

$\mathscr{T}$HE London in which the Devon-born Richard Cosway settled in 1754 – and in which Maria Hadfield arrived in 1779 – was the largest city in Europe, having recently overtaken Paris. Its population of over three quarters of a million probably also made it the most populous city in the world, although Tokyo (Edo) may have been bigger.[1]

Not merely Europe's largest city, London was becoming one of its most attractive. Torrents of tourists from the Old and New Worlds alike flooded in to see the sights and enjoy the diversions of the town. They found it vibrant, busy, brilliant, rather as New York was to seem to Europeans in the 1920s. Visiting celebrities and writers, from Voltaire onwards, loved the exhilarating whirl of life. Sophie von la Roche, the first German woman novelist of note, could hardly contain herself on first seeing London: it meant 'more to me than Paris and France'. She was a starry-eyed Anglomaniac, but others too were thrilled. 'At last I am in my beloved London, for which I have longed and schemed and pined', the German *philosophe*, Georg Christoph Lichtenberg, told a Göttingen friend in 1775. 'London is a giant', remarked the awe-struck Swiss-American, Jean-Louis Simond, in the Regency era.[2] London seemed supremely animated, ablaze with events and entertainments. Samuel Johnson, who had arrived from Lichfield in the 1730s, believed the full tide of human existence flowed at Charing Cross; but others – especially those somewhat younger, like Richard Cosway – would have chosen Piccadilly.[3]

For the centre of smart London was gravitating to the West End. The capital's history had long been a tale of two cities, the City itself, centred on the old Roman walled town, for centuries the focus of trade and manufactures; and Westminster, where sat King, Court and Parliament. The post-Fire age additionally brought the sprawl of the East End, stretching from Whitechapel east along the River through Wapping and Shadwell to Limehouse, teeming with sailors and labourers employed in and around the port. And, above all, it saw expansion westwards, with new stately houses – Buckingham House in Pall Mall, Arlington House in St. James's, Clarendon House in Piccadilly, erected by Lord Chancellor Clarendon – noble terraces and leafy squares, the exquisite haunts of patricians and plutocrats requiring an eligible urban residence. The West End was ideal for entertainments and entertaining, close to Parliament, to City mortgage brokers and to lawyers in the Inns of Court, and studded with stylish new shopping malls like Burlington Arcade.

It was thus no accident that Richard Cosway – who, as an artist, needed to be close to his patrons and, as a would-be man of mode, had in any case a yearning to shine in society – took up residence in 1768 at 4 Berkeley Street off Piccadilly, and then from 1784 at Schomberg House in Pall Mall, and finally (from 1791 virtually until his death in 1821) in Stratford Place, just off Oxford Street.

Stretching north from the park, and embracing Pall Mall (named after *palla a maglio*, a cross between croquet and bowls), St James's became the ultra fashionable quarter under Charles II: 'The inhabitants of St. James's', judged the *Spectator*, 'notwithstanding they live under the same laws and speak the same language, are a distinct people from those of Cheapside'. St James's was developed by Henry Jermyn, Earl of St Albans, who hatched up the idea of a square on the far side of Pall Mall. Speculators put up elegant buildings, and the whole development was sanctified by Wren's church, St James's Piccadilly, at the north end of York Street.

St James's Square became the model for the West End as a first-rate residential quarter, cramming much into compact spaces without sacrifice of tone. Development followed beyond, through Piccadilly and into Mayfair, where three great squares arose. First came Hanover Square – a topical name – laid out in 1713 with houses leased by prominent Whigs. Blessed by the fashionable church of St George, Hanover Square houses were spacious and inhabited by 'persons of distinction'. The Hanover Square Rooms were long famed for their concerts, at which J.C. Bach, Haydn, Paganini and Liszt all performed.

Berkeley Square then emerged in the 1730s, carved out of fields beyond the garden of Berkeley (later Devonshire) House, Piccadilly. Together with the streets to the west – Hill Street, Chesterfield Street, Charles Street, Brook Street (where Handel wrote the *Messiah*), John Street (now Chesterfield Hill) and Farm Street – Berkeley Square became the choice of the *beau monde*. Cosway could hardly have picked a more stylish location than Berkeley Street.

That development was followed by Grosvenor Square just to the west. Six acres in extent, it was London's largest square, its houses designed and decorated by Adam, Chambers, Soane, Wyatville, James and Samuel Wyatt and other leading architects. 'Oh, how I long to be transported to the dear regions of Grosvenor-Square!', sighed Miss Sterling in George Colman's popular comedy, *The Clandestine Marriage* (1766), 'far, far from the dull districts of Aldersgate, Cheap, Candlewick, and Farringdon Without and Within.'

Once Mayfair was built over, the area north of Oxford Street – Marylebone – was ripe for development. Cavendish Square and its surroundings emerged from the 1730s; and from the 1760s new blocks sprang up to its west. Henry William Portman developed two hundred acres of meadow descended from a Tudor ancestor:

OPPOSITE Plate 104 *William, 3rd Viscount Courtenay* 1791 [**93** detail]

Portman Square owed its popularity to Robert Adam, Wyatt and 'Athenian' Stuart, the architect of Montagu House.

'I believe the parallelogram between Oxford-street, Piccadilly, Regent-street, and Hyde Park encloses more intelligence and human ability, to say nothing of wealth and beauty,' bragged Sydney Smith, 'than the world has ever collected in such a space before.'[4] Cosway surely agreed, as did his contemporary and near neighbour, Edward Gibbon. The historian loved town: 'The metropolis affords many amusements which are open to all,' he wrote. 'It is itself an astonishing and perpetual spectacle to the curious eye; and each taste, each sense may be gratified by the variety of objects that will occur in the long circuit of a morning walk.' Gibbon rented a bachelor residence in Bentinck Street, and purred over his good fortune:

> *I had now attained the solid comforts of life, a convenient well-furnished house, a domestic table, half a dozen chosen servants, my own carriage, and all those decent luxuries whose value is the more sensibly felt the longer they are enjoyed. ... To a lover of books the shops and sales in London present irresistible temptations ... By my own choice I passed in town the greatest part of the year.*[5]

There, installed near Cavendish Square together with a lapdog and a parrot, he began the *Decline and Fall of the Roman Empire*.

These Georgian developments were crowned by the vision of Richard Cosway's greatest patron, the Prince of Wales, and his ingenious architect, John Nash. Dreaming of bestowing new grandeur and order upon the West End, the Prince and Nash visualised one long majestic south-north street, leading up from Carlton House (off Pall Mall) through Lower Regent Street, to a Quadrant (only much later called Piccadilly Circus), and then along Regent Street and into Portland Place to the Park. The development created a frontier between crowded and confused Soho on the east, and the elegant properties of Mayfair and Marylebone. Portland Place and Regent Street thus screened off the fashionable West End. 'No family of ton can breathe eastward of Berkeley Square', remarked the *World* magazine in 1787: it was a sentiment to which the Cosways might have added: *Amen.*[6]

Many of Europe's cities of course developed smart and superior quarters under the *ancien régime*. Nancy, Berlin, St Petersburg, Turin all sprouted great avenues, monumental architecture, views and vistas. But London was rather special. Elsewhere urban projects were typically launched by princes aiming to create a splendour that mirrored their power or pretensions; but in the West End developments were largely private speculations jointly planned by aristocratic landowners, property developers and builders, with a view to short-term profit and sound investments. It is thus no surprise that in the Cosways' West End the elegant dwellings of the rich abutted onto centres of chic enjoyment, where commerce and the Quality could intermingle.

Superior shops sprang up. Thomas Chippendale opened his workshops in Long Acre about 1745, later moving to St Martin's Lane. Piccadilly saw the establishment of such famous shops as Lock's the hatters, Hawkes the gentleman's outfitters, Asprey's, selling dressing cases and silverware, Fortnum and Mason's and Jackson's for provisions, Hatchard's the booksellers, and even

Hamley's toyshop, to say nothing of Christie's, the auctioneers. Recognising '*Fashion* is infinitely superior to *merit*', Josiah Wedgwood opened a showroom in 1765 in Grosvenor Square, aimed at the nobility and gentry. Dinner services were set out on tables 'as if to *do the needful* for the Ladys in the neatest, genteelest and best method'.[7]

The great London theatres had been in full swing since the Restoration. Stars like David Garrick, James Quin, Peg Woffington, and later Sarah Siddons, John Philip Kemble and Edmund Kean, gave the stage a new *éclat*. The capital possessed a thriving musical life, led by composers and impresarios like Handel, Heidegger, and, later, Salomon. Carlisle House in Soho Square was a leading musical venue, where Mrs Cornelys ran operatic concerts and masquerades – while just a warm summer evening's drive away down by the river were Vauxhall and Ranelagh. The British Museum was founded and picture galleries set up. Founded in 1768, the Royal Academy staged art exhibitions, first in Pall Mall and later at Somerset House. Madame Tussaud arrived from Paris in 1802.

In the West End cultural world, the ambience was mixed. The Cosways doubtless delighted in the capital's refined sophistication. There were dozens of clubs and societies where connoisseurs, savants, and gentlemen of taste could meet for recreation: White's, Boodle's and Crockford's, all in St James's Street, and Almack's in Pall Mall were aristocratic, the Society of Dilettanti and the Society of Antiquaries more art-orientated. Richard Cosway was active in the Society of Arts, sited in an Adam building off the Strand, a body established to encourage the interplay of art, commerce, technology, enterprise and aesthetics. Prizes from the Society helped launch his London career. In 1770 he was elected an associate of the Royal Academy, with full membership coming in the following year.[8]

But London's leisure world also had its racier side, especially conspicuous in a great swathe running from Soho and Leicester Square – where Hogarth and Reynolds lived – down to the Strand and Covent Garden. You could see Robert Powell's puppet shows in the Little Piazza, Covent Garden, or the 'wonderful tall Essex woman' at the Rummer in Three King's Court, Fleet Street, who was 'seven feet high'; while in Panton Street, the quack doctor, James Graham, was giving his celebrated displays of medicinal mud bathing, aided by a bevy of belles. In 1779 Robert Barker built his Panorama in Leicester Place, and nearby, in Lisle Street, Philippe-Jacques de Loutherbourg opened his Eidophusikon, or magic lantern. All formed part of a great archipelago of shows, spectacles and exhibitions.[9]

Richard Cosway had various connections with this more *risqué* side of things. The quack doctor, James Graham, had been the previous occupant of Schomberg House. Graham's Temple of Health, sited in the fashionable Adelphi Building on the Strand, offered lectures on and demonstrations of sexual rejuvenation, including a Celestial Bed, stuffed with stallion hair and wired up to electromagnets, which was hired out for fifty guineas a night to barren couples; Graham guaranteed that the use of the bed would ensure instant conception.[10]

Cosway also fell in with Philippe-Jacques de Loutherbourg. Not only an eminent scene-painter and theatrical artist, Loutherbourg was also an early pioneer of Mesmerism. Both Cosways indulged in the vogue for hypnotism, subscribing to the lectures of John B. de Mainauduc, a pupil of Dr Mesmer, the founder of 'animal magnetism'. A West Ender of fashion could thus have one foot in the most superior and select culture, while also dabbling in something more *outré* – in much the same way as Regency bucks amused themselves by occasionally slumming in the dives of Wapping.[11]

It was, in short, a fine time to be a fellow like Richard Cosway hoping to earn fame and fortune out of culture in the capital. There was a swelling community of cultural performers – writers, artists, critics, dealers – with the skill and business sense to promote fruitful interchange between wealth, art and fashion, commerce and culture – everything denounced by William Blake as a prostitution of genius. Handel, Hogarth, Reynolds, Garrick, Johnson, Gibbon and scores of lesser lights found London offered an invigorating cocktail of smart society, intellectual and artistic stimulus, and financial prospects. That was the London of Richard and Maria Cosway.

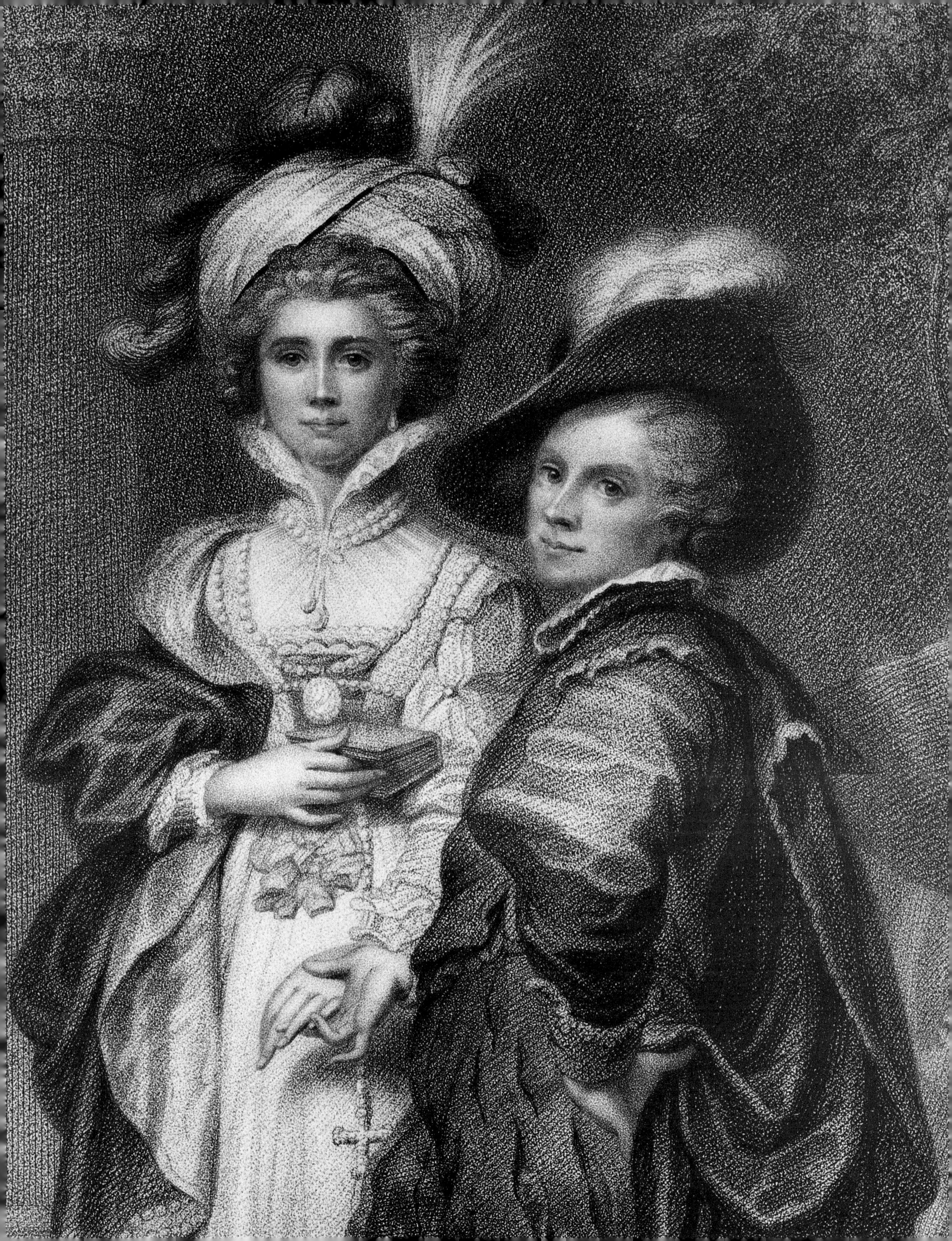

AILEEN RIBEIRO

PORTRAYING THE FASHION, ROMANCING THE PAST: DRESS AND THE COSWAYS

$\mathcal{D}$RESSED *like a peacock we can see him strutting it with the best in an age of artificiality and foppery. Ah! but those were grand times for portrait painters! Gallants in velvet coats edged with gold and silver lace! Beautiful women in dainty frills and laces, in picture hats over delicately curled and powdered tresses. Who in this year of*

grace wishes to paint a cropped head under a pudding basin? Cosway was not so far wrong in his estimate of his own genius, for in despite of flagrant faults of drawing, no other painter of his day recorded the spirit of that frivolous age with equal fascination and charm.[1]

Published in 1926, *The Art of the Miniature Painter*, with its somewhat breathless prose, reveals the perennial human tendency to see the past through rose-coloured spectacles, and in particular women's costume of the late eighteenth century, which is compared to the disadvantage of the often disturbingly androgynous female figure of the Twenties, with her short cropped hair and severe cloche hat. Equally so, the evolution of modern society and the development of the machine age caused some commentators to express regret (and at the same time reveal a slightly censorious note) when they looked back to what they saw as a 'frivolous age' in which men and women 'strutted' in 'peacock' finery, enjoying a raffish and elegant lifestyle. And it has to be admitted that the lives and careers of Richard and Maria Cosway lend credence to this widely held belief, popularised by romantic novels and movies, that the 'Regency' period (extended to stretch from the 1780s to the official Regency of 1811–20) was a time of stylish sophistication in costume and leisure activities, combined with a delight in theatrical role-playing.

Richard Cosway's early miniature *Self-portrait* [**18**] of *c*.1770 is an essay in sartorial luxury, the artist wearing a high powdered wig, and displaying fine French needle lace and an ermine lining to his coat. In Zoffany's famous painting of *The Academicians of the Royal Academy* of 1771–2, Cosway is conspicuous by his stylish clothes – a green suit, gold-coloured waistcoat, a gold-braided hat (*chapeau bras*) under his arm – and his somewhat affected pose, self-consciously on display, as though presenting his best side to the 'camera'; he is the only person, other than Reynolds, to wear a sword, an inappropriately grand and pretentious touch for a young artist who had only recently established his reputation.[2]

Cosway's love of fashion and his propensity for self-advertisement set him apart from his fellow-artists, and made him the target of amused and sometimes vitriolic comment. In J. T. Smith's affectionate memoir, *Nollekens and his Times*, there is a description of Cosway's appearance: 'full-dressed in his sword and bag; with a small three-cornered hat on the top of his powdered toupee, and a mulberry silk-coat profusely embroidered with scarlet strawberries'.[3] This striking and rather foppish image became increasingly out of step with the general trend of men's clothing in the late eighteenth century towards greater sobriety in fabric and style.

The 1770s was the decade of the macaronies, young men who adopted extravagant and brightly coloured fashions and towering wigs, on which perched tiny hats; they carried to excess every dissipation, and were known for their affected and effeminate manners. According to *The Lady's Magazine* (1773), the macaroni was

… a thing that has some resemblance to a man, as it is in appearance like a man. The difference between the two is precisely this. A man applies himself to the serious in life; the Macaroni to that which is trifling. The man is grace, the Macaroni full of levity. The former cultivates his mind, the latter studies to adorn his body; … [he] wears his hair powdered and curled, and never goes out till he has formed his countenance according to the rules of the latest fashions … He has a fine leg, and a very pretty foot … a very handsome watch set with precious stones, a snuff-box of the highest taste, and some other glittering trifles …[4]

This description might be the caption for the caricature of Cosway in *The macaroni painter or Billy Dimple sitting for his picture* [**27**] of 1772, where the artist has a 'feminine' appearance, like an actress *en travesti*. Although Cosway was reputed to have hated such caricatures, even if they might have been good for business, he seems to have seen himself as a 'pretty' man. The finely drawn *Self-portrait* [**103**] of *c*. 1800, shows an idealised youthful image, slightly soulful, with short delicately curling hair *à l'antique*, and a lightly sketched-in coat. At about the same time we can see a more dispassionate portrait of Cosway [**104**] drawn in 1793 by George Dance, which depicts a middle-aged man – still showing his best profile – in a smart, high-collared, double-breasted frock coat, a fashionably informal style of the end of the century.

In 1781 Cosway married Maria Hadfield at the fashionable church of St George's, Hanover Square. An accomplished artist and beauty, she is shown in her *Self-portrait* [**231**] of 1787 in a simple long-sleeved dress with a frilled collar, a turban on her fashionably curled *coiffure*; she has the elegant ease and direct glance of Vigée-Lebrun's self-portraits of the same period. Whatever the complex relationship of the Cosways, they were both aware of the importance of promoting their careers through the entertainment of patrons, and their influential salon was a popular meeting place for fashionable society, as well as for artists and collectors. Richard Cosway was a noted collector of both the fine and decorative arts, and his house – which Hazlitt called 'a fairy palace' – was the theatrical backdrop to his art and life.[5]

Any society artist has to excel in recording the likeness of his sitters as well as the details of clothing and accessories (though this is less important, obviously, in bust-length miniatures), and at the same time has to provide subtle flattery. *The World* in 1789 remarked how Cosway's 'Miniatures and small-lengths multiply as they should do – with as much exactness as Liotard – more grace than Rosalba'.[6] In the full-length portraits, although sometimes less successful artistically (Cosway sometimes had trouble with the proportions of the body), the artist could indulge his interest in fashion.[7] In his portrait of *Mrs Draper* [6] of *c.*1775, the details of the dress and accessories overpower the character of the sitter. Less Sterne's 'immortal Eliza' than a fashion doll, she sits in Cosway's sitter's chair [216] in a silk taffeta gown with a quilted skirt, her costume embellished with lace which trims her scarf, neck-kerchief, sleeve ruffles, apron and even the satin cloak, which hangs over a fire-screen, alongside a ribboned hat. In a less formal vein, Cosway's *Marianne Dorothy Harland, later Mrs Dalrymple* [7] of 1779, is shown in her dressing room in a simple morning costume, which is covered by a powdering mantle – the powder and puff lie on the dressing table. Playing the harp was a fashionable feminine pursuit in the late eighteenth century (Maria Cosway herself was a noted harp player),[8] and Cosway may have known of Gautier d'Agoty's gouache, *Marie-Antoinette dans sa chambre à Versailles* (Versailles), where the queen at her *lever*, wearing a simple morning toilette under a white powdering mantle, plays the harp in a pose like that of Mrs Dalrymple.

Some of Cosway's most successful portraits of women are those depicting the informal styles of dress coming into vogue in the 1780s, notably the simple chemise gown, which in its most basic form was a loose muslin shift (often white) with a drawstring neckline or frilled collar, and tied at the waist with a sash. It was a comfortable and flattering dress, suitable for Arcadian pastimes, and popular with Marie-Antoinette and her ladies. It was taken up in England by the leader of fashion, Georgiana, Duchess of Devonshire, who attended a concert in 1784 'in one of the muslin chemises with fine lace that the Queen of France gave me'.[9] Two years later Cosway painted a miniature of the duchess [76] in a chemise dress with a ruffled collar, and a large linen cap frilled round the edge, a charmingly informal, even pasto-

ral image. An element of rustic paradise can also be seen in Cosway's portrait of the morganatic wife of the Prince of Wales, *Mrs Fitzherbert* [142] of 1792, as a dryad or wood-nymph in a fanciful costume with Vandyke collar and pearl trimming, with oak-leaves in her hair. A fine drawing of the late 1780s by Cosway may also depict *Mrs Fitzherbert* [fig. 23]; it shows a fashionably dressed woman in an open chemise gown fastened with ribbon ties, a starched kerchief or *fichu* over her bosom, and at a modish slant one of the large plumed hats so typical of the decade, which we know as 'picture' hats.[10] Starched *fichus* also decorate the necklines of *Princess Galetzin and her two daughters* [98] of 1795; the mother and the younger (standing) girl wear simple chemise dresses bound round the waist with a sash, and the daughter's gown shows the rising waistline, which became a prominent feature of the neo-classical style of dress later in the decade, and which can be seen clearly in Cosway's painting of the Courtenay sisters [151] of 1805. Here, all three young women wear light muslin dresses, which fall in graceful draperies from the high waist. Mathilda (on the right) emphasises the classical theme by wearing a turban of swathed, gauzy fabric, and her sister Sophia (on the left, holding a parasol) has chosen a close-fitting bonnet, untied so that the ribbon strings fall over her breast.

The relative simplicity of women's dress of the late eighteenth and early nineteenth century echoes to some extent the movement initiated by men towards a refinement of silhouette and costume which, *à propos* the male wardrobe, resulted in a virtual uniform of dark suit (well tailored and usually of high-quality woollen cloth) and white starched linen. This is, on the whole, the male image conveyed in portraits of fashionable civilians of the period (as distinct from the glamorous braided uniforms of the military). Cosway's miniatures of his most important patron, the Prince of Wales, show this simple but elegant style. As a young man in the miniature of *c.*1780–2 [49], he wears a double-breasted cloth coat with the Garter star and a wide-lapelled waistcoat. A laced shirt ruffle can be seen below the black

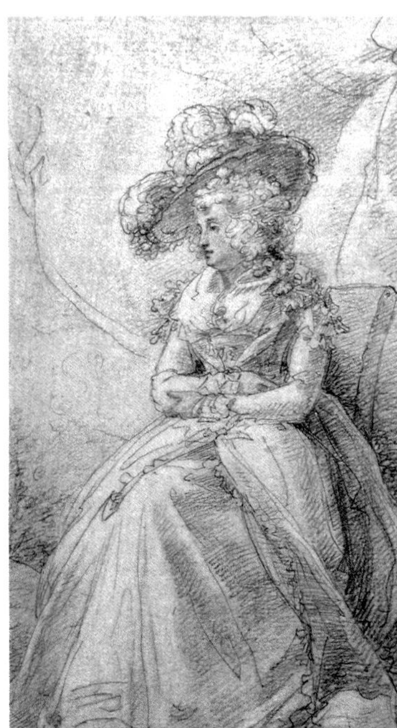

Fig. 23 *Mrs Fitzherbert, c.*1785–90 (The Duke of Devonshire and the Trustees of the Chatsworth Settlement)

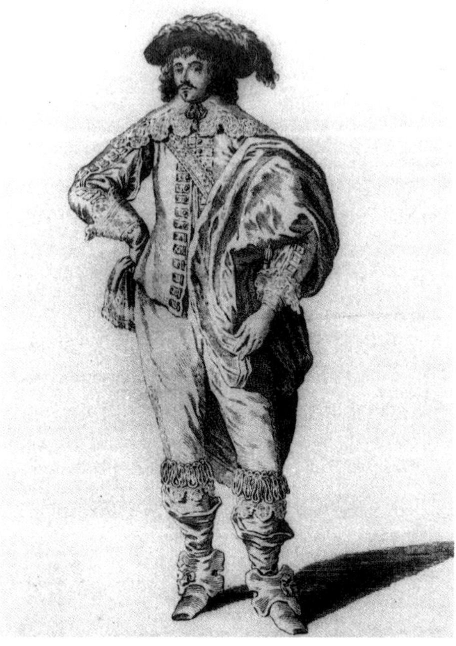

Fig. 24 *Habit of a Nobleman of England in 1640* from Thomas Jefferys *A Collection of the Dresses of Different Nations* ... II, 1757, pl.217

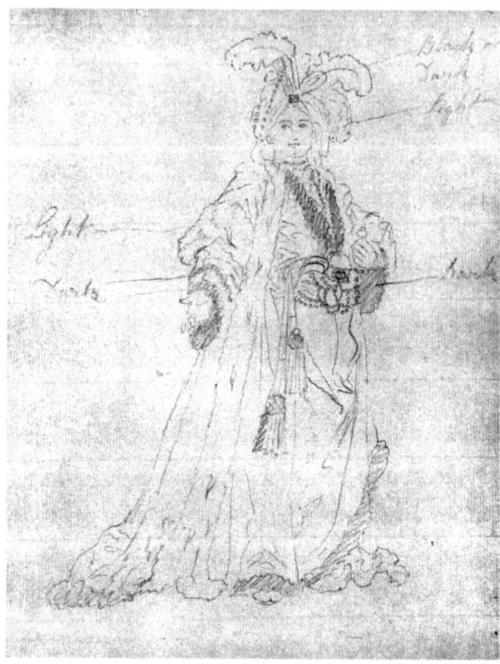

Fig. 25 *A figure in Turkish costume, c.*1780–90 (Fondazione Cosway, Lodi)

silk cravat, a military style which the prince (whose thwarted desire to be a soldier was channelled into the design of uniforms and the wearing of fancy dress) helped to popularise. At a dashing angle he wears a fashionable 'wide-awake' hat, which had replaced the long-established cocked hat, except at court and formal occasions.

The miniature already shows the Prince's inclination to corpulency which was to provide so much ammunition for the caricaturists, and also, perhaps, something of his sensitive side as a discerning patron of the arts. His 'feminine' cast of features was noted by the Duchess of Devonshire in 1782: 'He is inclined to be too fat, and looks too much like a woman in men's cloaths, but the gracefulness of his manner and his height certainly make him a pleasing figure'.[11] A later miniature of the *Prince of Wales* [**122**] of *c*.1792–3 shows no dramatic change in the basic elements of fashionable male costume; here again, is the double-breasted dark coat, but worn this time with two waistcoats with standing collars, and an elaborately knotted cravat. The prince's hair is frizzed and lightly powdered, rendered with the delicacy of touch that is characteristic of Cosway, who was as sensitive to the tactile qualities of hair as he was to the finer points of such items as lace and linen.[12] Cosway's flattering portraits of the heir to the throne must have been particularly appreciated when compared to the cruel visual comments made by the caricaturists on the prince's appearance and his extravagant lifestyle. In Gillray's *A voluptuary under the horrors of digestion* [**139**] of 1792, the bloated and dissipated prince almost bursts out of his clothes, a blue frock coat with buff-coloured waistcoat and breeches (buff and blue were Whig colours, an indication here of Foxite political sympathies), but nonetheless there is still a sense of style in his appearance, a monstrous elegance which he retained throughout his life.

Both prince and artist suffered from hostile comment about their appearance and proclivities, but in addition Cosway was criticised for an obsessional interest in his own image. The *Morning Post* (1788) noted sarcastically:

> *Dickey Cosway has published a great many likenesses of his own dear self, but whether to commemorate the beauties of his person, or to give posterity the external similitude of so amiable a man, it is difficult to say. The last portrait which this magnanimous artist made of himself is cloathed in a* Spanish *garb, which is well enough calculated to conceal the insignificance of his form ...* [13]

The reference is to an engraving of 1788 by Clarke after a *Self-portrait* drawing [**43**] by Cosway. Two years earlier Cosway had had another *Self-portrait* drawing engraved by Bova, entitled *R*dus *Cosway Armiger R.A.* [**83**] of 1786, in which the artist is shown in seventeenth-century costume (possibly Spanish, but this word also served to indicate any early seventeenth-century dress, such as that of Van Dyck or Rubens). The plumed hat and Spanish cape in this image are cruelly transformed into a ragged, slouched hat into which a pipe has been stuck, and a patched shapeless cloak, in an anonymous caricature, *Dicky Causway* [**84**], which depicts the artist as a Teniers-like boor or peasant.

Cosway's self-portraits in fanciful costume also include the full-length drawing of himself as *Esau* [**161**] of *c*.1806, wearing a strange amalgam of classical and 'Renaissance' dress, the draperies suggesting the former, and the latter evidenced by such early sixteenth-century features as the full upper-sleeve, square neck, and the tight-fitting hose which are nevertheless indented at the knee to suggest contemporary breeches. The mask at the bottom left indicates

Cosway's life-long interest in disguise and the theatrical which he transforms into fanciful costume, or into fancy dress which relates to the reality of the masquerade, that most popular and influential (in terms of its impact on portraiture) eighteenth-century pastime. It is very likely that Cosway, along with his fashionable society friends, attended such diversions, and his *Self-portrait in Vandyke dress* [**4**] of *c*.1770 may represent an actual costume worn at a masquerade; it consists of a buff silk suit with Vandyke lace collar and cuffs and a blue cloak wrapped over one shoulder. 'If you were to come over', wrote Horace Walpole in 1774 to Sir William Hamilton in Naples, 'you would find us a general masquerade. The maccaronis [*sic*], not content with producing new fashions every day, and who are great reformers, are going to restore the Vandyck dress ...'[14] That is meant, no doubt, to be tongue-in-cheek, but it indicates the infiltration into fashionable life, in terms of costume and cultural pursuits, of the historical, the romance of the past. For men, in particular, as their everyday clothing became simpler, unadorned and generally more practical, the masquerade and fancy dress portraiture provided escapist routes from the mundane to the romantic.

Vandyke costume was a favourite with Cosway and his sitters. In his full-length portrait of the *Prince of Wales* [**88**] of 1787, Cosway displays an empathy with the early seventeenth century, a feel for the *sense* of the period in his accurate depiction of the slashed doublet and breeches, standing lace-trimmed collar, and the cloak with the Garter star, bundled over the shoulder.[15] The pose, with plumed hat in one hand and cane in the other, is taken from Van Dyck's portrait of Charles, Prince of Wales, of the late 1630s at Goodwood.

Another portrait by Van Dyck, that of *William Villiers, 2nd Viscount Grandison* (collection of the Duke of Grafton) inspired the pose of Cosway's portrait in oils of *William, 3rd Viscount Courtenay* [**93**] of 1791, where the sitter wears a real Vandyke costume, in black trimmed with gold braid, which he wore at his coming-of-age celebrations. The Grandison portrait is engraved under the title of the 'Habit of a Nobleman of England in 1640' [fig. 24] in Thomas Jefferys's *A Collection of the Dresses of Different Nations both Ancient and Modern, and more particularly Old English Dresses after the designs of Holbein, Vandyke, Hollar*. This important work, published in four volumes in 1757 and 1772, was not just the first history of costume in English (although it contained many plates of contemporary dress also), but it was intended to be a major source book for masquerade and theatre costume, as well as a guide to artists portraying historic and exotic figures. Cosway owned a copy of this work, along with other useful sources for historic clothing, such as a collection of seventeenth-century costume prints, including 'Hollar's Dresses'.[16] Almost as popular as historical costumes for masquerades was oriental dress, and from Jefferys, Cosway copied a figure in Turkish costume [fig. 25], in a flowing fur-trimmed gown and turban decorated with feathers and jewels.[17]

The title of Jefferys's book quoted above indicates the prevailing fascination, which Cosway shared, for the costume of the sixteenth and early seventeenth centuries; this period was far enough removed in time to be 'romantic', and yet close enough to be familiar through the portraits by such artists as Holbein and Van Dyck, which were on view in the great aristocratic collections, and popularised though engravings. Cosway made a number of costume studies of the sixteenth century, including that of *Mary, Queen of Scots* [fig. 26], a romantic heroine of history painting, and a popular choice for

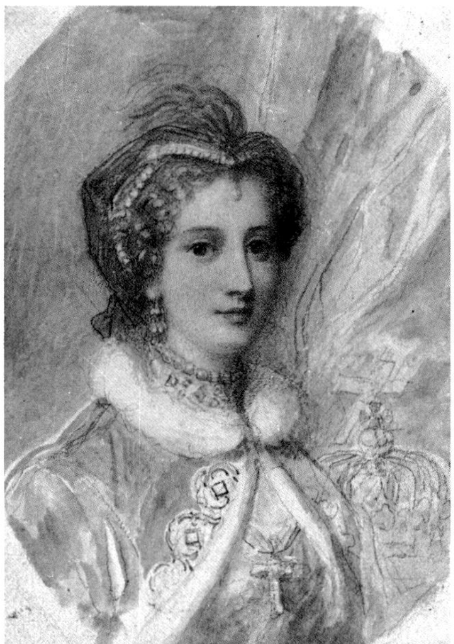

Fig. 26 *Mary, Queen of Scots, c.1780–90*
(Fondazione Cosway, Lodi)

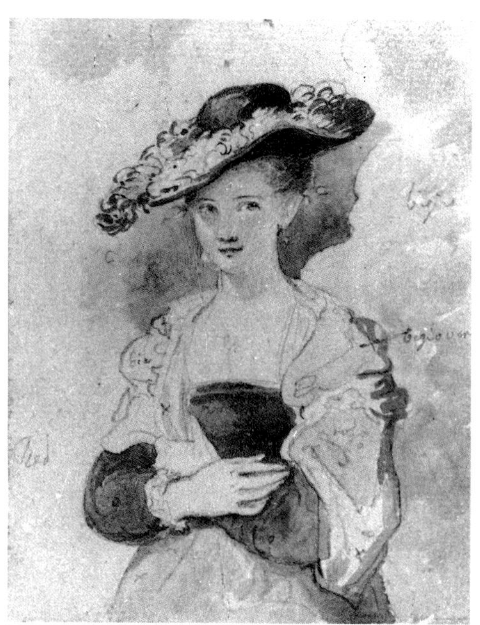

Fig. 27 *Study for a portrait of Maria Cosway in the
costume of Rubens's* Chapeau de Paille, 1786
(Fondazione Cosway, Lodi)

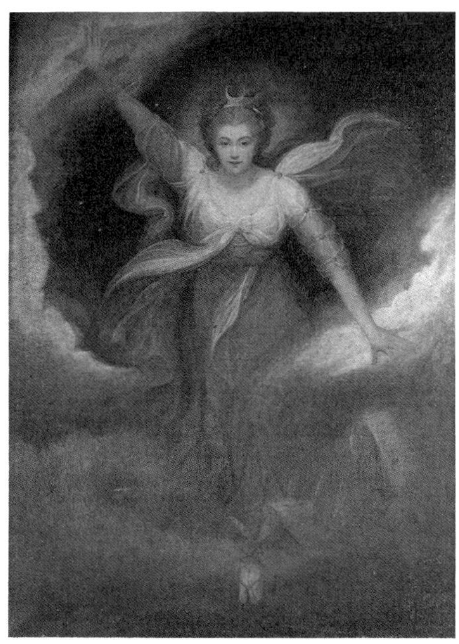

Fig. 28 *Georgiana, Duchess of Devonshire* 1782
by Maria Cosway (The Duke of Devonshire and
the Trustees of the Chatsworth Settlement)

masquerade dress. The collection at Lodi also contains sketches of late sixteenth-century Italian and French costume copied from Vecellio's famous Venetian costume book of the 1590s.[18]

Of all the Old Masters, Rubens was the most consistent source of inspiration to Richard Cosway, who portrayed Maria in the costume of the *Chapeau de Paille*[19] [fig. 27]. The wide-brimmed feathered hat and the scarf thrown loosely around the shoulders indicate an informal pastoral mood, very much in tune with the ease and simplicity of late eighteenth-century dress. The relaxed yet opulent costume depicted by Rubens in his self-portraits informs Cosway's images of himself, such as his *Self-portrait with busts of Michelangelo and Rubens* [36] of c.1789. This shows the Spanish-influenced style of the southern Netherlands with trunk hose, and a doublet with ribbon ties at the waist. In early seventeenth-century male costume these ties were both decorative and functional, serving to secure doublet to breeches. The ensemble is completed by a Spanish cloak and a soft velvet hat with segmented brim in Renaissance style.[20] Rubens's portrait of himself and his bride Isabella Brant, known as *The Honeysuckle Bower* (Alte Pinakothek, Munich) of 1609–10, suggested the pose and costume in Cosway's drawn *Self-portrait with Maria Cosway* [34] of c.1785. Similarly influenced by Rubens was Cosway's etched self-portrait with Maria [82] of 1784, where , again, the artist depicts himself in reasonably accurate dress of the period, figured doublet and breeches, a standing collar of plain linen, a cloak bundled over his arm, and the inevitable plumed hat looped up to one side.

Maria's costume is a more generalised interpretation of the early seventeenth century, for with Cosway it seems apparent that where women are concerned, he preferred the *idea* of the historic past lightly indicated rather than spelt out in accurate detail. Thus in *Maria Cosway with a bust of Leonardo* [37] of c.1789, she might be seen as the muse of Time Past with her curious invented costume, comprising an 'antique' tunic girdled at the waist in the classical Greek overfold (*kolpos*), a quasi-Renaissance bodice and over-gown

with braided upper sleeves, and an exotic headdress of swathed ribbon, lace and feathers. A simplified version of this *ensemble*, where the historical features merge into the general line of fashion of the late 1780s, is to be seen in the stipple engraving of the *Cosways* [92], also of 1789, where Richard depicts himself with greater Rubensian consistency.

A sense of historical detail, lightly sketched in and subordinate to the overall fashionable image can be seen in Cosway's *Elizabeth Milbanke, Viscountess Melbourne* [30] of 1784, where the dress mixes contemporary elements such as the hairstyle, the shape of the bodice and the silk band at the neck (*The Lady's Magazine* for August 1780 recommends 'narrow black Collars buckled round the neck') with features from costume of the time of Rubens. These include the open lace-edged collar and Vandyke cuffs, and the feathered hat decorated with ostrich plumes and pinned up at one side with a jewelled loop, which was inspired by a portrait by Rubens of his second wife, Helena Fourment (now in the Gulbenkian Foundation, Lisbon), which for much of the eighteenth century hung at Houghton Hall and was the source of a great deal of masquerade costume and countless fancy dress portraits. Like a number of other eighteenth-century artists, Cosway found inspiration in Rubens's great cycle of paintings on the life of Marie de Médicis (now in the Louvre),[21] for poses and costumes. In particular, number thirteen in the series, *The Capture of Juliers*, may have been the source for the dress and the composition (reversed) in Cosway's *An unknown lady on horseback* [31] of c.1788.

Although Cosway's own taste was coloured by his love of the Renaissance and the Baroque, it was impossible to avoid the fashion, popularised by the theories and practice of Reynolds, for depicting women either in generalised draperies, which were intended to signify 'timeless' dress, that is above the vagaries of ever-changing styles of costume; or more specifically as classical muses or goddesses. Thus the actress *Mrs Abington as the Comic Muse Thalia* [56] of c.1783, is shown with just a hint of 'antique' draperies. *Georgiana,*

Duchess of Devonshire [fig. 28], of 1782, is envisaged by Maria as the goddess Diana, flying through the clouds in swirling draperies based on the Greek tunic called the *chiton*, which fastened along the top of the arm with small clasps. She wears sandals on her feet, and her attribute, the crescent moon, is fixed to her hairband.

The character of Diana was a popular choice at masquerades, although the actual costume worn on such occasions would have been more structured and related to high fashion of the time than the glamorous but perhaps unconvincing 'classical' dress in which the duchess is depicted. It is equally hard to decipher what *Emma, Lady Hamilton* [102] of *c.*1800 wears in Cosway's lively pencil sketch of the portly (perhaps even pregnant) *demi-mondaine* performing one of her famous Attitudes in flowing draperies *à l'antique* bare-footed, and with a scarf bound round her head and under her chin. By this time, the late 1790s, life had caught up with art, and the kind of classical shift fastened on the shoulder with a brooch, leaving the arm bare, as in Cosway's *An unknown lady* [52] of the early 1780s, became the vogue, so that it is often difficult to distinguish fashion from fiction. The portrait of *Susan Beckford, later Duchess of Hamilton* [155] of *c.*1800 may represent a classical goddess, but her short-sleeved and high-waisted gown are totally *à la mode*. Cosway's drawing of an *An unknown lady as Juno* [159] of 1806 could equally derive from a fashion plate (the peacock an optional accessory). Even the drapery turns out to be a cloak with a tasselled end, and the diadem holding her veil in place is a contemporary jewelled version of the classical fillet or bandeau.

By the end of the eighteenth century the classical inspiration dominated female portraiture precisely *because* it conformed to real dress, the fashionable aesthetic of the time. The same did not happen in male portraiture, where the taste for historical costume prevailed, particularly for that of the Elizabethan period. This is reflected in a number of Cosway portraits, such as the oil painting of *George, Marquis of Blandford* [94], of 1797, where the sitter is shown in an early Elizabethan velvet doublet with a high collar. At about the same time the drawing of *Charles, 4th Earl of Harrington* [153] of *c.*1800–5 demonstrates the long-limbed late Elizabethan look in his short doublet, trunk hose and Spanish cape; his hair is artistically tousled in the new neo-classical way, which echoes the short Elizabethan style

that had to accommodate high collars and ruffs. There is also an Elizabethan air about Cosway's drawing of *George, 5th Earl of Jersey* [164] of *c.*1815, who appears, perhaps, in the guise of a Spanish knight or pilgrim at a courtly tournament.

All these costumes, like most of those in Cosway's fanciful portraits, are imaginary, although based on historical examples. His drawing of the *Hon. Peter Robert Burrell, later 2nd Baron Gwydyr* [162], of 1807, is another example of such romantic *ensembles*, consisting of a high-collared Elizabethan doublet, Vandyke cloak and plumed hat, but with an up-to-date touch, tight pantaloons tucked into somewhat theatrical hussar boots. At the accession of George IV in 1820, however, fantasy became fact, and although Cosway was no longer in royal favour, it is clear that his Elizabethan and Vandyke costume designs provided the inspiration for the theatrical extravaganza of the most expensive coronation in British history, when the new king was crowned in 1821. If one looks at the engraving of Cosway's *Duke of Orleans* [89] of 1788, this prince of fashion (and at the time a great crony of the Prince of Wales) in his slashed doublet and breeches, plumed hat, and ermine-lined cloak with the star of the Order of St Esprit[22] is not only a reminder of the artist's self-images, such as his *Self-portrait with busts of Michelangelo and Rubens* [36] but also of the 'fancy dress', as Sir Walter Scott called it, worn at the coronation. This consisted of an Elizabethan doublet and hose, over which was worn a cloak, as in the depiction of *A Member of the Privy Council* [fig. 29] or as in Lord Gwydyr in peer's robes [fig. 30] At the coronation Lord Gwydyr was deputy Lord Chamberlain, and he is shown carrying the white staff of his office. The whole dramatic and colourful *mise-en-scène* of the coronation was ordained by the new king, whose taste for fancy dress, along with his instincts as a collector of historic and exotic objects, had been nurtured as a young man by Cosway.[23]

The artist's last years were darkened by mental illness, his over-romantic imagination having turned towards the occult and other forms of the supernatural. As an old man he retained his sense of finicking *ancien régime* style. When Hazlitt saw him he noted that 'such was the jauntiness of his air and manner that to see him sit to have his half-boots laced on, you would fancy ... that instead of a little withered old gentleman it was Venus attired by the Graces'.[24]

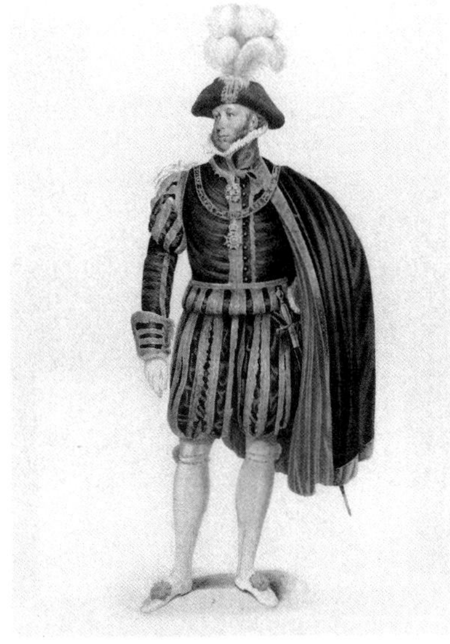

Fig. 29 *A Member of the Privy Council at the Coronation of George IV, 1821*, from Sir George Nayler, *The Coronation of His Most Sacred Majesty King George the Fourth*, London 1837

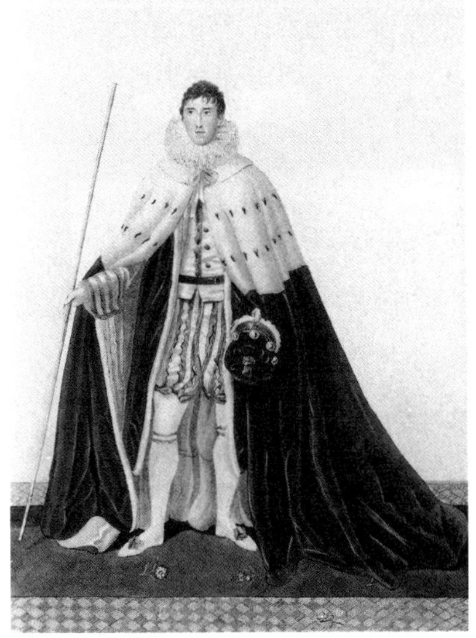

Fig. 30 *Lord Gwydyr as Deputy Lord Chamberlain at the Coronation of George IV, 1821*, from Sir George Nayler, *The Coronation of His Most Sacred Majesty King George the Fourth*, London 1837

NOTES AND REFERENCES

INTRODUCTION

1 Thomas Jefferson to Maria Cosway, his 'head' addressing his 'heart', letter written in Paris, 12 October 1786, in Jefferson 1950–82, x, p.446

2 Roworth 1992; Haskell 1980, pp.25–38

3 Blake 1987, ch.8, lines 37–44

4 Daniell 1890; York 1992; George 1948, pp.11–12, 'M. and B. Haydon, Stationers and Printers to his Royal Highness Prince William Henry, at No.2 Pike-street, Plymouth ...'

5 Lloyd 1991; Dethloff 1992

6 Millar 1977, pp.129–62; Watkin 1984, pp.98–126; London 1991–2; Lloyd 1993

7 *Library of Fine Arts* 1832, p.185

8 Letter dated 6 August 1773 from John Towneley [*sic*] to his nephew Charles Townley in Rome, Townley MSS, British Museum, London.

9 Smith 1828; *Library of Fine Arts* 1832; *Fraser's Magazine* 1840; Cunningham 1846; Fairholt 1858; Thornbury 1860; London 1865; Christie's, London, 24–27 June 1935

10 Williamson 1897 and 1905; London 1895

11 Reynolds 1992; Williamson 1906–8, II; Thorpe 1994

12 *Catalogue of the famous Collection of Miniatures of the British and Foreign Schools, the property of J. Pierpont Morgan, Esq ...*, Christie's, London, 24–27 June 1935, lots 245–303, specifically lots 248, 256, 254 and 249; Waterhouse 1947, p.50; Waterhouse 1981, pp.88–90; Waterhouse 1994, p.322

13 London 1991; London 1992–3; Shawe-Taylor 1990; Pointon 1993. For an exception cf. Piper 1992 and New Haven 1979.

14 Juninus 1812; Pasquin 1796, p.118; Cunningham 1829–33, VI, p.20; Bermingham 1993

RICHARD COSWAY: EARLY LIFE AND CAREER IN DEVON AND LONDON, 1742–70

1 Smith 1828, II, pp.392–3

2 Devon Record Office, Exeter

3 Farington 1978–84, 21 January 1820 and 16 July 1821; *Register of Burials (1819–21) St Marylebone Church*, Greater London Record Office; Nicholson 1931, pp.326–8; Farington 1978–84, 5 August 1809

4 Dunsford 1790; Harding 1845 and Snell 1892

5 Williamson 1897, pp.13–14; Williamson 1905, p.16; and Cunningham 1829–33, VI, pp.1–2

6 Miles 1979; Penny 1986

7 Sotheby's, London, 20 July 1981, lot 137, oval, height 5.6 cm, signed *RC / 1760* on obverse

8 For Peard (d.1765) see Williamson 1897, pp.4–5 and Williamson 1905, p.5; for Newte (d.1781) see Pasquin 1796, p.118

9 Allan 1979; RSA Minutes 1755

10 Black chalk, 15¾ × 35¼ in, Sir John Soane's Museum, London (no.P351). In Soane's 1835 *Description* of his house, in the section on the model room, 'amongst the pictures is a copy by R. Cosway RA of the Aurora of Guido'.

11 Nicholson 1931; Lippincott 1983; Pears 1988; Bignamini 1988; Colley 1992, pp.90–5

12 *The Public Advertiser*, 25 June 1757, quoted in Allan 1979, p.80; *The Gentleman's Magazine*, XXVI, 1756, quoted in Allan 1979, p.81

13 Foskett 1964; Foskett 1987; Waterhouse 1981; Waterhouse 1994; Whinney 1988

14 Haskell and Penny 1981, esp. pp.221–4; London 1991, esp. pp.8–15 and 49–64; Benjamin Ralph's comments of 1759 are quoted *loc. cit.* p.16

15 Cunningham 1829–33, VI, p.5

16 Joseph Moser in *The European Magazine*, September 1803, quoted in Allan 1979, p.128; New Haven 1983

17 Cunningham 1829–33, VI, p.2; Williamson 1897, p.5; London 1979; Cosway apprenticed to Shipley on 19 August 1755, quoted in Foskett 1964, p.3

18 Smith 1828, II, p.392; Graves 1907, p.65; Mortimer 1763, p.8

19 Mortimer 1763, pp.26, 15, 8, and 18; Noon 1981; Foskett 1987; Reynolds 1988; Pointon 1984, pp.187–205; Pointon 1993, pp.36–52

20 Reynolds 1988, pp.105–14

21 Boutet 1752

22 Smith 1828, II, pp.392–3, also quoted in Cunningham 1829–33, VI, p.3 and Williamson 1897, p.5; letter dated 1 June 1830, London, Sir John Soane's Museum, MS Priv. Corresp. III.c.4.31

23 Liverpool Central Libraries, Picton Collection, MS Humphry, fol.211, quoted in London 1974, pp.27–8; London 1984–5, no.99

24 *Miss Eleanor Falkingham*, signed and dated *London March ye 18th 1764, Rd. Cosway Pinxit*, height 1⅛ in, sold Sotheby's, London, 3 July 1958, lot 63, now Art Institute of Chicago (no.1959.63); *Randyll Peck*, signed and dated *1765, Cosway Pinxt.*, height 1⅜ in, sold Sotheby's, London, 11 December 1958, lot 43

25 Noon 1981, pp.183–4; Reynolds 1988, pp.126–7

26 Sterne 1984, pp.163 (entry for 11 June 1767), 131 and 183 (14 July 1767)

RICHARD COSWAY: ROYAL ACADEMICIAN, 1770–80

1 Hutchison 1960–2, pp.127–35; Hutchison 1986, pp.29–31; Royal Academy MSS, Council and Assembly Minutes 1770 and 1771; certificate rolled together with that of the flower painter Mary Moser; diploma work stolen between 1810 and 1818 and again in 1984 (currently untraced)

2 Millar 1969, I, pp.152–4; Haskell and Penny 1981, pp.148–51, no.8; British Museum, Townley MSS (acquired 1993), letter dated 24 February 1772

3 Engraved by C. Grignion, cf. George 1967, p.27; *Library of Fine Arts* 1832, IV, p.185

4 Williamson 1897, p.31, and 1905, p.38, Cosway moved to 22 Stratford Place in 1794; Constable 1953, p.53

5 British Museum, Townley MSS, 6 August 1773, letter from John Towneley to Charles Townley in Rome

6 Smith 1828, II, p.393 and Cunningham 1829–33, VI, p.4

7 Pointon 1984; Pointon 1993, pp.36–52; Bromley 1793, p.400 and Daniell 1890, p.9, no.33

8 For fancy dress cf. Ribeiro 1975, Edinburgh 1978, pp.19–30, Cherry and Harris 1982

9 Smith 1828, II, p.393, and Cunningham 1829–33, VI, p.184

10 Angelo 1828, pp.357–9

11 Cunningham 1829–33, VI, pp.3–4

12 The earliest reference to the attribution to Cosway occurs in a notebook belonging to the owner of the painting. Dated 1906 and titled 'Odds and ends about the Holland family and their possessions now belonging to H.W.L. Holland', it mentions 'Lancelot Browne the Landscape Gardener his portrait by Cosway (fol.3r). The portrait by Dance is at the National Portrait Gallery, London.

13 'The Choice of Hercules' was also the subject praised by the 3rd Earl of Shaftesbury in his criticism, *A Notion of the Historical Draught or Tablature of the Judgement of Hercules* (1713). A painting of this subject was commissioned by Shaftesbury from Paolo de Matteis (now Ashmolean Museum, Oxford), an engraving of which illustrated the writer's influential *Characteristicks of Man, Manners, Opinions, Times ...* (1714). Cosway was also likely to have been aware of the treatments of this subject by Poussin (Stourhead, The Hoare Collection, The National Trust), and by Benjamin West (1764; now Victoria and Albert Museum), as well as Reynolds's mock-heroic portrait of *Garrick between Tragedy and Comedy* (1762; Private Collection).

14 Townley's extensive archive of papers relating to the formation of his collection was acquired by the British Museum in 1993. It includes a number of letters from Richard Cosway to Townley.

15   This was formerly at the Fondazione Cosway, Lodi, where it was photographed by Diana Wilson in the late 1970s.

16   Vaughan 1989, I, pp.374–5, II, fig.2

17   Smith 1890–1904, III, pp.32–2, 72 and 382

18   Vaughan 1989, I, p.180

19   The drawing is in the Department of Greek and Roman Antiquities, British Museum. The letter is in the Fondation Custodia, Paris.

20   Sterne 1984, p.163

21   Sidney Sabin has informed me that a letter from Cosway addressed to Mrs Draper, which mentioned the arrangements for a sitting, once accompanied the picture.

22   Ribeiro 1983, p.100, no.109

23   1–4 May 1779, p.4

24   28–30 April 1772

25   The drawing of the *Choice of Hercules* is at the Fondazione Cosway, Lodi, no.III, 9

MARIA HADFIELD: ANGLO-FLORENTINE, 1760–80

1   Northcote 1898, p.149, letter of 26 December 1778; Whitley 1928a, p.312

2   I am grateful for a discussion on this matter with Julia King, who is undertaking research on Maria's brother, George Hadfield, the architect who later worked in Washington DC.

3   Moloney 1969; Florence 1971; Whitehead 1983, I, pp.287–307; *A Brief Account* 1775, p.25

4   Dentler 1964; Gibbon 1961, pp.118, 254, 175 and 187, n.5

5   Dunham Massey, Stamford Collection, National Trust; Watson 1939–40, p.32; Washington 1985–6, pp.297–8; Hibbert 1987; Black 1992; Brinsley Ford Archive of British Visitors to Italy in the 18th-century, Paul Mellon Centre for Studies in British Art, London

6   The Raphael is now in the National Gallery of Art, Washington DC, the Rubens is still in the Palazzo Pitti and the Zoffany is at Windsor Castle.

7   Borroni Salvadori 1985–6 (records from the archives of the Uffizi); Lodi, Fondazione Cosway, MS Inventory, 1820, fol.188r (copies located in Maria Cosway's room on the second floor at Stratford Place, London); Wynne 1990, p.537 (records of the Accademia del Disegno membership in the Archivio di Stato in Florence)

8   London 1974; Whitley 1928a, II, p.312; Bell 1902, pp.21–2; Northcote 1898, p.164

9   London, Royal Academy, MS Humphry HU/2/51 (4 February 1777), HU/2/55 (8 March 1777); Whitley 1928a, II, pp.312–13

10   Bell 1902, p.24; Wynne 1990, p.537 (records of foreign passports in the Archivio del Stato, Florence); New Haven, Yale University, Beinecke Library, Osborn MS (letter dated 11 July 1779); Florence 1971, no.54 (oil portrait in the Uffizi of *William Hadfield* by Pietro Labruzzi)

MR AND MRS COSWAY: LONDON AND PARIS, 1780–90

1   Northcote 1898, pp.149–50; Williamson 1897, p.11, and 1905, p.13; Fondazione Cosway, MS, legal indenture, 11 July 1822; Williamson 1897, p.17, and 1905, p.21

2   Postle 1995, pp.265 and 341, n.29

3   *The Morning Chronicle and London Advertiser*, 9 May 1782

4   Bordes 1983, pp.133–4; Bordes 1992, p.485; Carr 1993

5   Bordes 1994, p.102, no.30

6   Williamson 1897, p.11, and 1905, pp.13–14; Cunningham 1829–33, VI, p.10

7   The painting by Rubens is in the Alte Pinakothek, Munich (*c.*1630). For Quobna Ottobah Cugoano, cf. Potkay and Burr 1995, pp.125–8.

8   This widespread image set the mocking tone of critics towards Cosway, which continued from after his death up until the revival of interest in his life and work at the end of the nineteenth century.

9   Abelard 1781

10   Farington 1978–84, p.763 (4 February 1797), repeated, p.3445 (1 May 1809); Hazlitt 1930–4, XVIII, p.180

11   Pasquin 1786; Cosway 1832, p.186; Sheppard 1960, pp.368–77; Porter 1982

12   Shroyer 1979; Blake 1987, ch.8, lines 37–44 (MS fols 4v-5r); Potkay and Burr 1995, pp.125–8

13   For Marchesi cf. Highfill, Burnim and Langhans 1984, X, pp.89–91. Contemporary gossip asserted that Maria Cosway fell in love with Marchesi and followed him to Italy in 1790. However this trip was undertaken on account of what is most likely to have been serious post-natal depression.

14   New Haven, Yale University, Beinecke Rare Book and Manuscript Library, Osborn MS files, letter dated 2 February 1788, partially published in Noon 1981, pp.184 and 222, n.37. Charlotte Hadfield married William Combe, the writer of the popular verse series, based on his character Dr Syntax, which was published by Ackermann with illustrations by Rowlandson. Charles-Alexandre de Calonne (1734–1802) was Contrôleur-Général des Finances to Louis XVI, and, after his dismissal in 1787, retired to England.

15   Morris 1939, I, pp.197–8

16   Walpole 1937–83, XII, p.228 (17 August 1784); XL, p.285 (8 June 1791); XLII, p.200 (28 October 1787); XV, 1952, p.646 (20 May 1786); George Nassau, 3rd Earl Cowper (1738–89) was a notable collector and patron of the arts, who facilitated access for British artists to copy in the Galleria of the Uffizi and at the Pitti Palace (cf. Florence 1971, no.39).

17   Walpole 1937–83, XXXIII, pp.510–11 (27 January 1786). François Barthélemy (1747–1830) was secretary to the French embassy in London from 1785 to 1787 and minister plenipotentiary from 1787 to 1788. Michal Kasimierz (1731–1800), Prince Oghinski and hetman of Lithuania, was a candidate for the throne of Poland in 1764. The head of the Moravian Church in England from 1765 to 1786 was the Rev. Benjamin Latrobe (*c.*1728–86). Letters from d'Ageno, the Genoese envoy in London, dating from the mid-1780s, are preserved in the Fondazione Cosway, Lodi. For d'Eon, cf. Schuchard 1992a.

18   Boswell 1986, p.122 (diary entry 18 March 1787); Boswell 1981 (see diary entries for May to September 1785); Boswell 1928–34, XVI, pp.278–9 (letter dated 28 July 1785)

19   Vivian 1949, p.49; oil on panel, 69 x 45.5 cm, inv. 1890 n.577; Richard Cosway had earlier portrayed Paoli in a portrait miniature or drawing (untraced), which was engraved in stipple by C. Townley in 1784, cf. Daniell 1890, p.29, no.113; Foladare 1979, p.107; Lodi, Fondazione Cosway, MS Inventory, 1820, fol.188r; Florence 1971, no.40

20   Foladare 1979; for Louisa of Stolberg's letter of acceptance, cf. Oxford, Bodleian Library, MS Eng Lett., c.411, fol.53r; Williamson 1897, pp.72–5, and 1905, pp.94–8; Paoli's correspondence with Maria Cosway is preserved in the Fondazione Cosway, Lodi. I am grateful to Frances Vivian for permitting me to read the chapter on their relationship from her unpublished biography of Paoli, where she postulates that the General was the father of Louisa Cosway.

21   Lodi, Fondazione Cosway, Maria Cosway MS Diaries, frequent references to 'Madame Mère', 1802–3, cf. Cazzulani and Stroppa 1989, pp.61–9. Correspondence between Isabella Teotochi Albrizzi and Maria Cosway is to be found at Lodi, Fondazione Cosway, and Milan, Biblioteca Nazionale Braidense.

22   Bullock 1945; Jefferson 1950–82; Brodie 1974; Byrd 1993; Bordes 1992; Adams 1936; Rice 1976; Adams 1983, p.2; Stein 1993; Shackelford 1995

23   Trumbull 1953, p.120

24   The original letter of 12 October 1786 has not been traced. However Jefferson's press-copy letter written entirely by Jefferson himself – with his left hand – survives in the Library of Congress, Washington DC. The letter was first published in London in Jefferson, 1829, II, pp.46–56. The definitive edition of the letter is in Jefferson 1950–82, X, pp.443–53. Other transcriptions are found in Bullock, 1945, pp.29–42 and Brodie 1974, pp.483–92.

25   Bullock 1945, p.115; Jefferson 1950–82, XV, p.143; Cometti 1952

26   Haskell 1987; d'Hancarville's correspondence to Maria Cosway from 1787 to 1791 is at the Biblioteca Comunale Laudense at Lodi, mainly published in Ferrari 1913–14; the greeting is quoted from a letter of 21 April 1789, ibid., 1914, p.85

27   Ibid., 1914, p.41 (letter of 22 November 1787); Lloyd 1991; Bordes 1992, pp.484–5; Bordes 1983, pp.132–4; Boase 1963, p.151

28   Whitley 1928, II, p.101; Cazzulani and Stroppa 1989, pp.67–8; Oxford, Bodleian Library, MS Douce, d.24, fols. 126r-127v (letter dated 19 February 1823)

MARIA COSWAY: ITALY AND LONDON, 1790–1801

1 MS letter 1830, fol.2r; for George Hadfield, cf. Placzek 1982, II, p.283 (entry by D.D. Rieff); Walpole 1937–83, XI, p.285 (letter dated 8 June 1791); four watercolours at the Fondazione Cosway, Lodi, nos x.46–9

2 Lodi, Fondazione Cosway, Maria Cosway MSS, letters dated 13 June 1791 (from Venice) and 1 March 1793 (from Genoa)

3 Maria Cosway described her relationship with her daughter at length in a letter, a contemporary copy of which is at Lodi, Fondazione Cosway, Maria Cosway MSS, cf. Cosway 1926

4 Lodi, Fondazione Cosway, nos x.5–7; Boase 1963

5 Ford 1983; Essen 1992, pp.97–110

RICHARD COSWAY: COLLECTOR, CONNOISSEUR AND VIRTUOSO

1 Lloyd 1991; Smith 1828, II, pp.401–2; Wainwright 1989

2 This may also be 'A bust of M. Angelo, in terra-cotta', which was sold in Cosway's sale of *Miscellaneous Articles of Taste and Virtù* (Stanley's, London, 22 May 1821, lot 124). Cosway also owned a bronze bust of Tintoretto (ibid., 23 May 1821, lot 86).

3 Paris, Fondation Custodia, MS letter, undated [1805], from Richard Cosway to an unidentified nobleman in Paris; St Clair 1967, pp.149–50; letter from Hunt, dated 9 January 1805, quoted in Smith 1916, p.296

4 Quoted from Hardy 1973; drawing illustrated in Hayward 1973, p.269, fig.2

5 *Mrs Delany* (collections: Francis Wellesley; Leverhulme sale, Anderson's, New York, 2–4 March 1926, lot 91); *Frederick, 5th Earl of Carlisle* (at Castle Howard; and stipple engraving by A. Cardon, cf. Daniell 1890, p.6, no.21); *Hyacinthe Gabrielle Roland, later Countess of Mornington and Marchioness Wellesley* (sold Christie's, London, 17 November 1992, lot 26)

6 Lloyd 1993; Millar 1986

7 Lodi, Fondazione Cosway, MS inventory 1820, fols. 221r-222r; Windsor, Royal Archives, MSS Geo. 26460 and 26792

8 Schomberg House picture catalogue of 1791, in breakfast room on third floor, no.46; sold by Cosway to William, 3rd Viscount Dudley and Ward for £150, cf. note in Sir John Soane's copy of Cosway 1791 catalogue; according to a letter from a J.Carter in 1817 the picture was bought by Cosway at the sale of the collection of Sir Robert Bernard held at Christie's in 1789, and which then came into the possession of the Prince of Wales, cf. Lloyd 1991, pp.400–1 and 405, n.12; Davies 1968, pp.109–13, no.4681.

9 London 1991–2; Lloyd 1991 and 1993; Thogmorton Trust, Combe MSS, II, fol.174r; Fenaille 1904, III, pp.236–7, 242, 263 and 266; de Bellaigue 1968, pp.179 and 222–3; Robinson 1994, col. ill. p.27

10 Schomberg House picture catalogue of 1791, p.19, according to which they were currently at the Gobelins manufactory

11 Guiffrey 1879

12 Later auctions of Cosway's Old Master pictures were held at Christie's, London, 2–3 March 1792, and before and after his death by Mr Stanley, London, 17–19 May 1821 and 8–9 March 1822 [222], cf. Lloyd 1991, pp.400 and 405, nn.10–11

13 Schomberg House picture catalogue of 1791, p.49, no.50, p.4, no.21, p.2, no.9, and p.3, no.14, p.12, nos 56 and 57, p.16, no.91, cf. note in Sir John Soane's copy of this catalogue

14 Ibid., p.12, no.61, p.17, no.99, p.44, no.3, p.49, no.54, and p.17, no.102

15 Ibid., p.1, no.5, p.50, no.56, and p.21, no.16

16 Hazlitt 1930–4, XVIII, pp.173 and 179 and XII, pp.95–6

17 Published by permission of the Earl of Radnor; cf. Lloyd 1991, p.403

18 Some items were illustrated in Grose 1786–9, pls 11, 14, 33 and 35; reference provided by A.V.B. Norman

19 Lodi, Fondazione Cosway, MS Inventory, 1820, fol.205r ('A large Piano Forte – by Bredwood', 'A Carpet of the Sablonnerie – Manufactory – French, A very fine Chimney piece the – Sculpture by Banks R.A. after the drawing of Mr. Cosway'), fol.207r ('A Piano Forte Organ by Polinan', 'A large Sarcophagus – wood gilt', '2 Miniature Painting desks', 'A Curious Colour Box which – belonged to Rubens'), fol.209r ('A desk for Painting in miniature'), fol.210r ('A Case with Glass door with a skeleton in it'), fol.191r ('A Harp by Naderman'), and fol.212r ('A Great number of Heads, Hands, Feet, small Figures – Basso Relievo, Studies for Artists &c –')

20 The titlepage details continued: *Which will be Sold by Auction, / BY MR. STANLEY, / At MR COSWAY's late Residence, / No.20, Stratford Place, Oxford Street, / ON TUESDAY MAY 22, 1821, / AND TWO FOLLOWING DAYS, / At Twelve o'Clock. / CATALOGUES ONE SHILLING EACH, / To be had on the Premises, and of MR. STANLEY, at his Auction Rooms, 21, Old Bond-street.*

21 Cosway MS Inventory 1820, fol.6r; Wainwright 1989, pp.71–107 and pp.27–30 for earlier collections

22 Thornton and Dorey 1992, p.126

23 I am grateful to Clive Wainwright, Simon Jervis and Peter Thornton for their comments.

24 The letter dated 14 March 1804, cf. Buchanan 1982, pp.182–5; Lodi, Fondazione Cosway, MS Inventory 1820, fols. 161r and 163r; Reynolds 1929, p.189, no.CXXIX

25 Soane 1927, pp.334–9, 465–72 and 484

26 'Twenty-two wax models by Giov. da Bologna', sculpture sale of 'Fitzhugh' (William Lock), Christie's, London, 16 April 1785, lot 19, bought by Cosway for 1 guinea; 'A small Terra Cotta model by Nalekins', and 'A very fine Chimney piece the – Sculpture by Banks R.A. after the drawing of Mr. Cosway', cf. Lodi, Fondazione Cosway MS Inventory 1820, fols. 185r and 205r

27 22 May 1821, lot 120 (13 shillings); 23 May 1821, lot 15 (£2 6s), lot 17 (£2 4s), lot 19 (1 guinea), lot 30 (£2 4s), lot 47 (1 guinea), lots 53 and 54 (£1 4s together), lot 56 (6 shillings), lot 59 (£2 4s), lot 63 (2s 6d), lot 67 (£2 12s 6d), lot 68 (£2 10s), lot 70 (£1 13s) and lot 83 (£1 13s), cf. Sir John Soane's Museum, MS account from Mr Watson, who was paid £21 9s in total

28 Department of Greek and Roman Antiquities, British Museum

29 Haskell 1987, p.43, fig.30

30 For the fine baroque statue of Charles II, see Thornton and Dorey 1992, p.55, fig.51

31 London, Royal Academy, MS Lawrence, LAW/1/289/ fols. 1v-2r; partially cited in Reynolds 1988, p.126

32 Lodi, Fondazione Cosway, MS Inventory 1820, fols. 158r-164r; Lugt 1921 and 1956; Sciolla 1992, pp.88, 142–61 and 195–201; Dethloff 1992

33 *The Death of Leonardo in the arms of Francis I,* c.1815–20, monochrome and grey wash, 29.8 × 24.2 cm ($11^{3/4} \times 9^{1/2}$ in), formerly Alfred A. de Pass collection given (1914) to the Royal Institution of Cornwall, County Museum and Art Gallery, Truro; sold Christie's, London, 22 February 1966, lot 5, bought by Allen; Bonham's, London, 14 June 1995, lot 80, bought by A. J. Stirling; cf. Rosenblum 1967, pp.34–6

34 London, Stanley's, 4 February 1822, lot 154

35 Daniell 1890, p.45, no.181

36 London, Sir John Soane's Museum, MS Priv. Corresp. II.c.4.32, letter dated 19 August 1830

37 Oxford, Bodleian Library, MS Douce d.24, letter written in London, dated 21 April 1822, fol.1v

38 Ibid., letter written in Lodi on 25 November 1822, fols. 1r-1v. Maria Cosway then went on to describe the effect that Antonio Canova's death had caused in Italy.

39 Ibid., letter written in Lodi on 19 February 1823, fol.2r. The *Cupid & Psyche* by David is now in the Cleveland Museum of Art. For a study of G.B. Sommariva see Haskell 1987, pp.47–64.

40 An exhibition and publication of the holdings at the Fondazione Cosway is to be undertaken in Lodi.

MARIA COSWAY: PARIS, LYONS, LONDON AND LODI, 1801–38

1 For this period of the Louvre's history see Gould 1965; van Nimmen 1986; Wescher 1988; McClellan 1994; London, Sir John Soane's Museum, Prospectuses 1802/14 (this was kindly brought to my attention by Nick Savage); Soane also subscribed to both colour and monochrome copies, now in his museum.

2 The album became one of the treasures of Maria Cosway's Collegio in Lodi. After her death it was signed over the course of the nineteenth century by a number of eminent visitors including Garibaldi on 26 May 1862.

3 Lloyd 1992, p.125; Farington 1978–84, p.1863 (20 September 1802), pp.1825–6 (3 September 1803), and p.1909 (8 October 1803)

4 Farington 1978–84, pp.1878–80 (entry for 27 September 1802)

5 Lodi, Fondazione Cosway, MSS Maria Cosway, diaries and letterbooks, 1802–17; partially published in Cazzulani and Stroppa 1989, pp.23–51 and 59–104; for Fesch's collection see Haskell 1980, pp.57–8 and Thiébaut 1987, pp.5–47

6 Charvet 1905; Cazzulani and Stroppa 1989, pp.31–9 and 71–81; Lodi, Biblioteca Comunale Laudense, MSS Cosway and Lodi, Fondazione Cosway, MSS Fesch, partially published in Barghazi 1925

7 Bassano, Museo Civico, MS Canoviani, III.301, nos 2929–32 (9 February, 24 March and 25 May 1807); and Lodi, Biblioteca Comunale Laudense, MS cartella autografi XVIII–XIX, MS 446 (24 April 1807)

8 Lozzi and Stroppa 1985, pp.9–24; Cazzulani and Stroppa 1989, pp.40–6, 81–92 and 97–104

9 Maria Cosway's extensive correspondence with Annette Prudon, dating from 1811 to 1834, is preserved in the Biblioteca Communale Laudense in Lodi. For its partial publication see Ferrari 1913–14.

10 I am grateful to G.E. Bentley Jr for allowing me to reproduce this passage from the Cumberland MSS, Commonplace Book, fol.54r, cf. Bentley 1991, Foscolo 1970, p.226, no.2187, letter from Albrizzi in Paris to Foscolo in London, dated 5 September 1817. For a letter from Foscolo to Maria, probably datable to 1819, cf. Manfredi 1988.

11 For this letter, dated 6 September 1817, from Foscolo, then in England, to the Countess of Albany, cf. Foscolo 1970, p.368, no.2295.

12 Francis Douce (1757–1834) and the writer and traveller, Sir John Carr (1772–1832), were the executors of Richard Cosway's estate. Legal documents concerning the estate of both Richard and Maria Cosway are preserved at the Fondazione Cosway in Lodi.

13 London, Daphne Ottaway, MS bill from Richard Jarvis and receipt dated 21 July 1821; Busco 1994, pp.154–5, fig.171; Britton and Pugin 1825, I, pp.178–9; Bolton 1927, p.338; for the shrine at the Collegio in Lodi see Williamson 1897, ill. opp. p.58, and Williamson 1905, ill. opp. p.78

14 Oxford, Bodleian Library, MS Douce d.24, fols. 32v–33r, letter of 22 April 1822 from Maria Cosway to Francis Douce, cf. Oxford 1984; London, Sir John Soane's Museum, priv. corresp. III, c.4.32, fol.IV, letter of 19 August 1830 from Maria Cosway to Sir John Soane, cf. Soane 1927

15 The painting by Seghers, then considered to be a Rembrandt, bequeathed by Maria Cosway to the Uffizi; Cosway 1826; Porro 1833, pp.20–1; Cosway 1825, published in Cazzulani and Stroppa 1989, pp.107–10

16 Cosway 1838

17 After Maria's death, her estate in London was claimed by her last executor there, Newbold Kinton. The Collegio delle Dame Inglesi in Lodi, led by its new superior, Annette Prudon, and also by Gaetano Giudici, the specific legatee, fought the case to reclaim this particular sum, as well as the rest of the estate based in London, cf. Lodi, Fondazione Cosway, MSS.

18 Maria Cosway's life and work in Lodi are suitably remembered in the epitaphs on the two monuments, the first in the church, the second in the Collegio: PIE RELIGIOSE / DIVOTE GIOVANETTE / QVI RACCOLTE AD ORARE / PREGATE PER L'ANIMA / DELLA BARONESSA / MARIA HADFIELD VEDOVA COSWAY / LA QUALE / NEL MDCCCXII ERESSE / QVESTO COLLEGIO DELLE GRAZIE / PER LVNGHI ANNI / PRVDAMENTE LO GOVERNO / E CON SAVIO CONSIGLIO / VOLLE FIDARLO ALLE DAME INGLESI / NEL MDCCXXXI / PASSATA AL SIGNORE / IL GIORNO V GENNAJO MDCCCXXXVIII / DEPOSTA NEL SOTTERRANEO / DI QUESTA SACRA EDICVLA / OVE NELLA COMMUNIONE / DELLE VOSTRE GRATE E FERVIDE PRECI / ASPETTA LA BEATA RISVRREZIONE [Pious religious / devoted young girls / gathered here for worship / pray for the soul / of Baroness / Maria Hadfield, widow, Cosway / who / in 1812 founded / this College of the Graces / and who for many years / prudently governed it / and with wise counsel / wished to entrust it to the Order of the English Women / in 1831 / she went to Our Lord / on the day of the 5th of January 1838 / she is placed in the crypt / of this sanctified building / where in the communion / of your thanks and fervid prayers / she awaits the blessed resurrection]

ALLA MEMORIA / DELLA CELEBRE DONNA / BARONESSA MARIA COSWAY / FONDATRICE / DI QUESTO FIORENTE COLLEGIO / ERETTO NEL MDCCCXII / PROVVEDUTO DI CENSO PERENNE / NEL MDCCCXXIX / CONFIDATO CON SOVRANO ASSENSO / ALL' INSTITUTO DELLE DAME INGLESI / NEL MCCCCXXXVIII / AMPLIATO NEL MDCCCXXXVIII / IL CONSIGLIO COMUNALE DI LODI / CONSERVATORE DI TANTO BENEFICIO / POSE RICONOSCENTE / NEL MDCCCXXXIX [To the memory / of the famous woman / Baroness Maria Cosway / founder / of this flourishing college / erected in 1812 / provided with a perennial endowment / in 1829 / entrusted with sovereign assent / to the Institute of the English Women / in 1830 / expanded in 1838 / the town council of Lodi / guardian of her endowment / erected this monument in recognition of her / in 1839]

1 For general accounts of the Cosways' London, see George Rudé, *Hanoverian London, 1714–1808*, London: Secker and Warburg, 1971; M.D. George, *London Life in the Eighteenth Century*, Harmondsworth: Penguin 1966; there is an up-to-date bibliographical essay in Roy Porter, *London: A Social History*, London: Hamish Hamilton, 1994.

2 See Francesca M. Wilson (ed), *Strange Island: Britain through Foreign Eyes 1395–1940*, London: Longmans, Green & Co., 1940; Clare Williams (ed and trans), *Sophie in London, 1786, Being the Diary of Sophie v. La Roche*, London: Jonathan Cape, 1933, p.85; Margaret L. Mare and W.H. Quarrell (eds and trans), *Lichtenberg's Visits to England as Described in his Letters and Diaries*, Oxford: Clarendon Press, 1938, p.79; Christopher Hibbert (ed), *Louis Simond: An American in Regency England: The Journal of a Tour in 1810–1811*, London: Robert Maxwell, 1968, p.20

3 Richard B. Schwartz, *Daily Life in Johnson's London*, Madison, Wisc.: University of Wisconsin Press, 1983; André Parreaux, *Smollett's London*, Paris: A.G. Nizet, 1968

4 Lady Holland (ed), *A Memoir of the Reverend Sydney Smith*, 2 vols, London: Longman, Brown, Green and Longmans, 1855, I, p.261

5 Edward Gibbon, *Memoirs of My Life*, ed G.A. Bonnard, London: Nelson, 1966, p.183

6 T.Davis, *John Nash*, Newton Abbot: David and Charles, 1973; Hermione Hobhouse, *A History of Regent Street*, London: Macdonald and Jane's, 1975; and the classic: Sir John N. Summerson, *The Life and Work of John Nash Architect*, London: Allen and Unwin, 1980

7 For Wedgwood, see N. McKendrick, 'Josiah Wedgwood: An Eighteenth Century Entrepreneur in Salesmanship and Marketing Techniques', *Economic History Review*, ns 12, 1960, pp.408–33

8 Robert Joseph Allen, *The Clubs of Augustan London*, Cambridge, Mass.: Harvard University Press, 1933; the interplay between artists, gentlemen and physicians is explored in Anne Darlington, 'The Teaching of Anatomical Instruction at the Royal Academy of Arts and the Cultural Consequences of Art-Anatomy Practices, circa 1768–1782; Ph.D. thesis, University of London 1991. For spectacles, see R.D. Altick, *The Shows of London: A Panoramic History of Exhibitions, 1600–1862*, Cambridge, Mass.: Belknap Press, 1978

9 Roy Porter, 'John Hunter Showman', *Transactions of the Hunterian Society*, xx, 1995, pp.xx–xxx

10 Roy Porter, 'The Sexual Politics of James Graham', *British Journal for Eighteenth Century Studies*, v, 1982, pp.201–6; Roy Porter, 'Sex and the Singular Man: the Seminal Ideas of James Graham', *Studies on Voltaire & the Eighteenth Century*, CCXXVIII, 1984, pp.3–24

11 Jonathan Miller, 'Mesmerism', *The Listener*, 22 Nov. 1973, pp.685–90; Roy Porter, '"Under the Influence": Mesmerism in England', *History Today*, xxxv, September 1985, pp.22–9

PORTRAYING THE FASHION, ROMANCING
THE PAST: DRESS AND THE COSWAYS

1 G.C.Williamson and P.Buckman, *The Art of the Portrait Miniature*, London 1926, p.214. As this quotation suggests, it is the work of Richard Cosway which concerns the fashion historian, rather than that of Maria, whose *forte* was more in the realm of subject pictures than in portraiture. The emphasis in this essay will therefore be on Richard Cosway, although it must be pointed out that Maria's scenes of Regency life give some sense of the period, albeit a slight glossy and sentimentalised one *à la* Angelica Kauffman.

2 The sword was a fashionable accoutrement for a gentleman during the first half of the eighteenth century, but from that time, as Englishmen's costume became less formal, its use declined, to be replaced by the cane. It is appropriate, in the context of Zoffany's painting, for Reynolds as an older man and President of the Royal Academy to wear a sword, but rather pompous for a young artist. The sword was taken up in the 1770s as a fashion accessory by the macaronis, although satirists claimed that such effeminate men were unlikely to use such weapons. Learning how to cope with the sword in full dress was not easy, and had to be taught, as part of deportment, by the dancing master. Cosway was reputed to have fallen over on one formal occasion, when his sword became entangled between his legs (Reported in Henry Angelo, *Reminiscences of …* , London 1828, pp.357–9, quoted in Williamson, *Richard Cosway* RA … , London 1897, p.28.)

3 J.T. Smith, *Nollekens and his Times*, London 1828, II, p.402. The bag, made of black silk, contained the back hair of the wig; such bag wigs were part of formal menswear during the eighteenth century, and Cosway wears one, for example, in Zoffany's painting of *The Academicians*. The toupée (or toupet) was the elevated front section of the wig; it can also refer to the natural hair at the front combed over a padded roll.

4 *The Lady's Magazine*, London 1773, p.371. See also Aileen Ribeiro, 'The Macaronis', *History Today*, XXVIII, no.7, July 1978, pp.463–8

5 S. Lloyd, 'Richard Cosway, RA: The artist as Collector, Connoisseur and *Virtuoso'*, *Apollo*, CXXXIII, no.352, June 1991, pp.398–405

6 *The World*, 4 June 1789, quoted in *The Whitley Papers*, IV, p.370, Department of Prints and Drawings, British Museum

7 Cosway's collections included some of the most stylish fashion plates of the late eighteenth century. Among these was J.-M. Moreau's *Monument du Costume Physique et Moral de la fin du dix-huitième siècle, ou Tableaux de la Vie* (1789) with a text by the French pornographer and writer Retif de la Bretonne, cf. Lodi, Fondazione Cosway, MS Inventory 1820.

8 Maria Cosway had 'A harp by Naderman' in her room at 20 Stratford Place, cf. Lodi, Fondazione Cosway, MS Inventory 1820, fol.19r

9 Earl of Bessborough (ed), *Extracts from the Correspondence of Georgiana, Duchess of Devonshire*, London 1955, p.91

10 There is a mention in *The Morning Post*, 27 March 1789, of a portrait of Mrs Fitzherbert: 'Cosway has a most beautiful and striking likeness of Mrs Fitzherbert; which to the regret of all amateurs is not quite finished. It is a drawing of most exquisite softness and expression and far beyond the usual productions of the artist.' (Quoted in the *Whitley Papers*, IV, p.368, Department of Prints and Drawings, British Museum.)

11 Quoted in V. Cumming, *Royal Dress*, London 1989, p.73

12 See, for example, the engraving after Cosway's drawing of *Mademoiselle La Chevalière d'Eon de Beaumont* [**87**] of 1787, where the sitter is shown in a mob cap of linen with a fluted and goffered edge, and decorated with ribbons and embroidered muslin; the portrait miniature of *Elizabeth, Countess of Hopetoun* [**68**], of 1789, with her frilled neck-kerchief which fastens with a black ribbon tie; and the miniature of an *Unknown Gentleman* [**119**] of 1793, with his fringed cravat tied in a bow.

13 *The Morning Post*, 16 June 1788, quoted in the *Whitley Papers*, IV, p.367, Department of Prints and Drawings, British Museum

14 The Yale Edition of Horace Walpole's *Correspondence*, XXXV, 1973, eds W.S. Lewis, A.D. Wallace and R.A. Smith, pp.418–19

15 The costume of the Order of the Garter was redesigned after the restoration of Charles II in 1660, and consisted of a doublet-style jacket and short round breeches (trunk hose) both of cloth of silver, to be worn under a surcoat and mantle. There is a series of drawings by Cosway of the Prince of Wales in Garter costume (*c*.1788) at the Fondazione Cosway, Lodi. The historical elements of Garter costume, particularly the quasi-Elizabethan doublet and hose, appealed to the romantic imagination of artists such as Cosway, and fitted in well with the vogue for Vandyke dress in the eighteenth century. A number of portraits exist (and not just by Cosway) in which Garter costume is subsumed into fanciful Vandyke dress.

16 For Thomas Jefferys's *Dresses of Different Nations* and Hollar's costume prints, which could either be the *Ornatus Muliebris Anglicanus* (1640) or the *Theatrum Mulierum* (1643), or – most probably – a mixture of both, cf.Lodi, Fondazione Cosway, MS Inventory 1820, and Cosway's 'Drawings and Prints' sale catalogue of 1822.

17 Cosway's drawing is copied from the engraving in Jefferys's *Collections of the Dresses of Different Nations*, I, 1757, pl.4, which is called 'Habit of the Sultaness Queen'. The source for Jefferys's plate is the series of etchings made by J.M. Vien for the oriental masquerade held in 1748 by the students of the French Academy in Rome; these were published as the *Caravanne du Sultan à la Mecque, Mascarade Turque donnée à Rome par Messieurs les Pensionaires de l'Académie de France et leurs Amis au Carnaval de l'année 1748*. Cosway's interest in oriental, and particularly Turkish, dress is evidenced by his ownership of a copy of the *Recueil de Cent Estampes représentant différentes Nations du Levant* (listed in the 1822 'Drawings and Prints' auction catalogue). This is the most important collection of illustrations of the costumes of the Ottoman empire of the eighteenth century, engraved after J.B. Vanmour and published in 1714.

18 *Habiti Antichi et Moderni di tutto il Mondo* by Cesare Vecellio, Venice 1598. An earlier edition, under a slightly different title, was published in 1590. There is no reference to Vecellio in Cosway's effects, but he was clearly familiar with this work, plates from which might have been part of his large collection of prints. The 1820 inventory at Lodi *does* mention another important late sixteenth-century costume book, Hans Weigel's *Habitus praecipuorum populorum*, published in Nuremberg in 1577.

19 Probably Rubens's sister-in-law Susanna Fourment. Richard Cosway's collections included many prints after Rubens, particularly of Rubens himself and his family. Maria Cosway was also interested in Rubens. There is another portrait of Maria in *Chapeau de Paille* costume (with Knoedler, London 1931) which may be by Richard or Maria.

20 A similar hat occurs in Cosway's portrait drawing of himself [**43**] of *c*.1788, which relates to an earlier self-portrait in similar costume at Lodi (no.1.7)

21 The Cosway inventory of 1820 at Lodi lists the 'Luxembourgh [*sic*] Gallery of Rubens'.

22 The costume of the St Esprit, the premier French order of chivalry, founded in 1578, consisted of doublet and trunk hose worn under a cloak or mantle; it was fairly close in spirit to the revamped English Garter costume, and it could thus be linked, in terms of historical period, to a combination of Elizabethan and Vandyke dress.

23 Lloyd, *op. cit.*, note 5 above. The 1821 sale catalogue of 'Miscellaneous Articles of Taste and Virtù' lists a 'large sandal-wood fan', and an 'embroidered glove, formerly Charles the First's', which is evidence of Cosway's fascination with that monarch.

24 William Hazlitt, *The Complete Works of …*, 21 vols, London and Toronto, 1930–4, ed P.P. Howe after A.R. Waller and Arnold Glover, XVIII, pp.173–9, quoted in G.C. Williamson, *Richard Cosway RA …*, London 1897, p.42

CATALOGUE

This catalogue is divided into six sections, which correspond to the layout of the exhibition. In each section the works are grouped chronologically in the following order: oil paintings; drawings; miniatures; prints; and other items.

All works are by Richard Cosway unless otherwise stated.

* Exhibited in Edinburgh only

† Exhibited in London only

I RICHARD COSWAY: 1742–80

1 *William Shipley* 1759-60

[colour plate 1]
Oil on canvas, 72 × 59cm (28⅜ × 23¼in)
COLLECTIONS: donated by the artist in 1785 through the intervention of Caleb Whitefoord
REFERENCES: London, RSA, Society of Arts MS Letter-book 16 December 1785, and Committee Minutes (Misc.) 22 August 1787; Whitley 1928a, I, p.168, II, pp.247–8; Nicholson 1931, p.326; Allan 1979, pp.123, 145 and 233–4
EXHIBITED: London, Society of Artists, 1760, no.9 ('Mr. Shipley')
ILLUSTRATED: Hudson and Luckhurst 1954, p.15; Webster 1970, p.3
ROYAL SOCIETY OF ARTS, LONDON

William Shipley (1715–1803) was one of the most important figures in the development of art institutions in London during the mid-eighteenth century. A drawing master, who ran a well-known school, he also founded the Society for the Encouragement of Arts, Manufactures and Commerce, which exists to this day. Cosway was one of his most successful pupils.

2 *The Witts family* 1769-70

Oil on canvas in fictive octagon, 118 × 104cm (46½ × 40⅞in)
COLLECTIONS: probably commissioned by Elizabeth or Sarah Witts; by family descent
REFERENCES: *Tate Report* 1994, pp.17–18 and 89
EXHIBITED: London, Royal Academy, 1770, no.49 ('The portraits of a gentleman, his wife, and sister, in the character of Fortitude introducing Hope as the companion to Distress')
TATE GALLERY, LONDON
(Inv. T06969)

This unusual and ambitious allegorical portrait was painted to commemorate the early death of Broome Witts (1738–69), a successful linen draper in the City of London. He is shown posthumously as Fortitude in the centre of the painting, introducing his sister Sarah Witts (1745-97) as Hope, as a companion to his wife Elizabeth (1739-1837), née London, depicted as Distress.

RICHARD COSWAY AFTER NATHANIEL DANCE (1735-1811)

3 *Lancelot 'Capability' Brown* c. 1770

Oil on canvas, 53 × 42.5cm (20⅞ × 1 6¾in)
COLLECTIONS: presumably to the sittter's son-in-law, the architect, Henry Holland; by family descent
ILLUSTRATED: Hinde 1986, opp. p.112
PRIVATE COLLECTION

Lancelot Brown (1715–83), was a landscape gardener and architect, known as 'Capability' Brown, who was the founder of the modern or English style of landscape gardening. This portrait, which has traditionally been attributed to Cosway, is clearly based on the oil by Nathaniel Dance of c.1769, which belongs to the National Portrait Gallery, London (see London 1977b, no.27, ill.).

4 *Self-portrait in Vandyke dress c.* 1770

Oil on canvas, 129.5 × 101.6cm (51 × 40in). Inscribed on plaque: RICHARD COSWAY R.A. / B. 1740 / D.1821 / PORTRAIT OF THE ARTIST AS HIMSELF
COLLECTIONS: probably acquired by the 1st, 2nd or 3rd Lord Berwick; bequeathed to the National Trust by the 8th Lord Berwick in 1947
EXHIBITED: London 1962, p.22, no.50; Bregenz and Vienna 1968-9, p.100, no.179; Liverpool 1994-5, p.73, no.130
ATTINGHAM PARK, THE BERWICK COLLECTION (THE NATIONAL TRUST)

Cosway shows himself wearing Vandyke dress, which was fashionable – especially in the mid-eighteenth century – for formal portraiture and masquerade balls. By placing the masks on the table, Cosway presents himself as if he is about to attend one of these fashionable events.

5 *Charles Townley with a group of connoisseurs* 1771-5

[colour plate 21]
Oil on canvas, 85.1 × 110.5cm (33½ × 43½in)
COLLECTIONS: commissioned by Charles Townley, £100 paid to Cosway on 14 October 1775 (see London, British Museum, Charles Townley's MS account book); by family descent; the 3rd Lord O'Hagan's sale, Christie's, London, 19 May 1939, lot 93; Christie's, London, 1 June 1956, lot 75; purchased through Thos. Agnew's and Sons Ltd, London
REFERENCES: Manners and Williamson 1920, pp.124 and 223–4, ill. opp. p.124; Vaughan 1989, I, pp.374–5, II, fig.2
ILLUSTRATED: Saxl and Wittkower 1948, pl.58, fig.5; Lloyd 1991, p.399, fig.2
TOWNELEY HALL ART GALLERY AND MUSEUMS, BURNLEY BOROUGH COUNCIL
(Inv. PA/oil 195)

Cosway painted this group portrait as a commission from his friend Charles Townley (1737-1805). One of the lascivious connoisseurs, Chase Price, is shown sitting in the artist's *Sitter's chair* [216] designed by Matthias Lock, which can be seen also in the portrait of *Mrs Draper* [6]. The quality of Cosway's painting was recognised, throughout the first half of this century, by the erroneous attribution of this painting to Johann Zoffany.

6 *Mrs Draper c.* 1775

[colour plate 19]
Oil on canvas, 74.3 × 56.7cm (29¼ × 23½in)
COLLECTIONS: Sotheby's, London, 29 May 1963, lot 91; Messrs Sabin, London
REFERENCES: Hardy 1973, p.705, fig.2; Hayward 1973, p.271
ILLUSTRATED: Ribeiro 1983, p.100, no.109
PRIVATE COLLECTION

Mrs Draper (1744-88) is better known as Sterne's 'Immortal Eliza', the subject of the writer's infatuation in *The Journal to Eliza*, mediated through an untraced portrait miniature of her by Cosway. She was born Elizabeth Whitehill, and married Daniel Draper, an official with the East India Company. Cosway has shown her in fashionable dress, seated in his *Sitter's chair* [216], also represented in the *Townley group* [5].

7 *Marianne Dorothy Harland, later Mrs Dalrymple* 1779

[colour plate 30]
Oil on canvas, 71.1 × 91.8cm (27½ × 35½in)
COLLECTIONS: Charles E. Dashwood, Wherstead Park, Ipswich; his sale Christie's, London, 26 June 1914, lot 94, sold to Frederick Pollard; Christie's, London, 20 May 1917, lot 24; Mrs W.S. Salting, her sale Christie's, London, 20 May 1927, lot 44, sold to Arthur Tooth; Daniel H. Farr Company, New York, by 1930
REFERENCES: *The St. James Chronicle*, 1–4 May 1779, p.4
EXHIBITED: Royal Academy, London 1779, no.58 ('A Lady playing on the harp; small whole length')
THE METROPOLITAN MUSEUM OF ART, NEW YORK
Gift of Mrs William M. Haupt, from the Collection of Mrs James B. Haggin, 1969
(Inv. 69.104)

Marianne Dorothy Harland (1759-85) was the second daughter of Admiral Sir Robert Harland, Bt (c.1715-84) of Sproughton Hall, Suffolk, and his second wife Susan Reynolds. In 1783 Marianne Harland married General William Dalrymple (1735-1807), who was appointed Lieutenant-Governor of the Chelsea Hospital in 1798, the same year he was promoted to General. They had one child, John William Henry, who succeeded as 7th Earl of Stair (1784-1840).

8   *Robert, 4th Duke of Ancaster and Kesteven, with his sister Lady Georgiana Bertie c.*1779–80

[colour plate 42]
Oil on canvas, 125.7 × 100.4cm (49½ × 39½in).
Signed on base of right hand column: *R Cosway R A*. Inscribed on shield: A / K (for Ancaster and Kesteven)
COLLECTIONS: probably commissioned by Mary Panton, Duchess of Ancaster, mother of the sitters; by family descent
GRIMSTHORPE AND DRUMMOND CASTLE TRUST

In this double portrait Cosway represents, posthumously, Robert Bertie, 4th Duke of Ancaster (1756–79), being crowned with a laurel wreath (see Tudsbery-Turner 1991) by one of his younger sisters Lady Georgiana Bertie (1764–1838), who is depicted as the winged figure of Fame, holding a palm branch in her right hand. Cosway copied the portrait of the Duke from his earlier miniatures, two of which are set in patch boxes [**21**][**47**], while dressing the figure anachronistically in armour. This ambitious composition is based on Rubens's iconography of armoured heroes being crowned by Fame, combined with Van Dyck's framed settings for portraits of Charles I and his family. A preparatory drawing survives at the Fondazione Cosway in Lodi, in which Cosway depicts another sister of the 4th Duke, Lady Priscilla Bertie (1761–1828), later Baroness Willoughby de Eresby, attaching a cloak over the armour of her brother, while a child plays with his helmet.

9   *Rinaldo and Armida* 1772

[colour plate 28]
Oil on canvas, 45.5 × 56.7cm (17⅞ × 22¼in).
Engraved: (variant composition without putti) mezzotint by H. Dawe, *Rinaldo and Armida*, 1780 (see Daniell 1890, p.49, no.200)
EXHIBITED: Royal Academy, London 1772, no.56 ('Rinaldo and Armida, from Tasso')
PRIVATE COLLECTION

This recently rediscovered painting is a rare surviving example of Richard Cosway's subject paintings. The subject is taken from Tasso's popular Renaissance epic poem *Gerusalemme Liberata*. This particular scene was commonly painted by seventeenth-century Italian and French artists, such as Poussin, a tradition of which Cosway was well aware. Cosway also interpreted this scene of idyllic eroticism in a watercolour [**10**].

10*   *Rinaldo and Armida c.*1772

[colour plate 29]
Pen and ink with watercolour, 18.4 × 22.5cm (7¼ × 8⅞in); with original mount 25.7 × 29.8cm (10⅛ × 11¾in). Signed in pencil on mount below drawing: *Rᵈᵘˢ: Cosway Primarius Pictor Serenissimi Walliae Principis fecit*. Inscribed in pencil on mount above drawing: *Rinaldo & Armida*
COLLECTIONS: acquired (between 1785 and before 1822) for Duke Albert von Sachsen-Teschen
REFERENCES: Hermann 1992, p.25, no.10
EXHIBITED: Bregenz and Vienna 1968-9, p.100, no.182, fig.273
GRAPHISCHE SAMMLUNG ALBERTINA, VIENNA (Inv. 13010)

Duke Albert von Sachsen-Teschen acquired two drawings by Cosway, this sheet and the *Perseus and Medusa* [**44**], although this must have occurred after 1785, when Cosway was entitled to use his full Latin signature. Patrick Noon has described this one among several superb British figure drawings collected by the Duke, and has also stated that this sheet 'may well rank as [Cosway's] most charming extant watercolor'.

11   *Anthony and Cleopatra c.*1770–80

Pen and ink, brush with grey wash, watercolour, 22.3 × 17.5cm (8¾ × 6⅞in). Signed on ledge below sphinx: *RC*. Inscribed on verso: *Richard Cosway / Anthony and Cleopatra / From the Hodgkins Collection Paris*
COLLECTIONS: E.M. Hodgkins, Paris; Christie's, New York, 15 January 1992, lot 178 (as by Edward Francis Burney)
THOMAS WILLIAMS, LONDON

This study of *Anthony and Cleopatra* is one of Cosway's rare watercolours, which he executed early in his career. It can be related to the finished *Rinaldo and Armida* [**10**], as well as to two sheets from the 1770s of 'Sappho committing Suicide' and 'The Choice of Hercules' (both Fondazione Cosway, Lodi, nos IV.40 and III.10). It is notable for the delicate line in pen and ink, as well as for the muted application of watercolour.

12   *Thomas Cosway c.*1761

[colour plate 4]
Watercolour on ivory, height 3.2cm (1¼in)
COLLECTIONS: his daughter Mary Kingsmill Cosway (married Henry Whiting), by family descent
PRIVATE COLLECTION

Thomas Cosway, who was a naval officer, was either the uncle or a first cousin of the artist. His second wife, whom he married in 1761, was *Katharine Cosway*, née Proby [**13**], whom Richard Cosway also portrayed in a miniature. These are two of the artist's earliest surviving miniatures, which are painted in the style of the so-called 'modest school'.

13   *Katharine Cosway c.*1761

[colour plate 6]
Watercolour on ivory, height 3.4cm (1⅜in)
COLLECTIONS: her daughter, Mary Kinsgmill Cosway (married Henry Whiting), by family descent
PRIVATE COLLECTION

Katharine Cosway (née Proby) was the second wife of *Thomas Cosway* [**12**].

14   *An unknown divine c.*1760–70

[colour plate 8]
Watercolour on ivory, diam. 2.8cm (1⅛in)
ILLUSTRATED: Foskett 1972, II, pl.60, no.170
PRIVATE COLLECTION

RICHARD COSWAY AFTER SIR JOSHUA REYNOLDS (1723-92)

15   *Henry, 3rd Duke of Buccleuch, and his brother the Hon. Campbell Scott* 1764.

[colour plate 7]

Watercolour on ivory, height 3.5cm (1⅜in).
Signed and dated on verso: *R. Cosway / Pinxit / 1764*
COLLECTIONS: by family descent
HIS GRACE THE DUKE OF BUCCLEUCH AND QUEENSBERRY, KT

This is a partial copy after an oil portrait by Reynolds (1758; private collection) of the two brothers together with their sister, Lady Frances Scott, the children of Francis, Earl of Dalkeith. The elder brother was Henry Scott, 3rd Duke of Buccleuch and 5th Duke of Queensberry (1746–1812). The other brother, the Hon. Campbell Scott (1747–66), was also portrayed by Cosway in a miniature (*c.*1767; private collection), after a portrait by Greuze (*c.*1766).

16   *Lady Sarah Bunbury c.*1765-70

[colour plate 9]
Watercolour on ivory, height 5.8cm (2¼in).
Inscribed on verso in pen and ink on paper: *Lady Sarah Napier*
COLLECTIONS: purchased from W.J. Hartley
VICTORIA AND ALBERT MUSEUM, LONDON (Inv. P64-1935)

Sarah Lennox, later Lady Sarah Napier (1745–1826), who is best known as Lady Sarah Bunbury, was the daughter of the 2nd Duke of Richmond. In 1762 she married Sir Thomas Charles Bunbury MP, with the marriage being dissolved in 1776. She went on to marry the Hon. George Napier in 1781. She was the subject of one of Reynolds's best-known full-length female portraits, shown sacrificing to the Graces (1765; Art Institute of Chicago).

17   *Miss Elliot in the character of Pallas* 1769

[colour plate 5]
Watercolour on ivory, height 11.2cm (4⅜in)
EXHIBITED: London, Society of Artists, 1769, no. 27 ('A Portrait in miniature of a Lady as Pallas')
ILLUSTRATED: J. Saunders, MISS ELLIOT *in the Character of* MINERVA, mezzotint, published by H. Bryer 1772, 2nd state 1774 (see Bromley 1793, p.435 and Daniell 1890, p.16, no. 64)
FONDAZIONE COSWAY, LODI

Ann Elliot (1743–69) was an actress. The mezzotint may alternatively be after Cosway's untraced oil portrait of the same sitter, which was exhibited at the Royal Academy in 1770, no. 48 ('A portrait in the character of Minerva').

18   *Self-portrait in profile c.*1770

[colour plate 17]
Watercolour on ivory, height 5cm (2in)
COLLECTIONS: acquired by the Metropolitan Museum of Art in 1962
THE METROPOLITAN MUSEUM OF ART, NEW YORK
Gift of Miss Charlotte Guilford Muhlofer, 1962 (Inv. 62.49)

Cosway is here imitating the closely painted technique and style of his great rival at court, the German born Jeremiah Meyer. In a *tour de force* of miniature painting, the artist presents himself, with his distinctive profile, as one of the supremely fashionable macaronies or dandies, who were often caricatured at this period [**26**][**27**]. Graham Reynolds has verbally suggested that this might be an early self-portrait by Cosway.

19 *Anne, Countess Winterton c.*1775–80

[colour plate 14]
Watercolour on ivory, height 4.6cm (1⅞in)
REFERENCES: Reynolds 1988, p.127, pl. 78
BERNARD FALK COLLECTION ON LOAN TO THE
FITZWILLIAM MUSEUM, CAMBRIDGE
Graham Reynolds has pointed out that this is
an important transitional miniature by
Cosway, between the tightly close-hatched and
dark hues of his early work and the lighter
tonality and freer brushwork demonstrated
from the 1780s onwards. This miniature is a
good example of the artist's soft and rhythmic
drawing. It is also an early demonstration of
one of Cosway's favourite later techniques, the
enlargement of the size of the pupil in the eye.

20 *Thomas, 2nd Lord Lyttleton c.*1775–9

[colour plate 15]
Watercolour on ivory in gold and enamelled
frame; on verso, watercolour and diamond
setting with woman and Cupid grieving at a
monument), height 4.4cm (1¾in)
ILLUSTRATED: Williamson 1904, I, pl.lvi
PRIVATE   COLLECTION
Thomas, 2nd Lord Lyttleton (1744–79), was one
of the most notorious rakes of the 1770s, whose
strange early death was recorded in a posthumous oil portrait by Cosway, which was later
engraved [79]. The verso, which dates from
*c.*1780, shows a mythological female figure and
Cupid mourning at a monument comprised of a
coronet mounted on an urn on a plinth, which
is adorned with the Lyttleton coat of arms.
Godfrey Evans has verbally suggested that the
miniature's very fine setting may be the work of
James Morisset.

21 *Robert, 4th Duke of Ancaster and
Kesteven c.*1775–9

[colour plate 18]
Watercolour on ivory miniature, framed with
diamonds in silver setting, surrounded by
plaited hair, set under glass into lid of shuttle-
shaped gold patch box; miniature, height 3.2cm
(1¼in); box, depth 5.1cm, length
12.1cm, height 1.3cm high (2 × 4¾ × ½in).
Inscribed inside rim: *Robert, 4th Duke of
Ancaster*
ILLUSTRATED: Williamson 1897, p.82; Cazzulani
and Stroppa 1989, opp. p.104
GRIMSTHORPE AND DRUMMOND CASTLE TRUST
Robert Bertie, 4th Duke of Ancaster (1756–79),
was the only surviving son of Peregrine, 3rd
Duke, and his second wife, Mary (née Panton).
In 1778 he fought briefly in America, before
returning to succeed his father. His early death
(see Tudsbery-Turner 1991) was commemo-
rated by Cosway in an oil painting, in which he
was depicted together with his sister, Lady
Georgiana Bertie [8], as well as by the inclusion
of a copy of his portrait by Cosway in 'The
Ancaster Box' [47].

RICHARD COSWAY AFTER THOMAS
GAINSBOROUGH (1727–88)

22 *William Bouverie, 2nd Viscount
Folkestone and 1st Earl of Radnor* 1812

[colour plate 11]

Watercolour on ivory, height 8.5cm (3⅜in)
COLLECTIONS: probably commissioned by Jacob,
2nd Earl of Radnor, in 1812; by family descent
REFERENCES: Radnor and Squire 1909, p.112
PRIVATE   COLLECTION
William, 1st Earl of Radnor (1725–76), was the
inaugural President of the Society of Arts. The
original portrait by Gainsborough, of which
Cosway's portrait is a free interpretation, is in a
private collection. The sitter's son Jacob, the
2nd Earl [62], was one of Cosway's most
important patrons and a major purchaser of
Old Master pictures from the artist.

JOHN BOGLE (C.1746–1803)

23 *Commodore George Johnstone
c.*1767–74

[colour plate 12]
Watercolour on ivory, height 9.9cm (3⅞in).
Signed: *I Bogle / Pinxt*
COLLECTIONS: Edward Grosvenor Paine
REFERENCES: Smailes 1990, p.162
EXHIBITED: Edinburgh 1965, no. 267, pl. 66
SCOTTISH NATIONAL PORTRAIT GALLERY
(Inv. PG 2523)
Commodore George Johnstone (1730–87) was
the fourth son of Sir James Johnstone of
Westerhall, Dumfriesshire. He distinguished
himself in the attack on Port Louis in 1748. He
was the Governor of West Florida in 1765 and
elected a Director of the East India Company in
1783. This miniature was the basis for later oil
paintings of Johnstone by an artist in the circle
of Zoffany (Greenwich) and by Raeburn
(private collection). John Bogle was one of the
finest Scottish miniaturists working in London
during the later eighteenth century.

RICHARD CROSSE (1742–1810)

24 *Self-portrait c.*1780

[colour plate 10]
Watercolour on ivory, height 15.2cm (6in)
COLLECTIONS: acquired from the Rev. W. E.
Crosse, North Devon
REFERENCES: Noon 1981, p.181, pl. 195
VICTORIA AND ALBERT MUSEUM, LONDON
(Inv. P147-1929)
Richard Crosse, a deaf-mute, was, like Cosway,
a Devonian, and a fellow student at Shipley's
drawing school. Crosse was a key figure in the
generation of younger artists who emerged in
the 1760s and transformed this genre of
portraiture over the next generation. This self-
portrait is Crosse's masterpiece, which displays
his tightly controlled, linear draughtsmanship.

T. CHAMBARS (*c.*1724–89)
AFTER RICHARD COSWAY

25 *Edward Goldney* 1759

Line engraving, 19.8 × 11.3cm (7¾ × 4½in).
Lettered: *R. Cosway del. / T. Chambars sculp. /
Edward Goldney Sen.ʳ Gent. / Love without
Dissimulation / Past four a'Clock, star-light
Morning*
REFERENCES: Bromley 1793, p.387; Daniell 1890,
p.21, no. 84
ILLUSTRATED: Goldney 1759, frontispiece
BRITISH MUSEUM, LONDON
(Inv. 1875-8-14-1262)

Edward Goldney (b.1710) was a printer based in
Bristol. This is the earliest of Cosway's works to
have been engraved, and was the frontispiece to
Goldney's *Epistles to Deists and Jews,* first
published in London in 1759, with a second
edition following a year later. An impression at
Windsor has the additional lettering under the
title, *Widower,* and also the publication line,
*London New Years Morn. 1.ˢᵗ Jan. 1759 S.ᵗ Paul's
Church Yard.*

M. DARLY (*fl.*1750–78)

26 *The miniature macaroni* 1772

Etching, 17.6 × 12.5cm (6⅞ × 4⅞in)
REFERENCES: Smith 1828, II, p.393
PRIVATE   COLLECTION
Matthew Darly was a printseller, etcher,
designer of chinoiserie, drawing master and
caricaturist who specialised in depicting
macaronies, or fashionable young dandies of
the early 1770s. An impression in the Department of Prints and Drawings, British Museum
(George 1935, no.5031), gives the publication
date as 24 September 1772.

P. DAWE (*fl.c.*1768–80)

27 *The macaroni painter, or Billy Dimple
sitting for his picture* 1772

Mezzotint without letters, 33.3 × 25cm
(13⅛ × 10¼in)
REFERENCES: Smith 1828, II, p.393
THE HON. CHRISTOPHER LENNOX-BOYD
This mezzotint was engraved by Philip Dawe,
although an early tradition noted that it had
been drawn by R. Dighton and engraved by R.
Earlom. It is exceptionally rare and it appears
that Cosway may have sought to acquire and
then destroy as many copies as possible. An
impression in the Department of Prints and
Drawings at the British Museum (George 1935,
no.4582) is lettered: *The* MACARONI PAINTER, *or*
BILLY DIMPLE *sitting for his* PICTURE. / *Printed for
Bowles & Carver, Map & Printsellers N.º 69 in
St. Paul's Church Yard, London.*

G. STUBBS (1724–1806)
OR G. T. STUBBS (1756–1815)
AFTER RICHARD COSWAY

29 *Gaetano Manini ('Il Milanese')* 1780

Etching, 24.1 × 19.1cm (9½ × 7½in).
Lettered: *Il Milanese / Published as the Act
Directs may ᵗʰ 25 1780 / God damn much the
devil a bit nothing at all Signify to me / you be
one damn Rat you broil very well / for supper .*
Inscribed in pen in a contemporary hand:
Nobody know wat sort a Man I be
REFERENCES: Daniell 1890, p.25, no. 99
LENT BY HER MAJESTY THE QUEEN
The Chevalier or Cavalier Gaetano Manini
(*c.*1730 – *c.*1780/90) was a Milanese artist who
came to London around 1755 and practised as a
minor enameller and history painter, exhibiting subject pictures at the Free Society of
Artists as well as at the Society of Artists from
1761 to 1775. According to Daniell he was also a
picture dealer with whom Cosway quarrelled.
An impression of this etching – formerly
belonging to Sir Philip Currie – was inscribed
in a contemporary hand 'Cosway had this print
etched in ridicule of him'. However, it is not

clear what the nature of the quarrel was, whether to do with a dispute over commissions or clients, or concerning a more personal matter. An impression in the New York Public Library is inscribed in a contemporary hand 'G Stubbs fecit', while another with Norman Blackburn (1992) states 'G.T. Stubbs fecit'. It is unclear which of the Stubbs, father or son, actually etched what is one of Cosway's very rare surviving caricatures.

II RICHARD AND MARIA COSWAY: 1780-90

29 *John, 5th Duke of Argyll c.*1780-5

[colour plate 43]
Oil on canvas, 127 × 101.6cm (50 × 40in).
Signed: *R^d Cosway RA*
COLLECTIONS: by family descent
ILLUSTRATED: Cornforth and Hughes-Hartman 1990, p.23 (colour)
TRUSTEES OF THE 10TH DUKE OF ARGYLL

John, 5th Duke of Argyll (1723-1806), commanded a number of Scottish regiments before becoming a Field Marshal. He married Elizabeth Gunning, a great beauty of her day, and they made considerable improvements to Inveraray Castle. In what is one of Cosway's boldest swagger portraits the artist has depicted the Duke in imaginary seventeenth-century armour.

30 *Elizabeth Milbanke, Viscountess Melbourne* 1784

[colour plate 44]
Oil on panel, 76.4 × 62.9cm (30 × 24¾in).
Signed in monogram: *RC*
COLLECTIONS: commissioned by the Prince of Wales in 1784 for £31.10s, 'A Portrait of a Lady in Oil' (Windsor Castle MSS, Cosway's account 1781-6, RA 26792)
REFERENCES: Williamson 1897, p.117; Millar 1969, I, p.21, no. 716, II, pl.137
EXHIBITED: London 1991-2, p.63, no.14
LENT BY HER MAJESTY THE QUEEN

Elizabeth Milbanke (1752-1818) married the 1st Viscount Melbourne, who was Lord to the Bedchamber to the Prince of Wales, at which stage she became the Prince's mistress, and later she was much admired by Byron. Her son became the Prime Minister, Lord Melbourne (1778–1848), who was a close adviser to the young Queen Victoria. Cosway portrayed Lady Melbourne in fancy seventeenth-century costume, which was particularly fashionable in the 1780s.

31 *An unknown lady on horseback c.*1788

[colour plate 45]
Oil on panel, 67 × 51.7cm (26⅜ × 20⅜in)
COLLECTIONS: Philip Mead; Victor Spark, New York; purchased 1973
THE DUKE OF DEVONSHIRE AND THE CHATSWORTH SETTLEMENT TRUSTEES

This unfinished panel, in which Cosway utilises stylistic and compositional motifs from the paintings of Rubens and Van Dyck, has also been attributed to Gainsborough Dupont. The sitter has traditionally been identified as Lady Elizabeth Foster, later Duchess of Devonshire, although she may be a Mrs Hill painted in 1788. In that year an equestrian portrait by Cosway of this sitter was criticised in three verses from a contemporary newspaper (Long 1929, p.97).

32 *William, 3rd Earl of Radnor, with his sister the Hon. Mary Anne Pleydell-Bouverie* 1785

[colour plate 46]
Oil on canvas, 100 × 126cm (39⅜ × 49⅝in). Signed in lower right corner with monogram: *CR*. Engraved: in stipple as *Infancy* by C. White, 1787 (Daniell 1890, p.46, no. 187)
COLLECTIONS: commissioned by Jacob, 2nd Earl of Radnor, in 1785; by family descent
REFERENCES: Radnor and Squire 1909, II, pp.88-9, no.LXXXIII
PRIVATE COLLECTION

According to Lord Radnor's account books, on 24 October 1785 the sum of £115 was paid to 'Cosway for the Pictures of my 3 eldest Children', which included the pair of the Hon. Duncombe Pleydell-Bouverie (later Admiral) as the Infant Baptist. From 1781 to 1812 Jacob, 2nd Earl of Radnor, was one of Cosway's most significant clients, both in terms of portrait commissions and in purchasing important Old Master paintings from the artist. William, 3rd Earl of Radnor (1779-1869), and his sister Lady Mary Anne Pleydell-Bouverie (1778-90) are shown in an idyllic composition that is based on a Rubensian prototype. This painting is one of Cosway's most charming essays in child portraiture, a genre in which the artist excelled.

33 *Maria Cosway c.*1781-3

[colour plate 31]
Pencil with watercolour, 28.6 × 24.2cm (11¼ × 9½in), oval. Inscribed on mount (partially cut): *Maria*
BERYL KENDALL

This is Richard Cosway's earliest and one of his most direct portraits of Maria. The drawing has been altered at some stage, possibly by Cosway himself later in life.

34 *Self-portrait with Maria Cosway c.*1785

[colour plate 33]
Red and black chalk with wash over pencil, 31.4 × 22.4cm (12⅜ × 8⅞in); with original mount 46.7 × 35.7cm (18⅜ × 14in)
COLLECTIONS: Richard Cosway; Maria Cosway; Collegio delle Dame Inglesi, Lodi
FONDAZIONE COSWAY, LODI

This is the most deliberately Rubensian of all Richard Cosway's self-portraits together with Maria, and is closely inspired by the famous Rubens self-portrait with his first wife, Isabella Brant (Alte Pinakothek, Munich). It is not clear why Cosway left Maria's face unfinished.

35 *The Duchesse de Polignac* 1786

Pencil with watercolour, 23.2 × 14.2cm (9⅛ × 5⅝in); with original wash-lined mount 33.1 × 23.1cm (13 × 9⅛in). Inscribed in pencil on mount: *La Duchesse de Polignac*
PRIVATE COLLECTION

Yolande Martine Gabrielle de Polastron (*c.*1749-93), the wife of Armand Jules François Polignac, was one of the leading figures in Parisian society, and intimate with Marie Antoinette. The drawing was one of the very portraits that Cosway deigned to execute – despite being greatly in demand – on his visit to Paris with Maria in 1786. It was through the Duchesse that Cosway was able to examine the Rubens cycle of paintings celebrating the life of Marie de Médicis, which were still in the dilapidated Palais du Luxembourg (now in the Louvre). John Trumbull, who accompanied the Cosways on their visit on 9 August, noted in his diary, 'I owe this almost greatest pleasure I ever received from the arts, to his politeness' (Trumbull 1953, p.108).

36 *Self-portrait with busts of Michelangelo and Rubens c.*1789

[colour plate 40]
Pen and ink on original mount, 24.2 × 13.8cm (9½ × 5½in); mount, 39.3 × 28.5cm (15½ × 11¼in). Signed in monogram: *RC*. Inscribed: NATURA / *sculptura*
COLLECTIONS: Maria Cosway; Collegio delle Dame Inglesi, Lodi
REFERENCES: Lloyd 1991, p.398, pl. 1
EXHIBITED: Washington 1976, p.199, no. 343 (entry by Ross Watson)
ILLUSTRATED: Lloyd 1993, p.193, pl. 2 (p.125); Sciolla 1993, p.95, pl. 101
FONDAZIONE COSWAY, LODI
(Inv. I.1)

Two related studies in pen and ink exist for this portrait (private collection).

37 *Maria Cosway with a bust of Leonardo c.*1789

[colour plate 41]
Pen and ink on original mount, 23.7 × 15.4cm (9⅜ × 6¼in); with mount 39.7 × 29cm (15⅝ × 11⅜in)
COLLECTIONS: Maria Cosway; Collegio delle Dame Inglesi, Lodi
EXHIBITED: Washington 1976, p.198, no.341 (entry by Ross Watson)
FONDAZIONE COSWAY, LODI
(Inv. I.2)

38 *Lady Mildmay* 1789

Pencil with watercolour on original mount, 30 × 22.5cm (11¾ × 8⅝in) with mount. Signed on mount: *R.^dus Cosway R.A. Primarius Pictor Serenissimi Principis Pictor fecit 1789*
COLLECTIONS: by family descent
PRIVATE COLLECTION

39 *Vincent Lunardi* 1784

Pencil with wash, framed as a miniature, height 10.8cm (4¼in). Engraved: in stipple by F. Bartolozzi, VINCENT LUNARDI ESQ^r., 1784 (Daniell 1890, p.24, no. 96)
COLLECTIONS: Joseph Propert; Lord Tweedmouth; acquired by Henry E. Huntington through Duveen in 1927
REFERENCES: Reynolds 1992, pp.121-2, fig. 54
HENRY E. HUNTINGTON LIBRARY AND ART GALLERY, SAN MARINO, CALIFORNIA
(Inv. 27.152)

Vincent Lunardi (1759-1806), as the lettering on the 1784 engraving stated, was 'Secretary to the Neapolitan Ambassador, and the first aerial traveller in the English Atmosphere Septr. 15. 1784'. This ballooning exploit made Lunardi a phenomenal celebrity. In his portrait sketch Cosway suggests Lunardi's aerial feat through the windswept hair and the unusual angle of the head and figure.

40 *Hannah Cowley c.*1785-90

Pencil, framed as a miniature, height 9.5cm (3^7⁄8in). Inscribed on verso: *Mrs. Hannah Cowley*
COLLECTIONS: Joseph Propert; Lord Tweedmouth; acquired by Henry E. Huntington through Duveen in 1927
HENRY E. HUNTINGTON LIBRARY AND ART GALLERY, SAN MARINO, CALIFORNIA (Inv. 27.146)
Hannah Cowley (1743-1809) was a dramatist and, like Cosway, a native of Tiverton in Devon.

41 *Anne Damer c.*1785-90

Pencil with watercolour, framed as a miniature, 12.1 × 7.6cm (4^3⁄4 × 3in)
COLLECTIONS: Joseph Propert; Lord Tweedmouth; acquired by Henry E. Huntington through Duveen in 1927
REFERENCES: Reynolds 1992, pp. 121-2, fig. 55
HENRY E. HUNTINGTON LIBRARY AND ART GALLERY, SAN MARINO, CALIFORNIA (Inv. 27.147)
Anne Seymour Damer (1749-1828), née Conway, was the most notable sculptress of her generation in Britain (Whinney 1988, pp.319-20 and 465; Noble 1908). As cousin, friend and residual legatee of Horace Walpole, she inherited Strawberry Hill and most of its contents. The Cosways were close friends of Mrs Damer, and Richard portrayed her on at least two other occasions [57][95].

42 *The Comte d'Hautefeuille c.*1785-90

Pencil drawing with watercolour, framed as a miniature, height 11.2cm (4^3⁄8in). Inscribed on verso: *Charles Louis Felicité Texier Comte d'Hautefeuille*
COLLECTIONS: Joseph Propert; Lord Tweedmouth; acquired by Henry E. Huntington through Duveen in 1927
HENRY E. HUNTINGTON LIBRARY AND ART GALLERY, SAN MARINO, CALIFORNIA (Inv. 27.150)
The Comte d'Hautefeuille (1755-1814) was a noted dramatist, admired by Voltaire. He later lived in Holland, London and Germany where he presented a successful series of public lectures on drama. This portrait sketch is one of Cosway's most incisive male character studies.

43 *Self-portrait in Spanish dress c.*1788

Pencil with watercolour, framed as a miniature, 12.1 × 7.7cm (4^3⁄4 × 3in). Engraved: in stipple by J. Clarke, *Richd Cosway, Esq.*, 1788 (Bromley 1793, p.400; Daniell 1890, p.9, no. 32)
COLLECTIONS: The Countess of Yarborough; Joseph Propert; Lord Tweedmouth; acquired by Henry E. Huntington through Duveen in 1927
REFERENCES: Reynolds 1992, p.121, fig. 53
HENRY E. HUNTINGTON LIBRARY AND ART GALLERY, SAN MARINO, CALIFORNIA (Inv. 27.141)

44* *Perseus and Medusa c.*1785-90

Pen and ink with watercolour, 18.7 × 27.1cm (7^3⁄8 × 10^5⁄8in); with original mount 25.1 × 33.7cm (9^7⁄8 × 13^1⁄4in). Signed on mount in pencil: *R.^{dus} Cosway Primarius Pictor Serenissimi Walliae Principis Fecit.* Inscribed on mount: *R. Cosway.*
COLLECTIONS: acquired (between 1785 and before 1822) for Duke Albert Sachsen-Teschen
REFERENCES: Hermann 1992, p.24, no.9
GRAPHISCHE SAMMLUNG ALBERTINA, VIENNA (Inv. 13009)

45 *Andromache and Astyanax* 1789

Watercolour over pencil, 14.6 × 12.1cm (5^7⁄8 × 4^3⁄4in). Signed with monogram: *RC.*
Engraved: in stipple (1789) by J. Condé, ANDROMACHE AND ASCANIUS (Daniell 1890, p.42, no. 167)
COLLECTIONS: Richard Cosway; Sir John Soane
REFERENCES: Soane Museum, MS Inventory 1837, Picture Room ('Andromache & Astyanax')
SIR JOHN SOANE'S MUSEUM, LONDON (Inv. P120)
The subject is taken from Homer's *Iliad* (VI: 394-496), where Hector takes leave of his wife and child prior to his final and fatal encounter with Achilles in the Trojan War. Cosway has portrayed Andromache restraining Astyanax as he says farewell to his father. The composition is based on a famous drawing by Raphael, of a seated woman embracing a standing child, which belonged to Sir Thomas Lawrence and is now in the Ashmolean Museum, Oxford (no. P.II.561). The print was published as a pair with one of the lovers *Polindo and Albarosa*, likewise engraved in stipple by J. Condé.

46 *An unknown lady c.*1780

[colour plate 16]
Watercolour on ivory, height 6.3cm (2^1⁄2in)
COLLECTIONS: probably acquired for the Royal Collection on 2 July 1858
REFERENCES: Walker 1992, pp. 98-9, no.194
EXHIBITED: London 1970, no.53
LENT BY HER MAJESTY THE QUEEN
This watercolour was acquired for the Royal Collection as a 'Miniature of Lady Hamilton by Romney'. It may well represent the young Emma (1765-1815), who at this time was an assistant to the sex-therapist Dr James Graham at his Temple of Health and Hymen, which occupied the premises at Schomberg House prior to the Cosways moving there in 1784.

47 *'The Ancaster Box' inset with miniatures of the Ladies Priscilla and Georgiana Bertie; Robert, 4th Duke of Ancaster; and Mary Panton, Duchess of Ancaster c.*1780

[colour plates 22a, b and c]
Shuttle-shaped patch box of ivory with gold and enamel decoration, inset with three watercolour on ivory portrait miniatures, on outside and inside of lid, and on the base, respectively; box, depth 5.5cm, length 11.7cm, height 1.5cm (2^1⁄8 × 4^5⁄8 × ^{5}⁄8in); miniatures, heights 1^7⁄8in, 1^3⁄4in, 1^5⁄8in. Inscribed around rim inside box: MARY DUCHESS OF ANCASTER / *Baroness Willoughby d'Eresby / Robert Duke of Ancaster / Marchioness / of Cholmondeley*
COLLECTIONS: probably commissioned by Mary Panton, Duchess of Ancaster; by family descent
REFERENCES: Williamson 1897, pp.40 and 81; Williamson 1905, p.52
GRIMSTHORPE AND DRUMMOND CASTLE TRUST
This outstanding box was likely to have been commissioned by Mary Panton, Duchess of Ancaster (1725-93), to commemorate the early death of her son Robert, 4th Duke of Ancaster (1756-79). It was a more intimate form of familial remembrance than the allegorical oil by Cosway [8]. On the outside of the lid is set the miniature by Cosway of the sisters Lady Priscilla Barbara Bertie (1761-1828), who became Baroness Willoughby de Eresby, together with Lady Georgiana Charlotte Bertie, who later became Marchioness of Cholmondeley. On the inside of the lid is a copy of a miniature by Cosway of Robert, Duke of Ancaster, in uniform (dated *c.*1776-7). On the base of the box is a miniature by an unknown artist of Mary, Duchess of Ancaster.

48 *An unknown officer c.*1780-90

[colour plate 25]
Watercolour on ivory, height 4cm (1^1⁄2in)
COLLECTIONS: with Nyberg, bought by Louis C.G. Clarke, LL.D.; bequeathed to the Fitzwilliam Museum, Cambridge
REFERENCES: Bayne-Powell 1985, p.43
FITZWILLIAM MUSEUM, CAMBRIDGE (Inv. PD197-1961)
This officer wears the uniform of the 1st (or King's) Regiment of Dragoon Guards. The miniature is set in a gold frame decorated with white and blue enamel, with plaited hair between the borders.

49 *The Prince of Wales, later George IV c.*1780-2

[colour plate 51]
Watercolour on ivory, height 9.8cm (3^7⁄8in). Signed with monogram: *RC*
ILLUSTRATED: Piper 1992, p.185, pl.192
NATIONAL PORTRAIT GALLERY, LONDON (Inv. 5890)
This is one of the earliest miniatures by Cosway of the Prince of Wales (1762-1830). Cosway has shown his patron at his most dashing and somewhat effeminate, and the portrait may have been intended for the Prince's then mistress, Mary 'Perdita' Robinson.

50 *Frederick, 3rd Earl of Bessborough* c.1780

[colour plate 23]
Watercolour on ivory, height 3.4cm (1⅜in)
COLLECTIONS: Salting bequest
VICTORIA AND ALBERT MUSEUM, LONDON
(Inv. P44-1910)
This portrait of Frederick Ponsonby, 3rd Earl of
Bessborough (1758–1844), is a pair to the
portrait also by Cosway of *Henrietta Frances,
Countess of Bessborough* [**51**]. Both miniatures
are set with diamonds.

**51 *Henrietta Frances, Countess of
Bessborough* c.1780**

[colour plate 24]
Watercolour on ivory, height 3.4cm (1⅜in)
COLLECTIONS: Salting bequest
VICTORIA AND ALBERT MUSEUM, LONDON
(Inv. PD.45-1910)
This a pendant to the portrait by Cosway of her
husband, *Frederick, 3rd Earl of Bessborough*
[**50**].

**52 *An unknown lady of the Sotheby or
Isted family* c.1780-5**

[colour plate 26]
Watercolour on ivory, height 6.3cm (2½in)
COLLECTIONS: The Sotheby Collection;
Sotheby's, London, 11 October 1955, lot 14;
Louis C.G. Clarke, LL.D.; bequeathed to the
Fitzwilliam Museum in 1960
REFERENCES: Bayne-Powell 1985, p.44
FITZWILLIAM MUSEUM, CAMBRIDGE
(Inv. PD.199-1961)

**53 *Thomas, Viscount Wentworth of
Wellesborough* c.1780-5**

[colour plate 27]
Watercolour on ivory, height 5.8cm (2¼in)
PRIVATE COLLECTION
Thomas Wentworth (1745–1815) succeeded to
the peerage in 1774. He married Mary, Dowager
Countess Ligonier of Clonmell in 1788.

**54 *Georgiana, Duchess of Devonshire*
c.1782**

Watercolour on ivory, height 6.2cm (2½in)
COLLECTIONS: appears in royal inventories in
1870, though repaired by Faija in 1863
REFERENCES: Walker 1992, p.96, no. 192
ILLUSTRATED: Williamson 1897, opp. p.38, and
Williamson 1905, opp. p.56
LENT BY HER MAJESTY THE QUEEN
Georgiana, Duchess of Devonshire (1757–1806),
was Richard Cosway's first major client for his
portrait miniatures. The substantial bill for
work executed between 1776 and 1789 was still
unpaid in 1820 (Lodi, Fondazione Cosway, MS
Inventory 1820, fols. 217r–218r).

**55 *The Prince of Wales, later George IV*
c.1782-3**

[colour plate 49]
Watercolour on ivory, diam. 3.3cm (1¼in)
COLLECTIONS: Duchess of Gloucester; in 1857
bequeathed by her to Queen Victoria
REFERENCES: Walker 1992, p.88, no.176
LENT BY HER MAJESTY THE QUEEN
The Prince of Wales sports his newly fashionable
'frizzed' hairstyle.

56 *Mrs Abington as the Comic Muse* c.1783

[colour plate 55]
Watercolour on ivory, height 14.5cm (5¾in).
Signed in monogram: *RC*. Inscribed: SAC / THALIA
THE RT HON. THE EARL OF SHELBURNE
Mrs Abington (c.1737–1815) was one of the
foremost comic actresses of her generation. The
mood, pose and composition of Cosway's
portrait are inspired by Reynolds's full-length oil
portrait of *Mrs Abington as the Comic Muse*,
which was painted c.1768 and revised in 1773, now
at Waddesdon Manor (London 1986, p.247, no.
72). Cosway could have seen the painting when it
was exhibited at the Royal Academy in 1771 (no.
161). See two letters from Mrs Abington to
Cosway (Williamson 1897, p.38, and Williamson
1905, pp. 48-9). Cosway also drew a full-length
portrait of her as Thalia, now at Waddesdon
Manor, which was engraved in stipple by
Francesco Bartolozzi in 1783 (Daniell 1890, p.1,
no. 1). A related, but less finished, drawing by
Cosway is in the Fogg Art Museum at Harvard
University.

57 *Anne Damer* 1785

[colour plate 58]
Watercolour on ivory, height 6.1cm (2⅜in).
Signed with monogram: *RC*; signed and dated on
reverse: *Hon:lis Anna Damer / Rich:dus De
Cosway, Armgr R.A. / et serenissimi Walliae
Principis / Primarius Pictor / Pinxit 1785*
COLLECTIONS: Christie's, London, 28 November
1978, lot 36
REFERENCES: Walker 1985, I, p.143, II, pl.336
NATIONAL PORTRAIT GALLERY, LONDON
(Inv. 5236)
Richard Cosway painted Anne Damer on at least
two other occasions [**41**][**95**].

**58 *The Prince of Wales, later George IV*
c.1785-90**

[colour plate 53]
Watercolour on ivory, height 8.3cm (3¼in).
Engraved on verso: *George Frederick Augustus /
Prince of Wales*
COLLECTIONS: commissioned by the Prince of
Wales, given to Mrs Fitzherbert; Minnie
Seymour, the adopted daughter of George IV and
Mrs Fitzherbert; by family descent
EXHIBITED: London 1961-2, no.3, ill.
PRIVATE COLLECTION
This miniature is a pair to the portrait of the
Prince's morganatic wife *Mrs Fitzherbert* [**59**].
They are preserved with Cosway's miniature of
Mrs Fitzherbert's eye [**60**], and a double gold
wedding ring engraved 'George Augustus
Frederick' (not exhibited). Both miniatures are
set in gold frames inset with the plaited hair of
the sitters.

59 *Mrs Fitzherbert* c.1785-6

[colour plate 52]
Watercolour on ivory, frame set with sitter's
hair, height 8.3cm (3¼in)
COLLECTIONS: commissioned by the Prince of
Wales; Mrs Fitzherbert; Minnie Seymour, the
adopted daughter of George IV and Mrs
Fitzherbert; by family descent
EXHIBITED: London 1961-2, no.3, ill.
PRIVATE COLLECTION
Mrs Fitzherbert (1756–1837) was the morganatic
wife of the Prince of Wales. This miniature is a
pair to his portrait by Cosway [**58**]. The two
miniatures are preserved with the artist's
portrait of her *Eye* [**60**], and the double
wedding ring (not exhibited).

60 *Mrs Fitzherbert's eye* 1786

[colour plate 54]
Watercolour on ivory, height 3.2cm (1¼in)
COLLECTIONS: commissioned by the Prince of
Wales; Mrs Fitzherbert; Minnie Seymour, the
adopted daughter of George IV and Mrs
Fitzherbert; Captain L. Seymour Dawson-
Damer MP; by family descent
PRIVATE COLLECTION
This *Eye*, which is set in a gold locket, is the
only authentic such miniature by Cosway that
has been traced. It is almost certainly the one
Cosway charged five guineas for in 1786 (Lodi,
Fondazione Cosway, MS Inventory 1820,
fol.220r). The artist specialised in painting not
only miniature eyes, but also mouths. Mrs
Fitzherbert's eye miniature is preserved with
Cosway's portrait miniatures of the *Prince of
Wales* [**58**] and of *Mrs Fitzherbert* [**59**].

**61 *Henrietta Scott, later Duchess of
Portland* 1785**

Watercolour on ivory in gold setting, height
4.9cm (2in). Signed and dated on verso in pen
and ink on paper: *Miss Har. Scott. / CR*
(monogram) / *1785*
COLLECTIONS: given to the 5th Duke of Portland
by Lord Murray in 1855
REFERENCES: Goulding 1914-15, pp.160-1,
no.237; pl.XXIII, fig.237
ILLUSTRATED: Foskett 1972, II, pl.60, no.172
PRIVATE COLLECTION
Henrietta Scott (1774–1844) was the eldest
daughter of General John Scott of Balcomie. In
1795 she married William Henry Cavendish
Bentinck, Marquess of Tichfield, who became
the 4th Duke of Portland in 1809. This miniature of her provided the basis for a portrait of
her – together with her mother – in a full-length
oil painting by Richard Cosway, now at
Harewood House. An authentic replica
miniature by Cosway survives in a private
collection.

62 *Jacob, 2nd Earl of Radnor* 1786

Watercolour on ivory, height 6.1cm (2⅜in)
REFERENCES: Radnor and Squire 1909, II, p.113
PRIVATE COLLECTION
Jacob, 2nd Earl of Radnor (1750–1828), was one
of Cosway's most important clients. He not
only commissioned portraits of himself –
including a full-length oil (private collection) –
and of various members of his family, but he

also acquired important Old Master paintings.
Lord Radnor's account book noted on 8 July
1786 that Cosway had been paid £23 2s for this
miniature, in which the sitter is shown wearing
Vandyke dress.

63 *Mary Russell, later Mrs Domvile* 1787

[colour plate 59]
Watercolour on ivory with lock of hair in pearl
clasp on reverse, height 7.2cm (2¾in). Signed
with monogram: *RC*. Signed on verso: *R.dus
Cosway RA / Primarius Pictor / Serenissimi
Walliae / Principis / Pinxit / 1787*. Inscribed on
urn: *M.R. / 1786*
COLLECTIONS: F.E. Perowne in 1934; on loan to
the Victoria and Albert Museum from 1948
VICTORIA AND ALBERT MUSEUM, LONDON
(Inv. P51–1984)
Mary Russell (d.1856) was the daughter of
William Russell and his first wife Mary (née
Lock). Cosway has shown her mourning at an
urn containing the remains of her mother.

64 *Sir Thomas Stepney c.*1787

[colour plate 60]
Watercolour on ivory, 7 × 5.7cm (2¾ × 2¼in).
Signed on verso: *R:dus Cosway / R.A. / et
Primarius Pictor / Serenissimi Walliae /
Principis / Pinxit / 1787*. Inscribed on verso:
Cosway / 1787 / Sir Thomas / Stepney
COLLECTIONS: presented by Dorothy Manners
ILLUSTRATED: Noon 1981, p.179, pl.34
VICTORIA AND ALBERT MUSEUM, LONDON
(Inv. P45–1953)
Sir Thomas Stepney (*c.*1760–1825), the 8th
Baronet, was the last male descendant of Van
Dyck in the direct line (Whitley 1930, p.96)

65 *Warren Hastings* 1787

[colour plate 65]
Watercolour on ivory, height 5.7cm (2¼in)
COLLECTIONS: Alan Evans bequest to the
National Gallery (1975); formerly on loan to the
National Portrait Gallery (no. L152[34])
NATIONAL PORTRAIT GALLERY, LONDON
(Inv. 6286)
Warren Hastings (1732–1818) was Governor-
General of Bengal and the architect of the
British Empire in India. One of the most
famous men of his time, he frequently sat for
portraits. The sitting for this portrait was said
to have taken place as Edmund Burke made his
opening speech against Hastings at the
beginning of his seven-year trial for impeach-
ment over alleged corruption in India.

66 *Captain, the Hon. Edmund Phipps* 1788

Watercolour on ivory, height 5.1cm (2in).
Signed and dated on verso: *R:dus Cosway / R.A.
/ Primarius Pictor / Serenissimi Walliae /
Principis / Pinxit / 1788*. Engraved around the
upper rim of gold frame: CAPT THE HON.ble
EDMUND PHIPPS, 1st FOOT GUARDS. 1788, and lower
centre: R. COSWAY, R.A. PINXIT
COLLECTIONS: Sotheby's, London, 20 November
1945, lot 44; Robert H. Rockliffe; his sale
Sotheby's, London, 11 November 1947, lot 101;
where purchased by Louis C.G. Clarke, LL.D.;
bequeathed 1960
REFERENCES: Bayne-Powell 1985, p.40

FITZWILLIAM MUSEUM, CAMBRIDGE
(Inv. PD.198–1961)
Captain, the Hon. Edmund Phipps (1760–1837),
was the fourth and youngest son of the 2nd Lord
Mulgrave and his wife Lepell, the eldest
daughter of Lord Hervey of Ickworth. He
became a General Officer in the Army and
Colonel-Commandant in the 60th Foot. He is
shown here by Cosway in the uniform of a
Grenadier Company Officer, 1st Regiment of
Foot Guards.

67 *James, 3rd Earl of Hopetoun* 1789

[colour plate 57]
Watercolour on ivory, height 7.9cm (3⅛in).
Signed on verso: *James / Earl of Hopetoun /
R.dus Cosway R.A. / Primarius Pictor /
Serenissimi Walliae / Principis / Pinxit / 1789*
COLLECTIONS: A.P. Cunliffe; Sotheby's, London,
20 November 1945, lot 37, bought Sydney; anon.
sale, Christie's, London, 18 February 1969, lot
118, bought Fry
REFERENCES: New Haven 1979–80, p.50, no.52
YALE CENTER FOR BRITISH ART, NEW HAVEN,
PAUL MELLON COLLECTION
(Inv. B1974.2.19)
James Hope (1741–1816) was the second son of
John, 2nd Earl of Hopetoun, and he succeeded
his father in 1781. He was Lord-Lieutenant of
Linlithgowshire from 1794 to 1816. This is a
pendant to Cosway's miniature of *Elizabeth,
Countess of Hopetoun* [**68**], portraits conveying
an effect of reserved flattery at which the artist
was so adept.

68 *Elizabeth, Countess of Hopetoun* 1789

[colour plate 56]
Watercolour on ivory, height 7.6cm (3in)
COLLECTIONS: see [**67**]
EXHIBITED: New Haven 1979–80, p.50, no.53
YALE CENTER FOR BRITISH ART, NEW HAVEN,
PAUL MELLON COLLECTION
(Inv. B1974.2.18)
Elizabeth Carnegie (1750–93) was the daughter
of George, 6th Earl of Northesk. She was also
portrayed by Cosway in a drawing with two of
her children [**97**]. This miniature is a pendant
to Cosway's portrait of *James, 3rd Earl of
Hopetoun* [**67**]. The journalist Sir Henry Bate,
on seeing another portrait of the Countess,
painted two years earlier by Gainsborough,
commented: 'her ladyship, though not in the
bloom of life possesses that elegance, grace and
beauty which form the best combination a
picture can have'.

69 *The Duke of Clarence, later William IV* 1789

[colour plate 62]
Watercolour on ivory, height 7.8cm (3⅛in)
LT-COL. R.L. JENKINS (ON LOAN TO THE
NATIONAL PORTRAIT GALLERY, LONDON)
(Inv. L176)
After the Prince of Wales, his younger brother,
the Duke of Clarence, was Cosway's most
important client, mainly sitting to the artist in
1789 and 1791 [**115**], although, as with the
Prince of Wales, he had still not paid the artist
by 1820 (Lodi, Fondazione Cosway, MS
Inventory 1820, fol.224r). This miniature more

probably dates to 1789, as that year the Duke sat
five times to Cosway, three times for a larger
miniature (£31.10s) and twice for smaller ones
(£21.10s).

70 *General, the Viscount Fielding c.*1790

Watercolour on ivory, height 6.1cm (2⅜in).
Engraved on verso: *General / The Viscount
Fielding / by Cosway*
COLLECTIONS: Louis C.G. Clarke, LL.D., be-
queathed to the Fitzwilliam Museum in 1960
REFERENCES: Bayne-Powell 1985, p.42
FITZWILLIAM MUSEUM, CAMBRIDGE
(Inv. PD.195–1961)
General, the Viscount Fielding (1760-99) was
the eldest son of Basil Fielding, Earl of Denbigh
and Desmond. He was promoted to Major-
General in 1795.

71 *Self-portrait in Elizabethan costume* c.1785-90

[colour plate 63]
Watercolour on ivory, height 7.1cm (2¾in)
COLLECTIONS: bequeathed by Miss M. Grace in
1949
ILLUSTRATED: Foskett 1972, II, pl.60, no.169
NATIONAL GALLERY OF IRELAND, DUBLIN
(Inv. 3024)
A lock of the artist's hair is set into the reverse
of the miniature.

72 *Edward, 12th Earl of Derby c.*1785-90

Watercolour on ivory, height 6.1cm (2⅜in)
EXHIBITED: London 1956-7, p.91, no.279
PRIVATE COLLECTION (ON LOAN TO
MANCHESTER CITY ART GALLERIES)
Edward Stanley (1752–1834), 12th Earl of Derby,
married the noted actress *Elizabeth Farren* [**73**]
in 1797. An authentic replica of this miniature is
in a private collection.

73 *Elizabeth Farren, later Countess of Derby c.*1785-90

Watercolour on ivory, height 5.7cm (2¼in)
EXHIBITED: London 1956-7, p.91, no.274
PRIVATE COLLECTION (ON LOAN TO
MANCHESTER CITY ART GALLERIES)
Elizabeth Farren (1763–1829) was the wife of
Edward, 12th Earl of Derby [**72**].

74 *Henry, 2nd Earl of Carrick c.*1785-90

[colour plate 64]
Watercolour on ivory, height 7.7cm (3in)
COLLECTIONS: E.G. Raphael, London; acquired
by Henry. E. Huntington through Duveen in
1926 or 1927
ILLUSTRATED: Reynolds 1992, col. pl.VIII
HENRY E. HUNTINGTON LIBRARY AND ART
GALLERY, SAN MARINO, CALIFORNIA
(Inv. 26.16)
Henry Thomas, 2nd Earl of Carrick (1746–1813),
was the eldest son of Somerset Hamilton, 8th
Viscount Ikerrin and 1st Earl of Carrick, and his
wife Juliana, daughter of Henry, Earl of
Shannon. In 1774 he married Sarah, second
daughter of Edward Taylor of Asheaton, by
whom he had eight children.

75 *An unknown gentleman c.*1785-90

Watercolour on ivory, height 6.4cm (2½in).
Inscribed on tag: *Marcus Kappel / see Catalogue V. Bode / 46*
COLLECTIONS: Mrs Edward R. Wardwell, New York

YALE UNIVERSITY ART GALLERY, NEW HAVEN
Gift of Mrs Edward R. Wardwell for the Lelia and John Hill Morgan Collection
(Inv. 1976.12.1)

The sitter's plaited hair is contained within the verso of the miniature.

76 *Georgiana, Duchess of Devonshire* 1786

[colour plate 61]
Watercolour on ivory, height 8.9cm (3½in)
REFERENCES: Williamson 1897, p.107
EXHIBITED: Bregenz and Vienna 1968-9, p.100, no.180; Richmond 1979-80, p.34, no. 23
ILLUSTRATED: Williamson 1905, p.114 and ill. opp. p.26; Williamson 1904, I, pl. LVIIIA.i

THE DUKE OF DEVONSHIRE AND THE TRUSTEES OF THE CHATSWORTH SETTLEMENT
(Inv. 71)

Lady Georgiana Spencer (1757-1806) married the 5th Duke of Devonshire in 1774. She was a leading figure in fashion and Whig society during the late 1770s and 1780s. She sat to Cosway for miniatures frequently between 1776 and 1789 [54], and was charged £36 for this large miniature in 1786. Maria Cosway portrayed the Duchess as Cynthia in a critically acclaimed full-length oil painting which is still at Chatsworth, and which was engraved by Valentine Green [229].

JOHN SMART (1741-1811)

77 *The Prince of Wales, later George IV c.*1783

Watercolour on vellum, 6 × 5.3cm (2⅜ × 2⅛in).
Inscribed on verso in ink: *His Royal Highness the Prince of Wales*. Engraved: in stipple by L. Sailliar, 1785
COLLECTIONS: by descent from the artist; Christie's, London, 26 November 1937, lot 24; acquired by Queen Mary
REFERENCES: Foskett 1964, p.82; Walker 1992, p.155, no.309

LENT BY HER MAJESTY THE QUEEN

Walker refers to a finished version of this composition, signed and dated 1783 (formerly in the David-Weill collection and with Wildenstein in Paris in 1938), which is more likely to be the version that was exhibited at the Society of Arts in 1783 (no.228).

JOHN SMART (1741-1811)

78 *Maria Cosway* 1784

Watercolour on ivory; plaited hair behind glass on verso, height 5.2cm (2⅛in). Signed on verso: *JS / 1784.* Inscribed on verso with initials in gold: *MC*
COLLECTIONS: Martin Hecksher Collection in 1898; Messrs Durlacher; George Salting bequest (no.4574)
REFERENCES: Foskett 1964, p.65
ILLUSTRATED: Williamson 1904, pl.LXXI, no.2

VICTORIA AND ALBERT MUSEUM, LONDON
(Inv. P59-1910)

When this miniature was in the Hecksher Collection it was identified as the Countess of Jersey, presumably Frances, wife of the 4th Earl, although Williamson proposed Maria Cosway as the subject. The solid modelling and realism seen in Smart's work is in direct contrast with the feathery brushwork and idealisation seen in the miniatures of his rival Cosway.

C. TOWNLEY (1746-*c.*1800)
AFTER RICHARD COSWAY

79 *Thomas, 2nd Lord Lyttleton* 1781

Mezzotint engraving, proof before letters,
38.7 × 29.3cm (15¼ × 11½in)
REFERENCES: Daniell 1890, p.25, no.98

LENT BY HER MAJESTY THE QUEEN

Thomas, 2nd Lord Lyttleton (1744-79), a notorious rake, was elected MP for Bewdley in 1768 and succeeded his father in 1773 (Blunt 1936). Cosway, who had already portrayed the sitter in a miniature [20], painted the head of the sitter in a full-length portrait in oils (formerly at Hagley Hall), with the rest of the body painted by Richard Brompton. The engraved posthumous portrait illustrates Lord Lyttleton's notorious prediction of his own death within three days, which he claimed had been foretold by a bird that flew into his room, whereupon it turned into a visionary woman (Frost 1876, pp.343-7). The lettering on an impression of this mezzotint in the New York Public Library reads: *R. Cosway R.A. pinxt. 1780. / Engraved by Chas. Townley 1781 /* THOMAS LORD LYTTLETON */ From the Original Picture in the Possession of the Right Honble. / Elizath. Lady Dowager Lyttleton / Publish'd as the Act Directs 21st. Novem. 1782 and Sold by C. Townley in Arlington Street, Piccadilly.*

80 *The Right Hon. Charles James Fox* 1782

Etching, 26.8 × 20.3cm (10½ × 8in). Lettered:
Rd: Cosway R.A: pinxt: ad vivum, et sculpt: 1782. / The Right Honble: / Charles James Fox, One of His Majesty's Principal Secretaries of State. / Publish'd June 4th: 1782, by C: Townley, in Arlington Street, Piccadilly.
REFERENCES: Daniell 1890, p.20, no.77

LENT BY HER MAJESTY THE QUEEN

Charles James Fox (1749-1806), the third son of Lord Holland, was the most famous Whig politician of the period, and a key supporter of the Prince of Wales. He was as admired for his oratory as he was notorious for his dissolute personal life. This is one of only two etchings executed by Cosway himself, the other being the self-portrait with Maria in the garden of Schomberg House [82]. A proof impression, with the lettering added by the artist in pen and ink, is in a private collection.

UNKNOWN ARTIST

81 *A smuggling machine or a convenient Cosauway for a man in miniature* 1782

Line engraving, 27.2 × 23.7cm (10¾ × 9⅜in).
Lettered: (in bubble) *Tis geting nothing / — nay — tis geting / worse than nothing*; (beneath picture) *Lowliness is giving Ambitions Ladder, / Whereto the climber upward turns his Face, / But when he once attain the upmost round, / He then unto the Ladder, turns his back, / Looks into the clouds — scornin the base degrees / By*

which he did ascend — / Shak. Jul. Caesar; (title) A SMUGGLING MACHINE */ or / a Convenient Cosauway for a Man in Miniature. / Publish'd Jany: 1782 by H Humphry New Bond Street No. 18.*
Inscribed in pen: *51.9.1.60*
REFERENCES: George 1935, pp.638-9, no. 6102

BRITISH MUSEUM, LONDON
(Inv. George 6102)

This caricature of the diminutive Richard Cosway refers to his rapid social ascent after his marriage the previous year.

82 *Mr and Mrs Cosway* 1784

[colour plate 35]
Etching, 20.9 × 24.8cm (8¼ × 9¾in). Inscribed:
Cosway 1784
REFERENCES: Daniell 1890, p.11, no. 42
EXHIBITED: Liverpool 1994-5, p.74, no.21

WHITWORTH ART GALLERY, UNIVERSITY OF MANCHESTER
(Inv. P.20239)

M. BOVA AFTER RICHARD COSWAY

83 *Rdus. Cosway Armiger R.A. Primarius Pictor Serenissimi Walliae Principis* 1786

[colour plate 39]
Stipple engraving, 27.9 × 16.5cm (11 × 6½in).
Lettered: (on book) *Vita / Di Rubens*; (title) *Ipse delt. / Mno. Bova sct. Pupil to F. Bartolozzi / RDUS.* COSWAY ARMIGER R.A. */ Primarius Pictor Serenissimi Walliae Principis / Publish'd as the Act directs March 20th. 1786 by Mno. Bova & E. Diemar No. 114 Strand.*
REFERENCES: Daniell 1890, p. 9, no. 31

LENT BY HER MAJESTY THE QUEEN

Cosway here celebrates both his status as arms-bearer to the Royal Academy, and his entitlement — granted the previous year — to sign his work with the Latin title, translated as 'Principal Painter to His Highness The Prince of Wales'. Cosway based his pose — seated on steps and wrapped in a cloak — on Marcantonio Raimondi's engraved portrait of Raphael, though adding some Rubensian flourishes: the hat decorated with ostrich feathers and the biography of Rubens placed beside him on the step.

UNKNOWN ARTIST

84 *Dicky Causway. In Plain English.* 1786

[colour plate 36]
Etching, 23.8 × 15cm (9⅜ × 5⅞in).
Lettered: (on bundle) *Life of / Witting / :ton / New Song*; (title) *Ipse pinxt. / Tipsy sculpt. /* DICKY CAUSWAY. *In Plain English. — Pubd. 1st May. 1786. by E. Jackson. Mary-le-bone Street Golden Sqr.*
REFERENCES: George 1935, p.340, no.7020

BRITISH MUSEUM, LONDON
(Inv. George 7020)

In this cruel caricature, Cosway's self-portrait as arms-bearer to the Academy is transmogrified into a drunken beggar. Gone are the Latin appendage to his signature and the biography of Rubens, to be replaced by 'plain English' and a life of Dick Whittington. The publication of this satire was noted in *The Daily Universal Register* (17 May 1786): 'Among the impudent exhibitions of the day, is the print of *diminutive Dickey the convenient*, which every one may see who chuses to peep into the great shop in Pall Mall as he goes along the causeway'.

F. BARTOLOZZI (1727–1815)
AFTER RICHARD COSWAY

85 *Maria Cosway* 1785

[colour plate 38]
Stipple engraving, 24.2 × 16.5cm (9½ × 6½).
Lettered: *R. Cosway R.A. Delin*t*. / F. Bartolozzi
Sculp*t*. /* MARIA COSWAY */ Publish'd as the Act
directs 29 Jan*y*. 1785. by G. Bartolozzi & to be had
at M*r*. Torres Hay Market 28*
REFERENCES: Bromley 1793, p.434; Daniell 1890,
p.9, no.34; Monticello 1993, pp.176–7, no.44

LENT BY HER MAJESTY THE QUEEN

In this stipple engraving of Maria shown seated
in a garden, which is a pair to his self-portrait
[83], Cosway has posed his wife in the manner
of Rubens's portraits of his first wife, Isabella
Brant, while presenting her in one of her most
spectacular hats.

UNKNOWN ARTIST

86 *Maria Costive at her studies.* 1786

[colour plate 37]
Etching, 21.7 × 14.2cm (8½ × 5⅝in).
Lettered: (picture titles) GIANTS OF OSSIAN /
EOLUS / SAMSON / *Deluge* / DICKY CAOS; (title)
MARIA COSTIVE. / *at her Studies.* Inscribed in
pencil: *1786*
REFERENCES: George 1935, p.339, no.7019

BRITISH MUSEUM, LONDON

The publication of this satirical etching was
noted in *The Morning Herald* (30 May 1786):
'What has the good-natured *Maria Cosway*
done, that she should be caricatured as well as
Dicky? The satire, it is true, rather affects her
cara sposa, than herself; and the introduction
of the Sarcophagus, or Chamber Urn, it must
be confessed is a tolerable stroke, at Dicky's
taste for the antique.' An impression of this
caricature (Royal Library, Windsor Castle) of
Richard's stipple portrait of Maria [85], which
is a pendant to [83], has the publication details:
*London Pub*h*d April 29 1786 by E. Jackson N. 14
Mary-le-bone St*t*: Golden Sq*r*.*

T. CHAMBARS (*c*.1724–89)
AFTER RICHARD COSWAY

87 *Mademoiselle La Chevalière d'Eon de
Beaumont* 1787

Stipple engraving, 17.6 × 11.3cm (7 × 4½in).
Lettered: *R. Cosway R.A. del*t*. 1787 / Tho*s*.
Chambars Sculp*t*. / Published July 12*th* 1787 by
B. Beale Evans, Poultry, London*
REFERENCES: Daniell 1890, p.17, no.65

PRIVATE COLLECTION

The Chevalière d'Eon de Beaumont (1728–1810)
was a notorious French diplomat, freemason
and transvestite, who, after settling perma-
nently in London in 1785, caused a sensation by
giving public fencing displays in women's dress
(Schuchard 1992a). He/she was one of the most
exotic presences at the Cosways' *salon* during
the late 1780s. A close friend of Richard's, he
was satirised as 'Mr Femality' in William
Blake's unpublished play 'An Island in the
Moon' (Blake 1987, pp.6–8). An impression of
this stipple engraving in the New York Public
Library bears the title lettering: *Mademoiselle
La Chevaliere /* D'EON *de* BEAUMONT.

L. SAILLIAR (1748-95)
AFTER RICHARD COSWAY

88 *His Royal Highness George, Prince of
Wales* 1787

[colour plate 67]
Stipple engraving, 32.9 × 23.9cm (12¾ × 9½in).
Lettered: *R. Cosway R.A. pinx*t*. / L. Saïlliar Sc.
/* HIS ROYAL HIGHNESS GEORGE PRINCE OF WALES */
R*dus*. Cosway. R:A; et Primarius Pictor
Serenissimi Walliae Principis delin*t*: et Excu*t /
Pub*d*. as the Act directs Aug*t*: 24*th*. 1787.*
REFERENCES: Daniell 1890, p.20, no.81
ILLUSTRATED: Cazzulani and Stroppa 1989,
fig.20

PRIVATE COLLECTION

In Jacques-Louis David's amorous letter to
'Mistress Cosway', written in early 1788, he
asked Maria to thank her husband for having
the engraver J.Condé bring him an impression
of this print. The anglophile David went on to
say that he had the print framed, and placed in
his *salon*, where he said it was admired by
everyone who saw it. David continued by saying
that in return he was sending the Cosways 'un
petit dessin de moi en souvenir du plaisir que
j'ai eu à faire votre connaissance' (Bordes 1983,
p.133, and 1992, p.485). This was published as a
pendant with the stipple after Cosway's portrait
drawing of the Duc d'Orléans [89].

G. HADFIELD (1763–1826)
AFTER RICHARD COSWAY

89 *His Most Serene Highness Louis Phillip
Joseph Duke of Orleans* 1788

[colour plate 66]
Stipple engraving, 33.8 × 24cm (13¼ × 9½in).
Lettered: *R. Cosway R.A. pinx*t*. / G. Hadfield
Sculp*t*. /* HIS *most* SERENE HIGHNESS LOUIS PHILLIP
JOSEPH DUKE *of* ORLEANS. / R*dus*. Cosway R.A. et
Primarius Pictor Serenissimi Walliae Principis
delin: et Excu*t*. / Publish'd as the Act directs
1788, by R. Cosway.*
REFERENCES: Daniell 1890, p.28, no.112; Bordes
1992
ILLUSTRATED: Lloyd 1993, p.194 (p.126)

PRIVATE COLLECTION

The notoriously dissolute Duc d'Orléans (1747-
93), First Prince of Blood Royal of France (and
known as Philippe-Égalité during the Revolution), was an anglomaniac, who made numerous visits to England during the 1780s. He
became firm friends with the Prince of Wales,
who had a portrait by Reynolds hung at Carlton
House (London 1986, pp.309–10, no.137). The
Duc commissioned a group portrait drawing of
his children [fig. 9] from Richard Cosway,
which was undertaken during the Cosways'
visit to Paris in 1786. The engraver, George
Hadfield, was a younger brother of Maria
Cosway, who, under the patronage of Thomas
Jefferson, spent the second half of his life
working as an architect in Washington.

W. BIRCH (1755-1834)
AFTER WILLIAM HODGES (1744-97)
AND RICHARD COSWAY

90 *A view from Mr Cosway's breakfast-
room, Pall Mall, with the portrait of
Mrs Cosway* 1789

[colour plate 34]

Stipple engraving, 15 × 17.2cm (5⅞ × 6¾in).
Lettered: A VIEW from M*R*. COSWAY'S BREAKFAST-
ROOM PALL MALL, / WITH THE PORTRAIT OF M*RS*.
COSWAY. / *The Landscape Painted by W*m*.
Hodges RA and the Portrait by R*d*. Cosway R.A.
/ & engraved by W. Birch Enamel Painter /
Published Feb*y*. 1. 1789 by W*m*. Birch Hampstead
Heath & sold by T. Thornton, Southampton
Str*t*. Cov*t*. Garden.*
REFERENCES: Daniell 1890, p.10, no.38
ILLUSTRATED: Walkley 1994, p.18, no.13

PRIVATE COLLECTION

A more detailed descriptive lettering accompa-
nies an impression of the print at the New York
Public Library with an altered title: *A View from
Mr Cosway's Breakfast-Room, Pall Mall With
the Portrait of Mrs. Cosway at the Window,
viewing the Procession in the Park of His
Majesty going to the Parliament-House.* The
accompanying description reads: *The prospect
from hence is curious, and uncommonly fine, for
a town-house. The tops of the trees hiding the
inferior buildings, nothing appears to the sight
but which is rich and grand. It extends over the
Duke of Marlborough's Gardens and St. James's
Park, to Westminster Hall, St. Margaret's
Church, Westminster Abbey, the Treasury, St.
John's Church, and the Surry Hills. The
landscape is painted by Mr. Hodges, and the
portrait by Mr. Cosway. The size of the picture is
three feet ten inches wide, by two feet eight high;
was painted in the year 1787, and is in Mr.
Cosway's possession.* The original painting can
be identified as a *View of S. Park by Hodges*
(exhibited, Royal Academy, London, 1787,
no.53) hanging in the bedroom at Stratford
Place (Lodi, Fondazione Cosway, MS Inventory
1820, fol.196r).

R. THEW (1758-1802)
AFTER RICHARD COSWAY

91 *Abelard and Eloisa in the gardens of
Fulbert's country residence at Corbeil*
1789

Stipple engraving, 38.6 × 26.4cm (15 × 10¼in).
Lettered: *R*d*. Cosway RA delin / R*t* Thew Sc /
Abelard and Eloisa in the Gardens of Fulbert's
Country Residence at Corbeil / Published 1 June
1789. by M. Lawson No. 96. Strand corner of
Beaufort Buildings*
REFERENCES: Lloyd 1992, fig.2

LENT BY HER MAJESTY THE QUEEN

The second state of this print was titled
Portraits of Mr. & Mrs. Cosway [92].

R. THEW (1758-1802)
AFTER RICHARD COSWAY

92 *Portraits of Mr & Mrs Cosway* 1789

[colour plate 105]
Stipple engraving, 38.6 × 26.4cm (15 × 10¼in).
Lettered: *R*d*. Cosway RA delin / R*t*. Thew Sc /
Portraits of Mr. & Mrs. Cosway. / Published
1 June 1789. by M. Lawson No. 96. Strand corner
of Beaufort Buildings*
REFERENCES: Lloyd 1992, fig. 2
ILLUSTRATED: Cazzulani and Stroppa 1989, fig. 4

PRIVATE COLLECTION

The first state of this print was titled *Abelard
and Eloisa* [91].

III RICHARD COSWAY: 1790–1800

93 *William, 3rd Viscount Courtenay* 1791

[colour plate 104]
Oil on canvas, 230 × 172cm (92 × 68in). Signed and dated: *Rdus Cosway R.A. / P. Gallia Pictor Pinxit / 1791.* Engraved: in mezzotint by C. Turner 1799–1801, published by J. Murphy 1809 (Whitman 1907, p.74)
COLLECTIONS: commissioned by sitter 1790–1; artist charged £136 10s in 1791 (Powderham Castle MSS); Maria Cosway successfully had bill paid in 1820; by descent at Powderham Castle (Girouard 1963)
EXHIBITED: London 1956–7, no.347
ILLUSTRATED: Waterhouse 1981, p.89
LORD COURTENAY

The notoriously extravagant William Courtenay (1768–1835) succeeded his father as 3rd Viscount Courtenay in 1788. In the early 1780s he had sat for his portrait from Romney, which had been commissioned by his admirer, the writer and traveller William Beckford. Lord Courtenay became one of Cosway's most faithful clients, also commissioning portraits of six of his sisters [151]. Here the artist portrayed his flamboyant young patron in the spectacular Vandyke dress which he had worn during his coming-of-age ceremonies at Powderham in 1790. He fled to America in 1811 to escape his creditors, residing at the Claremont on the Hudson, before purchasing the Château Dreveil in Paris in 1825–6, where he lived in great style until his death. Twelve days before Lord Courtenay's death the House of Lords revived in his favour the Earldom of Devon, which had been considered extinct for nearly three centuries.

94 *George, Marquis of Blandford, later 5th Duke of Marlborough* 1797

Oil on mahogany panel, 75.5 × 60.9cm (29¾ × 24in). Signed: R COSWAY R.A. *Pictor Principiensis.* Inscribed: with motto, DIEU DEFEND LE DROIT; (erroneously) GEORGE 4TH DUKE / OF MARLBOROUGH / 1766–1840. Engraved: mezzotint by W. Barney, dedicated to the Marchioness of Blandford (Daniell 1890, p.4, no.12)
COLLECTIONS: commissioned by the sitter in 1797; by family descent
REFERENCES: Lodi, Fondazione Cosway, MS Inventory 1820, fol.226r (from the list of Outstanding Debts: (1797) 'Marquis of Blandford – His portrait in oil – £31.10.0'
HIS GRACE THE DUKE OF MARLBOROUGH

The extravagant Marquis of Blandford (1766–1840) succeeded his father as the 5th Duke in 1817 (Soames 1987). He married Susan, daughter of the Earl of Galloway, in 1791. A noted bibliophile, Blandford assembled a celebrated library for his house White-Knights near Reading.

95 *Anne Damer* 1790

Pencil and watercolour, 23 × 14cm (9 × 5½in). Signed and dated (transferred from recto to verso): *Rdus. R.A. Primarius Pictor Serenissimi Walliae Principis Fecit. 1790.* Inscribed: (in typed label on recto) *The Honble. [Mrs] Anne Damer*; (by Horace Walpole in pen and ink label adhered to verso) *Mrs Damer / in the middle / of having just finished / her bust of the young Paris / drawn by Richd. Cosway 1790. / H.W.* Engraved: in lithograph by W. Greatbatch after a copy-drawing by G.P. Harding, and published in 1840 as THE HONBLE. ANNE SEYMOUR DAMER; Lewis 1961, p.34, no.13
COLLECTIONS: Horace Walpole at Strawberry Hill; by descent
PRIVATE COLLECTION

Richard Cosway portrayed Anne Damer on at least two other occasions [41][57]. Two preparatory drawings for this study belong to the Fondazione Cosway, Lodi (nos 1.47 and 48).

96 *Dorothy Jordan* c.1790

Pencil and watercolour, 11.5 × 8.9cm (4½ × 3½in)
BRITISH MUSEUM, LONDON
(Inv. 1922-4-10-4)
Dorothy Jordan (1761–1816) was one of the most notable comic actresses of her generation in the British theatre. In 1790 she became the mistress of the Duke of Clarence, later King William IV, and bore him ten children (Tomalin 1994).

97 *Elizabeth, Countess of Hopetoun, and her children* c.1790

Pencil and watercolour, 23.5 × 14.3cm (9¼ × 5⅜in)
COLLECTIONS: Christie's, London, 11 November 1993, no. 66
EXHIBITED: London 1994, no. 15
NATIONAL GALLERY OF SCOTLAND
(Inv. D5370)
The original wash-lined mount, from which the drawing is now separated, is inscribed in pencil: *Countess of Hopetoun & her children.* Lady Elizabeth Carnegie (1750-93) was the daughter of the 6th Earl of Northesk. In 1766 she married James Hope, 3rd Earl of Hopetoun (1741–1816). Richard Cosway also painted a pair of miniatures of the *Earl and Countess of Hopetoun* [67 and 68].

98 *Princess Galetzin and her two daughters* 1795

Pencil drawing with watercolour, 29.5 × 21.8cm (11⅝ × 8⅝in)
COLLECTIONS: commissioned for £94 10s by the Prince of Wales in 1795 (Lodi, Fondazione Cosway, MS Inventory 1820, fol.222r); by descent
REFERENCES: Oppé 1950, no.150
LENT BY HER MAJESTY THE QUEEN

99 *Louisa Cosway on her deathbed* 1796

[colour plate 70]
Pencil and watercolour; on original wash-lined mount 14 × 23.1cm (5½ × 9½in); with mount 25.2 × 34.7cm (9⅞ × 13⅝in)
FONDAZIONE COSWAY, LODI
In this moving drawing that records the death of the Cosways' only child Louisa (1790–6), Richard may have been aware of Samuel Cooper's drawing of a *Dead Child* (London 1974b, p.69, no.137). The drawing may also be seen as a remarkably proto-Victorian image of death in childhood.

100 *General Thaddeus Kosciuszko* 1797–8

Pencil and watercolour, 18.8 × 23.5cm (7⅜ × 9¼in); with original wash-lined mount 33.9 × 38.9cm (13⅜ × 15⅜in). Engraved: in stipple and published by Anthony Cardon in 1798, dedicated to the Whig Club of England (Daniell 1890, p.23, no.92)
FONDAZIONE COSWAY, LODI

The great Polish patriot General Thaddeus Kosciuszko (1756–1817) accompanied Lafayette to America. In 1794 he commanded the Polish army in the attempt to gain independence. He died in Switzerland a year after settling there. Benjamin West painted a Kosciuszko in a similar pose (Von Erffa and Staley 1986, pp.525–6, no.650, col. ill. p.133), which is now in the Allen Memorial Art Museum, Oberlin College, Oberlin, Ohio (Hamilton 1952). Cosway was reputed to have sketched Kosciuszko through the keyhole of his room in London, on account of the sitter's aversion to sitting for portraits.

101 *Caroline, Princess of Wales, and Princess Charlotte* 1797

Pencil with wash and watercolour, 22.7 × 14.1cm (8⅞ × 5½in)
COLLECTIONS: commissioned by the Prince of Wales in 1797 for £47 5s (Lodi, Fondazione Cosway, MS Inventory 1820, fol.222r); by descent
REFERENCES: Oppé 1950, no.151
LENT BY HER MAJESTY THE QUEEN
Caroline of Brunswick (1768–1821), married the Prince of Wales in 1795. Despite their unhappy marriage, both parents lavished attention on their only daughter Princess Charlotte (1796–1817), who was portrayed on numerous occasions by Cosway.

102 *Emma, Lady Hamilton* c.1800

Pencil with watercolour, 22.3 × 14cm (8¾ × 5½in)
COLLECTIONS: bequeathed by Capt. H.W. Murray, 1938
EXHIBITED: Bregenz and Vienna 1968–9, p.100, no.181, fig.236; Edinburgh 1978, no.48; Nottingham and London 1991, p.61, no.35
NATIONAL PORTRAIT GALLERY, LONDON
(Inv. 2941)
Emma Hart (c.1761–1815) later married Sir William Hamilton, the British Resident in Naples, who became a noted vulcanologist and a great collector of classical antiquities (Sontag 1992). Emma is best known for her relationship with Nelson. Cosway has shown her adopting one of her famous 'Attitudes', a series of well known poses which she choreographed and performed as tableaux vivants.

103 *Self-portrait leaning on hand* c.1800

[colour plate 73]
Pencil, 23.7 × 19cm (9¼ × 7½in). Inscribed: *R Cosway*
COLLECTIONS: Private Collection, USA
EXHIBITED: New Haven 1979, p.114, no.116; New York 1986, no.21
PRIVATE COLLECTION, COURTESY OF BERGGRUEN AND ZEVI LIMITED

GEORGE DANCE (1741–1825)

104 *Richard Cosway R.A.* 1793

Chalk and pencil with watercolour, 25.3 × 19.2cm (9⅞ × 7½in). Inscribed: *April 6th. 1793 / Geo: Dance.* Engraved: in chalk manner by W. Daniell, *Richard Cosway R.A.* (Dance and Daniell 1809–14)
REFERENCES: Gaunt 1963, pp.182–3
ILLUSTRATED: Williamson 1897, opp. p.6, and Williamson 1905, opp. p.30
ROYAL ACADEMY OF ARTS, LONDON

105 *Mars and Venus c.*1790–1800

Pen and ink, 22.2 × 18.1cm (8¾ × 7⅛in); with original wash-lined mount, 30.5 × 26.1cm (12 × 10¼in)
YALE CENTER FOR BRITISH ART, NEW HAVEN, PAUL MELLON COLLECTION
(Inv. B1977.14.5226)

106 *Prometheus c.*1790–1800

Pen and ink on original wash-lined mount, 30.5 × 26.2cm (12 × 10¼in)
COLLECTIONS: Francis Peabody 1952
EXHIBITED: New Haven 1979–80, no.117
NEW YORK PUBLIC LIBRARY
(Inv. 159)

107 *Sextus, the son of Pompey, applying to Erictho to know the fate of the Battle of Pharsalia c.*1790–1800

Pen and ink, 18.4 × 22.8cm (7¼ × 9in) on original wash-lined mount
COLLECTIONS: Francis Peabody 1952
EXHIBITED: New Haven 1979–80, no.118
NEW YORK PUBLIC LIBRARY
(Inv. 154)

In terms of the dense pen and ink draughtsmanship and the unusual choice of subject matter, Cosway may well have intended this drawing as a homage to the late John Hamilton Mortimer, his contemporary at Shipley's drawing school. Mortimer's version of this subject was exhibited at the Society of Artists in 1771 (no. 84) and engraved in mezzotint by R. Dunkarton in 1776 (Sunderland 1986, pp. 142–3, no. 51, fig. 81). Paul Gwynne has identified Cosway's original source as from Lucan, *De Bello Civile*, VI: 620ff.

108 *Hero and Leander in the temple c.*1790–1800

Pen and ink with brush and pencil, 18.4 × 23.5cm (7¼ × 9¼in)
REFERENCES: Blayney-Brown 1982, p.229, no.461
ASHMOLEAN MUSEUM, OXFORD
(Inv. DBB 461)

Paul Gwynne has identified the source of this scene – and the following two [**109**][**110**] – as part of a series of drawings by Cosway, which illustrate Musaeus's poem *Hero and Leander* as translated by Sir Robert Stapylton (Musaeus 1647). Cosway's bound and monogrammed copy of the classical poem is in the library of the Fondazione Cosway at Lodi. The romantic and tragic story was very popular in English Renaissance poetry and also with neo-classical artists across Europe (Mouilleseaux 1974 and Reid 1993).

109 *Hero and Leander by the Hellespont c.*1790–1800

Pen and ink with watercolour on original wash-lined mount, 24.8 × 28.8cm (9¾ × 11⅜in)
COLLECTIONS: bequeathed by E.H.W. Meyerstein, 1953
EXHIBITED: London 1972, p.325, no.545
BRITISH MUSEUM, LONDON
(Inv. 1953.4.11.2)

Leander, a young man from Abydos, fell in love with Hero, who was the beautiful priestess of Venus at her temple in Sestos, which was on the other side of the Hellespont. Every night he swam across the straits to be with her in her tower, where she was accompanied by an old nurse. Eventually Leander drowned and Hero committed suicide by throwing herself off the cliffs onto his body.

110 *Hero's dream c.*1790–1800

Pen and ink with wash, 18.4 × 22.3cm (7¼ × 8⅞in)
PRIVATE COLLECTION

Before Leander drowned at the denouement of the story, Hero had had a premonitionary dream of a beached dolphin.

RICHARD COSWAY AFTER SIR PETER PAUL RUBENS (1577–1640)

111 *The death of Hippolytus c.*1790–1800

Pen and ink over pencil, on original wash-lined mount, 32 × 44.8cm (12⅝ × 17⅝in); with mount 37.1 × 50cm (14⅝ × 19⅝in). Etched: by Maria Cosway (impression at the Fondazione Cosway, Lodi)
COLLECTIONS: Richard Cosway, Maria Cosway; Collegio delle Dame Inglesi, Lodi (stamped with circular monogram in ink: COLLEGIO FEMMINILE COSWAI / LODI)
FONDAZIONE COSWAY, LODI

This is the largest of Richard Cosway's drawings to survive. He copied it from the oil sketch by Rubens, currently in the Courtauld Institute Galleries, rather than the more finished panel now in the Fitzwilliam Museum, Cambridge. This is an interesting example of the artistic collaboration between the Cosways, which usually entailed Maria etching her husband's drawings.

112 *Self-portrait c.*1790

Pencil and watercolour, framed as a miniature, height 10.3cm (4in)
COLLECTIONS: given by Miss G.M. Zornlin, 1870
ILLUSTRATED: Piper 1992, p.185
NATIONAL PORTRAIT GALLERY, LONDON
(Inv. 304)

A copy by Henry Stubble is in the Henry E. Huntington Library and Art Gallery, San Marino, California.

113 *An unknown lady* 1790

[colour plate 91]
Watercolour on ivory, height 7cm (2¾in). Signed and dated: *Rdus Cosway / R.A. / Primarius Pictor / Serenissimi Walliae / Principis / Pinxit / 1790*
COLLECTIONS: with H.E. Backer, where purchased in 1947 by Louis C.G. Clarke, LL.D., by whom bequeathed in 1960
REFERENCES: Bayne-Powell 1985, p.42
FITZWILLIAM MUSEUM, UNIVERSITY OF CAMBRIDGE
(Inv. PD.196-1961)

114 *Maria Fagnani, later Marchioness of Hertford* 1791

Watercolour on ivory with lock of hair in back of setting, height 7.6cm (2⅞in). Signed and dated in pen and ink on verso: *Rd. Cosway / R.A. / Primarius Pictor / Serenissimi Walliae / Principis / Pinxit / 1791.* Inscribed on verso over lock of hair: *Maria Fagniani by Cosway 1791*
COLLECTIONS: probably Richard, 4th Marquess of Hertford; Sir Richard Wallace; Lady Wallace; Sir John Murray Scott sale, Christie's, London 24–26 June 1913, lot 26; with Arthur Tite, London; purchased in 1959 by the NACF, by whom presented to the Library of Hertford House
REFERENCES: Reynolds 1980, p.341
LIBRARY OF HERTFORD HOUSE, LONDON
(Inv. MAI)

Maria Emily Fagnani (1771–1856) was the daughter of the singer and dancer Costanza Brusati, and almost certainly the 4th Duke of Queensberry, known as 'Old Q'. Both he and his friend George Selwyn left her considerable fortunes. This greatly enhanced the Hertford family's wealth after her marriage in 1798 to Francis, 3rd Marquess of Hertford, who was a great friend of the Prince of Wales. Their only son Richard, later the 4th Marquess, was extremely fond of his mother, and is reputed to have slept with a miniature of her – most probably the one by Cosway – under his pillow.

115 *The Duke of Clarence, later William IV* 1791

Watercolour on ivory, height 7.6cm (3in). Signed and dated on original backing card in ink: *Rdus Cosway / R.A. / Primarius / Pictor / Serenissimi Walliae / Principis / Pinxit / 1791*
COLLECTIONS: one of the miniatures of the Duke of Clarence painted in 1791, costing £31 10s (Lodi, Fondazione Cosway, MS Inventory 1820, fols 224r–225r; Duke of Gloucester; bequeathed by the Duchess of Gloucester to Queen Victoria in 1857
REFERENCES: Millar 1986, p.587; Walker 1992, pp.91–2, no.182
EXHIBITED: London 1970, no. 45
ILLUSTRATED: Cazzulani and Stroppa 1989, fig.23
LENT BY HER MAJESTY THE QUEEN

The Duke of Clarence (1765–1837), later King William IV, wears the Star of the Order of the Garter on his coat.

116 *Princess Mary, Duchess of Gloucester* 1792

Watercolour on ivory, height 7.9cm (3⅛in)
COLLECTIONS: commissioned by the Prince of Wales in 1792 for 30 guineas (Lodi, Fondazione Cosway, MS Inventory 1820, fol.221r); recorded in royal inventory of 1844
REFERENCES: Millar 1986, p.587; Walker 1992, p.93, no.185
ILLUSTRATED: Williamson 1897, opp. p.78
LENT BY HER MAJESTY THE QUEEN

Princess Mary (1776–1857) was the fourth surviving daughter of George III and Queen Charlotte. In 1816 she married William Frederick, Duke of Gloucester.

117 *Princess Sophia* 1792

Watercolour on ivory, height 7.9cm (3⅛in).
Signed and dated: *R^dus Cosway / R.A. / Primarius Pictor / Serenissimi Walliae / Principis / Pinxit / 1792*
COLLECTIONS: commissioned by the Prince of Wales in 1792 for £31 10s (Lodi, Fondazione Cosway, MS Inventory 1820, fol.221r); recorded in a royal inventory in 1851
REFERENCES: Millar 1977, pp.131–2; Millar 1986, p.587; Walker 1992, pp.93–4, no.186
EXHIBITED: London 1970, no.50
ILLUSTRATED: Williamson 1897, opp. p.38, and Williamson 1905, opp. p.111; Millar 1977, p.132, fig.147; Cazzulani and Stroppa 1989, fig.22
LENT BY HER MAJESTY THE QUEEN
Princess Sophia (1777–1848) was the fifth daughter of George III and Queen Charlotte.

118 *The Prince of Wales, later George IV* 1792

[colour plate 50]
Watercolour on ivory, height 8.1cm (3¼in).
Signed in pen and ink on paper on verso: *R^dus Cosway RA / Primarius Pictor / Serenissimi Walliae / Principis / Pinxit / 1792.*
Inscribed on reverse of case: GP and HONI SOIT QUI MAL Y PENSE
COLLECTIONS: commissioned by the Prince of Wales in 1792 for £31 10s; Sotheby's, London, 28 April 1981, lot 230, bought by Leggatt for the National Portrait Gallery
REFERENCES: Walker 1985, I, pp.200–1, col. ill. 12; II, pl.464
NATIONAL PORTRAIT GALLERY, LONDON
(Inv. 5389)
Set in a gold locket, Cosway's miniature represents the Prince wearing the Garter cloak and costume.

119 *An unknown gentleman* 1793

Watercolour on ivory, height 8.8cm (3½in).
Signed and dated on original backing card in pen and ink on verso: *R^dus. Cosway, / R.A. / Primarius Pictor / Serenissimi / Walliae / Principis / Pinxit / 1793*
COLLECTIONS: bequest of George Salting 1910
VICTORIA AND ALBERT MUSEUM, LONDON
(Inv. P46-1910)

120 *Mrs Fitzgerald* 1794

[colour plate 89]
Watercolour on ivory, height 8.3cm (3¼in).
Signed and dated in pen and ink on paper on verso: *R^dus Cosway, / R.A. / Primarius Pictor / Serenissimi Walliae / Principis / Pinxit / 1794*
COLLECTIONS: Henry E. Huntington 1927
ILLUSTRATED: Wark 1986, p.43; Reynolds 1992, col. pl.x
HENRY E. HUNTINGTON LIBRARY AND ART GALLERY, SAN MARINO, CALIFORNIA
(Inv. 26.21)
Catherine Fitzgerald (d.1832) was the younger daughter of the Rev. Henry Vesey. She married the Rt Hon. James Fitzgerald (1742–1835), a noted Irish politician. When he refused a peerage she was created Baroness Fitzgerald and Vesey in 1826. Her eldest son, William Vesey Fitzgerald, succeeded to her Irish peerage in February 1832 as Lord Fitzgerald.

121 *An unknown lady* 1794

Watercolour on ivory, height 8.8cm (3½in).
Signed and dated in pen and ink on paper on verso: *R^dus Cosway, / R.A. / Primarius Pictor / Serenissimi Walliae / Principis / Pinxit / 1794*
COLLECTIONS: Edward Joseph; Frank Woodroffe; J. Pierpont Morgan; his sale, Christie's, London, 24 June 1935, lot 256
ILLUSTRATED: Foskett 1987, p.321, col. pl.26c
PRIVATE COLLECTION

122 *The Prince of Wales, later George IV* c.1792

[colour plate 48]
Watercolour on ivory, height 7.3cm (2⅞in).
Inscribed on verso of case: *Prince of Wales, afterwards, George IV*
COLLECTIONS: one of the miniatures painted in 1792 costing £31 10s (Lodi, Fondazione Cosway, MS Inventory 1820, fol.221r)
GRIMSTHORPE AND DRUMMOND CASTLE TRUST

123 *Isaac Blackburne* c.1790–5

Watercolour on ivory with plaited hair set in reverse, height 7cm (2⅞in)
COLLECTIONS: Miss Ireland Blackburne, 9 Belgrave Road, London (in 1897); Christie's, London, 8 July 1987, lot 378
REFERENCES: Williamson 1897, p.101
EXHIBITED: London 1895, no.69
COMMANDER GERALD BARNETT, RN (RETD)

124 *Lady Elizabeth Bingham* c.1790–5

[colour plate 90]
Watercolour on ivory, height 8.9cm (3½in).
Inscribed in pen and ink on paper on verso: *Lady / Elizabeth Bingham / afterwards / Vernon Harcourt / Cosway*
PRIVATE COLLECTION

125 *Miss Sophia Bankes* c.1795

[colour plate 88]
Watercolour on ivory with pearl mount, height 8.9cm (3½in)
COLLECTIONS: Henry E. Huntington 1927
ILLUSTRATED: Wark 1986, p.43; Reynolds 1992, col. pl.ix
HENRY E. HUNTINGTON LIBRARY AND ART GALLERY, SAN MARINO, CALIFORNIA
(Inv. 26.9)
Miss Sophia Bankes (dates unknown), shown wearing men's clothing, was the second daughter of the politician and author Henry Bankes (1757–1834). Her mother was Frances, daughter of William Woodley, Governor of the Leeward Islands.

126 *John Philip Kemble* 1795

[colour plate 93]
Watercolour on ivory, height 7cm (2¾in).
Inscribed in pencil on paper on verso: *1795* and in pen and ink *Cosway*
COLLECTIONS: Sotheby's, London, 5 March 1956, part of lot 18; acquired from H.E. Backer, London
VICTORIA AND ALBERT MUSEUM, LONDON
(Inv. P13-1956)
John Philip Kemble (1757–1823) was one of the most famous actors of his generation. Cosway has portrayed Kemble in the dress *all'antica* of one of his most famous roles, Coriolanus.

127 *Louisa Paolina Angelica Cosway* c.1795

[colour plates 68 and 71]
Watercolour on ivory, height 6.8cm (2⅝in).
Inscriptions on three labels adhered to reverse: *Cosway, 18, 42*
COLLECTIONS: Maria Cosway; Collegio delle Dame Inglesi, Lodi; Signore Varese, Milan; Christie's, London, 1 June 1896
ILLUSTRATED: Williamson 1897, opp. p.86 and 1905, opp. p.24
CITY OF PLYMOUTH MUSEUMS AND ART GALLERY
(Inv. 1977.6.6)
Louisa was the only daughter of Richard and Maria Cosway.

128 *The Prince of Wales, later George IV* 1795

[colour plate 47]
Watercolour on ivory, height 7.8cm (3in)
COLLECTIONS: commissioned by the Prince of Wales in 1795 for 30 guineas – one of three miniatures 'in uniform'; Durlacher; his sale 1898; F. Leverton Harris, by whom bequeathed in 1926
REFERENCES: Bayne-Powell 1985, p.41 and col. pl.v
FITZWILLIAM MUSEUM, CAMBRIDGE
(Inv. 3752)
An authentic replica is at Windsor (Walker 1992, pp.89–90, no.179). The Prince of Wales wears the uniform of the 10th (or Prince of Wales's) Light Dragoons of which he was Colonel from 1796 to 1820. He is wearing a short frogged jacket laced with silver, over which are his shoulder-belt and plate, together with his cap or pelisse lines. He also wears the Ribbon and Star of the Order of the Garter.

129 *Charlotte, Princess Royal, later Queen of Württemberg* 1795

Watercolour on ivory, height 9.8cm (3⅞in).
Inscribed on verso: *H.R.H. / Princess Royal / Cosway*
COLLECTIONS: commissioned by the Prince of Wales in 1795 for 30 guineas (Lodi, Fondazione Cosway, MS Inventory 1820, fol.222r)
CITY OF PLYMOUTH MUSEUMS AND ART GALLERY
(Inv. 1977.6.4)
Charlotte, Princess Royal, later Queen of Württemberg (1766–1828) was the eldest daughter of King George III and Queen Charlotte. There is a copy of this miniature by George Engleheart at Windsor (Walker 1992, pp.111–12, no.221).

130 *Princess Amelia* 1795

Watercolour on ivory, height 9cm (3½in).
Inscribed on backing card: *H.R.H. Princess
Amelia R^d Cosway*
COLLECTIONS: commissioned by the Prince of
Wales for 30 guineas; probably Duke of Sussex;
Lord Truro; his sale Christie's, London, 11 May
1893, lot 39, bought for the Royal Collection
REFERENCES: Lodi, Fondazione Cosway, MS
Inventory 1820, fol.222r; Millar 1986, p.587;
Walker 1992, p.94, no.187
EXHIBITED: London 1970, no.52
ILLUSTRATED: Williamson 1897, opp. p.78, and
1905, opp. p.104
LENT BY HER MAJESTY THE QUEEN
Princess Amelia (1783–1810) was the youngest
daughter of George III and Queen Charlotte.
Cosway painted another miniature of her seven
years later [**177**].

131 *Queen Charlotte* 1795

[colour plate 87]
Watercolour on ivory, height 9cm (3½in).
Inscribed on original backing card in pen and
ink on paper: *Queen Charlotte by Cosway*
COLLECTIONS: commissioned by George, Prince
of Wales, in 1795 for 30 guineas; recorded in
royal inventory of 1870
REFERENCES: Lodi, Fondazione Cosway, MS
Inventory 1820, fol.222r; Millar 1986, p.587;
Walker 1992, p.87, no.174
EXHIBITED: London 1970, no.41
ILLUSTRATED: Williamson 1897, opp. p.78
LENT BY HER MAJESTY THE QUEEN
Charlotte of Mecklenburg-Strelitz (1744–1818)
married George III in 1761.

132 *Mrs Arbuthnot* 1796

Watercolour on ivory in pearl mount, height
6.9cm (2¾in). Signed and dated on original
backing card in ink: *R. Cosway / R.A. /
Primarius Pictor / Serenissimi Walliae /
Principis / Pinxit / 1796*
COLLECTIONS: Drouot, Paris, 29 May 1937, lot 24;
Louis C.G. Clarke, LL.D., by whom bequeathed
in 1960
REFERENCES: Bayne-Powell 1985, p.45
FITZWILLIAM MUSEUM, UNIVERSITY OF
CAMBRIDGE
(Inv. PD.200.1961)
Bayne-Powell has suggested the sitter is the first
wife of Charles Arbuthnot, rather than Harriet
Arbuthnot, the friend of Wellington.

133 *Richard, Admiral Earl Howe* 1798-9

[colour plate 97]
Watercolour on ivory, height 5.4cm (2⅛in)
PRIVATE COLLECTION (ON LOAN TO THE
NATIONAL MARITIME MUSEUM, GREENWICH)
Richard, Admiral Earl Howe (1726-99), was one
of the most distinguished naval commanders of
the period.

134 *Princess Charlotte of Wales* c.1799

[colour plate 86]
Watercolour on ivory, with a lock of hair on
back; on verso, watercolour on ivory by a
follower of Richard Cosway of *George, Prince of
Wales*, height 6cm (2⅝in)

REFERENCES: Walker 1992, p.95, no.189
LENT BY HER MAJESTY THE QUEEN
Princess Charlotte of Wales (1796–1817) was the
only daughter of the Prince of Wales and
Princess Caroline of Brunswick.

135 *An unknown boy* 1799

Watercolour on ivory, height 8.9cm (3½in).
Signed and dated in pen and ink on paper on
verso: *R^{dus}. / Cosway / R.A. / Primarius Pictor
/ Serenissimi Walliae / Principis / Pinxit / 1799*
COLLECTIONS: given by Mrs Samuel S. Joseph
VICTORIA AND ALBERT MUSEUM, LONDON
(Inv. P7–1941)
This portrait of a boy, aged about five, has
traditionally been identified as Sir Frederick
Augustus d'Este (1794–1848), the son of H.R.H.
Frederick Augustus, Duke of Sussex, and Lady
Augusta Murray.

ANDREW PLIMER (1763–1837)

136 *The Hons Anne, Harriet and Elizabeth
Rushout ('The Three Graces')* c.1790

Watercolour on ivory, 12.2 × 14.6cm
(4¾ × 5¾in)
COLLECTIONS: J.L. Propert; sold to George J.
Gould (by Agnew); acquired by Henry E.
Huntington through Duveen
REFERENCES: Reynolds 1992, pp.116–18
ILLUSTRATED: Wark 1986, p.47
HENRY E. HUNTINGTON LIBRARY AND ART
GALLERY, SAN MARINO, CALIFORNIA
(Inv. 24.22)
The three Rushout sisters were the daughters of
John, 1st Baron Northwick. Andrew Plimer was
Cosway's most gifted pupil. His brother
Nathaniel Plimer was also a miniaturist.

JOHN SMART (1741–1811)

137 *Self-portrait* 1797

[colour plate 13]
Watercolour on ivory with plaited hair behind
glass on verso, height 8.6cm (3⅜in). Signed and
dated on recto: *I.S. / 1797*. Inscribed on verso
with initials in gold: *JS*
COLLECTIONS: purchased from Messrs Frost and
Reed, London
VICTORIA AND ALBERT MUSEUM, LONDON
(Inv. P11–1940)
John Smart, like Cosway, was one of the
generation of talented artists who were trained
at William Shipley's drawing school and who
transformed the genre of portrait miniature
painting in Britain over the last third of the
eighteenth century. This perfectly preserved
Self-portrait – one of Smart's masterpieces –
reveals his meticulously veristic style which is
in direct contrast with Cosway's evanescent
handling.

W. SHARP (1749–1824) AFTER RICHARD
COSWAY

138 *George, Prince of Wales* 1790

Line engraving, 24.3 × 16.5cm (9½ × 6½in).
Lettered: R^{DUS}. COSWAY *Pictor Principis Pinxit /
GULIELMUS SHARP Sculpsit / ICH DIEN / GEORGE /
Prince of Wales. / Engraved & Publish'd by W^m.
Sharp, N°.8, Charles Street Middlesex Hospital;
& Sold by W. Skelton, Haymarket, Aug: 12. 1790.*

REFERENCES: Bromley 1793, p.320; Daniell 1890,
p.20, no.80
ILLUSTRATED: Lloyd 1993, p.192 (p.124), fig.1
PRIVATE COLLECTION
The miniature from which this engraving was
made also provided the model for the 1787 stipple
engraving by T. Burke. This print was probably
the most widely disseminated of Cosway's images
of the Prince.

JAMES GILLRAY (1757–1815)

139 *A voluptuary under the horrors of
digestion* 1792

Coloured etching, 35.8 × 28.5cm (13¼ × 10¾in).
Lettered: *J^s. G^y. design et fecit. / Pub^d. July 2^d.
1792. by H. Humphrey N°. 18 Old Bond Street.* A
VOLUPTUARY *under the horrors of Digestion.*
NATIONAL PORTRAIT GALLERY, LONDON
One of Gillray's best-known images, this is also
one of the most famous caricatures of the
sybaritic and overweight Prince of Wales, which
manages to capture something of his monstrous
elegance. Gillray based his portrayal of the Prince
on one of Cosway's miniatures [**118**].

L. SCHIAVONETTI (1765–1810)
AFTER RICHARD COSWAY

140 *Mrs Cosway* 1791

Stipple engraving, 25.9 × 18.1cm (10¼ × 7in).
Lettered: *R. Cosway R.A. del^t. / L. Schiavonetti
sculp^t. / Mrs. Cosway / London Publish'd. Feby. 1:
1791 by Molteno Colnaghi. & Co. N°.132 Pall Mall.*
REFERENCES: Daniell 1890, p.10, no.35
PRIVATE COLLECTION

D. ORME (C.1766–1802)
AFTER RICHARD COSWAY

141 *William Bromfield, Esqr.* 1792

Line engraving, 43 × 29cm (16⅞ × 11⅜in).
Lettered: *Cosway R.A. Pinx^t. / D. Orme Sculp^t. /
William Bromfield, Esqr. /* DUCIT OPES ANIMUMQUE
FERO */ Sold & Published by D. Orme & Co. N^o: 14.
Old Bond Street London July 21. 1792.*
REFERENCES: Daniell 1890, p.5, no.15; Burgess 1973
WELLCOME INSTITUTE LIBRARY, LONDON
(Inv. 428.1)
William Bromfield (1712–92) was surgeon to
Queen Charlotte. In 1741 he gave a series of
popular lectures on anatomy and surgery, and he
published regularly.

J. CONDÉ (D.1794)
AFTER RICHARD COSWAY

142 *Mrs Fitzherbert* 1792

Stipple engraving, 29.7 × 22cm (11⅝ × 8⅝in).
Lettered: *R. Cosway R.A. pinxt. / John Condé
sculp^t. / London. Published Feby. 7. 1792, by J.
Condé. N°.63. Queen Anne Street East / and M^{rs}.
Lay. N°.38, Dean Street, Soho.*
REFERENCES: Bromley 1793, p.436; Daniell 1890,
p.19, no.76
SCOTTISH NATIONAL PORTRAIT GALLERY
(Inv. E.P.V.59-3)
An impression (Royal Library, Windsor Castle) of
this well-known image of Mrs Fitzherbert (1756–
1837), the morganatic wife of the Prince of Wales,
is titled: M^{RS}. FITZHERBERT.

A. CARDON (1722–1813)
AFTER RICHARD COSWAY

143 *Louisa Paolina Angelica Cosway aged five* 1797

Stipple engraving, 33.7 × 25.4cm (13¼ × 10in). Lettered: *R. Cosway R.A. delin^t. / Anth^y. Cardon sculp^t. /* LOUISA PAOLINA ANGELICA COSWAY *Etatis 5.*
REFERENCES: Daniell 1890, p.12, no.45
LENT BY HER MAJESTY THE QUEEN

P. CONDÉ (*fl.*1795–1824)
AFTER RICHARD COSWAY

144 *I.B. De Mainauduc M.D. Member of the Corporation of Surgeons* 1798

Stipple engraving, 22.9 × 17.5cm (9 × 6⅞in)
REFERENCES: de Mainauduc 1798, frontispiece; Daniell 1890, p.25, no.100; Burgess 1973, p.231
WELLCOME INSTITUTE LIBRARY, LONDON (Inv.1877.1)
An impression is in the New York Public Library with the publication details: *R. Cosway R.A. pinx^t. / P. Condé sculp^t. / I.B. De* MAINAUDUC */ M.D. / Member of the Corporation / of /* SURGEONS. */ Published as the Act directs.*

J. CONDÉ (*d.*1794)
AFTER RICHARD COSWAY

145 *Docet amor* 1791

Stipple engraving, 28 × 21.3cm (11 × 8⅜in). Lettered: *R^d.. Cosway R.A. Delin. / In^o. Condé Sculp^t. /* DOCET AMOR */ Published as the Act directs, Ap^l. 26th. 1791. by R. Cosway.*
REFERENCES: Landon 1802, II, pp.141–2; Daniell 1890, p.43, no.175
ILLUSTRATED: Richard Cosway's *Catalogue of...Pictures*, 1791, frontispiece [**219**]; Richard Cosway's *Catalogue of... Pictures*, 17–19 May 1821; Landon 1802, opp. p.141 and 1809 frontispiece (line engraving after Cosway by Mme Lefevre, née Lingée)
PRIVATE COLLECTION
Cosway used this print as the frontispiece in the catalogue to promote his private contract sale of Old Master pictures in 1791, and Maria used it again in a similar way for the 1821 auction catalogue of his pictures. Landon stated that Cosway intended to use it as a frontispiece for an edition of the 163 separate prints after his original compositions. As to the image itself, Cosway adapted the more normal composition, which is a legendary story from classical antiquity, to have the man trace the shadow thrown from the woman's profile (Rosenblum 1957 and Bermingham 1992). This image is central to an understanding of not only Richard Cosway's persona as an artist, but also Maria's relationship to him – as a woman, wife, artist and muse.

UNKNOWN MEDALLIST

146* *Richardus Cosway R.A. c.*1790

Gilt bronze medallion, diam. 12.2cm (4¾in). Lettered: RICHARDUS COSWAY R.A. PRIMARIUS PICTOR PRINCIPIS
COLLECTIONS: Richard Cosway, London; Maria Cosway, Lodi, bequeathed by her to the Galleria degli Uffizi in 1839
REFERENCES: Brown 1980, I, p.79, no.341

EXHIBITED: Florence 1971, no.240
MUSEO NAZIONALE DEL BARGELLO, FLORENCE (Inv.10409)

UNKNOWN MEDALLIST

147† *Richardus Cosway. R.A. c.*1790

Bronze medallion, diam. 12.2cm (4¾in). lettered: RICHARDUS COSWAY. R.A. PRIMARIUS PICTOR PRINCIPIS
COLLECTIONS: presented by Messrs Peel and Humphris
REFERENCES: Brown 1980, I, p.79, no.341
VICTORIA AND ALBERT MUSEUM, LONDON (Inv. A–8–1962)

UNKNOWN MEDALLIST

148* *Maria Cosway* 1797

Uniface gilt-bronze medallion, diam. 11.6cm (4½in). Lettered: MARIA COSWAY 1797
COLLECTIONS: Maria Cosway, London and Lodi, bequeathed by her to the Galleria degli Uffizi in 1839
REFERENCES: Brown 1980, I, p.100, no.423
EXHIBITED: Florence 1971, no.241
MUSEO NAZIONALE DEL BARGELLO, FLORENCE (Inv. 10408)
Only one other – damaged – version of this extremely rare medallion has so far been traced (Department of Coins and Medals, British Museum).

IV RICHARD COSWAY: 1800–21

149† *George, Earl of Sunderland and his brother Lord Charles Spencer* 1800

Oil on canvas, 129.5 × 104.1cm (51 × 41in). Engraved: W. Barney, *Geo. Spencer, Earl of Sunderland and Lord Charles Spencer*, 1805, mezzotint (Daniell 1890, p.35, no.138). Inscribed: (on left, erroneously) GEORGE 5TH DUKE / OF MARLBOROUGH /; (right) LORD CHARLES / S. CHURCHILL
COLLECTIONS: commissioned in 1800 by George, Marquis of Blandford, for £105 (Lodi, Fondazione Cosway, MS Inventory 1820, fol.226r); White-Knights, Reading; by family descent at Blenheim Palace, Oxfordshire
EXHIBITED: Royal Academy, London, 1800, no.221 ('Portraits of the two sons of the Marquis of Blandford'); London 1951–2, no.390
HIS GRACE THE DUKE OF MARLBOROUGH
George Spencer (1793–1857), later 6th Duke of Marlborough, is depicted by Cosway playing with armour, in the company of his younger brother, Lord Charles Spencer (1794–1840). They were both sons of George, Marquis of Blandford, who succeeded as 5th Duke in 1817. At Blenheim Palace there is also an authentic reduced version miniature of this composition.

150* *Archibald, 9th Duke of Hamilton c.*1800

Oil on panel, 74.3 × 60.9cm (29¼ × 24in). Inscribed: *Archibald 9th Duke of Hamilton by R Cosway*
COLLECTIONS: by family descent
HIS GRACE THE DUKE OF HAMILTON AND BRANDON, KT

Archibald, 9th Duke of Hamilton (1740–1819), was the father of the 10th Duke, a noted collector, who married *Susan Beckford* [**155**]. She was the daughter of the great connoisseur and writer William Beckford, who built the ill-fated neo-Gothic extravaganza, *Fonthill Abbey* [**166**] in Wiltshire.

151 *The Hons Sophia, Louisa and Mathilda Courtenay* 1805

Oil on canvas, 147.3 × 177.8cm (70 × 92in)
COLLECTIONS: commissioned by William, 3rd Viscount Courtenay in 1805 for £262 10s (Powderham Castle MSS); by family descent
LORD COURTENAY
The sitters were three of the daughters of the 2nd Viscount Courtenay, and sisters of the 3rd Viscount [**93**]. Sophia married Nathaniel Foy in 1804; Louisa (d.1823) married Lt-Gen. Lord Robert Henry Somerset, fourth son of the Duke of Beaufort, in 1805; while Mathilda (d.1848) married Lt-Gen. John Locke. The composition is ambitious and graceful, although it is unusual in a triple portrait to have the sitters seated on the ground.

152 *Harriet Mellon, later Duchess of St Albans, as a sibyl c.*1805

Oil on panel, 76.4 × 62.4cm (30 × 24¼in). Inscribed in pencil on verso: *Duchess of St. Albans* and *1138*
COLLECTIONS: Sotheby's, London, 10 July 1985, lot 58 (repr. in col.); bought by Leggatt for the Tate Gallery in 1985
REFERENCES: Tate Gallery 1988, pp.61–2
TATE GALLERY, LONDON (Inv. T04114)
Harriet Mellon (1777–1837) was an actress, who in 1827 married the 9th Duke of St Albans (1801–49). As was argued in 1985 the picture bears a very strong resemblance to other portraits of Harriet Mellon (Walker 1985, I, pp.433–4). This painting was attributed to Richard Cosway by the late Sir Ellis Waterhouse and Jacob Simon, independently, prior to its auction in 1985.

153 *Charles, 4th Earl of Harrington c.*1800–5

Pencil with watercolour, 23.2 × 14.1cm (9¼ × 5⅝in). Signed in monogram: *CR.* Inscribed on dog's collar: *Peter*
COLLECTIONS: purchased from Colnaghi, London, 1970
CECIL HIGGINS ART GALLERY, BEDFORD
Charles, 4th Earl of Harrington (1780–1851), better known by his earlier title of Lord Petersham, was a notable Regency eccentric.

154 *Mrs Udney c.*1800–5

Pencil with watercolour on original mount, 22.9 × 14cm (9 × 5½in). Signed on middle step: *R. Cosway.* Engraved: in stipple in the manner of A. Cardon (Daniell 1890, p.37, no.150)
BRITISH MUSEUM, LONDON (Inv. 1904-6-14-6)
Mrs Udney was the young wife of Robert Udney (1725–1802), who was a collector of Old Master paintings and friend of Richard Cosway. The artist painted a portrait miniature (untraced)

of his friend, which was engraved (Daniell 1890, p.37, no.150). He also designed a memorial to his friend, which was composed of Minerva instructing various putti, in front of a group of roundels portraying the greatest Old Masters (Royal Museum, Copenhagen), and which was also engraved (Daniell 1890, p.48, no.194). Richard Cosway was particularly close friends with Mrs Udney, and it was she who was in his carriage when he died of a sudden seizure in 1821.

155 *Susan Beckford, later Duchess of Hamilton c.*1800-5

Pencil with watercolour, 21.8 × 10.7cm (9 × 5³⁄₈in)
COLLECTIONS: Phillips, London, 21 December 1987, lot 7
EXHIBITED: London 1990, no.26
PRIVATE COLLECTION
Susan Beckford (d.1859) was the second daughter of the famous collector and writer William Beckford and his wife Lady Margaret Gordon. In 1810 Susan Beckford married the collector and antiquarian, Alexander, 10th Duke of Hamilton (1767-1852), son of *Archibald, 9th Duke of Hamilton* [**150**]. An unfinished bust-length portrait drawing of the 10th Duke by Richard Cosway is in the Henry E. Huntington Library and Art Gallery, San Marino, California.

156 *John Braham with Harriet Abrams and her two daughters c.*1800-5

Pencil with watercolour on original wash-lined mount, 22 × 30cm (8⁵⁄₈ × 11³⁄₄in). Signed: ʀᵈ. COSWAY
COLLECTIONS: Phillips, London, 7 November 1994, lot 31
PRIVATE COLLECTION
This drawing is thought to portray Harriet Abrams (b. *c.*1760) and her two daughters. Harriet and her sister Theodosia Abrams (*c.*1761 – after 1834) were soprano and contralto singers, who performed regularly at concerts in London, and were often accompanied by a third sister Eliza (b. *c.*1763). John Braham (*c.*1774-1856) was a well-known tenor.

157 *George III c.*1805-10

Pencil with watercolour, 23.3 × 13.5cm (9¹⁄₈ × 5³⁄₈in), on original wash-lined mount 35.5 × 26.4cm (14 × 10³⁄₈in)
PRIVATE COLLECTION
Because of King George III's (1738-1820) antagonism towards his eldest son, it is very unlikely that the monarch actually sat to Cosway for this portrait drawing. The artist probably interpreted the face from a coin or medal. Cosway may have intended that this drawing act as a pair to that of the Prince of Wales [**158**].

158 *The Prince of Wales, later George IV c.*1805-10

Pencil with watercolour, 23 × 13.5cm (9 × 5³⁄₈in), with original wash-lined mount 29.1 × 20.2cm (11½ × 8in). Inscribed on verso: *Madama Cosway f[—] Gabrielle Bettini / a Lucien[-] July[-]*

COLLECTIONS: Sir J. Goldsmid in 1895
EXHIBITED: London 1895, no.121 ('Duke of Gloucester')
PRIVATE COLLECTION
Cosway may well have intended that this drawing act as a pendant to that of *George III* [**157**].

159 *An unknown lady as Juno* 1806

Pencil with watercolour, 29.2 × 21.5cm (11½ × 8½in). Signed and dated: *Richardus Cosway R.A. F.S.A. Primarius Pictor Serenissimi Walliae Principi Fecit Londini Anno 1806*
REFERENCES: Blayney-Brown 1982, pp.225-6, no.450
EXHIBITED: Bregenz and Vienna 1968-9, p.100, no.183
ASHMOLEAN MUSEUM, OXFORD
(Inv. DBB 450)
A copy of this drawing is in the Fitzwilliam Museum, Cambridge.

160* *Mystical self-portrait c.*1805

Pencil drawing with watercolour, 10.8 × 7.9cm (4¼ × 3¹⁄₈in)
COLLECTIONS: Maria Cosway; Collegio delle Dame Inglesi, Lodi; Christie's, London, 1 July 1896
ILLUSTRATED: Williamson 1897 and 1905, frontispieces
WORCESTER ART MUSEUM, WORCESTER, MASSACHUSSETTS
(Inv.1921.57)
In this late mystical self-portrait Cosway has set himself before a heavenly sunrise, and positioned himself between the two Masonic columns, while pointing to the Star of David, which is revealed in a manuscript he holds open [**187**].

161* *Self-portrait as Esau* 1806

Pencil with watercolour, 25.7 × 21.5cm (10¹⁄₈ × 8½in). Inscribed on recto: (six Hebraic characters, translated as 'His Name is Esau'). Inscribed on label on verso: *Richard Cosway Esq., R.A. &c &c, Drawn in 1812 by Himself;* (on another label on verso) *Ritratto / di Riccardo Cosway delle Accadᵐⁱᵃ. Rˡᵉ di Londra / Primo pittore di S.A.R. il Principe di Galles / dipinto da se medᵐᵒ. l'anno 1806. Età 65 / Presentato alla I.R. Galleria di Firenze / dalla vedova Maria Cosway / l'anno 1824 / Morto a Londra l'anno 1821 / di anni 80*
COLLECTIONS: Richard Cosway (Lodi, Fondazione Cosway, MS Inventory 1820, fol.158r); presented by Maria Cosway to the Galleria degli Uffizi in 1824 (Florence, Uffizi MS, ASC, Filza XLVIII, 1824, 23)
EXHIBITED: Florence 1971, no.52
GALLERIA DEGLI UFFIZI, FLORENCE
(Inv.1890 n.3257)
In this extraordinary and complex self-portrait as Esau, Richard Cosway reveals his profound involvement in Christian mysticism. The whole image is a manifesto of his highly syncretic religious beliefs. These are signified by references to esoteric Freemasonry and the Cabbala, in the form of the two columns of the Temple of Jerusalem, on the bases of which are represented the two Tablets of the Old Testa-

ment Law (on the left) and the two interlocking triangles (on the right), the latter a reference to the artist's fascination with the occult tradition. Cosway in later life was a practising magician and faith healer, who claimed to have prophetic powers. His identification with Esau is explained by the fact that the elder twin of Jacob – and son of Isaac – was considered to be a precursor of the Gnostic and Masonic traditions of hidden knowledge. Cosway, who amassed a substantial library on all aspects of conventional religion and the occult [**220**], presents himself as trampling on the earthly powers, indicated by the globe, coins, manuscripts, and the mask which is infested by a snake. The significance of this particular image to the Cosways was also shown by the fact that of all his many self-portraits this was the one that Richard had framed and displayed at Stratford Place, and it was also the one which Maria decided to present to the famous collection of self-portraits at the Uffizi. In stylistic terms the massive pose that Cosway strikes combines elements from the figure studies of Michelangelo and Fuseli, as well as from the heroic male portraiture of Lawrence (*Coriolanus*, 1801, Tate Gallery, London).

162 *The Hon. Peter Robert Burrell, later 2nd Baron Gwydyr and 19th Baron Willoughby de Eresby* 1807

Pencil with watercolour, on original wash-lined mount, 29.2 × 22.2cm (11½ × 8¾in). Signed and dated in pencil: *Rᵈᵘˢ. Cosway R.A. F.S.A. Primarius Pictor Serenissimi Walliae Principis Fecit Londini 1807*
COLLECTIONS: Christie's, London, 6 June 1972, lot 52
EXHIBITED: Edinburgh 1978, no.17
ILLUSTRATED: Williamson 1897, opp. p.22
PRIVATE COLLECTION
The Hon. Peter Robert Burrell (1782-1865) succeeded his father in 1820 as 2nd Baron Gwydyr and his mother in 1828 as 19th Baron Willoughby de Eresby. In 1807 he married Clementina Sarah, daughter and sole heiress of James Drummond, 1st Lord Perth. Burrell is shown in Vandyke costume, resting his right arm on the staff of the Joint Hereditary Lord Chamberlain.

163 *An unknown lady as a sibyl* 1808

Pencil drawing with watercolour, 29.3 × 21.3cm (11½ × 8½in); on original wash-lined mount 42.8 × 34.6cm (10⁷⁄₈ × 13⁵⁄₈in). Signed and dated: *Rᵈᵘˢ Cosway. R.A. et F.S.A. Primarius Pictor Serenissimi Walliae Principis Fecit 1808*
EXHIBITED: Edinburgh 1978, p.33, no.32
HIS GRACE THE DUKE OF HAMILTON AND BRANDON, KT

164 *George, 5th Earl of Jersey and 8th Viscount Grandison c.*1815

Pencil and black chalk with watercolour, 29 × 21.5cm (11³⁄₈ × 8½in)
REFERENCES: Williamson 1897, p.111
THE RT HON. THE EARL OF JERSEY
George Villiers, 5th Earl of Jersey (1773-1859), shown in fancy dress, succeeded his father in 1805. The 5th Earl was a passionate fox-hunter

and a notably successful breeder of champion horses at his Oxfordshire estate of Middleton. In 1804 he married Sarah Sophia, eldest daughter of John Fane, 10th Earl of Westmorland, by Anne, daughter and sole heiress of the banker Robert Child of Osterley Park, Middlesex. He added Child to his family name in 1819.

165 *George, Viscount Villiers, later 6th Earl of Jersey and his brother the Hon. Augustus John Villiers c.1815*

Pencil with watercolour, 29.5 × 22cm (11⅝ × 8⅝in). Signed: R COSWAY
REFERENCES: Williamson 1897, p.112
THE RT HON. THE EARL OF JERSEY

George Augustus-Frederick, Viscount Villiers (1808–59), succeeded his father as 6th Earl of Jersey but died three weeks later. In 1841 he had married Julia, the eldest daughter of Sir Robert Peel. The Hon. Augustus John Villiers (1810–47) was the second son of the 5th Earl of Jersey. A Captain in the Royal Horse Guards, in 1831 he married Georgiana, daughter of Viscount Keith.

166 *Fonthill Abbey 1807*

Pen and ink, 24.8 × 19.9cm (9¾ × 7⅞in); with original wash-lined mount with gilt border 38.1 × 32.2cm (15 × 12⅝in). Watermark: *1803*
FONDAZIONE COSWAY, LODI
(Inv. IX.38)

As he described in a letter to Jacob, 2nd Earl of Radnor [62], in 1807 Richard Cosway spent ten days as a guest of the great collector, writer and recluse, William Beckford, at his remarkable folly in Wiltshire designed by Wyatt. This is a very rare landscape by Cosway, which must have been executed on that visit.

167 *Venus mourning Adonis c.1805-15*

Watercolour over pencil, 13 × 8.9cm (5⅛ × 3½in)
COLLECTIONS: Richard Cosway; Sir John Soane
REFERENCES: London, Sir John Soane's Museum, MS Inventory 1837, Picture Room ('Mars reposing in the lap of Venus')
SIR JOHN SOANE'S MUSEUM, LONDON
(Inv. P116)

Cosway interpreted this tragic scene from one of the most popular of all the classical myths (Ovid, *Metamorphoses*, x: 708–39). After being accidentally grazed by one of Cupid's arrows, Venus fell hopelessly in love with the beautiful mortal Adonis. Out hunting one day he was killed by a wild boar. As is the case here, Venus was usually shown grieving over the body of her dead lover. By means of the nudity and reclining pose of Venus, Cosway emphasised the eroticism of the myth, while also referring to the denouement of the story through the distraught figures of Cupid and the hound.

168 *Love chaining Time 1812*

Pencil, red chalk and watercolour, 20.8 × 15.8cm (8¼ × 6¼in). Signed and dated on back of old frame: *Rdus. Cosway R.A. Primarius Pictor Serenissimi Walliae Principis Delt. 1812*
COLLECTIONS: Maria Cosway; Collegio delle Dame Inglesi, Lodi; Colnaghi, London (1950)

REFERENCES: Lodi, Fondazione Cosway, MS Inventory 1820, fol.158r ('Love chaining Time'); Blayney-Brown 1982, pp.227–8, no.455
ASHMOLEAN MUSEUM, OXFORD
(Inv. DBB 455)

The influence of Italian Mannerism is particularly emphasised in this drawing. In combining a sense of frenzied eroticism and extreme anatomical distortion, Cosway may well have been aware of Bronzino's famous painting of the *Allegory of Love* (National Gallery, London).

169 *An allegory of Love and Death c.1810-15*

Pencil with wash, 12 × 16.2cm (4¾ × 6⅜in) on original wash-lined mount
REFERENCES: Blayney-Brown 1982, pp.227–8, no.455
ASHMOLEAN MUSEUM, OXFORD
(Inv. DBB 454)

170 *Joseph and Potiphar's Wife 1810*

Pencil with wash, 14 × 17.7cm (5½ × 7in) on original wash-lined mount. Signed and dated: *Ricus. Cosway R.A. Primarius Pictor Serenissimi Walliae Principis Delt. 1810*
REFERENCES: Blayney-Brown 1982, pp.226–7, no.453
ASHMOLEAN MUSEUM, OXFORD
(Inv. DBB 453)

This composition is closely based on an etching by Rembrandt.

171 *Madonna and Child c.1805-15*

Watercolour over pencil, 23.3. × 18.9cm (9⅛ × 7⅜in). Inscribed in pencil on mount: *R Cosway*
YALE CENTER FOR BRITISH ART, NEW HAVEN
Gift of Mr and Mrs Stuart P. Feld
(Inv. B1978.24.1)

172 *The Flight into Egypt c.1805-10*

Pencil, pen and ink, red chalk, grey wash, with touches of brown wash and green ink, 23.4 × 19.2cm (9¼ × 7⅝in). Inscribed in pencil on mount: *R Cosway*
COLLECTIONS: Maria Cosway; Collegio delle Dame Inglesi, Lodi
YALE CENTER FOR BRITISH ART, NEW HAVEN
Gift of Mr and Mrs Stuart P. Feld
(Inv. B1978.24.7)

A painting of this subject was exhibited at the Royal Academy (1802, no.119).

173 *Christ blessing the little children c.1810-15*

Pencil, red chalk, brush and grey ink, on original wash-lined mount with gilt border, 20.2 × 16.5cm (8 × 6½in); with mount 34.7 × 28.5cm (13⅝ × 11¼in). Signed in pencil: *R Cosway*
COLLECTIONS: Maria Cosway; Collegio delle Dame Inglesi, Lodi
YALE CENTER FOR BRITISH ART, NEW HAVEN
Gift of Mr and Mrs Stuart P. Feld
(Inv. B1978.24.8)

174 *The Descent from the Cross c.1810-15*

Pencil, pen and ink, red chalk, brown and grey wash, on original wash-lined mount with gilt border, 22.8 × 17.8cm (9 × 7in); with mount 34.9 × 28.4cm (13¾ × 11⅜in)
COLLECTIONS: Maria Cosway; Collegio delle Dame Inglesi, Lodi
REFERENCES: Lodi, Fondazione Cosway, MS Inventory 1820, fol.158r ('The Descent of the Cross')
YALE CENTER FOR BRITISH ART, NEW HAVEN
Gift of Mr and Mrs Stuart P. Feld
(Inv. B1978.24.6)

175 *The Anointing of the Dead Christ c.1800*

Black chalk, 26 × 39cm (10¼ × 15⅜in). Signed: with monogram *CR*. Inscribed: *51*
COLLECTIONS: Maria Cosway; Collegio delle Dame Inglesi, Lodi; Signore Varese, Milan; Christie's, London, 1 June 1896, lot 129 ('Study for an Entombment – black chalk'), sold with lot 128; Dr George C. Williamson; Christie's, London, 9 November 1993, lot 2
EXHIBITED: New York 1994, no.9
NATIONAL GALLERY OF SCOTLAND
(Inv. 5378)

An untraced drawing of the 'Descent from the Cross' in a similar technique was also owned by Williamson (Williamson 1897, ill. opp. p.44 – in large paper copies only, and 1905, ill. opp. p.122). A similar pose for the body of Christ was adopted by Cosway for the composition of *Christ's Passion*, which was engraved by William Sharp and published in 1791 (Macklin 1791–1816; and Paley 1986).

176 *The Supper at Emmaus c.1810*

Watercolour over pencil, 15.6 × 20.7cm (6⅛ × 8⅛in)
COLLECTIONS: Maria Cosway; Collegio delle Dame Inglesi, Lodi
YALE CENTER FOR BRITISH ART, NEW HAVEN
Gift of Mr and Mrs Stuart P. Feld
(Inv. B1978.24.2)

This drawing relates to the altarpiece of the same subject commissioned by William, 3rd Viscount Courtenay, for the church at Powderham in Devon. Greatly damaged, this large canvas has recently been restored and is currently at Powderham Castle. In the painting Cosway included his own portrait in the guise of the innkeeper, inscribing his signature on the front of Christ's tunic.

177 *Princess Amelia 1802*

Watercolour on ivory, height 6.8cm (2⅝in). Signed and dated: *Rdus Cosway / R.A. et F.S.A. / Primarius Pictor / Serenissimi Walliae / Principi[s] / Pinxit / 1802*
COLLECTIONS: bequest from George Salting in 1910
REFERENCES: Reynolds 1988, pp.130–1, fig.81
VICTORIA AND ALBERT MUSEUM, LONDON
(Inv. P67-1910)

Princess Amelia (1783–1810) was the youngest daughter of George III and Queen Charlotte. Cosway had painted a miniature of her seven years earlier [130].

178 *Louis-Philippe, Duc d'Orléans, later King of France c.1805*

[colour plate 92]
Watercolour on ivory, octagonal, height 5.3cm (2⅛in)
COLLECTIONS: first recorded in royal inventories in 1837
REFERENCES: Walker 1992, p.96, no.191
LENT BY HER MAJESTY THE QUEEN

Louis-Philippe (1773-1850) was the eldest son of *Louis-Philippe, Duc d'Orléans* [89], known during the revolution as Philippe-Egalité. In 1808 he married Princess Maria Amelia of Naples. In 1830, after the deposition of Charles X, he was proclaimed King of France. After the Revolution of 1848 he was exiled in England, living at Claremont House where he died. As a boy Louis-Philippe was drawn with his brothers and sister in a group portrait [fig. 9] by Cosway which was made in France during the visit in 1786, and which is now in the Musée Condé, Chantilly. This miniature was probably painted when the Orléans family was living in exile at Twickenham between 1800 and 1806. Henry Bone copied it in enamel as he recorded in a drawing, which is inscribed *Le Duc d'Orleans – after Cosway / Feby. 1805.* (London, National Portrait Gallery Archive, Album I, fol.48r). A less idealised portrait miniature by Cosway of Louis-Philippe is in the Cleveland Museum of Art, Ohio.

179 *Princess Charlotte of Wales* 1807

Pencil with watercolour on paper, framed as a miniature, height 10.2cm (4in). Dated on recto: *1807.* Signed in pen and ink on verso: *Rd. Cosway R.A. / Feby. 1807 / Princess Charlotte.* Engraved: in stipple by M.A. Bourlier in 1807 with title *H.R.H. The Princess Charlotte of Wales*
COLLECTIONS: Weigall Collection; Edward Joseph; Frank Woodroffe; J. Pierpont Morgan; his sale, Christie's, London, 24-27 June 1935, lot 265; Christie's, London, 11 May 1994, lot 89
LITERATURE: Williamson 1906-8, II, no.253, pl.CXI; Long 1929, p.101; Walker 1985, I, p.109
PRIVATE COLLECTION

Princess Charlotte of Wales (1796-1817) was the only daughter of the Prince of Wales and Princess Caroline. In 1816 she married Prince Leopold of Saxe-Coburg, afterwards Leopold I of Belgium, but died in childbirth the following year.

180 *Thomas, 7th Earl of Elgin* 1807

[colour plate 96]
Watercolour on ivory, height 6.3cm (2½in)
COLLECTIONS: by family descent
THE RIGHT HON. THE EARL OF ELGIN AND KINCARDINE, KT

Thomas, 7th Earl of Elgin, is shown wearing the uniform of the Lord Lieutenant of Fife, an appointment which he held for two months in 1807. On the arrival of the Elgin marbles in London, Cosway attempted – unsuccessfully – to have them displayed in public (Paris, Institut Néerlandais, Fondation Custodia, MS letter from Richard Cosway (1805)). This miniature has traditionally been attributed to Nathaniel Hone.

181 *Arthur Wellesley, later 1st Duke of Wellington* 1808

[colour plate 94]
Watercolour on ivory, height 7.1cm (2¾in). Signed and dated in pen and ink on verso: *Rdus. Cosway / R.A. et F.S.A. / Pimarius Pictor / Serenissimi / Walliae / Principi[s] / Pinxit / 1808*
COLLECTIONS: given by Mrs Samuel S. Joseph
REFERENCES: Reynolds 1988, pp.130-1, fig.82
VICTORIA AND ALBERT MUSEUM, LONDON (Inv. P6-1941)

Arthur Wellesley (1769-1852), 1st Duke of Wellington, Field-Marshal and Prime Minister, was portrayed in the scarlet and gold-braided coat of the 33rd Regiment. His sitting to Cosway took place just prior to his departure for Spain and the Peninsular War campaign.

182 *Self-portrait in old age c.*1805-10

[colour plate 95]
Watercolour on ivory, height 6cm (2⅜in)
COLLECTIONS: Louis C.G. Clarke, LL.D., by whom bequeathed in 1960
REFERENCES: Bayne-Powell 1985, p.46
EXHIBITED: Cambridge 1981-2, p.32
FITZWILLIAM MUSEUM, CAMBRIDGE (Inv. PD.203-1961)

HENRY BONE (1755-1834)
AFTER RICHARD COSWAY

183 *Richard, 2nd Earl of Lucan* 1808

Enamel on porcelain, height 7.6cm (3in)
THE RT HON. THE EARL OF WEMYSS AND MARCH, KT

Henry Bone was principally an enamellist, who specialised in copies of portraits by other artists as well as copying works by the Old Masters. Bone recorded his copy of Cosway's untraced miniature in a drawing in one of his sketchbooks (London, National Portrait Gallery, Bone Album III).

ATTRIBUTED TO THOMAS RICHMOND (1771-1837)

184 *Sir William Richard Cosway c.*1800-10

Watercolour on ivory, 8.6cm (3⅜in)
COLLECTIONS: by family descent
PRIVATE COLLECTION

Sir William Richard Cosway, a cousin of Richard Cosway, was also a naval officer, who served with Admiral Collingwood at the Battle of Trafalgar. He was the recipient of Maria Cosway's autobiographical letter, written in 1830 [255].

ANDREW ROBERTSON (1777-1845)

185 *Self-portrait* 1811

Watercolour on ivory set in octagonal brooch, height 3.2cm (1¼in)
COLLECTIONS: by family descent; Christie's, London, 12 July 1988, lot 142
REFERENCES: Smailes 1990, p.246
SCOTTISH NATIONAL PORTRAIT GALLERY (Inv. PG 2741)

Andrew Robertson, who was born in Aberdeen but made his career in London, was the leading miniaturist in the first decades of the nine-teenth century. His technique of imitating the effects of oil painting replaced the flattering and evanescent brilliance of Cosway's minia-tures.

186 *Letter to Jacob, 2nd Earl of Radnor* 1807

Pen and ink on paper, 23.5 × 19.7cm (9¼ × 7¾in) closed
REFERENCES: Lloyd 1991, pp.403 and 405, n.14
PRIVATE COLLECTION

In one of the rare letters to have survived from the artist's own hand, the artist apologises to one of his most important patrons for not visiting him in Wiltshire, his excuse being that he had been offered – and had accepted – the chance to spend some days with the reclusive William Beckford, studying the fabulous art collections at Fonthill Abbey [166].

(DIONYSIUS ANDREAS FREHER)

187 *Microcosmos, or the Little World Man in his Primeval and Fallen state, to his Adoption to be the Son of God. Mens in Coelis, quies in Terris c.*1700

Manuscript with engravings, leather binding with spine tooled: THE / LITTLE WORLD / MAN & C., 546 +8 fols, open at titlepage, and at *The Third Table* of insert, 24.4 × 18.5cm (9⅝ × 7¼in)
COLLECTIONS: Richard Cosway; John Philips; John Ferguson; acquired with the major part of his library in 1921
GLASGOW UNIVERSITY LIBRARY (Inv. MS Ferguson 125)

Adam Maclean, who has catalogued this manuscript, has noted that this is a commen-tary on the Three Tables, illustrated in the William Law edition of Jacob Boehme's works. These three engravings, which have sections that open up to reveal other underlying images, are contained at the beginning of the manu-script. This mystical text was of particular significance to Cosway in that – according to his introductory inscriptions – he believed it to have been composed by Rubens, noting that it had been 'Faithfully translated from the Original Latin work by Petrus Paulus Rubenius'. In support of this claim, Cosway pasted in a self-portrait engraving opposite an engraved portrait of Rubens. This manuscript also includes, on page 427 a drawing of two interlocking triangles that form the six-pointed Star of David, is the one Cosway points to in his *Mystical self-portrait* [160].

188 *Sketchbook c.*1770-1810, showing *Self-portrait painting at an easel c.*1805

Volume of 119 drawings open at fol.200r; 23 × 18.5cm (9⅛ × 7¼in)
BRITISH MUSEUM, LONDON (Inv. 1941-2-8-191/307)

This is the only one of Cosway's sketchbooks that has survived intact, and it offers a vivid insight into Cosway's working practices as an artist and draughtsman. It includes early academic copies, caricatures, compositional sketches and figure studies. In this self-portrait painting at an easel, Cosway represents himself in a Michelangelesque pose, as if inspired by artistic *furor*.

UNKNOWN NOTARY

189 *A Catalogue, Schedule, or Inventory of the Household Goods … made between Richard Cosway, of Stratford Place … and Maria his Wife … 15 April 1820*

Manuscript of 229 fols, open at fol.158r (list of 'Mr. Cosway's own Drawings'), 31.5 × 22.3cm (12⅜ × 8¾in). Inscribed on fol.1r: *A Catalogue, Schedule, or Inventory / of the Household Goods and Furniture, Books, – / Maps, Pictures, Prints, Statues, Busts, Models, Linen, / China, Plate and Plated Articles, Cases, Drawers, / Presses, Cabinets, and Outstanding Debts, comprised / (with the respective Contents of the said Cases, / – Drawers, Presses, and Cabinets.) in a certain Indenture / of Assignment, bearing date the 15th day of April, / 1820, and made between Richard Cosway, of / Stratford Place, in the County of Middlesex[,] Esq. R.A. / and Maria his Wife, of the one part; and Sir / John Carr, of New Norfolk Street, in the parish / of St. George Hanover Square, in the same / County. Knight, and Francis Douce, of Charlotte / Square, Portland Road, in the same County, / Esquire, of the other part: Upon certain Trusts / in the said Indenture expressed, for the benefit / of the said Richard Cosway and Maria his / wife, and the Survivor of them.*
COLLECTIONS: Maria Cosway; Collegio delle Dame Inglesi, Lodi
REFERENCES: Lloyd 1991, pp.403 and 405, n.16; to be published in part by *The Walpole Society*
FONDAZIONE COSWAY, LODI

V RICHARD COSWAY: COLLECTOR, CONNOISSEUR AND VIRTUOSO

SIR PETER PAUL RUBENS (1577–1640)

190 *King James VI and I uniting the kingdoms of Scotland and England c.1629*

[colour plate 78]
Oil on panel, 63.5 × 48.3cm (25 × 19in)
COLLECTIONS: F.A.E. Bruynincx, Antwerp; Richard Cosway; probably in his sale of *Pictures*, Stanley's, London, 19 May 1821, lot 71 ('Study for one of the Paintings at Whitehall'), and his sale of *Pictures and Vertù*, Stanley's, London, 9 March 1822, lot 67, sold for £26 5s (priced sale catalogue in Frick Art Reference Library, New York); Colonel T.M. Davies
EXHIBITED: London 1977a, p.135, no.180
BIRMINGHAM MUSEUMS AND CITY ART GALLERY
This is a finished sketch and model for a part of the huge canvas on the Whitehall ceiling.

SIR PETER PAUL RUBENS (1577–1640)

191 *The Rape of Ganymede c.1636–7*

[colour plate 79]
Oil on panel, 33.4 × 24.5cm (13⅛ × 9⅝in)
COLLECTIONS: Count Charles de Proli, Antwerp, 1785; François Pauwels, Brussels, 1803; Richard Cosway; his sale of *Pictures*, Stanley's, London, 17 May 1821, lot 65; offered for sale at Sotheby's, London, 6 July 1994, lot 43

REFERENCES: Cosway's Catalogue of Pictures 1791 [**219**], p.50, no.56 (on the staircase, Schomberg House); Jaffé 1989, p.357, no.1271
MR DARIO ZENDRALLI COLLECTION, LUGANO
This is the preliminary oil sketch for the larger canvas of the same subject (Museo del Prado, Madrid). This was one of more than sixty large canvases produced by Rubens between 1636 and 1637 for the decoration of the Torre de la Parada, Philip IV's newly built hunting lodge, which was close to Madrid.

ATTRIBUTED TO WILLIAM DOBSON (1610/11–46)

192 *An unknown gentleman, formerly identified as Nathaniel Lee c.1642–6*

Oil on canvas, 56.5 × 46.3cm (22¼ × 18¼in). Engraved: in mezzotint by John Watts in 1778, titled, *Dobson pinxt. / J. Watts fecit /* NATH^L. LEE *the* MAD POET. */ From an Original Picture in the Collection of Rich^d. Cosway Esqr. R.A. / Author of Eleven Tragedies, which were received with applause, two of them were written after he had been confin'd in Bedlam / four Years, he Attempted Acting, but did not succeed, he was found dead on the Street Anno 1690 after a Night of Riot and Extravagance. / Through all the inmost Chambers of the Sky / May there not be a glimpse or Starry Spark, / But Gods meet Gods & jostle in the Dark / Lee's Aedipus. / Pub^d. as the Act directs Sept. 3^d. 1778. by John Watts Printseller opposite the Mews Charing Cross London.*
COLLECTIONS: Richard Cosway; his sale of *Pictures*, Stanley's, London, 18 May 1821, lot 80, and his sale of *Pictures and Vertù*, Stanley's, London, 9 March 1822, lot 58, sold for £5 15s (priced copy of sale catalogue in Frick Art Reference Library, New York)
REFERENCES: Cosway's Catalogue of Pictures 1791 [**219**], p.1, no.5 (in the eating room, ground floor, Schomberg House); Lodi, Fondazione Cosway, MS Inventory 1820, fol.203r (drawing room, first floor, Stratford Place, 'Portrait of Lee the poet')
GARRICK CLUB, LONDON
This was attributed to Dobson by Cosway and described by him in his 1791 Catalogue of Pictures as 'A most capital and singularly expressive portrait of Nat. Lee the poet, equal to Vandyke, and much in his style, particularly the marking of the hand'. While the attribution of the painting to Dobson can still be sustained, the identity of the sitter cannot be Nathaniel Lee (c.1653–92), on acount of his being born after Dobson had already died.

REMBRANDT VAN RIJN (1606–69)

193 *A Franciscan friar c.1655*

[colour plate 80]
Oil on canvas, 89 × 66.5cm (35 × 26¼in).
Signed: *Rembrandt. f. 165[?]*
COLLECTIONS: Richard Cosway; his sale of *Pictures*, Stanley's, London, 18 May 1821, lot 93 ('A Capucin Friar'), sold for £63; presented to the National Gallery by the Duke of Northumberland in 1838
REFERENCES: Lodi, Fondazione Cosway, MS Inventory 1820, fol.206r (back drawing room, first floor, Stratford Place, 'A Head of a Capuchin by Rembrant'); Maclaren 1993, I, pp.334–5, no.166, II, pl.283

NATIONAL GALLERY, LONDON
(Inv. 166)
While there are other versions of this subject by Rembrandt, it is likely that the London painting was the one in Cosway's collection.

GEORGE STUBBS (1724–1806)

194† *Portrait of a Spanish dog belonging to Mr Cosway 1774–5*

[colour plate 2]
Oil on panel, 54 × 69.9cm (21¼ × 27½in).
Signed: *Geo: Stubbs / 1775.* Engraved: see **195**
COLLECTIONS: Richard Cosway, his sale of *Pictures and Vertù*, Stanley's, London, 9 March 1822, lot 13 ('STUBBS A Dog chacing a Butterfly'), sold for £1 13s (priced catalogue at Frick Art Reference Library, New York); William Darby; Jocelyn Fielding
REFERENCES: Lodi, Fondazione Cosway, MS inventory 1820, fol.182r (back parlour, ground floor, Stratford Place, 'A White dog – by Stubbs'); Parker 1971, pp.115 and 198
EXHIBITED: Royal Academy, London, 1775, no.303 ('Portrait of a Spanish Dog belonging to Mr Cosway'); London 1984a, no.99
PRIVATE COLLECTION
Judy Egerton (London 1984a) has plausibly suggested that Stubbs may have painted this most charming of his canine portraits as a gesture of thanks to his friend Cosway for instructing him in the technique of enamel painting. This breed of dog, which was a cross between a Chihuahua and a King Charles Spaniel, was known as the Papillon because its ears and face were considered to look like a butterfly, which Stubbs incorporated within the composition.

E. FISHER (1722–c.1785) AFTER GEORGE STUBBS (1724–1806)

195* *Mr Cosway's dog 1782*

[colour plate 3]
Mezzotint engraving, proof before letters, 25.1 × 35.8cm (9⅞ × 14¼in)
REFERENCES: Lennox-Boyd, Dixon and Clayton, 1989
FONDAZIONE COSWAY, LODI
This mezzotint was published on 12 July 1782. It reproduces the oil portrait by Stubbs [**194**] in reverse.

BACCIO BANDINELLI (1493–1560)

196 *Design for a bed 1518–19*

Pen and brown ink over stylus indentations, 28.6 × 20.9cm (11¼ × 8¼in)
COLLECTIONS: Nicholas Lanier; Richard Cosway (Lugt 1921, no. 628), *Drawings and Prints* sale, Stanley's, London, 19 February 1822, lot 1026, 'A Design for a Bed, adorned by Cupids, &c.', sold in group of drawings by 'Raphael and Analogists'; Sir Thomas Lawrence (part of his Raphael series)
REFERENCES: Parker 1956, pp.47–8, no.80
EXHIBITED: Cambridge 1988, p.43, no.20, ill. p.104
ASHMOLEAN MUSEUM, OXFORD
(Inv. P.II.80)
Both Cosway and Lawrence, who later owned this drawing, considered it to be by Raphael. Cosway preserved it in his book of 44 drawings

by 'Raphael & school' (Lodi, Fondazione Cosway, MS Inventory 1820, fol.163r). He owned another book of 52 drawings by Bandinelli. 66 drawings by Bandinelli, which included what was claimed to be a pen and ink portrait of Michelangelo, were sold in his *Drawings and Prints* sale (Stanley's, London, 15 February 1822, lots 342–56). Bandinelli made this drawing as a study for a bed which he incorporated in a relief sculpture of the Birth of the Virgin at the Basilica della Santa Casa at Loreto.

ATTRIBUTED TO GIROLAMO ROMANINO (c.1485-1562)

197 *Four studies of groups of musicians and soldiers c.1530-40*

Pen and brown ink on an eighteenth-century mount, 3.6 × 4.6cm (1³/₈ × 1³/₄in), 4.0 × 5.3cm (1¹/₂ × 2¹/₈in), 3.4 × 5.1cm (1³/₈ × 2in), 3.4 × 5.1cm (1³/₈ × 2in), 3.4 × 4.3cm (1³/₈ × 1⁵/₈in); 14.5 × 29.7cm (5³/₄ × 11⁵/₈in) card mount. Inscribed by Richardson or Cosway: *Titiano*
COLLECTIONS: Jonathan Richardson the younger; Richard Cosway (Lugt 1921, no.629); Maria Cosway; Collegio delle Dame Inglesi, Lodi

FONDAZIONE COSWAY, LODI

This previously unpublished drawing was probably among the 29 drawings attributed to Titian in the 1822 sale of Cosway's *Drawings and Prints* (lots 530-3). It is the only Old Master drawing formerly owned by Richard Cosway, which is still at Lodi, and was therefore one of the few that Maria Cosway took to Italy in 1822, after the sale of her husband's collection. The attribution to Romanino has been supported by David Ekserdjian and Gianni Carlo Sciolla. These four compositional studies are executed in the vigorous pen and ink technique used by Romanino in his drawings of this decade (Nova 1995).

ATTRIBUTED TO BARTOLOMEO BAGNACAVALLO (1484-1542)

198 *Diana and Actaeon c.1530-40*

Pen, brown ink and wash with white heightening on blue paper, 20.2 × 28.3cm (8 × 11¹/₈in)
COLLECTIONS: Jonathan Richardson the younger; Richard Cosway (Lugt 1921, no.629)
REFERENCES: Andrews 1968, I, p.10; II, p.15, fig.96

NATIONAL GALLERY OF SCOTLAND
(Inv. RSA 197)

Aidan Weston-Lewis has commented that, in view of so little being known about Bagnacavallo's draughtsmanship, the traditional attribution to this Ferrarese artist should be questioned.

GIULIO ROMANO (c.1492-1546)

199 *A woman standing on a dragon c.1530-40*

Pen and brown ink and wash, heightened with white, squared for enlargement in black chalk, 31.2 × 24.6cm (12¹/₄ × 9⁵/₈in). Inscribed on verso: *Di Giulio Romano mano propria*
COLLECTIONS: Sir Peter Lely; Richard Cosway; his sale of *Drawings and Prints*, Stanley's, London, 15 February 1822, lot 365 ('A highly finished Drawing of Psyche with the Dragons')

REFERENCES: Pouncey and Gere 1962, I, p.63, no.82; II, pl.75

BRITISH MUSEUM, LONDON
(Inv. 1946-7-13-30)

This was in Cosway's 1822 posthumous sale of *Drawings and Prints* as part of a group of seventeen works by Giulio Romano (lots 363-72).

GIULIO CAMPI (1502-72)

200 *Salome carrying the head of St John the Baptist c.1540-50*

Black chalk, heightened with white, 25.6 × 40.9cm (10¹/₈ × 16¹/₈in). Inscribed: *Primasitio after Raphael*
COLLECTIONS: Richard Cosway (Lugt 1921, no.628); Francis Douce
REFERENCES: Parker 1956, pp.121-2, no.252; Macandrew 1980, p.263
EXHIBITED: London 1994, pp.93-4, no.116
ILLUSTRATED: Metz 1789, pl.21, and 1798, pl.50 (as by Giulio Romano)

ASHMOLEAN MUSEUM, OXFORD
(Inv. P.II.252)

GIOVANNI BATTISTA NALDINI (1537-91)

201 *Study of a reclining nude man (with an additional study for the legs of the same figure) c.1570-80*

[colour plate 81]
Red chalk (corners cut diagonally), 21.6 × 32.9cm (8¹/₂ × 13in)
COLLECTIONS: Richard Cosway (Lugt 1921, no.628); Sir James Knowles in 1908; given by G.T. Clough in 1913
REFERENCES: Cox Rearick 1964, I, p.361, cat.A12

FITZWILLIAM MUSEUM, CAMBRIDGE
(Inv. 2914)

This very fine drawing has been previously attributed to Casolani, Parmigianino and Pontormo, although a consensus among drawings' experts has now formed around Naldini. Although this sheet cannot be connected with a finished work by Naldini, it seems characteristic of an early example of his draughtsmanship, when he was influenced by Michelangelo.

PIETRO FACCINI (c.1562-1602)

202 *The mystic marriage of St Catherine c.1580-90*

[colour plate 83]
Pen and brown ink with brown wash, 26.8 × 19.6cm (10¹/₂ × 7⁷/₈in)
COLLECTIONS: Richard Cosway (Lugt 1921, no.629)
EXHIBITED: Cambridge 1985, no.23

FITZWILLIAM MUSEUM, CAMBRIDGE
(Inv. 2611)

LODOVICO CARRACCI (1555-1619)

203 *A seated angel playing the harp c.1605*

Black chalk, 28.7 × 22cm (11¹/₄ × 8⁵/₈in)
COLLECTIONS: Richard Cosway (Lugt 1921, no.628); Sir Thomas Lawrence
REFERENCES: Popham 1957, p.183, no.A62 (attributed to an artist in style near to Roncalli)

BRITISH MUSEUM, LONDON
(Inv. 1895-9-15-729)

Aidan Weston-Lewis has commented that this drawing is by Guido Cagnacci (1601-63), and suggests that it should be associated with the canvases of the *Glory of San Valeriano* and the *Glory of San Mercuriale* now in the Pinacoteca in Forlì.

HANS HOLBEIN THE YOUNGER (1497/8-1543)

204 *Study of a woman with four children c.1530-40*

Pen and black ink, with grey and black wash over traces of under-drawing in black chalk, 13.4 × 16.9cm (5¹/₄ × 6⁵/₈in)
COLLECTIONS: Richard Cosway (his sale of *Drawings and Prints*, Stanley's, London, 16 February 1822, probably among lot 437, 'Three washed Drawings, by Holbein')
REFERENCES: Rowlands 1993, I, pp.146-7, II, pl.209
EXHIBITED: London 1988, pp.231-2, no.198
ILLUSTRATED: Metz 1798, pl.60 (lettering to etching describes the drawing as by Holbein and belonging to Richard Cosway)

BRITISH MUSEUM, LONDON
(Inv. 1852-5-19-1)

Cosway owned another drawing by Holbein of 'Trumpeters on a Balcony' (British Museum), which was similarly etched for a luxury edition of reproductions after Old Master drawings (Metz 1798).

SIR PETER PAUL RUBENS (1577-1640) AFTER MICHELANGELO BUONARROTI (1475-1564)

205 *Studies after the 'Madonna de' Medici' c.1600-10*

[colour plate 85]
Black chalk, 20 × 27.8cm (7⁷/₈ × 10⁷/₈in)
COLLECTIONS: Richard Cosway, his sale of *Drawings and Prints*, Stanley's, London, 18 February 1822, possibly lot 674 ('A Madonna suckling the Child, in black chalk')
REFERENCES: Andrews 1985, I, p.71, II, p.118, fig.470
EXHIBITED: New York 1988, pp.77-8, no.18

NATIONAL GALLERY OF SCOTLAND
(Inv. D712)

The original sculpture by Michelangelo is in the New Sacristy of the church of San Lorenzo in Florence.

SIR PETER PAUL RUBENS (1577-1640)

206 *Pieter van Hecke*; (verso) *Two Studies for St Cecilia c.1620-30*

Black chalk, 41.3 × 34.5cm (16¹/₄ × 13⁵/₈in)
COLLECTIONS: Jonathan Richardson the elder; Thomas Hudson; Richard Cosway (Lugt 1921, no.629), possibly in his sale of *Drawings and Prints*, Stanley's, London, 18 February 1822, lot 853 ('Portrait of a Gentleman, in black chalks')
REFERENCES: Vlieghe 1987, p.118, no.107a
EXHIBITED: London 1977, pp.76-7, no.81

BRITISH MUSEUM, LONDON
(Inv. 1885-5-9-48)

This sheet is a preparatory study for the oil portrait that was formerly in the collection of Edmond de Rothschild in Paris. The drawing has also been attributed to Van Dyck.

SIR PETER PAUL RUBENS (1577-1640)

207 *Frans Rubens c.*1630-40

Red and black chalk, 20 × 14.9cm (7⅞ × 5⅞in). Inscribed on recto: *P.P. Rubens*; and on verso: *43. Peter Paul Rubens. A small head one of the children of Rubens, with cap and feather: red black chalk. Size 8" × 6". From the Collections of Mariette, Sandby. Cosway and Sir Thomas Lawrence. Signed* [deleted]*; black and red chalk* (catalogue entry for exhibition in 1835-6). Engraved: in stipple by L. Schiavonetti, titled ALBERT RUBENS and belonging to R. Cosway
COLLECTIONS: Paul Sylvester; Richard Cosway (Lugt 629), his sale of *Drawings and Prints*, Stanley's, London, 18 February 1822, lot 673, 'The Portrait of Young Albert, in red and black chalk', sold for 15 shillings (see annotated copy of sale catalogue in Department of Prints and Drawings, British Museum); Sir Thomas Lawrence; Lord Francis Egerton, 1st Earl of Ellesmere
REFERENCES: Vlieghe 1987, no.99c, fig.102
EXHIBITED: London 1835-6 (first exhibition), no.43
PRIVATE COLLECTION

Frans Rubens was the younger son of the artist by his second wife Hélène Fourment, with Albert being the elder brother. Another portrait drawing by Rubens of his son Frans is in the Museum Boymans-van Beuningen, Rotterdam. The drawing was clearly one of Cosway's prized possessions as it was the only one he had engraved separately.

JEAN-ANTOINE WATTEAU (1684-1721)

208 *A gentleman standing in a park*
*c.*1710-20

[colour plate 82]
Red chalk, 11 × 7.1cm (4⅜ × 2¾in). Etched: by Watteau and Thomassin for *Figures de Modes*
COLLECTIONS: probably Richard Cosway; Maria Cosway; Collegio delle Dame Inglesi, Lodi; Charles Fairfax Murray
EXHIBITED: Cambridge 1981-2, pp.1-2
FITZWILLIAM MUSEUM, CAMBRIDGE
(Inv. PD.III.1961)

According to a note on the mount of this drawing written by a later owner, Dr Louis C.G. Clarke, who bequeathed this and its pair [**209**] to the Fitzwilliam Museum, they were both acquired by Fairfax Murray at Lodi around the turn of the century.

JEAN-ANTOINE WATTEAU (1684-1721)

209 *A lady standing in a park c.*1710-20

[colour plate 84]
Red chalk, 10.9 × 7.1cm (4¼ × 2¾in). Etched: by Watteau and Thomassin for *Figure de Modes*
COLLECTIONS: probably Richard Cosway; Maria Cosway; Collegio delle Dame Inglesi, Lodi; Charles Fairfax Murray
REFERENCES: Washington, Paris and Berlin 1984-5, p.233
EXHIBITED: Cambridge 1981-2, pp.1-2
FITZWILLIAM MUSEUM, CAMBRIDGE
(Inv. PD.110.1961)

UNKNOWN ARTIST

210 *The Triform Diana,* late Hellenistic or Roman period

Hollow-cast bronze on late eighteenth-century marble base with gilt-metal decoration, height 39cm (15⅜in); bronze height 13.5cm (5⅜in)
COLLECTIONS: Richard Cosway; his sale of *Miscellaneous Articles of Taste and Virtù*, Stanley's, London, 23 May 1821, lot 68 ('The triform Diana, on a marble pedestal*)*, sold for £2 10s to Sir John Soane
SIR JOHN SOANE'S MUSEUM, LONDON
(Inv. A50)

UNKNOWN ARTIST

211 *The bull breaking the egg*
classical period

[colour plate 76]
Bronze on seventeenth-century Italian marble base bearing the arms of the Trapani family, height 18.3cm (7¼in); diam. of base 16.5cm (6½in)
COLLECTIONS: Richard Cosway; his sale of *Miscellaneous Articles of Taste and Virtù*, Stanley's, London, 23 May 1821, lot 67 ('The Bull breaking the egg, on a marble stand'), sold for £2 12s 6d to Sir John Soane
SIR JOHN SOANE'S MUSEUM, LONDON
(Inv. s136)

DANIELE (RICCIARELLI) DA VOLTERRA (*c.*1509-66)

212 *Michelangelo Buonarroti c.*1560-4

Bronze bust, height 28cm (11in)
COLLECTIONS: possibly Richard Cosway; Sir Thomas Lawrence; his sale of *Modern Drawings*, Christie's, London 19 June 1830, lot 392 ('A fine original Bust of Michelangiolo Buonaroti, in bronze – size of life'), bought by Woodburn for £40; presented in 1845 by William Woodburn
REFERENCES: Lodi, Fondazione Cosway, MS Inventory 1820, fol.204r (drawing room, first floor, Stratford Place; '4 large Busts – 1 Michael Angiolo 3 Roman Emperors'); Penny 1992, I, pp.159-61, no.109
ASHMOLEAN MUSEUM, OXFORD
(Inv. NBP 109)

GIOVANNI BATTISTA GUELFI (*fl.*1714-34)

213 *Figure for the monument to James Craggs in Westminster Abbey c.*1727

[colour plate 77]
Terracotta with wooden face, height 38.9cm (15⅜in)
COLLECTIONS: Richard Cosway; his sale of *Miscellaneous Articles of Taste and Virtù*, Stanley's, London, 23 May 1821, lot 47 ('A figure resting on an urn, in T.C.'); sold for 1 guinea to Sir John Soane
REFERENCES: Gunnis 1953, p.183; Whinney 1988, pp.160-1 and p.449; Thornton and Dorey 1992, p.27, fig.18 (col.)
SIR JOHN SOANE'S MUSEUM, LONDON
(Inv. MP 190)

James Craggs the younger (1686-1721) was a Secretary of State.

UNKNOWN ENGLISH GOLDSMITH

214 *The Cosway salt* 1584-5

[colour plate 74]
Silver gilt, height 21cm (8¼in)
COLLECTIONS: possibly Richard Cosway; Sir Jesse Hind, his sale, Sotheby's, London, 15 May 1947, lot 61; purchased from How of Edinburgh
REFERENCES: Wilson 1990, pp.78-80
ILLUSTRATED: Wilson 1989, pl.6
BRITISH MUSEUM, LONDON
(Inv. 3479)

While there is no concrete evidence that this ornate, important piece of Elizabethan silver gilt belonged to Cosway, it has been associated with his name for many years, and would have been an object that fitted very well with the artist's refined taste for highly decorative luxury objects.

CABINET-MAKER, PROBABLY WORKING IN THE EAST INDIES

215 *The Rubens colour box*
mid-seventeenth century

[colour plate 75]
Inlaid corimandel with brass fittings, height 22cm, width 60cm, depth 42cm (8⅝ × 23⅝ × 16½in) closed. Inscribed: on brass plaque affixed to underside of lid:
This Box came from Antwerp,
& belonged to P.P. Rubens.
It was purchased by Rd. Cosway Esqr. R.A.
Principal Painter to H.R.H. the Prince of Wales.
He used it for Many Years as his Colour Box.
Maria Cosway, his Widow,
Presents it to Sir Thomas Lawrence.
Principal Painter to his Majesty George 4th.
President of the Royal Academy &c
(1822)
COLLECTIONS: [Peter Paul Rubens?]; acquired by Richard Cosway in Antwerp in 1786; Maria Cosway; given by her to Sir Thomas Lawrence in 1822; his sale of *Modern Drawings*, Christie's, London, 19 June 1830, lot 448 ('RUBENS'S COLOUR-BOX, with a mahogany Stand; upon a brass plate inside is an Inscription, dated 1822, purporting that after having been used many years by Richard Cosway, it was presented by his Widow to Sir Thomas Lawrence'); bought by Scrope for 25 guineas
REFERENCES: Lodi, Fondazione Cosway, MS Inventory 1820, fol.207r (back drawing room, first floor, Stratford Place, 'A Curious Colour Box which – belonged to Rubens'); Lloyd 1991, pp.403-5
PRIVATE COLLECTION

MATTHIAS LOCK (*c.*1710-65)

216 *Cosway's sitter's chair c.*1755-60

[colour plate 20]
Gilt wood armchair with crimson damask upholstery, the seat and arm pads close-nailed, height 111cm, width 66cm, depth 69.8cm (43½ × 26 × 27½in)
COLLECTIONS: Messrs Asprey, London; acquired by the Victoria and Albert Museum in 1973
REFERENCES: Hardy 1973; Hayward 1973
EXHIBITED: London 1984b, pp.169-70, no.L25, entry by John Hardy
VICTORIA AND ALBERT MUSEUM, LONDON
(Inv. W1-1973)

J.B. VIGNOLA (1507-73)

217 *Règles des Cinq Ordres d'Architecture*, Utrecht 1736

Printed book (open at titlepage); spine tooled with gold lettering monogram RC and VIGNOLE, 12.7 × 7.8cm (5 × 3in) closed. Inscribed in pen in Cosway's hand on fol.1r: *Dec.r. 1 1811 / from Rd Cosway / to his esteem'd / Friend. J. Soane Esq.r.* frontispiece lettering to portrait of Vignola: *Regles / des / Cinq Ordres d'Architecture / de Jacques Barozzio de Vignole / A LEIDE / chez PIERRE VAN DER AA. 1712.* Titlepage lettering: *Regles des Cinq Ordres d'Architecture de J.B. de Vignole, avec les augmentations de Michel Ange Buonaroti: nouvelle édition revuë, corrigé e augmentée. / A UTRECHT / Chez Etienne Neaulme / MDCCXXXVI*
COLLECTIONS: given by Richard Cosway to Soane in 1811
SIR JOHN SOANE'S MUSEUM, LONDON (Inv. AL 35G)

SISTO BADALOCCHIO (1581-1647) AND GIOVANNI LANFRANCO (1581-1647) AFTER RAPHAEL (1483-1520)

218 *Historia del Testamento Vecchio* 1698

Volume of 54 etchings, 17.5 × 24cm (6⅞ × 9½in) open at etching no.19 ('Lot's Escape'). Signed in pencil opposite opening: *W Blake 1779*
REFERENCES: Essick 1994, pp.107 and 115–16
COLLECTIONS: William Blake (cover inscribed: *W Blake / 1773*)
PRIVATE COLLECTION
This volume of etchings by Badalocchio and Lanfranco, which was dedicated to Annibale Carracci, reproduced the famous series of Raphael's frescoes for the Vatican loggia. Copies of this important visual resource for artists, especially for those who did not visit Italy – belonged to Richard Cosway (Lodi, Fondazione Cosway, MS Inventory 1820, fol.3r), and also – as here – to William Blake. The paths of these two religious artists crossed on many occasions; Blake engraved Cosway's composition of *Venus dissuades Adonis from Hunting* in 1787 (Daniell 1890, p.51, no.211), while Cosway was a keen supporter of Blake. Michael Phillips has indicated that the six glue spots visible on this opening are revealing of Blake's technique for transferring images for etching. While Blake on economic grounds must have been limited to a modest library, Cosway had a substantial collection of books of prints. These were a constant source for his own mannered but deeply felt religious compositions, that were so inbued with the spirit, style and composition of Raphael and of the Renaissance and Baroque Old Masters.

(RICHARD COSWAY)

219 *A Catalogue of the Entire Collection of Pictures of Richard Cosway, Esq. R.A. …*, London 1791

Private contract catalogue, open at frontispiece of DOCET AMOR [**145**] and at titlepage, 28.3 × 22.2 × 2.5cm (11¼ × 8¾in)
COLLECTIONS: Maria Cosway; Collegio delle Dame Inglesi, Lodi
REFERENCES: Lloyd 1991, pp. 400 and 405, n.9
FONDAZIONE COSWAY, LODI

(GEORGE STANLEY)

220 *A Catalogue of the very curious, extensive, and valuable Library of Richard Cosway, Esq. R.A. …*, Stanley's, London, 8-12 June 1821

Volume of auction catalogues, open at Cosway sale titlepage, 22.2 × 14.5cm (8⅞ × 5¾in)
COLLECTIONS: Richard Ford (various inscriptions); gift of F.H. Cripps in 1928
REFERENCES: Lloyd 1991, p.405, n.13
LONDON LIBRARY

(GEORGE STANLEY)

221 *The Cosway Collection. A Catalogue of … Drawings and Prints … the genuine property of the late Richard Cosway, Esq. R.A. …*, Stanley's, London 14-22 February 1822

Volume of auction catalogues, open at titlepage 21.5 × 13.5cm (8½ × 5⅜in)
REFERENCES: Lloyd 1991, pp.404-5, n.22
BODLEIAN LIBRARY, UNIVERSITY OF OXFORD (Inv. Douce CC 293/5)

(GEORGE STANLEY)

222 *A Catalogue … of Pictures by Ancient Masters … the property of the late Richard Cosway, Esq. R.A. … also a number of valuable articles of vertù…*, Stanley's, London, 8-9 March 1822

Volume of auction catalogue, open at Cosway sale titlepage, 26.4 × 18.5cm (10⅜ × 7¼in)
REFERENCES: Lloyd 1991, p. 405, n.11
BODLEIAN LIBRARY, UNIVERSITY OF OXFORD (Inv. Douce FF 65[8])

VI MARIA COSWAY: ARTIST, MUSICIAN AND EDUCATIONALIST

JOHN TRUMBULL (1756-1843)

223 *Thomas Jefferson* 1788

Oil on panel, 11.4 × 8.3cm (4½ × 3¼in). Inscribed on verso: *Thomas Jefferson / owned by John C. Cruger*
COLLECTIONS: Mrs Angelica Schuyler Church; the Cruger family; bequeathed by Cornelia Cruger in 1922
REFERENCES: Kimball 1944, p.503, fig.2; Cometti 1952, pp.152-4
METROPOLITAN MUSEUM OF ART, NEW YORK Bequest of Cornelia Cruger, 1922 (Inv. 24.19.1)
This small oil on panel of Thomas Jefferson (1743-1826) was painted by John Trumbull, as a replica from the *Declaration of Independence* (Yale University Art Gallery, New Haven), expressly for an admirer, Mrs Angelica Schuyler Church. Another replica was painted for Maria Cosway in the same year (at the Collegio in Lodi until 1976, when presented by the Italian government as a Bicentennial gift to the people of the United States). Trumbull, who privately couriered many of the love letters between Jefferson and Maria in Paris and London, was clearly sensitive to the remarkable attachments between the two. Not only does this miniature recall the 'pre-eminent icon of Jefferson's imposing position in the birth of the Amercian nation', but it also commemorates the most extraordinary friendship in the lives of both Jefferson and Maria Cosway.

MARIA COSWAY

224 *The death of Miss Gardiner* 1789

[colour plate 32]
Oil on canvas, 101.2 × 127cm (39¾ × 50in). Signed and dated: *Maria Cosway P. / 1789*
REFERENCES: unknown critic, *The World*, 13 April 1789, p.3
EXHIBITED: Royal Academy, London, 1789, no.101 ('A dying child, summoned by the spirit of its deceased parents: an historical fact')
MUSÉE DE LA RÉVOLUTION FRANÇAISE, VIZILLE (Inv. 1994-30)
Horace Walpole noted that this represented the 'Portraits of Miss Gardnor and Lady Townshend' (Williamson 1905, p.133). A critic in *The World* who commented on this painting and one of Medusa, which was also exhibited at the Academy in 1789, noted 'From the all accomplished MARIA, there is MEDUSA, with what is as far from Terror, as Pity is, poor Miss GARDINER and Lady TOWNSHEND'.

MARIA COSWAY AND SIR THOMAS LAWRENCE (1769-1830)

225 *Caroline, Princess of Wales, and Princess Charlotte,* 1800, retouched in 1801

[colour plate 72]
Oil on panel 59 × 49.5cm (23¼ × 19½in). Inscribed on verso: *Caroline, Princess of Wales aged 32, and Princess Charlotte her daughter; designed and painted by Maria Cosway (wife of Mr Cosway), around 1800. The heads afterwards touched and altered by Lawrence in 1801. The Princesses sat to both the painters. Given by HRH The Princess of Wales, Feb. 1801 to Lady Glenbervie when she was about to embark for the Cape of Good Hope*
PRIVATE COLLECTION
The two faces were retouched by Lawrence, who was a close friend of Princess Caroline. The spectacular original frame is surmounted with the Prince of Wales's crest of the three ostrich feathers.

MARIA COSWAY

226 *Giulia Beccaria* 1802-3

[colour plate 101]
Oil on panel, 21.3 × 16cm (8⅜ × 6¼in). Inscriptions: (on verso in ink from hand of Teresa Manzoni Stampa) *Bozzo cavato / dal verso, per / Mad. Cosway / della figlia di Beccaria / madre di Manzoni / a Parigi / l'anno 11*
COLLECTIONS: Teresa Manzoni Stampa; acquired for Biblioteca Nazionale Braidense in 1923 by Pio Istituto per Figli della Providenza
REFERENCES: Griffini Rosnati 1993, p.50
EXHIBITIONS: Milan 1985-6, p.104, no.161 (entry

by F. Mazzocca) and p.109 (col.); Milan 1991, p.291, no.1.238, and p.144 (col.)
ILLUSTRATED: Parenti 1942, p.13 (col.); Citati and Milani 1973, p.15; Ginzburg 1983, pl.6 (col.); Bezzola 1985, on jacket (col.); Batori and Goffredo De Robertis 1994, p.53 (col.)

BIBLIOTECA NAZIONALE BRAIDENSE, MILAN

Giulia Beccaria (1762–1841) was the mother of the great Italian writer Alessandro Manzoni (1785–1873) [**227**]. An important *salon* hostess in her own right, Maria Cosway had met Beccaria in Paris during the Peace of Amiens in 1802, from when this lively portrait dates. Maria also drew a portrait of an older Giulia Beccaria in *c*.1823 (Scherillo 1923, ill. opp. p.16). Maria educated Vittoria, who was the seventh child of Alessandro Manzoni by his first wife, Enrichetta Blondel. The family as a whole is portayed in Ernesta Bisi's pencil drawing of *c*.1823. Maria Cosway also drew a delicate portrait in red chalk of Manzoni's and Blondel's sixth child, Clara (1821–3), which is now at the Villa Manzoni, Brusuglio (Milan 1985-6, no.15).

UNKNOWN ARTIST (FORMERLY ATTRIBUTED TO MARIA COSWAY)

227 *Alessandro Manzoni c.*1805

[colour plate 100]
Oil on canvas, 59.5 × 48cm (23³⁄₈ × 18⁷⁄₈in)
COLLECTIONS: bequeathed by Giulia Costantini Manzoni in 1912
REFERENCES: Griffini Rosnati 1993, p.50
EXHIBITED: Milan 1985-6, no.39 (entry by F. Mazzocca); Milan 1991, p.292, no.1.241
ILLUSTRATED: Parenti 1942, p.215; Citati and Milani 1973, p.38; Ginzburg 1983, pl.10; Soldarini 1985, on cover (col.); Tettamanzi 1985, p.20, fig.12

BIBLIOTECA NAZIONALE BRAIDENSE, MILAN
(On loan to the Centro Nazionale di Studi Manzoniani, Milan)

Alessandro Manzoni (1785–1873) was the greatest Italian novelist of the nineteenth century. His mother was *Giulia Beccaria* [**226**]. His daughter, Vittoria, was educated by Maria Cosway at the Collegio in Lodi from 1831 to 1835 [**228**].

GABRIELE ROTTINI (1797–1858)

228 *Baroness Maria Hadfield Cosway listening to Vittoria Manzoni c.*1835

[colour plate 103]
Oil on canvas, 142.9 × 203.5cm (55⁷⁄₈ × 80¹⁄₄in)
COLLECTIONS: probably commissioned by Maria Cosway; Collegio delle Dame Inglesi, Lodi
EXHIBITED: Milan 1985-6, p.110-11, no.162 (entry by F. Mazzocca); Biblioteca Nazionale Braidense, Milan 1993 (no catalogue, but see Griffini Rosnati 1993)
ILLUSTRATED: Williamson 1897, opp. p.60, and 1905, opp. p.80; Cazzulani and Stroppa 1989, fig.15; Lloyd 1992, fig.8; Batori and Goffredo De Robertis 1994, p.49 (col.)

FONDAZIONE COSWAY, LODI

Little is known about the commissioning of this extraordinary painting, which encapsulates Maria Cosway's life and work at her Collegio in Lodi. However, it is most likely that it was painted at her request to commemorate the departure from the Collegio in 1835 of Vittoria

Manzoni (1822–92), one of the younger daughters and seventh child of the great writer Alessandro Manzoni and his first wife Enrichetta Blondel (Ginzburg 1983). Vittoria had been a pupil at the Collegio since 1831, and was constantly written to by her mother and grandmother, Giulia Beccaria (Scherillo 1923, pp.8-31). The painting would also have been intended to mark Maria Cosway's creation as a Baroness by the Austrian Emperor, as she is shown seated on an ermine cloak. Vittoria Manzoni is shown standing and addressing Maria Cosway. They are surrounded by a group of sisters and pupils. None of them has yet been securely identified, although the prominent sister in the centre of the composition may well be Annette Prudon. The Brescian painter Gabriele Rottini was a leading neo-classical painter in Lombardy, who specialised in the portrayal of large-scale figure groups.

V. GREEN (1739–1813)
AFTER MARIA COSWAY

229 *Georgiana, Duchess of Devonshire, as Cynthia* 1783

Mezzotint engraving, 61 × 39.4cm (24 × 15¹⁄₈in). Lettered: *Painted by Maria Cosway. / Engraved by V. green. Mezzotinto Engraver to his Majesty, and to the Elector Palatine / Published Janry. 1st 1783, by V. Green, No 29, Newman Street, Oxford Street, London.*
REFERENCES: Whitman 1902, p.102, no.122

LENT BY HER MAJESTY THE QUEEN

The original full-length painting (220 × 160cm) was exhibited at the Royal Academy in 1782 (no.17), and is now at Chatsworth [fig. 28]. Horace Walpole described the picture as the 'Duchess of Devonshire as Diana in the air. Extravagant'. Maria Cosway represented her as Cynthia, taken from Spenser's *Faerie Queene* (book III, canto 43). The Duchess of Devonshire, who was one of the leading figures in society and Whig politics at this period, was also – from 1776 to 1789 – one of Richard Cosway's main patrons. A copy of this painting was recorded hanging on the staircase at Stratford Place (Lodi, Fondazione Cosway, MS Inventory 1820, fols. 195r and 213r). Maria Cosway utilised a similar pose in her oil portrait of Henry Lubomirski as Eros, which was formerly at the castle of Láncut in Poland (Honour 1994).

V. GREEN (1739–1813)
AFTER MARIA COSWAY

230 *Like Patience on a monument, smiling at Grief* 1783

Mezzotint engraving, 50.2 × 40.7cm (19³⁄₄ × 16in)
REFERENCES: Whitman 1902, p.152, no.129 (published: 4 June 1783)

LENT BY HER MAJESTY THE QUEEN

The original painting was exhibited with this title at the Royal Academy in 1781 (no.139), while the subject was developed from a line in Shakespeare's *A Midsummer Night's Dream*. The crouching figure of Grief is shown entwined in a serpent. The pose of this figure is derived from one of Michelangelo's frescoed ancestors in the lunettes of the Sistine Chapel.

V. GREEN (1739–1813)
AFTER MARIA COSWAY

231 *Mrs Cosway* 1787

[colour plate 69]
Mezzotint engraving, 41.8 × 32.8cm (16¹⁄₂ × 12⁷⁄₈in). Lettered: *Painted by Maria Cosway. / Engraved by V. Green, Mezzotinto Engraver to his Majesty, and to the Elector Palatine. Mrs. Cosway. Published by V. and R. Green, Newman Street, Oxford Street, London, Sepr 1st 1787.*
REFERENCES: Whitman 1902, p.107, no.130
EXHIBITED: Royal Academy, London, 1787, no.251 ('Portrait of a lady')
ILLUSTRATED: Lloyd 1992, opp. p.22, fig.1.

LENT BY HER MAJESTY THE QUEEN

Reviewers who noted this – since untraced – painting when it was exhibited at the Academy in 1787, identified the sitter as Mrs Cosway (Williamson 1905, p.133).

F. BARTOLOZZI (1727–1815)
AFTER MARIA COSWAY

232 *The Hours* 1788

Stipple engraving, 35.6 × 45.2cm (14 × 17³⁄₄in)
BRITISH MUSEUM, LONDON
(Inv. 1859-7-9-730)
The subject is taken from Gray's *Ode to Spring*.

F. BARTOLOZZI (1727–1815)
AFTER MARIA COSWAY

233 *Lodona* 1792

Stipple engraving, 34.8 × 44.6cm (13³⁄₄ × 17¹⁄₂in)
BRITISH MUSEUM, LONDON
(Inv. 1859-7-9-729)

MARIA COSWAY AFTER PHILIPPE-AUGUSTE HENNEQUIN (1762–1833)

234 *Sir Sidney Smith* 1797

[colour plate 99]
Etching, 24.3 × 19.1cm (9¹⁄₂ × 7¹⁄₂in)
REFERENCES: Bordes 1979, p.210, fig.18; Benoit 1994, p.230, no.G.5
SCOTTISH NATIONAL PORTRAIT GALLERY
(Inv. E.P.V.110.11)
Sir William Sidney Smith (1764–1840) was one of the major naval commanders in the Napoleonic Wars. The lettering on an impression of this etching at the Fondazione Cosway, Lodi, reads: *Sir Sidney Smith / imprisoned in the Abbaye Paris on the 23rd April 1796 / Transferred from thence to the Temple on the 3d July 1796.*

V. GREEN (1739–1813)
AFTER MARIA COSWAY

235 *The Descent from the Cross* 1800

Coloured mezzotint engraving, 67 × 55cm (26³⁄₈ × 21⁵⁄₈in)
BRITISH MUSEUM, LONDON
(Inv. 1877-6-9-1732)
The original altarpiece was painted in 1799, and still hangs in its original setting (private collection). A smaller variant survives at the Fondazione Cosway in Lodi. It is likely that this was the picture which was exhibited at the Royal Academy in 1801 (no.232) as *The*

exultation of the Virgin Mary, or the salvation of mankind, purchased by the death of Jesus Christ. This was one of the last paintings executed and exhibited by Maria Cosway. It not only reflects her intense Catholicism at this period, but can be seen as prefiguring her later dedication to girls' education within a religious context at Lyons and Lodi.

T. GIRTIN (1775-1802) AND J.S. AGAR (C.1776-C.1858) AFTER MARIA COSWAY

236 *Advertisement for Ackermann and Suardy's patent water-proof manufactories for wearing apparel* c.1800

Stipple engraving, 46.5 × 29.3cm (18¼ × 11½in). Lettering (partial): PATENT WATER-PROOF MANUFACTORIES, / FOR WEARING APPAREL / RAIN DEFIED. HEALTH PRESERVED. / M.*rs Cosway del.t* / *Girtin Scrip.t et sculp.t 56 Drury Lane / Agar sculp.t* / UPPER BELGRAVE PLACE, FORMERLY NEW SPRING GARDENS, / CHELSEA, / And at / CUPERS BRIDGE, LAMBETH. /*Patronised / BY / Their Majesties, Their Royal Highnesses The Prince of Wales / The Dukes of York, Clarence, Kent, Cumberland, Glocester; &c. &c. &c. /* ACKERMANN, SUARDY AND C.O / *Patentees for making all sorts of* CLOTH, *&c.* WATER-PROOF, UNMMPAIRABLE *by* HEAT, / *humbly beg leave to offer their services to the Public, upon the following moderate terms[...]*
BRITISH MUSEUM, LONDON
(Inv. 1898-3-24-6)
The preparatory drawing for this pluvial allegory is preserved in the Denham album (New Haven, Yale University, Beinecke Library, fol.123r). Maria Cosway also designed the image for another advertisement for Ackermann's Repository of Arts, 101 Strand, London, published on 4 May 1802 (Essen 1992, p.329, no.173).

P.W. TOMKINS (1760-1840)
AFTER MARIA COSWAY

237 *The birth of the Thames* 1803

Stipple engraving, 56.5 × 44cm (22¼ × 17¼in).
REFERENCES: Landon 1801, I, p.177 and 1802, II, p.209
ILLUSTRATED: Landon 1802, II, opp. p.209, reproduced as a line engraving: *Madme. Cosway pinxt. / Madme. Lefevre Sculp / La naissance de la Tamise*
BRITISH MUSEUM, LONDON
(Inv. 1873-8-9-232)
The original painting was exhibited at the Royal Academy in 1800 (no.23). It survives in a private collection in Ireland (Guinness and Ryan 1971, pp.182-91).

CAROLINE WATSON (1761-1814)
AFTER MARIA COSWAY

238-249 *The Winter Day* 1803

Series of twelve acquatints, each 22.7 × 28.4cm (8⅞ × 11⅛in). Lettering on each acquatint: *M. Cosway del.t / the Poetry by M.rs Robinson / Miss C. Watson sculp.t / Published 1.st March. 1803. at R. Ackermann's Repository of Arts: 101. Strand.*
COLLECTIONS: Sir Robert Witt
EXHIBITED: York 1993, p.45, no. 37 (plate 5 only)

ILLUSTRATED: Walker 1986
COURTAULD INSTITUTE GALLERIES, LONDON (WITT COLLECTION)
This book of twelve prints illustrates the poem *The Winter Day* by Mary 'Perdita' Robinson (1758-1800), which contrast 'the evils of poverty and the ostentatious enjoyment of opulence'. Mrs Robinson was a well-known actress and one of the Prince of Wales's earliest mistresses, later becoming a minor poet. She was portrayed by many artists including Richard Cosway (Ingamells 1978 and Perry 1995). In the odd numbered plates, Maria Cosway may have recorded the interiors and parties at Schomberg House and Stratford Place (the original drawings are in the New York Public Library).

MARIA COSWAY

250 *Songs and duets composed by Mrs Cosway*, London 1785

Printed book of music, open at titlepage, 28.3 × 37.2cm (11⅛ × 14⅝in)
ILLUSTRATED: Bullock 1945, p.50
NEW YORK PUBLIC LIBRARY
The titlepage image of Cupid reclining at the foot of a large tree in a forest, playing on pipes to a crouching lion, may have been designed by Richard or Maria Cosway, or by both the artists (Daniell 1890, p.48, no.197). There exists a stipple engraving by P. Bettelini after Richard Cosway of 1785 (14.5 × 17.2cm, 5¾ × 6¾in), while there is also a reversed etching by Maria Cosway (18.3 × 20.3cm, 7¼ × 8in).

A. CARDON (1742-1813)
AFTER MARIA COSWAY

251 *A Progress of Female Virtue* and *A Progress of Female Dissipation*, London 1800

Two volumes of acquatints bound together, open at plate 4 of first volume, 27.5 × 34cm (10⅞ × 13⅜in) closed
REFERENCES: Bermingham 1993
BRITISH MUSEUM, LONDON
(Inv. 1871-8-12-2303/2320)

MARIA COSWAY AND JULIUS GRIFFITHS

252 *Galerie du Louvre*, Paris 1802

[colour plate 98]
Volume of 50 pages and 7 plates of coloured etchings, open at first plate; 70.4 × 60.4cm (27¾ × 23¾in) closed
REFERENCES: Van Nimmen 1986, pp.127-39, 163, 165, 169, and 171; McClellan 1994, pp.141-3
BRITISH MUSEUM, LONDON
(Inv. 1983-U-2494 [1-7])

MARIA COSWAY

253 *Musée Central, Ou Galerie du Louvre à Paris* 1801-3

[colour plate 102]
Bound illuminated manuscript of 54 fols.; handwritten text on fols. 2r-5v and 50v-53v; 84 coloured etchings pasted onto fols. 6r-48r, open at fols. 2v-3r; 24.5 × 19 × 2.5cm (9⅝ × 7½ × 1in) closed. Inscribed on red morocco cover in gold lettering: MARIA COSWAY.

Inscribed on fol.2r: *Musée Central, / Ou / Galerie du Louvre, / à Paris. / On propose, par souscription, la Collection gravée à / l'eau = forte, par Madame Maria Cosway, de tous les chefs = d'oeuvres des Ecoles Italiene, − Flamande et Française, qui décorent aujourd'hui la Galerie du Louvre, accompagnée d'une notice historique sur chaque tableau, & sur son auteur, par / J. Griffiths ...*(rest of fols. 2r-3r describes detailed contents of work) *À Paris, ce 12. Fluviose An 10. / 1.er Fevrier 1802.*
Inscribed on fol.53v: *Gallery of the Louvre / at Paris. / It is proposed to publish by subscription highly finished / Etchings, / by Maria Cosway, of all the Pictures which / comprise the superb collection in the gallery of the Louvre, / comprising the most celebrated Chefs-d'Oeuvres of the / Italian, Flemish, and French schools; with an historical / account of each picture, and interesting anecdotes of the Artists, by / J. Griffiths, Esq:re* (rest of fols 53v-52v describes detailed contents of work) *1:st February 1802.*
COLLECTIONS: Maria Cosway; Collegio delle Dame Inglesi, Lodi
FONDAZIONE COSWAY, LODI

THOMAS JEFFERSON (1743-1860)

254 *Letter to Maria Cosway ('My Head and My Heart')* 12 October 1786

(photographic facsimile)
Pen and ink on paper, 23.5 × 17.8cm (9¼ × 7in), first page
LIBRARY OF CONGRESS, WASHINGTON DC

MARIA COSWAY

255 *Letter to Sir William Richard Cosway* 24 May 1830

Pen and ink on paper, fol.1r, 25.5 × 18.5cm (10 × 7¼in)
VICTORIA AND ALBERT MUSEUM, LONDON
(Inv. MS L.961-1953)

UNKNOWN AUSTRIAN ILLUMINATOR

256 *Document creating Maria Cosway as a Baroness* 1834

Illuminated vellum manuscript with wax seal in tin box, open at fols 4v-5r, 40.8 × 32.7 × 6.8cm (16¼ × 12⅞ × 2⅝in), closed box
COLLECTIONS: Maria Cosway; Collegio delle Dame Inglesi, Lodi
REFERENCES: Lloyd 1992, pp.126 and 138, n.130
FONDAZIONE COSWAY, LODI

CHRISTIAN-GOTTLIEB STIEHL (1708-92)

257* *Snuff-box* 1774

Gold inset with *pietre dure* from Saxony, with separate silver-gilt plaque, and booklet listing differing types of *pietre dure*; height 4.1cm (1⅝in). Signed: *CG Stiehl − Hoff Steinschneider.* Inscribed on box with numbers referring to differing *pietre dure* used and described in booklet. Inscribed on plaque: *l'ettore di Sassonia / Federigo Augusto III / inviò questa scatola per segno d'amicizia / al Generale Pasquale De' Paoli / in Corsica nell' anno 1774 / e fu da questo regalato / a Maria Cosway / in Londra 1789*

COLLECTIONS: probably commissioned by the Elector of Saxony for presentation to General Pasquale Paoli in 1774; given by him to Maria Cosway in 1789; presented by her to the Galleria degli Uffizi on 10 June 1829 (Florence, Uffizi, MS, AGF filza LXIII, 1839)
EXHIBITED: Florence 1979, p.139, no.55
MUSEO DEGLI ARGENTI, PALAZZO PITTI, FLORENCE
(Inv. 890)
Christian-Gottlieb Stiehl was one of the two outstanding gold box makers in Saxony during the second half of the eighteenth century. A virtually identical box of the same date is in the Louvre (Snowman 1990, pl.669)

UNKNOWN ARTISTS

258 *Two statuettes of Mars and Minerva and two figurines of mummies*, Roman and Egyptian (Ushabti or XXVI dynasty)

Bronze and porcelain, height 10cm (3⅞in), in wood and glass case
COLLECTIONS: Dominique Vivant-Denon; he presented the two Ushabti figurines to Maria Cosway; she presented all four objects to Sir John Soane
REFERENCES: Soane 1927, pp.465-7
SIR JOHN SOANE'S MUSEUM, LONDON
(Inv. S128, S148, S149 and S150)
In a letter at the Sir John Soane's Museum from Maria Cosway in Lodi to Soane, dated 19 February 1831, she wrote: 'When I was at Paris, my friend, Monsieur Denon, whom you must know by reputation, was just returned from Egypt, with B. He gave me two small Egyptian figures he found himself, they are in perfect preservation, and tho' small, the work is with much taste and beauty, and the hieroglyphics perfect and clear. I even left the Egyptian dust on them. These I put in a small box, with a Mercury and a Minerva found here at Lodi Vecchio, and consigned them to a person who is going to England, but am afraid they will be long on the road, but hope will be safe.'
Through these objects Maria Cosway linked her friends, the French archaeologist, Vivant-Denon, and the architect-*virtuoso* Soane, and at the same time demonstrated her own remarkable gift for friendship.

C. PICART AFTER RICHARD WESTMACOTT (1775-1856)

259 *Design for the tomb of Richard Cosway* 1821

Line engraving, 35.5 × 25.6cm (14 × 10in)
LENT BY HER MAJESTY THE QUEEN

FILIPPINI AFTER GABRIELE ROTTINI (1797-1858)

260 *Baronessa Maria Hadfield Cosway on her deathbed* 1838

Lithograph, 61.3 × 51.8cm (24¼ × 20⅜in).
Inscribed: BARONESSA MARIA HADFIELD COSWAY / *Mori in Lodi il 5 Gennajo 1838 / Rottini / Brescia Lit. Filippini*
COLLECTIONS: Collegio delle Dame Inglesi, Lodi
FONDAZIONE COSWAY, LODI

Maria Cosway died on 5 January 1838 at Lodi, whereupon Gabriele Rottini made a portrait drawing (untraced) of her on her deathbed. He had previously portrayed her in a group portrait, surrounded by pupils and sisters, while being read to by her best-known pupil Vittoria Manzoni [**228**], one of the younger daughters of the great writer, *Alessandro Manzoni* [**227**], and a grand-daughter of *Giulia Beccaria* [**226**].

ADDITIONAL EXHIBITS

UNKNOWN MEDALLIST

261† *Maria Cosway* 1797

Bronze medallion, diam. 11.6 cm (4½in)
Lettered MARIA COSWAY 1797
COLLECTIONS: Robert Reeve of Lowestoft; acquired by the British Museum in 1858
REFERENCES: Brown 1980, I, p.100, no.423
BRITISH MUSEUM, LONDON
(Inv.58-7-10-22)

262* *Mrs Ironmonger Troward and her children* 1801

Pencil and watercolour on original wash-lined mount, 33.3 × 51 cm (13⅛ × 20⅛in)
COLLECTIONS: by family descent
PRIVATE COLLECTION

According to his account book (Private Collection MS), Richard Ironmonger Troward, a prosperous solicitor and art collector, paid Cosway £94.10s on 19 December 1801 for this family picture of his wife and children. In what is his largest and most ambitious group portrait drawing, the artist has depicted Sarah Ironmonger Troward (1758–1838) with her youngest child, Albany (1799–1865), on her lap. The girl standing behind is Amelia (d.1854), the boy to the side is Thomas (1797–1856), while the girl on the stool is Sarah (1798–1884).

263 *The Death of Leonardo da Vinci in the arms of Francis I c.*1815

Monochrome and grey wash, 29.8 × 24.2 cm (11¾ × 9½in).
COLLECTIONS: Richard Cosway, London; Maria Cosway; Collegio delle Dame Inglesi, Lodi; Alfred A. de Pass, given in 1914 to the Royal Institution of Cornwall, County Museum and Art Gallery, Truro; Christie's, London, 22 February 1966, lot 5, bought by Allen; Bonham's, London, 14 June 1995, lot 80
REFERENCES: Rosenblum 1967, pp.34-6

A. J. STIRLING

BIBLIOGRAPHY

The bibliography includes works cited in the catalogue entries and as footnotes to the essay 'Richard and Maria Cosway: Regency Artists of Taste and Fashion'. Also included are works of importance for the study of the subject.

BOOKS AND ARTICLES

ABELARD 1781
Letters of Abelard and Heloise. With a particular account of their Lives, Amours, and Misfortunes: extracted chiefly from Monsieur Bayle, by John Hughes, Esq. To which are added four poems by Mr Pope and other hands., London 1781

ADAMS 1936
C.K. Adams, *A Catalogue of the Pictures in the Garrick Club*, London 1936

ADAMS 1983
William Howard Adams, *Jefferson's Monticello*, New York 1983

ALLAN 1974
D.G.C. Allan, *The Houses of the Royal Society of Arts: A History and A Guide*, rev. edn, London 1974 (1st edn, London 1966)

ALLAN 1979
D.G.C. Allan, *William Shipley, Founder of the Royal Society of Arts: A Biography with Documents*, 2nd edn, London 1979 (1st edn, London 1968)

ALPERS 1988
Svetlana Alpers, *Rembrandt's Enterprise: The Studio and the Market*, London 1988

ALTICK 1978
Richard D. Altick, *The Shows of London: A Panoramic History of Exhibitions 1600–1862*, Cambridge (Mass.) and London 1978

ANDREWS 1968
Keith Andrews, *National Gallery of Scotland: Catalogue of Italian Drawings*, 2 vols, Cambridge 1968

ANDREWS 1985
Keith Andrews, *Catalogue of Netherlandish Drawings in the National Gallery of Scotland*, 2 vols, Edinburgh 1985

ANGELO 1828
Reminiscences of Henry Angelo, with Memoirs of his late Father and Friends…, London 1828

AVERY 1987
Charles Avery, *Giambologna*, Oxford 1987

BAILY 1907
J.T. Herbert Baily, *Francesco Bartolozzi, R.A.: A Biographical Essay*, (extra number to the *Connoisseur*), London 1907

BARGHAZI 1925
P. B[arghazi]., 'Dalla corrispondenza di lettere con madama Baronessa Maria Hadfield Cosway', *Archivio Storico per la Città e i Comuni del Circondario e della Diocesi di Lodi*, XLIV, 1925, pp.107–20

BATORI and GOFFREDO DE ROBERTIS 1994
Armida Batori and Mariella Goffredo De Robertis, 'Ultime acquisizioni del Fondo Manzoniano della Biblioteca Nazionale Braidense', *Cà de Sass* (Trimestrale della CARIPLO, Casa di Risparmio delle Provincie Lombarde), no.128, December 1994, pp.49–53

BAYNE-POWELL 1985
Robert Bayne-Powell, *Catalogue of Portrait Miniatures in the Fitzwilliam Museum, Cambridge*, Cambridge 1985

BELL 1938
C.F. Bell, *Annals of Thomas Banks, Sculptor, Royal Academician…*, Cambridge 1938

de BELLAIGUE 1968
Geoffrey de Bellaigue (et al.), *Buckingham Palace and its Treasures*, New York 1968

BENOIT 1994
Jérémie Benoit, *Philippe-Auguste Hennequin 1762–1833*, Paris 1994

BENTLEY 1991
G.E. Bentley Jr, 'Mainaduc, Magic and Madness: George Cumberland and the Blake Connection', *Notes and Queries*, CXXXVI, September 1991, pp.294–6

BERMINGHAM 1992
Ann Bermingham, 'The Origin of Painting and the Ends of Art: Wright of Derby's "Corinthian Maid"', *Painting and the Politics of Culture: New Essays on British Art 1700–1850*, John Barrell (ed), pp.135–66

BERMINGHAM 1993
Ann Bermingham, 'The Aesthetics of Ignorance: The Accomplished Woman in the Culture of Connoisseurship', *Oxford Art Journal*, XVI, no.2, 1993, pp.3–20

BEZZOLA 1985
Guido Bezzola, *Giulia Manzoni Beccaria (1762–1841)*, Milan 1985

BIGNAMINI 1988
Ilaria Bignamini, 'George Vertue, Art Historian and Art Institutions in London, 1689–1768', *The Walpole Society*, LIV, 1988, pp.1–148

BLACK 1992
The British Abroad: The Grand Tour in the Eighteenth Century, Stroud and New York 1992

BLAIKLEY 1955
Ernest Blaikley, 'Richard Cosway, Miniaturist, Artist, Fop and Man of Fashion', *Apollo*, LXII, August 1955, pp.53–5

BLAKE 1987
William Blake: An Island in the Moon, a facsimile of the manuscript, Michael Phillips (ed), Cambridge 1987

BLAYNEY BROWN 1982
David Blayney Brown, *Ashmolean Museum, Oxford, Catalogue of the Collection of Drawings: Volume IV, the Earlier Drawings, British Artists and Foreigners Working in Britain born before c.1775*, Oxford 1982

BLUNT 1936
Reginald Blunt, *Thomas Lord Lyttleton: the Portrait of a Rake…*, London 1936

BOASE 1963
T.S.R. Boase, 'Macklin and Bowyer', *Journal of the Warburg and Courtauld Institutes*, XXVI, 1963, pp.14–77

BORDES 1979
Philippe Bordes, 'Les arts après la Terreur: Topino-Lebrun, Hennequin et la peinture politique sous le Directoire', *La Revue du Louvre et des Musées de France*, 1979, III, pp.199–212

BORDES 1983
Philippe Bordes, *Le Serment du Jeu de Paume de Jacques-Louis David: le peintre, son milieu et son temps de 1789 à 1792: Musée national du Château de Versailles*, (Notes et Documents des Musées de France, 8), Paris 1983

BORDES 1992
Philippe Bordes, 'Jacques-Louis David's anglophilia on the eve of the French Revolution', *The Burlington Magazine*, CXXXIV, no.1073, August 1992, pp.482–90

BORDES 1994
Philippe Bordes, 'Acquisitions', *Revue du Louvre*, 5/6, December 1994, p.102

BORRONI SALVADORI 1985-6
Fabia Borroni Salvadori, 'Artisti e viaggiatori agli Uffizi nel Settecento', *Labyrinthos: Studi e ricerche sulle arti nei secoli XVIII e XIX*, [part 1] IV, nos 7–8, 1985, pp.3–72, [part 2] VI, no 10, 1986, pp.38–92

BOSWELL 1928-34
Private Papers of James Boswell from Malahide in the collection of Lt.-Colonel Ralph Heyward Isham, G. Scott and F.A. Pottle (eds), 18 vols, New York 1928–34

BOSWELL 1981
Boswell, The Applause of the Jury, 1782–1785: The Yale Edition of the Private Papers of James Boswell, New Haven 1981

BOSWELL 1986
Boswell, The English Experiment, 1785–1789: The Yale Edition of the Private Papers of James Boswell, New Haven 1986

BOUTET 1752
Claude Boutet, *The Art of Painting in Miniature…*, 6th edn, London 1752

BREJON de LAVERGNÉE and THIÉBAUT 1981
Arnauld Brejon de Lavergnée and Dominique Thiébaut, *Catalogue sommaire illustré des peintures du musée du Louvre: II, Italie, Espagne, Allemagne, Grande-Bretagne et divers*, Paris 1981

BRIEF ACCOUNT 1775
A Brief Account of the Roads of Italy…, 2nd edn, London 1775 (1st edn 1774)

BRITTON and PUGIN 1825
John Britton and Augustus Pugin, *Illustrations of Public Buildings*, 5 vols, London 1825

BRODIE 1974
Fawn Brodie, *Thomas Jefferson: An Intimate History*, London 1974

BROMLEY 1793
Henry Bromley, *A Catalogue of Engraved British Portraits…*, London 1793

BROWN 1980
Laurence Brown, *A Catalogue of British Historical Medals 1760–1960*, 3 vols, London 1980

BUCHANAN 1982
William Buchanan and the 19th Century Art Trade: 100 Letters to his Agents in London and Italy, Hugh Brigstocke (ed), London 1982

BULLOCK 1945
Helen Duprey Bullock, *My Head and My Heart: A Little History of Thomas Jefferson and Maria Cosway*, New York 1945

BURGESS 1973
Renate Burgess, *Portraits of Doctors & Scientists in the Wellcome Institute of the History of Medicine*, London 1973

BUSCO 1994
Marie Busco, *Sir Richard Westmacott: Sculptor*, Cambridge 1994

BUSH 1976
Alfred L. Bush, 'The Life Portraits of Thomas Jefferson', *Jefferson and the Arts: an Extended View*, William Howard Adams (ed), Washington 1976, pp.9–100

BUTTERFIELD and RICE 1948
L.H. Butterfield and Howard C. Rice Jr, 'Jefferson's earliest note to Maria Cosway with some new facts and conjectures on his broken wrist', *The William and Mary Quarterly*, 3rd ser., V, no.1, January 1948, pp.26–33

BYRD 1993
Max Byrd, *Jefferson: A Novel*, New York 1993

CARR 1993
Gerald L. Carr, 'David, Boydell and Socrates: A Mixture of anglophilia, self-promotion and the press', *Apollo*, CXXXVII, no.375, May 1993, pp.307–15

CARTER 1817
J. Carter (published letter), *The Gentleman's Magazine*, LXXVII, i, May 1817, p.423

CAZZULANI and STROPPA 1989
Elena Cazzulani and Angelo Stroppa, *Maria Hadfield Cosway: Biografia, Diari e Scritti della Fondatrice del Collegio delle Dame Inglesi in Lodi*, Orio Litta 1989 (review by Stephen Lloyd, *The Burlington Magazine*, CXXXII, no.1052, November 1990, p.799)

CHARVET 1905
E.L.G. Charvet, 'Enseignement public des arts du dessin a Lyon 1804', *Bulletin du Comité de Sociétés des Beaux-Arts des Départements* (Réunion des Sociétés des Beaux-Arts des Départements), XXXV, 1905, pp.79–112

CHERRY and HARRIS 1982
Deborah Cherry and Jennifer Harris, 'Eighteenth-century portraiture and the seventeenth-century past: Gainsborough and Van Dyck', *Art History*, V, no.3, September 1982, pp.287–309

CITATI and MILANI 1973
Pietro Citati and Este Milani, *Immagini di Alessandro Manzoni*, Milan 1973

CLARKE 1995
Roger Clarke, 'Small Wonder: The artist, the Regent, his wife, and her lovers', *The Independent Magazine*, no.349, 27 May 1995, pp.40–1

COLDING 1953
Torben Holck Colding, *Aspects of Miniature Painting: Its Origins and Development*, Copenhagen 1953

COLLEY 1992
Linda Colley, *Britons: Forging the Nation 1707–1837*, New Haven and London 1992

COMBE 1822
(William Combe), 'Exhibition of the Works of the late Mr. Cosway', *The Repository of Arts, Literature, Fashions, Manufactures, &c*, 2nd series, XIII, no.76, 1 April 1822, pp.230–1

COMETTI 1952
Elizabeth Cometti, 'Maria Cosway's Rediscovered Miniature of Jefferson', *William and Mary Quarterly*, 3rd ser., IX, 1952, pp.152–5

CONSTABLE 1953
W.G. Constable, *Richard Wilson*, London 1953

COOK 1985
Brian F. Cook, *The Townley Marbles*, London 1985

CORNFORTH and HUGHES-HARTMAN 1990
John Cornforth and George Hughes-Hartman, *Inveraray Castle*, Derby 1990

COSWAY 1800
Imitations in Chalk, Etched by Mrs Cosway from Original Drawings by Richard Cosway, London 1800

COSWAY 1825
Anon., 'I quadri appartenenti a Maria Cosway conservati nel Collegio della Beata Vergine delle Grazie in Lodi', *Gazzetta della Provincia di Lodi e Crema*, 29 January, 12 March, 25 June and 2 July 1825

COSWAY 1826
Raccolta di Disegni originali scelti del Portafogli del celebre Riccardo Cosway R.A. e primo pittore del serenissimo Principe di Wallia, posseduti dalla di lui vedova la Signora Maria Cosway, e intagliati da Paolo Lasinio Figlio, Florence 1826

COSWAY 1838
Anon., 'Cenni Biografici sopra la Baronessa Maria Hadfield Cosway Fondatrice d'una casa religiosa di Dame Inglesi a Lodi morta il 5 Gennaio 1838...', (pamphlet inserted in the) *Gazzetta Privilegiata di Milano*, 11 February 1838

COSWAY 1926
'Lettera sull'educazione pratica dei piccoli fanciulli dai quattro anni ai sei: risposta ad una lettera di M.G. sopra l'educazione data dalla Baronessa Maria Cosway Fondatrice del Collegio delle Dame Inglesi in Lodi', *Archivio Storico per la Città e i Comuni del Circondario e della Diocesi di Lodi*, XLV, 1926, pp.36–51

COX REARICK 1964
Janet Cox Rearick, *The Drawings of Pontormo*, Cambridge (Mass.) 1964

CUNNINGHAM 1829–33
Allan Cunningham, *The Lives of the Most Eminent British Painters, Sculptors, and Architects*, 6 vols, London 1829–33

DABNEY 1981
Virginius Dabney, *The Jefferson Scandals: A Rebuttal*, New York 1981

DANCE and DANIELL 1809–14
A Collection of Portraits sketched from the Life since the year 1793 (drawn by George Dance and engraved by William Daniell), 2 vols, London 1809–14

DANIELL 1890
Frederick B. Daniell, *A Catalogue Raisonné of the Engraved Works of Richard Cosway, R.A.*, London 1890

DAVIES 1968
Martin Davies, *National Gallery Catalogues: The Early Netherlandish School*, London 1968 (1st edn, 1945)

DENTLER 1964
Clara Louise Dentler, *Famous Foreigners in Florence*, Florence 1964

DETHLOFF 1992
Diana Dethloff, 'Patterns of drawing collecting in late seventeenth- and early eighteenth-century England', *Drawings: Masters and Methods, Raphael to Redon, Papers presented to the Ian Woodner Master Drawings Symposium at The Royal Academy of Arts, London* (1987), Diana Dethloff (ed), London 1992, pp.197–207

DUNSFORD 1790
Martin Dunsford, *Historical Memoirs of the Town and Parish of Tiverton*, Exeter 1790

von ERFFA and STALEY 1986
Helmut von Erffa and Allen Staley, *The Paintings of Benjamin West*, New Haven and London 1986

ESSICK 1994
Robert N. Essick, 'Blake in the Marketplace, 1993, Including a Report on the Sale of the Frank Rinder Collection', *Blake: An Illustrated Quarterly*, XXVII, no.4, Spring 1994, pp.104–29

FAIRHOLT 1858
F.W. Fairholt, 'Tombs of English Artists. No.8 – Richard Cosway, R.A.', *The Art-Journal*, IV, September 1858, p.268

FARINGTON 1978–84
Joseph Farington: The Diary of Joseph Farington, Kenneth Garlick, Angus Macintyre and Kathryn Cave (eds), 16 vols, New Haven and London 1978–84

FELTHAM 1802
John Feltham, *The Picture of London, for 1802; being a correct guide to all the Curiosities, Amusements, Exhibitions, Public Establishments, and remarkable Objects, in and near London...*, London 1802

FENAILLE 1903–12
Maurice Fenaille, *Etat Général des Tapisseries de la Manufacture des Gobelins depuis son origine jusqu'à nos jours: 1600–1900*, 4 vols, Paris 1903–12

FERRARI 1913
Emma Ferrari, 'I disegni di Riccardo Cosway nella Biblioteca di Lodi', *Rassegna d'Arte*, XIII, no.9, September 1913, pp.144–7

FERRARI 1913–14
Emma Ferrari, 'Di alcuni documenti riguardanti Riccardo Cosway nella Biblioteca di Lodi', *Archivio Storico per la città di Lodi*, XXXII, [part 1] 1913, pp.171–86; [parts 2–3], XXXIII, 1914, pp.25–48 and 75–93

FLETCHER 1901
E. Fletcher (ed), *Conversations of James Northcote R.A. with James Ward on Art and Artists*, London 1901

FOLADARE 1979
Joseph Foladare, *Boswell's Paoli*, Hamden (Connecticut) 1979

FORD 1983
John Ford, *Ackermann 1783–1983: The Business of Art*, London 1983

FOSCOLO 1970
Edizione Nazionale delle Opere di Ugo Foscolo, XX, *Epistolario*, VII, M. Scotti (ed), Florence 1970

FOSKETT 1964
Daphne Foskett, *John Smart, the Man and his Miniatures*, London 1964

FOSKETT 1972
Daphne Foskett, *A Dictionary of British Miniature Painters*, 2 vols, London 1972

FOSKETT 1987
Daphne Foskett, *Miniatures: Dictionary and Guide*, Woodbridge 1987 (incorporates *A Dictionary of British Miniature Painters*, 1st edn, London 1972, and *Collecting Miniatures*, 1st edn, London 1979)

FRASER'S MAGAZINE 1840
Anon., 'The Greater and Lesser Stars of Old Pall Mall', *Fraser's Magazine for Town and Country*, XXII, no.131, November 1840, pp.556–9

FROST 1876
Thomas Frost, *The Life of Thomas Lord Lyttelton*, London 1876

GAUNT 1963
William Gaunt, 'George Dance's Royal Academy', *The Connoisseur*, CLIII, no.617, July 1963, pp.182–7

GEORGE 1948
Eric George, *The Life and Death of Benjamin Robert Haydon*, Oxford 1948

GEORGE 1935 and 1938
M.D. George, *British Museum, Department of Prints and Drawings, Catalogue of Political and Personal Satires*, V (1771–1783) and VI (1784–1792), London 1935 and 1938

GEORGE 1967
M. Dorothy George, *Hogarth to Cruikshank: Social Change in Graphic Satire*, London 1967

GIBBON 1961
Gibbon's Journey from Geneva to Rome: His Journal from 20 April to 2 October 1764, Georges A. Bonnard (ed), London 1961

GINZBURG 1983
Natalia Ginzburg, *La Famiglia Manzoni*, Turin 1983

GIROUARD 1963
Mark Girouard, 'Powderham Castle, Devon: the seat of the Earl of Devon', *Country Life*, CXXXIV, nos 3461–63, 4–18 July 1963, pp.18–21, 80–3 and 140–3

GOLDNEY 1759
Edward Goldney, *Epistles to Deists and Jews...*, London 1759 (2nd edn, 1760)

GOULD 1965
Cecil Gould, *Trophy of Conquest: The Musée Napoléon and the Creation of the Louvre*, London 1965

GOULDING 1914–15
R.W. Goulding, 'The Welbeck Abbey Miniatures', *The Walpole Society*, IV, 1914–15

GRAVES 1905–6
Algernon Graves, *The Royal Academy of Art: a complete Dictionary of Contributors and their work from its foundation in 1769 to 1904*, 8 vols, London 1905–6

GRAVES 1907
Algernon Graves, *The Society of Artists of Great Britain, 1760–1791; The Free Society of Artists, 1761–1783; a complete dictionary of contributors and their work from the foundation of the societies to 1791*, London 1907

GRIFFINI ROSNATI 1993
Grazia Maria Griffini Rosnati, 'Lettere di Giulia Beccaria e di Enrichetta Blondel', *Manzoni a Brera*, Armida Batori (ed), Milan 1993, pp.45–57

GROSE 1786–9
Francis Grose, *A Treatise on Ancient Armour and Weapons...*, 5 vols, London 1786–9

GUIFFREY 1879
'Cartons de Jules Romains pour la Tenture de Scipion offerts au Roi Louis XVI par le peintre Anglais Richard Cosway (Août-Septembre 1786)', *Nouvelles Archives de l'Art Français* (Société de l'Histoire de l'Art Français), 2nd series, VII, 1879, pp.263–8 and 467–8

GUINNESS and RYAN 1971
Desmond Guinness and William Ryan, *Irish Houses and Castles*, London 1971

GUNNIS 1953
Robert Gunnis, *Dictionary of British Sculptors 1660–1851*, London 1953 (rev. edn, London 1968)

HAMILTON 1952
Chloe Hamilton, 'A portrait of General Kosciuszko by Benjamin West', *Allen Memorial Art Museum Bulletin*, IX, 1952, pp.81–91

HAMILTON 1969
Harlan W. Hamilton, *Doctor Syntax: A Silhouette of Combe*, Kent (Ohio) and London 1969

HARDING 1845
Lt.-Col. Harding, *The History of Tiverton*, 2 vols, Tiverton 1845

HARDY 1973
John Hardy, 'The Discovery of Cosway's Chair', *Country Life*, CLIII, no.3951, 15 March 1973, pp.705–6

HASKELL 1980
Francis Haskell, *Rediscoveries in Art: Some Aspects of Taste, Fashion and Collecting in England and France*, 2nd edn, Oxford 1980 (1st edn, 1976)

HASKELL and PENNY 1981
Francis Haskell and Nicholas Penny, *Taste and the Antique*, New Haven and London 1981

HASKELL 1987
'The Baron d'Hancarville: an adventurer and art historian in eighteenth-century Europe', *Past and Present in Art and Taste: selected essays*, New Haven and London 1987, pp.30–45 (first published in *Oxford, China and Italy: Writings in Honour of Sir Harold Acton*, Edward Chaney and Neil Ritchie (eds), Florence 1984)

HAYWARD 1973
Helena Hayward, 'A Unique Rococo Chair by Matthias Lock', *Apollo*, xcviii, no.140, October 1973, pp.268–71

HAZLITT 1822
William Hazlitt, 'Fonthill Abbey', *The London Magazine*, November 1822

HAZLITT 1826
William Hazlitt, 'On the Old Age of Artists', *The Plain Speaker: opinions on books, men and things*, 2 vols, London 1826, pp.207–27

HAZLITT 1930–4
The Complete Works of William Hazlitt..., P.P. Howe after A.R. Waller and Arnold Glover (eds), 21 vols, London and Toronto 1930–4

HELD 1960
Julius S. Held, 'The Early Appreciation of Drawings', *Acts of the Twentieth International Congress of History of Art*, iii, New York 1960, pp.72–95

HERMANN 1992
Luke Hermann, *Beschreibender Katalog der Handzeichnungen in der Graphischen Sammlung Albertina. Die Englische Schule. Zeichnungen und Aquarelle Britischer Kunstler*, Vienna 1992 (review by Patrick Noon in *Master Drawings*, xxxii, no.1, 1994, pp.70–1)

HIBBERT 1976
Christopher Hibbert, *George IV*, 2nd edn, Harmondsworth 1976 (1st edn, 2 vols, London 1972–3)

HIBBERT 1987
Christopher Hibbert, *The Grand Tour*, London 1987

HIGHFILL, BURNIM AND LANGHANS 1984
'Luigi Marchesi', *A Biographical Dictionary of Actors, Actresses, Musicians, Dancers, Managers and other Stage Personnel in London 1660–1800*, P.H. Highfill Jr, K.A. Burnim and E.A. Langhans (eds), Carbondale and Edwardsville 1984, x, pp.89–91

HINDE 1986
Thomas Hinde, *Capability Brown: The Story of a Master Gardener*, London 1986

HIRST 1981
Michael Hirst, *Sebastiano del Piombo*, Oxford 1981

HOFLAND 1819
Mrs Hofland, *A Descriptive Account of the Mansion and Gardens of White-Knights. A Seat of his Grace the Duke of Marlborough...illustrated by T.C. Hofland*, London 1819

HONOUR 1994
Hugh Honour, 'Canova's "Amorini" for John Campbell and John David La Touche', *La Scultura: studi in onore di Andrew S. Ciechanowiecki (Antologia di Belle Arti, nuova serie, nn.48–51)*, Alvar González-Palacios (ed), Turin 1994, pp.129–39

HUDSON and LUCKHURST 1954
D. Hudson and K.W. Luckhurst, *The Royal Society of Arts, 1754–1954*, London 1954

HUTCHISON 1960–2
Sidney C. Hutchison, 'The Royal Academy Schools, 1768–1830', *The Walpole Society*, xxxviii, 1960–2, pp.123–92

HUTCHISON 1986
Sidney C. Hutchison, *The History of The Royal Academy: 1768–1986*, 2nd edn, London 1986 (1st edn 1968)

INGAMELLS 1978
John Ingamells, *Mrs Robinson and her Portraits*, Wallace Collection Monographs, i, London 1978

JAFFÉ 1975
Irma B. Jaffé, *John Trumbull: Patriot-Artist of the American Revolution*, Boston 1975

JAFFÉ 1989
Michael Jaffé, *Catalogo Completo: Rubens*, Milan 1989

JEFFERSON 1829
Memoirs, Correspondence, and Private Papers of Thomas Jefferson, late President of the United States, now first published from the original Manuscripts, Thomas Jefferson Randoph (ed), 4 vols, London 1829

JEFFERSON 1950–82
The Papers of Thomas Jefferson, Julian P. Boyd (general ed), 22 vols, Princeton 1950–82

JUNINUS 1812
Juninus, 'Conversations on the Arts', *The Repository of Arts, Literature, Commerce...*, vii, no.40, April 1812, pp.195–7

KELLY 1995
Ian F. Kelly, *Jefferson in Paris*, Film Education Study Guide, London 1995

KIMBALL 1944
Fiske Kimball, 'The Life Portraits of Jefferson and their Replicas', *Proceedings of the American Philosophical Society*, lxxxviii, no.6, December 1944, pp.497–506

KIMBALL 1950
Marie Kimball, *Jefferson: The Scene of Europe 1784 to 1789*, New York 1950

LA MARLE 1989
Hubert La Marle, *Philippe Égalité: 'Grand Maitre' de la Révolution*, Paris 1989

LANDON 1802
Ch.-P. Landon, *Nouvelles des Arts*, ii, 1801–2

LENNOX-BOYD, DIXON and CLAYTON 1989
C. Lennox-Boyd, R. Dixon and T. Clayton, *George Stubbs: The Complete Engraved Works*, London and New York 1989

LESLIE and TAYLOR 1865
C.R. Leslie and T. Taylor, *Life and Times of Sir Joshua Reynolds*, 2 vols, London 1865

LIBRARY OF FINE ARTS 1832
Anon., 'Recollections of Richard Cosway, Esq. R.A.', *Library of Fine Arts*, iv, London 1832, pp.184–91

LIPPINCOTT 1983
Louise Lippincott, *Selling Art in Georgian London: the Rise of Arthur Pond*, New Haven and London 1983

LLOYD 1991
Stephen Lloyd, 'Richard Cosway, RA: The Artist as Collector, Connoisseur and *Virtuoso*', *Apollo*, cxxxiii, no.352, June 1991, pp.398–405

LLOYD 1992
Stephen Lloyd, 'The Accomplished Maria Cosway: Anglo-Italian Artist, Musician, Salon Hostess and Educationalist (1759–1838)', *Journal of Anglo-Italian Studies*, ii, 1992, pp.108–39

LLOYD 1993
Stephen Lloyd, 'Forming the Taste of a Prince: Richard Cosway and George IV's early Collecting', *Apollo*, cxxxviii, no.378, September 1993, pp.192–4 (issue republished as *Buckingham Palace: A Complete Guide*, Robin Simon (ed), London 1993, pp.124–6)

LONG 1929
Basil S. Long, *British Miniaturists*, London 1929

LOZZI and STROPPA 1985
Maurizio Lozzi and Angelo Stroppa, *Il Collegio Cosway ieri e oggi*, Lodi 1985

LUCKHURST 1954
Kenneth W. Luckhurst, *The Royal Society of Arts: 1754–1954*, London 1954

LUGT 1921 and 1956
Frits Lugt, *Les Marques de Collections de Dessins & d'Estampes...*, Amsterdam 1921; *Supplément*, The Hague 1956

LUGT 1938
Frits Lugt, *Répertoire des Catalogues de ventes publiques...*, i, 1600–1825, The Hague 1938

MACANDREW 1980
Hugh Macandrew, *Catalogue of the Collection of Italian Drawings in the Ashmolean Museum*, iii, Italian Schools, Oxford 1980

MACKLIN 1791–1816
Thomas Macklin, *The Old Testament, Embellished with Engravings after Pictures and Designs by the Most Eminent English Artists*, London 1791–1816

MACLAREN 1993
National Gallery Catalogues: The Dutch School 1600–1900, 2 vols, rev. edn by Christopher Brown, London 1993 (1st edn, 1960)

de MAINAUDUC 1798
The Lectures of J.B. de Mainauduc, M.D., Member of the Corporation of Surgeons in London, Part the First, London 1798

MANFREDI 1988
Antonio Manfredi, 'Una lettera inedita di Ugo Foscolo nell' Archivio Cosway', *Archivio Storico Lodigiano*, cvii, 1988, pp.5–12

MANNERS and WILLIAMSON 1920
Lady Victoria Manners and George C. Williamson, *John Zoffany, R.A.: His Life and Works 1735–1810*, London 1920

MAUQUOY-HENDRICKX 1956
M. Mauquoy-Hendrickx, *L'Iconographie d'Antoine van Dyck: catalogue raisonné*, 2 vols, Brussels 1956

McCLELLAN 1994
Andrew McClellan, *Inventing the Louvre: Art, Politics, and the Origins of the Modern Museum in Eighteenth-century Paris*, London 1994

METZ 1789
Conrad Martin Metz, *Imitations of Ancient and Modern Drawings...*, London 1789 (2nd edn, 1798)

MILLAR 1969
Oliver Millar, *The Georgian Pictures in the Collection of Her Majesty the Queen*, 2 vols, London 1969

MILLAR 1977
Oliver Millar, *The Queen's Pictures*, London 1977

MILLAR 1986
Oliver Millar, 'George IV when Prince of Wales: his debts to artists and craftsmen', Documents for the History of Collecting: 2, *The Burlington Magazine*, cxxviii, August 1986, pp.586–92

MOLONEY 1969
Brian Moloney, *Florence and England*, Florence 1969

MORRIS 1939
Gouverneur Morris, *A Diary of the French Revolution*, Beatrix Cary Davenport (ed), 2 vols, Boston 1939

MORTIMER 1763
Thomas Mortimer, *The Universal Director*, London 1763

MOUILLESEAUX 1974
Jean Pierre Mouilleseaux, '"Léandre et Héro" de Taillasson, à propos d'un thème iconographique et littéraire', *Revue du Louvre*, xxiv, 1974, pp.411–16

MULLER 1989
Jeffrey M. Muller, *Rubens: The Artist as Collector*, Princeton 1989

MUSAEUS 1647
Musaeus, on the Loves of Hero and Leander, with Annotations upon the Originall, translated by Sir Robert Stapylton, London 1647

NAGLER 1836
C.K. Nagler, *Neues allgemeines Künstler-Lexicon...*, 22 vols, Munich 1836

NICHOLSON 1931
C.A. Nicholson, 'Richard Cosway and the Royal Society of Arts', *The Connoisseur*, lxxxviii, no.364, November 1931, pp.326–8

van NIMMEN 1986
Jane van Nimmen, 'Responses to Raphael's Paintings at the Louvre 1798–1848', unpublished Ph.D. thesis, University of Maryland 1986

NOBLE 1908
Percy Noble, *Anne Seymour Damer*, London 1908

NOON 1981
John Murdoch, Jim Murrell, Patrick J. Noon and Roy Strong, *The English Miniature*, New Haven and London 1981, pp.163–209

NORTHCOTE 1898
Memorials of an Eighteenth Century Painter, James Northcote, S. Gwynn (ed), London 1898

NORTHCOTE 1901
Conversations of James Northcote R.A. with James Ward on Art and Artists, E. Fletcher (ed), London 1901

NOVA 1995
Alessandro Nova, 'The Drawings of Girolamo Romanino', *The Burlington Magazine*, CXXXVII, no.1104, March 1995, pp.159–68 (Part I); and CXXXVII, no.1106, May 1995, pp.300–6 (Part II)

O'DONOGHUE 1908–25
Freeman O'Donoghue, *Catalogue of Engraved British Portraits preserved in the Department of Prints and Drawings in the British Museum*, 6 vols, London 1908–25

OPPÉ 1950
A.P. Oppé, *English Drawings, Stuart and Georgian Periods in the Collection of His Majesty The King at Windsor Castle*, London 1950

PALEY 1986
Morton D. Paley, *The Apocalyptic Sublime*, New Haven and London 1986

PARENTI 1942
Marino Parenti, *Immagini della Vita e dei Tempi di Alessandro Manzoni*, Milan 1942

PARKER 1956
K.T. Parker, *Catalogue of the Collection of Drawings in the Ashmolean Museum*, II, *Italian Schools*, Oxford 1956

PASQUIN 1786
Anthony Pasquin (John Williams), *The Royal Academicians: a Farce. As it was performed to the Astonishment of Mankind by his Majesty's Servants, at the STONE HOUSE, in UTOPIA, in the summer of 1786*, London 1786

PASQUIN 1796
Anthony Pasquin, *Memoirs of the Royal Academicians being an attempt to improve the national taste*, I, London 1796

PEARS 1988
Iain Pears, *The Discovery of Painting: The Growth of Interest in the Arts in England 1680–1768*, New Haven and London 1988

van PELT 1971
Charles B. van Pelt, 'Thomas Jefferson and Maria Cosway', *American Heritage*, XXII, no.5, August 1971, pp.22–9 and 102–3

PENNY 1992
Nicholas Penny, *Catalogue of European Sculpture in the Ashmolean Museum: 1540 to the Present Day*, 3 vols, Oxford 1992

PERRY 1995
Gill Perry, '"The British Sappho": Borrowed Identities and the Representation of Women Artists in late Eighteenth-Century British Art', *The Oxford Art Journal*, XVIII, no.1, 1995, pp.44–57

PINDAR 1794–6
The Works of Peter Pindar Esq. [John Wolcot], 4 vols, London 1794–6

PIPER 1992
David Piper, *The English Face*, Malcolm Rogers (ed), London 1992 (1st edn, 1978)

PLACZEK 1982
'George Hadfield', *Macmillan Encyclopedia of Architects*, A.K. Placzek (ed), New York and London 1982, II, p.293 (entry by Rieff)

POINTON 1984
Marcia Pointon, 'Portrait-Painting as a Business Enterprise in London in the 1780's', *Art History*, VII, no.2, June 1984, pp.187–205

POINTON 1993
Marcia Pointon, *Hanging the Head: Portraiture and Social Formation in Eighteenth Century England*, New Haven and London 1993

POPHAM 1957
A.E. Popham, *Correggio's Drawings*, London 1957

PORRO 1833
Cleto Porro, *Guida della Regia Città di Lodi compilata per uso de' forestieri*, Lodi 1833

PORTER 1982
Roy Porter, 'The Sexual Politics of James Graham', *The British Journal for Eighteenth Century Studies*, V, 1982, pp.201–6

PORTER 1985
Roy Porter, '"Under the Influence": Mesmerism in England', *History Today*, XXXV, September 1985, pp.22–9

PORTER 1994
Roy Porter, *London: A Social History*, London 1994

POSTLE 1995
Martin Postle, *Sir Joshua Reynolds: The Subject Pictures*, London 1995

POTKAY and BURR 1995
Adam Potkay and Sandra Burr, *Black Atlantic Writers of the Eighteenth Century: Living the New Exodus in England and the Americas*, New York 1995

POUNCEY and GERE 1962
Philip Pouncey and J.A. Gere, *Italian Drawings in the Department of Prints and Drawings in the British Museum: Raphael and his Circle*, 2 vols, London 1962

RADNOR and SQUIRE 1909
Helen Matilda, Countess of Radnor, and William Barclay Squire, *Catalogue of the Pictures in the Collection of the Earl of Radnor*, 2 vols, London 1909

REID 1993
Jane Davidson Reid, *The Oxford Guide to Classical Mythology in the Arts 1300–1900*, 2 vols, New York and Oxford 1993

REISET 1879
F. Reiset, 'Les Cartons de Jules Romain au Musée du Louvre', *Nouvelles Archives de l'Art français* (Société de l'Histoire de l'Art français), 2nd ser., 1879, pp.465–7

REYNOLDS 1929
The Letters of Sir Joshua Reynolds, F.W. Hilles (ed), Cambridge 1929

REYNOLDS 1980
Graham Reynolds, *Wallace Collection: Catalogue of Miniatures*, London 1980

REYNOLDS 1988
Graham Reynolds, *English Portrait Miniatures*, Cambridge 1988 (1st edn, 1952)

REYNOLDS 1992
Graham Reynolds, 'Late Eighteenth-Century Miniatures by Richard Cosway and Andrew Plimer', *British Art 1740–1820: Essays in Honor of Robert R. Wark*, Guilland Sutherland (ed), San Marino, California 1992

RIBEIRO 1975
Aileen Ribeiro, 'The Dress worn at Masquerades in England, 1730 to 1790, and its relation to Fancy Dress in Portraiture', Ph.D. thesis, Courtauld Institute of Art, University of London 1975

RIBEIRO 1983
Aileen Ribeiro, *A Visual History of Costume: The Eighteenth Century*, London 1983

RIBEIRO 1995
Aileen Ribeiro, *The Art of Dress: Fashion in England and France 1750–1820*, New Haven and London 1995

RICE 1976
Howard C. Rice Jr, *Thomas Jefferson's Paris*, Princeton 1976

ROSENBLUM 1957
Robert Rosenblum, 'The Origin of Painting: A Problem in the Iconography of Romantic Classicism', *The Art Bulletin*, XXXIX, December 1957, pp.279–90

ROSENBLUM 1967
Robert Rosenblum, *Transformations in Late Eighteenth Century Art*, Princeton 1967

ROSENBLUM 1993
Robert Rosenblum, 'Andy Warhol: Court Painter to the 70s', *Andy Warhol Portraits*, Henry Geldzahler (ed), London 1993, pp.139–50

ROWLANDS 1993
John Rowlands, *Drawings by German Artists in the Department of Prints and Drawings in the British Museum*, London 1993

ROWORTH 1992
Angelica Kauffman: A Continental Artist in Georgian England, Wendy Wassyng Roworth (ed), Brighton and London 1992

ROWORTH 1994
Wendy Wassyng Roworth, 'Anatomy is destiny: regarding the body in the art of Angelica Kauffman', *Femininity and Masculinity in Eighteenth-century Art and Culture*, Gill Perry and Michael Rossington (eds), Manchester 1994, pp.41–62

ST CLAIR 1967
William St Clair, *Lord Elgin and the Marbles*, London 1967

SAXL and WITTKOWER 1948
Fritz Saxl and Rudolf Wittkower, *British Art and the Mediterranean*, Oxford 1948 (reprinted 1969)

SCARISBRICK 1994
Diana Scarisbrick, *Jewellery in Britain 1066–1837: A Documentary, Social, Literary and Artistic Survey*, Norwich 1994

SCHELLER 1969
R.W. Scheller, 'Rembrandt en de encyclopedische verzameling', *Oud Holland*, LXXXIV, nos 2–3, 1969, pp.81–147

SCHERILLO 1923
M. Scherillo (ed), *Manzoni Intimo, I, Vittoria e Matilde Manzoni: Memorie di Vittoria Giorgini-Manzoni*, Milan 1923

SCHUCHARD 1975
Marsha Keith Schuchard, 'Freemasonry, Secret Societies, and the Continuity of the Occult Traditions in English Literature', Ph.D. thesis, 2 vols, University of Austin, Texas, 1975

SCHUCHARD 1989
Marsha Keith Schuchard, 'Blake's Healing Trio: Magnetism, Medicine, and Mania', *Blake: An Illustrated Quarterly*, XXIII, no.1, 1989, pp.20–32

SCHUCHARD 1992a
Marsha Keith Schuchard, 'Blake's "Mr. Femality": Freemasonry, Espionage, and the Double-Sexed', *Studies in Eighteenth-Century Culture*, XXII, 1992, pp.51–71

SCHUCHARD 1992b
Marsha Keith Schuchard, 'The Secret Masonic History of Blake's Swedenborg Society', *Blake: An Illustrated Quarterly*, XXVI, no.2, 1992, pp.40–51

SCIOLLA 1992
Gianni Carlo Sciolla, *Il Disegno*, II, *I grandi collezionisti*, Turin 1992

SCIOLLA 1993
Gianni Carlo Sciolla, *Il Disegno*, III, *Le collezioni pubbliche italiane*, part I, Turin 1993

SHACKELFORD 1995
George Green Shackelford, *Thomas Jefferson's Travels in Europe, 1784–1789*, Baltimore 1995

SHAFTESBURY 1713
Anthony Ashley Cooper, 3rd Earl of Shaftesbury, *A Notion of the Historical Draught or Tablature of the Judgement of Hercules*, London 1713

SHAFTESBURY 1714
Anthony Ashley Cooper, 3rd Earl of Shaftesbury, *Characteristicks of Men, Manners, Opinions, Times*, 2nd edn, London 1714

SHAWE-TAYLOR 1990
Desmond Shawe-Taylor, *The Georgians: Eighteenth Century Portraiture and Society*, London 1990

SHEPPARD 1960
F.H.W. Sheppard (general ed), *The Survey of London*, XIX, *The Parish of St. James Westminster*, I, *South of Piccadilly*, London 1960

SHROYER 1979
R. J. Shroyer, 'Mr Jacko "knows what riding is" in 1785: dating Blake's Island in the Moon', *Blake: An Illustrated Quarterly*, XII, 1979, pp.250–6

SMAILES 1990
Helen Smailes, *The Concise Catalogue of the Scottish National Portrait Gallery*, Edinburgh 1990

SMITH 1828
John Thomas Smith, *Nollekens and his Times: comprehending a life of that celebrated Sculptor; and Memoirs of several contemporary artists…*, 2 vols, London 1828

SMITH 1883
John Chaloner Smith, *British Mezzotinto Portraits…*, 4 vols, London 1883

SMITH 1890–1904
A.H. Smith, *A Catalogue of Sculpture in the Department of Greek and Roman Antiquities, British Museum*, 3 vols, London 1890–1904

SMITH 1916
A.H. Smith, 'Lord Elgin and his collection', *The Journal of Hellenic Studies*, XXXVI, 1916, pp.163–372

SNELL 1892
Frederick John Snell, *The Chronicles of Twyford, being a new and popular history of the town of Tiverton in Devonshire*, London 1892

SNOWMAN 1990
A. Kenneth Snowman, *Eighteenth Century Gold Boxes of Europe*, Woodbridge 1990 (1st edn, London 1966)

SOAMES 1987
Mary Soames, *The Profligate Duke: George Spencer-Churchill, fifth Duke of Marlborough, and his Duchess*, London 1987

SOANE 1835
Description of the House and Museum on the north side of Lincoln's Inn Fields, the residence of Sir J. Soane, London 1835 (1st edn, 1830)

SOANE 1927
The Portrait of Sir John Soane, R.A. (1753–1837) set forth in letters from his friends (1775–1837), Arthur T. Bolton (ed), London 1927

SOLDARINI 1985
Giovanni Soldarini (general ed), *Manzoni nella Terra Ambrosiana* (Atti del Convegno della Diocesi di Milano nel Bicentenario della nascita 19–21 Aprile 1985; Centro Ambrosiano di Documentazione e di Studi Religiosi), Milan 1985

SONTAG 1992
Susan Sontag, *The Volcano Lover: a Romance*, London 1992

STERNE 1984
Laurence Sterne, *'A Sentimental Journey' with 'The Journal to Eliza' and 'A Political Romance'*, Ian Jack (ed), Oxford 1984

SUGDEN 1922
Emily R. Sugden, 'An early reader of Swedenborg: Richard Cosway R.A.', *New Church Review*, XXIX, no.3, July 1922, pp.294–304

SUNDERLAND 1986
John Sunderland, 'John Hamilton Mortimer: his Life and Works', *The Walpole Society*, LII, 1986

TATE GALLERY 1988
Tate Gallery: Illustrated Catalogue of Acquisitions 1984–6, London 1988

TATE REPORT 1994
Tate Report: Tate Gallery Biennial Report 1992–94, London 1994

TETTAMANZI 1985
Laura Tettamanzi, *Lombardia di Manzoni*, Como 1985

THACKERAY 1968
William Makepeace Thackeray, *Vanity Fair*, Harmondsworth 1968 (1st publ. 1848)

THIÉBAUT 1987
Dominique Thiébaut, *Ajaccio, Musée Fesch, les primitifs italiens* (Inventaire des collections publiques françaises 32), Paris 1987

THORNBURY 1860
Walter Thornbury, 'Two fop artists: Sherwin and Cosway', *The Art-Journal*, VI, April 1860, pp.97–9

THORNTON and DOREY 1992
Peter Thornton and Helen Dorey, *A Miscellany of Objects from Sir John Soane's Museum*, London 1992

THORPE 1994
James Thorpe, *Henry Edwards Huntington: A Biography*, Berkeley 1994

de TOLNAY 1943
Charles de Tolnay, *History and Technique of Old Master Drawings*, New York 1943

TOMALIN 1994
Claire Tomalin, *Mrs Jordan's Profession: The Story of a great Actress and a future King*, London 1994

TRUMBULL 1941
Autobiography, Reminiscences and Letters of John Trumbull from 1756 to 1841, New York, London and New Haven 1941

TRUMBULL 1953
The Autobiography of Colonel John Trumbull, Patriot-Artist 1756–1843, Theodore Sizer (ed), New Haven 1953

TUDSBERY-TURNER 1991
Stephen Tudsbery-Turner, 'Robert, 4th Duke of Ancaster: "An Object of General Admiration"', *The Church Monuments Society Newsletter*, VI, no.2, Winter 1991, pp.42–4

VAUGHAN 1989
Gerard Vaughan, 'The Collecting of Classical Antiquities in England in the Eighteenth Century: a Study of Charles Townley and his Circle', D.Phil. thesis, 2 vols, University of Oxford 1989

VIVIAN 1949
Frances Vivian, 'General Paoli in England', *Italian Studies*, IV, 1949, p.49

VLIEGHE 1987
Hans Vlieghe, *Corpus Rubenianum Ludwig Burchard*, XIX, *Portraits*, II, *Antwerp, Identified Sitters*, 2 vols, Oxford 1987

WAINWRIGHT 1989
Clive Wainwright, *The Romantic Interior: the British Collector at Home, 1750–1850*, New Haven and London 1989

WALKER 1985
Richard Walker, *National Portrait Gallery: Regency Portraits*, 2 vols, London 1985

WALKER 1986
John Walker, 'Maria Cosway, an undervalued artist', *Apollo*, CXXIII, no.291, May 1986, pp.318–24

WALKER 1992
Richard Walker, *The Eighteenth and Early Nineteenth Century Miniatures in the Collection of Her Majesty The Queen*, Cambridge 1992

WALKLEY 1994
Giles Walkley, *Artists' Houses in London 1764–1914*, Aldershot 1994

WALPOLE 1937–83
The Yale Edition of Horace Walpole's Correspondence, W.S. Lewis (general ed), 48 vols, London and New Haven 1937–83

WARK 1986
Robert R. Wark, *The Huntington Art Collection: A Handbook*, San Marino 1986

WATERHOUSE 1947
Ellis Waterhouse, 'The Decline of the Miniature', *Penguin Parade*, 2nd ser., I, Harmondsworth 1947, pp.42–51

WATERHOUSE 1981
Ellis Waterhouse, *The Dictionary of British 18th Century Painters in Oils and Crayons*, Woodbridge 1981

WATERHOUSE 1994
Ellis Waterhouse, *Painting in Britain 1530 to 1790*, 5th edn, New Haven and London 1994

WATKIN 1984
David Watkin, *The Royal Interiors of Regency England*, London 1984

WATSON 1939–40
F.J.B. Watson, 'Thomas Patch (1725–1782): Notes on his Life, together with a Catalogue of his known Works', *The Walpole Society*, XXVIII, 1939–40, pp.15–50

WEBSTER 1970
Mary Webster, *Francis Wheatley*, London 1970

WELLESLEY (1919)
Catalogue of the Miniatures and Portraits in Plumbago or Pencil belonging to Francis & Minnie Wellesley, Woking and London, n.d. (1919)

WESCHER 1988
Paul Wescher, *I Furti d'Arte: Napoleone e la nascità del Louvre*, Turin 1988 (1st edn, Berlin 1976)

WHINNEY 1988
Margaret Whinney, *Sculpture in Britain: 1530 to 1830*, Harmondsworth 1988 (1st edn, 1964)

WHITE 1981
Christopher White, 'Rubens and British Art 1630–1790', *"Sind Briten hier?": Relations between British and Continental Art 1680–1880*, Munich 1981, pp.27–43

WHITEHEAD 1982
Jane S. Whitehead, 'The noblest collection of curiositys: British visitors to the Uffizi 1650–1789', *Gli Uffizi: quattro secoli di una galleria* (Atti del Convegno Internazionale di Studi, Florence, 20–24 September 1982), P. Barocchi and G. Ragionieri (eds), Florence 1983, I, pp.287–307

WHITLEY 1928a
William T. Whitley, *Artists and their Friends in England 1700–1799*, 2 vols, London and Boston 1928

WHITLEY 1928b
William T. Whitley, *Art in England 1800–1820*, Cambridge 1928

WHITLEY 1930
William T. Whitley, *Art in England 1821–1837*, Cambridge 1930

WHITMAN 1902
Alfred Whitman, *British Mezzotinters: Valentine Green*, London 1902

WHITMAN 1907
Alfred Whitman, *Charles Turner*, 1907

WILLIAMSON 1897
George C. Williamson, *Richard Cosway R.A. and his Wife and Pupils: Miniaturists of the Eighteenth Century*, London 1897 (2nd edn, 1905)

WILLIAMSON 1904
George C. Williamson, *The History of Portrait Miniatures*, 2 vols, London 1904

WILLIAMSON 1905
George C. Williamson, *Richard Cosway R.A.*, London 1905 (1st edn, 1897)

WILLIAMSON 1906–8
George C. Williamson, *Catalogue of the Collection of Miniatures, the property of J. Pierpont Morgan*, 4 vols, London 1906–8

WILLIAMSON 1934
George C. Williamson, 'English Light on Italian walls' (letter), *Country Life*, LXXV, no.1940, 24 March 1934, p.313

WILSON 1989
David M. Wilson, *The British Museum: Purpose and Politics*, London 1989

WILSON 1990
Timothy Wilson, 'The Cosway Salt', *National Art Collections Fund: Annual Review*, 1990, pp.78–80

WILSON, SASSOON and BREMER-DAVID 1982
Gillian Wilson, Adrian Sassoon and Charissa Bremer-David, 'Acquisitions by the Department of Decorative Arts, 1982', *The J. Paul Getty Museum Journal*, II, 1983, pp.13–66

WRIGHT 1824
T. Wright, *Some Account of the Life of Richard Wilson, Esq. R.A. …*, London 1824

WYNNE 1990
Michael Wynne, 'Members from Great Britain and Ireland of the Florentine Accademia del Disegno 1700–1855', *The Burlington Magazine*, CXXXII, no.1049,

EXHIBITION CATALOGUES

This list includes the abbreviated references to all the
exhibitions, with the exception of those held before
1830, which are noted separately in the footnotes and
catalogue entries.

BIRMINGHAM 1934
*Commemorative Exhibition of the Art Treasures of the
Midlands*, exh. cat., Birmingham City Museum and Art
Gallery, 1934

BREGENZ and VIENNA 1968–9
Angelika Kauffmann und ihre Zeitgenossen, exh. cat., O.
Sandner (ed), Vorarlberger Landesmuseum, Bregenz
und Osterreichisches Museum für Angewandte Kunst,
1968–9

CAMBRIDGE 1981–2
*Drawings from the Collection of Louis C.G. Clarke,
LL.D., 1881–1960*, exh. cat., Fitzwilliam Museum,
Cambridge 1981–2

CAMBRIDGE 1985
*The Achievement of a Connoisseur, Philip Pouncey:
Italian Master Drawings*, exh. cat., David Scrase and
Julien Stock (eds), Fitzwilliam Museum, Cambridge
1985

CAMBRIDGE 1988
*Baccio Bandinelli 1493–1560, Drawings from British
Collections*, exh. cat., Roger Ward (ed), Fitzwilliam
Museum, Cambridge 1988

EDINBURGH 1965
British Portrait Miniatures, exh. cat., Daphne Foskett
(ed), 11 Rothesay Terrace, Edinburgh 1965

EDINBURGH 1978
*Van Dyck in Check Trousers: Fancy Dress in Art and
Life, 1700–1900*, exh. cat., Helen Bennett and Sara
Stevenson (eds), Scottish National Portrait Gallery,
Edinburgh 1978

ESSEN 1992
Simon Jervis, 'Rudolph Ackermann', *London – World
City 1800–1840*, exh. cat., Celina Fox (ed), Villa Hügel,
Essen 1992

FLORENCE 1971
*Firenze e l'Inghilterra: rapporti artistici e culturali dal
XVI al XX secolo*, exh. cat., Mary Webster, Palazzo Pitti,
Florence 1971

FLORENCE 1979
*Curiosità di una reggia, vicende della guardaroba di
Palazzo Pitti*, exh. cat., Palazzo Pitti, Florence 1979

KYOTO 1989
Le Mode en France 1715–1815: De Louis XV à Napoléon Ier,
exh. cat., Musée National d'Art Moderne de Kyoto, 1989
(French edn, Paris 1990)

LIVERPOOL 1994–5
Face to Face, Three Centuries of Artists' Self-Portraiture,
exh. cat., Xanthe Brooke (ed), Walker Art Gallery,
Liverpool, 1994–5

LONDON 1835–6
*The Lawrence Gallery. First (– Tenth) Exhibition. A
Catalogue of...original Drawings...collected by Sir
Thomas Lawrence*, 10 exh. cats, S. Woodburn, London
1835–6

LONDON 1865
*Catalogue of the Special Exhibition of Portrait
Miniatures*, exh. cat., South Kensington Museum,
London 1865

LONDON 1895
*Catalogue of Miniatures, Oil Paintings, Drawings, and
Engravings by Richard Cosway, R.A. (1740–1821) and
Maria Cosway his wife*, exh. cat., George C. Williamson
(ed), Amateur Art Exhibition, Moncorvo House, 64
Ennismore Gardens, London 1895

LONDON 1956–7
British Portraits, exh. cat., Royal Academy of Arts,
London 1956–7

LONDON 1961–2
*Exhibition of Royal Gifts in aid of the Young Women's
Christian Association*, exh. cat., Christie's, London
1961–2

LONDON 1962
British Self-portraits: c.1580–c.1860, exh. cat., Arts
Council, London 1962

LONDON 1966
George IV and the Arts of France, exh. cat., The Queen's
Gallery, Buckingham Palace, London 1966

LONDON 1970
*Gainsborough, Paul Sandby and Miniature-Painters in
the Service of George III and his Family*, exh. cat., The
Queen's Gallery, Buckingham Palace, London 1970

LONDON 1972
The Age of Neoclassicism, exh. cat., Royal Academy and
Victoria and Albert Museum, London 1972

LONDON 1974a
British Artists in Rome 1700–1800, exh. cat., Lindsay
Stainton (ed), Kenwood, London 1974

LONDON 1974b
Samuel Cooper and his Contemporaries, exh. cat.,
Daphne Foskett (ed), National Portrait Gallery, London
1974

LONDON 1976
Johann Zoffany, exh. cat., Mary Webster (ed), National
Portrait Gallery, London 1976

LONDON 1977a
Rubens: Drawings and Sketches, exh. cat., John
Rowlands (ed), British Museum, London 1977

LONDON 1977b
Nathaniel Dance 1735–1811, exh. cat., David Goodreau
(ed), Kenwood, London 1977

LONDON 1978
Gainsborough and Reynolds in the British Museum, exh.
cat., Tim Clifford, Antony Griffiths and Martin
Royalton-Kisch (eds), British Museum, London 1978

LONDON 1979
*Thomas Hudson 1701–1779, Portrait Painter and
Collector*, exh. cat., Ellen G. Miles (ed), Kenwood,
London 1979

LONDON 1982
Van Dyck in England, exh. cat., Oliver Millar (ed),
National Portrait Gallery, London 1982

LONDON 1984a
George Stubbs 1724–1806, exh. cat., Judy Egerton (ed),
Tate Gallery, London 1984

LONDON 1984b
Rococo: Art and Design in Hogarth's England, exh. cat.,
Victoria and Albert Museum, London 1984

LONDON 1986
Reynolds, exh. cat., Nicholas Penny (ed), Royal
Academy of Arts, London 1986

LONDON 1988
*The Age of Dürer and Holbein: German Drawings 1400–
1550*, exh. cat., John Rowlands (ed), British Museum,
London 1988

LONDON 1990
*English Watercolours and Drawings: Agnew's 117th
Annual Exhibition*, exh. cat., 12 March – 6 April 1990

LONDON 1991
*The Portrait in British Art: Masterpieces bought with the
help of the National Art Collections Fund*, exh. cat., John
Hayes (ed), National Portrait Gallery, London 1991

LONDON 1991–2
Carlton House: The Past Glories of George IV's Palace,
exh. cat., The Queen's Gallery, Buckingham Palace,
London 1991–2

LONDON 1992–3
*The Swagger Portrait: Grand Manner Portraiture in
Britain from Van Dyck to Augustus John 1630–1930*, exh.
cat., Andrew Wilton (ed), Tate Gallery, London

LONDON 1994
*The Study of Italian Drawings: The Contribution of
Philip Pouncey*, exh. cat., Nicholas Turner (ed), British
Museum, London 1994

MILAN 1985
L'Officina dei Promessi Sposi, exh. cat., D. Isella and F.
Mazzocca (eds), Biblioteca Nazionale Braidense and
Pinacoteca di Brera, Milan 1985

MILAN 1985–6
Manzoni: Il Suo e il nostro tempo, exh. cat., Palazzo
Reale, Milan 1985–6

MILAN 1991
*La Braidense: La Cultura del libro e delle biblioteche
nella società dell'immagine*, exh. cat., Biblioteca
Nazionale Braidense, Milan 1991

MONTICELLO 1993
The Worlds of Thomas Jefferson at Monticello, exh. cat.,
Susan R. Stein (ed), Monticello 1993

NEW HAVEN 1979
*The Fuseli Circle in Rome: Early Romantic Art of the
1770s*, exh. cat., Nancy L. Pressly (ed), Yale Center for
British Art, New Haven 1979

NEW HAVEN 1979–80
English Portrait Drawings & Miniatures, exh. cat.,
Patrick J. Noon (ed), Yale Center for British Art, New
Haven 1979–80

NEW HAVEN 1983
Rembrandt in Eighteenth Century England, exh. cat.,
David Alexander, Ellen d'Oench and Christopher White
(eds), Yale Center for British Art, New Haven 1983

NEW YORK 1986
French and English Drawings 1700–1875, exh. cat.,
Zangrilli, Brady and Co. Ltd, New York 1986

NEW YORK 1988
*Creative Copies: Interpretative Drawings from
Michelangelo to Picasso*, Egbert Haverkamp-Begemann
and Carolyn Logan (eds), Drawing Center, New York
1988

NEW YORK 1994
Master Drawings 1760–1890, exh. cat., W.M. Brady &
Co., Inc., New York 1994

NOTTINGHAM and LONDON 1991
*The Artist's Model: Its Role in British Art from Lely to
Etty*, exh. cat., Ilaria Bignamini and Martin Postle
(eds), University Art Gallery, Nottingham, and the
Iveagh Bequest, Kenwood, London 1991

OXFORD 1984
*The Douce Legacy: An exhibition to commemorate the
150th anniversary of the bequest of Francis Douce (1757–
1834)*, exh. cat., Bodleian Library, Oxford

PARIS 1978
Jules Romain, l'histoire de Scipion: tapisseries et dessins,
exh. cat., Roseline Bacou and Bertrand Jestaz (eds),
Grand Palais, Paris 1978

RICHMOND 1979–80
*Treasures from Chatsworth: The Devonshire Inherit-
ance*, exh. cat., Virginia Museum of Fine Arts,
Richmond, Virginia 1979–80 (and five other US
museums)

TULSA 1993–5
Master Drawings from the National Portrait Gallery,
exh. cat., by Malcolm Rogers, The Philbrook Museum of
Art, Tulsa 1993 (touring various venues in US and UK,
1993–5)

WASHINGTON 1976
The Eye of Thomas Jefferson, exh. cat., William Howard
Adams (ed), National Gallery of Art, Washington DC
1976

WASHINGTON, PARIS and BERLIN 1984–5
Watteau 1684–1721, exh. cat., Margaret Morgan Grasselli
and Pierre Rosenberg (eds), National Gallery of Art,
Washington DC, and Grand Palais, Paris, and Schloss
Charlottenberg, Berlin 1984–5

WASHINGTON 1985–6
*The Treasure Houses of Britain: Five Hundred Years of
Private Patronage and Art Collecting*, exh. cat.,
National Gallery of Art, Washington DC 1985–6

YORK 1993
*Affecting Moments: Prints of English Literature made in
the Age of Romantic Sensibility 1775–1800*, David
Alexander (ed), King's Manor Gallery, York 1993

INDEX OF SITTERS

Photographic Credits

The photographs were supplied by the public
and private owners, and the photographers
listed here:

James Austin Photography

CJB Photography

Raffaello Bencini

The Bridgeman Art Library, London

Geremy Butler Photography

Richard W. Caspole

Robert Chapman Photography

A.C. Cooper Ltd.

Photographic Survey, Courtauld Institute of Art

L'Immagine

Antonia Reeve Photography

The Royal Collection
© 1995 Her Majesty The Queen

Rodney Todd-White & Son

© Max Whitaker 1991